Women's Life in Greece and Rome

WOMEN'S LIFE IN GREECE AND ROME

Mary R. Lefkowitz
and Maureen B. Fant

The Johns Hopkins University Press
Baltimore, Maryland

First published in the United States of America in 1982 by
The Johns Hopkins University Press

Fifth printing (paperback), 1987

The Johns Hopkins University Press
701 West 40th Street
Baltimore, Maryland 21211

Library of Congress Cataloging in Publication Data
Main entry under title:

Women's life in Greece and Rome.
Rev. and enl. ed. of: Women in Greece and Rome. 1977.
Includes bibliographical references and indexes.
1. Women—Rome. 2. Women—Greece.
I. Lefkowitz, Mary R., 1935-   .II. Fant, Maureen B.
HQ1127.W653   1982   305.4'0938   82-7756
ISBN   0-8018-2865-I   AACR2
ISBN   0-8018-2866-X (pbk.)

Contents

II WIVES, DAUGHTERS, FRIENDS

III ACCOMPLISHMENTS

IV OCCUPATIONS

PART TWO: ROME

X A POET, SULPICIA

XI WIVES, MOTHERS, DAUGHTERS

Contents

XVII DAILY LIFE

XVIII RELIGION

For our mothers
Mena Rosenthal and Nancy Brown

Preface

Histories of the ancient world have traditionally been written without much reference to women. The ancients themselves set the pattern: wars and politics, not social or domestic affairs, claimed the chief attention of educated men. But the politics of today's world urge our reconsideration of past practice, and studies of other cultures offer promising new analytical approaches to evidence that had formerly been discounted or ignored. This book is intended to make accessible to people who do not know the ancient languages the kinds of materials on which historians of women in the ancient world must base their work.

A glance through the contents will reveal that the materials are assembled from disparate sources, mostly the types of documents one does not expect to find in a 'history' book. Yet such are the materials on which the modern historian must rely to produce a comprehensive history of women in antiquity. They offer a spectrum of opinions, some possibly representative and often persistently influential; and a record, scattered over space and time, of personal feelings, often, because they are spoken in the stress of bereavement or in the formality of legal documents, unrepresentative of the conditions that ordinarily characterised family life. General trends of attitudes towards women and impressions of their status in society emerge, but these too should be considered in the larger context of 'men's' history. If, starting in the Hellenistic period, women appear to play a larger role in determining their own affairs and society's, it must be remembered that concomitant emphasis is given in contemporary documents and art to the achievements of ordinary *men*.

Many familiar texts, like Hesiod's story of Pandora, Aristotle's reflections on women, selections from Juvenal's sixth satire, are reproduced here for the reader's convenience. Other interesting documents, e.g. some of the papyrus letters and most of the dedicatory and funerary inscriptions, are not available elsewhere in translation. Special effort has been made to include a representative selection of medical documents, including (for the first time in English) cures not consonant with conventional ideas of Greek enlightenment. Omitted from the book are literary texts readily available in paperback that should be read in their entirety, and also mythological documents, like stories of the Amazons and the legends in the first books of Livy.

Most of the material in this book first appeared in our reader *Women in Greece and Rome* (Toronto/Sarasota 1977). To this we have added, along with new introductions and notes, more documents about women's occupations, legal status, and religious life.

Whenever possible we have tried to let the documents speak for themselves. We have provided background information in prefaces and notes primarily to explain the context of excerpts or the more fragmentary documents. But this (or any) collection will offer only impressions unless it is read in conjunction with history texts and with the aid of an experienced instructor. Every reader will want to consult S. Pomeroy's *Goddesses, Whores, Wives, and Slaves* (New York 1975), with its comprehensive bibliography, since our notes record only the works that we have found particularly helpful in interpreting the ancient texts.

Mary Lefkowitz had primary responsibility for the Greek and Christian sections, Maureen Fant for the Roman. We are both responsible for the topical arrangement of the sources, which we hoped would be more helpful than a strict chronological order for students reading this material for the first time. But a concordance of sources is provided for scholars who wish to use the materials in a different sequence.

Assembling materials from diffuse and often recondite sources, from two cultures, covering a period of a thousand years, involves more knowledge and expertise than any two people could easily possess. For improvements, corrections, and additions to our original collection of readings we are grateful to the reviewers of *Women in Greece and Rome*, to colleagues who have used that text with classes, and especially to J.H. D'Arms, J.C. Fant, D.M. Lewis, H. Lloyd-Jones, S. Pomeroy and J. Sullivan. Thanks are due also to the staff of the library of the American Academy in Rome.

We are grateful to the following for permission to reprint: Harvard University Press and the Loeb Classical Library (39, 67-8, 73-4, 82, 90, 92, 103, 113-15, 148, 154, 179, 180, 189, 192, 206, 208, 212, 218, 223-4, 230, 240-1, 244-5); Penguin Books (88, 93, 150-2, 203, 209, 227); Johns Hopkins University Press (64, 120, 178, 213, 217); AMS Press (193, 195-7, 219); University of Texas Press (187-8, 243); Cambridge University Press (112, 128, 265); Oxford University Press (194, 266, 267); Cornell University Press (106, 211); University of Illinois Press; University of Chicago Press (96); Random House (155).

M.R.L.
M.B.F.

PART ONE

GREECE

I
Poets

It is only fitting that the first speakers in a book about women should be women. Their words give some sense of the importance of women in women's lives, of the pleasures of owning and giving, of participating in festivals and in household games. But we must wait for men to tell us about the social, legal, and physical environments in which ancient women lived, since the course of women's lives, from birth to death, was set by men, fathers, husbands, brothers, uncles, by the male citizens by whom governments were formed and armies raised. It is men too who—selectively, we may presume—tell us most about women's achievements.

Aside from poetry, women's writing survives only in private letters written on papyrus, preserved, by an accident of nature, only from Hellenistic and Roman Egypt. Students of the ancient world are always acutely aware that only a fraction of the writings of antiquity has survived. Much of what remains was preserved because men in late antiquity and the Middle Ages felt it to have enduring value. It is then both logical and poignant that we should have so little of what women wrote. Surviving fragments and references in the work of male authors are tantalising indications that the intellectual efforts of women were, at least occasionally, committed to writing.

That women in all periods of antiquity could write sophisticated verse indicates that at least some women were educated. But the fact that from all antiquity only a few female authors' names and a few fragments of their poetry survive suggests that such intellectual attainments were at best exceptional. If all women had gone to school and had been able to record what they felt about their world, a very different, and surely less self-congratulatory, picture of ancient life would have emerged. As it is, what little remains of women's writings offers eloquent testimony not so much of an informing literary inheritance, as of a potential never realised.

The poetry of Sappho, in the sixth century B.C., had a profound influence both on the content and form of subsequent lyric. The emphasis on emotion and on the action of the mind that distinguished her poetry from that of her male contemporary Alcaeus set the pattern for the concerns of all later love poetry. The sensual appeal in her poetry of the natural world reappears in the careful landscape of Hellenistic pastoral. By imitating her stanza-form and metre, later poets could instantly convey the stance of the isolated lover and the pain of a friend's departure or loss.

Many of these poems describe a world that men never saw: the deep love women could feel for one another in a society that kept the sexes apart and the intense excitement of rituals in which only women could participate. Later women poets occasionally write of this other world: Erinna's *Distaff* speaks of a girlhood friendship lost through marriage and through death; Anyte's epitaphs describe the special offerings women leave goddesses at shrines. But in the Hellenistic age, when women gained new privileges and freedom, women poets began to write about men's subjects and for the same occasions for which male poets wrote. In many cases, if we did not know names, there would be no way to tell the author's gender.

Sappho. (Lesbos, 6th cent. B.C.)

1. *To Aphrodite. (Fr. 1. Tr. M.R.L.)*

Aphrodite on your intricate throne, immortal, daughter of Zeus, weaver of plots, I beg you, do not tame me with pain or my heart with anguish

but come here, as once before when I asked you, you heard my words from afar and listened, and left your father's golden house and came

you yoked your chariot, and lovely swift sparrows brought you, fast whirling over the dark earth from heaven through the midst of the bright air

and soon they arrived. And you, o blessed goddess, smiled with your immortal face and asked what was wrong with me, and why did I call now,

and what did I most want in my maddened heart to have for myself. 'Who now am I to persuade to your love, who, Sappho, has done you wrong? For if she flees, soon she'll pursue you, and if she won't take gifts, soon she'll give them, and if she won't love, soon she will love you, even if she doesn't want to.'[1]

Come to me now again, release me from my cruel anxiety, accomplish all that my heart wants accomplished. You yourself join my battle.

2. *The man opposite you. (Fr. 31. Tr. M.R.L.)*

The man seems to me strong as a god, the man who sits across from you and listens to your sweet talk nearby and your lovely laughter – which, when I hear it, strikes fear in the heart in my breast. For whenever I glance at you, it seems that I can say nothing at all

but my tongue is broken in silence, and that instant a light fire rushes beneath my skin, I can no longer see anything in my eyes and my ears are thundering,

and cold sweat pours down me, and shuddering grasps me all over, and I am greener than grass, and I seem to myself to be little short of death

But all is endurable, since even a poor man ...[2]

3. *Anactoria. (Fr. 16. Tr. M.R.L.)*

Some would say an army of cavalry, others of infantry, others of ships, is the fairest thing on the dark earth, but I say it's whatever you're in love with

It's completely easy to make this clear to everyone, for Helen, who far surpassed other people in beauty, left behind the most aristocratic

of husbands and went to Troy. She sailed away, and did not remember at all her daughter or her beloved parents, but [Aphrodite] took her aside

(*3 lines missing*)

which makes me remember Anactoria[3] who is no longer near,

her lovely step and the brilliant glancing of her face I would rather see than the Lydians' chariots or their infantry fighting in all their armour.

4. *Parting. (Fr. 94. Tr. M.R.L.)*

'The truth is, I wish I were dead.'[4] She left me, whispering often, and she said this, 'Oh what a cruel fate is ours, Sappho, yes, I leave you against my will.'

And I answered her: 'Farewell, go and remember me, for you know how we cared for you.

'If you do remember, I want to remind you ... and were happy ... of violets ... you set beside me and with woven garlands made of flowers around your soft neck

'and with perfume, royal, rich ... you anointed yourself and on soft beds you would drive out your passion

'and then . . . sanctuary . . . was . . . from which we were away . . .'

5. *Atthis. (Fr. 96. Tr. M.R.L.)*

... you, like a goddess renowned, in your song she took most joy. Now she is unique among Lydian women, as the moon once the sun sets

stands out among all the stars, and her light grasps both the salt sea and the flowering meadows

and fair dew flows forth, and soft roses and chervil and fragrant melilot bloom.

Often as she goes out, she remembers gentle Atthis, and her tender heart is eaten by grief ...

6. *The wedding of Hector and Andromache. (Fr. 44. Tr. M.R.L.)*

'... Hector and his comrades are bringing a girl with dark eyes from holy Thebes and ... Plakia, soft Andromache in their ships across the salt sea; many curved bands of gold and purple robes and intricate playthings, countless silver cups and ivory.' So he spoke. And [Hector's] beloved father quickly got up, and the story went out to his friends throughout the city [of Troy] with its wide dancing places. Then the Trojan women led mules to wheeled carts and a crowd of women came out, and also of ... -ankled maidens, and separately the daughters of Priam and men brought horses with chariots (*unknown number of lines missing*) ... and the sweet-sounding *aulos* was mixed with the noise of castanets, and the maidens sang a sacred song and the holy sound reached heaven ... bowls and goblets ... perfume and cassia and incense were mixed and all the older women shouted out, and all the men cried out a fair loud song, calling on Paean, the far-shooter, the lyre player, to sing of Hector and Andromache, who were like gods ...

Corinna. (Tanagra, Boeotia, 5th cent. B.C.?)

7. *The contest of Cithaeron and Helicon. (654 P. Tr. M.R.L.)*

This fragment from a much longer poem concentrates more on the feelings than on the tangible rewards of victory and defeat.

'... They hid the holy goddess' baby in a cave, a secret from Cronus the crooked-minded, when [his mother] blessed Rhea stole him away and won great honour from the immortals.' So he sang. Straightway the Muses got the blessed gods to bring their voting pebbles to the golden bowls, and then all were counted. Cithaeron won more. Hermes proclaimed with a shout that he had won the victory, and the gods decorated him with wreaths, and there was joy in his heart. But Helicon was overcome by harsh grief ... and he tore out a bare rock and from the height dashed it into countless stones.

8. *Reflections on a woman poet. (664 P. Tr. M.R.L.)*

I blame clear-voiced Myrtis, because – though a woman – she entered into rivalry with Pindar.

Erinna. (Telos, 4th cent. B.C.)

9. *Childhood. (GLP 3.120. Tr. M.R.L.)*

The surviving fragments of Erinna's three-hundred line *Distaff* appear to describe the girlhood of the speaker and her girl-friend Baucis and a separation caused first by Baucis' marriage and finally by her death.[5]

... into the sea, with mad running ... from white horses ... I shouted ... you as tortoise, leaping through ... the garden of the great courtyard. These ... poor Baucis ... I weep for you ... these traces lie still warm in my heart ... now embers ... of dolls in our bedrooms ... at dawn your mother, who ... with fleece; she came to you ... about the salted meat ... When we were little girls Mormo[6] brought panic ... her ears on her head; she ran on all fours ... she changed faces ... But when ... you forgot all that you heard as a child from your mother, dear Baucis ... forgetfulness ... Aphrodite. So weeping for you I leave aside ... my feet do not ... from my house permitted, nor to see ... or to lament with bare head; but blood-red shame tears about me ...

10. *Two epigrams for Baucis. (AP VII. 712, 710. Tr. M.R.L.)*

I am the tomb of Baucis the bride. This stone has heard much lamentation. As you pass by, tell this to Death beneath the ground: 'You are jealous, Death.' As you look, the fine inscription on the tomb tells you of Baucis' savage fate: how her husband's father lighted her funeral pyre with the torches they carried while they sang to Hymenaeus, the marriage god. And you, Hymenaeus, transformed the wedding dances into cries of lamentation.

Column and my sirens, and mourning urn, you hold my death, these few ashes. Tell all who pass by my tomb to greet me, be they from this city or another country: 'The tomb holds a bride, my father called me Baucis, I came from Tenos,'[7] so they will know. And tell them that my friend Erinna inscribed this epigram on my tomb.

Anyte. (Tegea, 3rd cent. B.C.)

Poems on a variety of topics by four women poets were included in the Byzantine collection of Greek epigrams known as the Palatine Anthology. Hedyle's mother and son were also poets; Moero, whose father was a tragic actor and husband a grammarian, also wrote epic poetry. But only Anyte and Nossis wrote epigrams on women's life.

11. *Miletus. (AP VII. 492. Tr. M.R.L.)*

We leave you, Miletus, dear homeland, because we rejected the lawless insolence of impious Gauls. We were three maidens, your citizens. The violent aggression of the Celts brought us to this fate. We did not wait for unholy union or marriage, but we found ourselves a protector in Death.[8]

12. *Antibia. (AP VII. 490. Tr. M.R.L.)*

I weep for Antibia, a virgin. Many suitors wanted her and came to her father's house, because she was known for her beauty and cleverness. But deadly Fate sent all their hopes rolling away.[9]

13. *Thersis. (AP VII. 649. Tr. M.R.L.)*

Instead of a bridal bed and holy rites of marriage, your mother set here on your marble tomb a maiden, like you in size and in beauty, Thersis. So now we can speak to you although you are dead.[10]

14. *Philaenis. (AP VII. 486. Tr. M.R.L.)*

Often here on her daughter's tomb, Cleina in her sorrow cried for her dear child who died too soon, calling back Philaenis' soul. Before she could be married, she crossed the pale stream of Acheron.

Nossis. (Locri, 3rd cent. B.C.)

15. *To Hera. (AP VI. 265. Tr. M.R.L.)*

Sacred Hera – since you often come down from heaven to see Lacinion with its fragrant incense – take this linen cloth. Theophilis, daughter of Cleocha, and her noble daughter Nossis, wove it for you.

16. *To Aphrodite. (AP VI. 275. Tr. M.R.L.)*

I think that Aphrodite will be happy to receive as an offering this band from Simaetha's hair, since it is intricate, and smells sweetly of the nectar that Aphrodite herself uses to anoint fair Adonis.

17. *To Artemis. (AP VI. 273. Tr. M.R.L.)*

Artemis, goddess of Delos and lovely Ortygia, set down your sacred bow in the Graces' laps, wash your skin clean in the Inopus, and come to Locri to deliver Alcetis from her hard labour pains.

18. *Polyarchis. (AP VI. 332. Tr. M.R.L.)*

Let's go to the temple of Aphrodite to see how her statue is intricately worked from gold. Polyarchis set it there, with the great wealth she won from her own body's splendour.

19. *Thaumarete. (AP IX. 604. Tr. M.R.L.)*

This picture captures Thaumarete's form – how well he painted her looks and her beauty, her gentle eyes. If your little watch-dog saw you, she would wag her tail, and think that she saw the mistress of her house.[11]

20. *Callo. (AP IX. 605. Tr. M.R.L.)*

This picture – the image she made of herself, Callo set here in blonde
Aphrodite's house. How gently she stands there. Her charm blooms. I
greet her: there is no blemish at all in her life.

1. Aphrodite's promise closely resembles the type of binding formula used in magical
incantations. See *Papyri Graecae Magicae*, ed. K. Preisendanz, I, pp. 122-4.
2. In the Greek there is more emphasis on imagination – the 'I' of the poem (a female, but not
necessarily Sappho herself) says 'he seems to me to be like one of the gods'. See M.R. Lefkowitz,
GRBS 14 (1973) 113-23.
3. Sappho's simile describes not just the moon's beauty but its sustaining effect on whatever its
light touches. The implication is that her absent friend will similarly beautify and nourish everyone
in her new environment. Cf. Alcman, Fr. 1. 39-43 (below, p. 119), where the sun is used simply as a
metaphor of pre-eminence, stressing physical appearance.
4. On the dramatic situation of this ode, see especially A.P. Burnett, *CP* 74 (1979) 16-27.
5. On interpretation, see especially S.B. Pomeroy, *ZPE* 32 (1978) 17-22.
6. A bogey-woman who was thought to kill children because she had lost her own.
7. Another island; her birthplace may be mentioned because she died away from home.
8. Miletus was sacked in 277 B.C. An epigram (*AP* VII. 493) by Antipater of Thessalonica
describes how a mother killed herself and her daughter when the Romans sacked Corinth in 146
B.C. Cf. Polyxena's willingness to sacrifice herself in Euripides, *Hecuba* 345-78.
9. For a female, death before marriage was considered particularly wasteful. For other examples
in extant inscriptions, see R. Lattimore, *Themes in Greek and Latin Epitaphs* (Urbana, Ill. 1942) 189-92.
10. A likeness of the dead person was carved on the tombstone; cf. FH 60 and p. 137.
11. The Greeks admired verisimilitude; cf. what the women say about the tableau of Adonis and
Aphrodite in Theocritus 15 (below, p. 109). The two women in Herodas 4 are equally effusive.

II
Wives, Daughters, Friends

Praise

Epitaphs preserve ideals more faithfully than historical fact, but as such constitute a record of models of approved public and private behaviour in women's lives.

21. *Phrasicleia. Athens, 6th cent. B.C. (Kaibel 6. Tr. M.R.L.)*

The tomb of Phrasicleia: I shall be called a maiden always. This is the name the gods gave me in place of 'wife'.

22. *Archedice. Athens, 5th cent. B.C. (FH 138/Thuc. 6.59. Tr. M.R.L.)*

This dust hides Archedice, daughter of Hippias,[1] the most important man in Greece in his day; but though her father, husband, brothers, and children were tyrants, her mind was never carried away into arrogance.[2]

23. *Aspasia. Chios, 5th cent. B.C. (FH 139. Tr. M.R.L.)*

Of a worthy wife this is the tomb – here, by the road that throngs with people – of Aspasia, who is dead; in response to her noble disposition Euopides set up this monument for her; she was his consort.

24. *Bitte. Amorgos, mid-5th cent. B.C. (SEG XV. 548. Tr. M.R.L.)*

I lie here, a marble statue instead of a woman, a memorial to Bitte, and of her mother's sad grief.[3]

25. *Biote. Athens, late 5th cent. B.C. (Peek 1415/IG II² 10954. Tr. M.R.L.)*

Because of your true and sweet friendship, your companion[4] Euthylla placed this tablet on your grave, Biote, for she keeps your memory with her tears, and weeps for your lost youth.

26. *Melite. Athens, 365/360 B.C. (Kaibel 79/IG II² 12067. Tr. M.R.L.)*

An inscription on a tablet that shows a woman holding out her hand to her husband. The verses awkwardly represent a dialogue between husband and wife.

'Farewell, tomb of Melite; a good woman lies here. You loved your husband Onesimus; he loved you in return. You were the best, and so he laments your death, for you were a good woman.'
'And to you farewell, dearest of men; love my children.'[5]

27. *Xenoclea. Piraeus, c. 360 B.C. (IG II² 12335. Tr. M.R.L.)*

Leaving two young girls, Xenoclea, daughter of Nicarchus, lies here dead; she mourned the sad end of her son, Phoenix, who died out at sea when he was eight years old.

There is no one so ignorant of grief, Xenoclea, that he doesn't pity your fate. You left behind two young girls and died of grief for your son, who has a pitiless tomb where he lies in the dark sea.

Blame

In an epic that explains how and why man's life is now so hard, read as a school text throughout antiquity, Hesiod describes how woman was given to man's representative Epimetheus ('Afterthinker') as punishment for his brother Prometheus' ('Forethinker') crimes against Zeus. Later in the poem he offers advice on picking a wife.

28. *Pandora. Boeotia, early 7th cent. B.C. (Hesiod, Works and Days 42-105 Tr. M.R.L.)*

For the gods have hidden away and are hiding from men the means of life. If they weren't, you could easily work just for a day to get what would keep you for a year, even if you remained idle – you could put your rudder away over the fireplace, and the work of oxen and of toiling mules would disappear.

But Zeus hid the means of life because he was angry in his heart, because crooked-minded Prometheus deceived him. That is why he devised for men these miserable sorrows. Zeus had hidden fire. But good Prometheus son of Iapetus stole it back for men, away from Zeus the Deviser; he hid it from Thunderer Zeus in a hollow reed.

So Zeus became angry at him and told him: 'Son of Iapetus, since you can devise better than everyone, are you glad that you stole fire and tricked my mind? That theft will be a big pain for you and for men in the future, for I'll give them in return for the fire an evil which they can all enjoy in their hearts while putting their arms round an evil of their very own.' So Zeus spoke, and laughed, father of god and men.

Zeus ordered famous Hephaestus to mix as fast as he could earth with water, and to put in it a human's voice and strength, and to make its face resemble a deathless goddess's, with the fair form of a virgin. And he ordered Athena to teach her her work, to weave on the intricate loom. And he ordered golden Aphrodite to shed grace on her head and cruel passion and worries that gnaw at the limbs. And he commanded Hermes, slayer of Argos, to put in her a bitch's mind and a thieving heart. So Zeus spoke, and they obeyed Zeus son of Cronus, their lord.

Immediately the famous lame god Hephaestus moulded from earth a thing like a chaste virgin, acting on Zeus' orders. He put life in her and the grey-eyed goddess Athena put clothing on her. Around her, goddesses, the Graces and queenly Persuasion, put golden bands on her skin, and the fair-haired Seasons crowned her with spring flowers. In her breast the Guide Hermes, slayer of Argos, put lies, tricky speeches, and a thieving heart; he did this in accordance with Zeus' plans. Hermes, the gods' herald, put in her a voice, and they named this woman Pandora,[6] because all gods who live on Olympus gave her a gift, a pain to men-who-eat-barley.

And when he had completed this steep trap from which there is no escape, Father Zeus sent famed Hermes, the gods' swift messenger, to Epimetheus, bringing this gift. Nor did Epimetheus think, as Prometheus had told him, not ever to accept a gift from Olympian Zeus but to send it right back again, so that it would not prove an evil for mortals. But he accepted it, and when he had taken the evil he understood what he'd done.

Before that the races of men had lived on the earth without evils and without harsh labour and cruel diseases which give men over to the Fates – for in evil times men grow old quickly. But the woman lifted in her hands the great lid from the jar and scattered these evils about – she devised miserable sorrows for men. Only Hope stayed there inside in her unbroken house beneath the rim of the jar. She did not fly out; before that the woman put back the lid of the jar, according to the plans of Zeus Aegis-holder, gatherer of clouds.

The other thousand miseries fly around among men. The earth is full
of evils, and the sea is full of them. Diseases come to men in the day, and
at night uninvited, bringing evils for mortals in silence, since Deviser
Zeus took away their voices. So there is no way to escape the mind of
Zeus.

29. *Advice on picking a wife. Boeotia, early 7th cent. B.C. (Hesiod, Works and
     Days 695-705. Tr. M.R.L.)*

You are at the right age to bring a wife to your house when you are not
much less than thirty, and not much more. This is the right time for
marriage. Your wife should be four years past puberty and be married to
you in the fifth. Marry a virgin, so you can teach her good habits. The
best one to marry is the girl who lives near you; look over her in detail, so
you don't marry one who'll bring joy to your neighbours.[7] For a man can
win nothing better than a good wife, and nothing more painful than a
bad one – a dinner-snatcher, who scorches her husband, strong as he
may be, without fire, and gives him over to a savage old age.

30. *The female mind. Amorgos, 6th cent. B.C. (Semonides, On Women. Tr. H.
     Lloyd-Jones)*

Although the context of this famous poem is lost, its use of animal and
inanimate metaphors suggests that it was intended, like Aesop's fables, as
social satire; see H. Lloyd-Jones, *Females of the Species* (London 1976). But it
is important to note that, as in Hesiod, good behaviour is defined in terms
of service to a woman's husband, not by its intrinsic value to the society as
a whole, or by a woman's worth to other women or to herself.

In the beginning the god made the female mind separately. One he made
from a long-bristled sow. In her house everything lies in disorder,
smeared with mud, and rolls about the floor; and she herself unwashed,
in clothes unlaundered, sits by the dungheap and grows fat. Another he
made from a wicked vixen; a woman who knows everything. No bad
thing and no better kind of thing is lost on her; for she often calls a good
thing bad and a bad thing good. Her attitude is never the same.

Another he made from a bitch, own daughter of her mother, who
wants to hear everything and know everything. She peers everywhere
and strays everywhere, always yapping, even if she sees no human being.
A man cannot stop her by threatening, nor by losing his temper and
knocking out her teeth with a stone, nor with honeyed words, not even if
she is sitting with friends, but ceaselessly she keeps up a barking you can
do nothing with.

Another the Olympians moulded out of earth, a stunted creature; you see, a woman like her knows nothing, bad or good. The only work she understands is eating; and not even when the god makes cruel winter weather does she feel the cold and draw a stool near to the fire.

Another he made from the sea; she has two characters. One day she smiles and is happy; a stranger who sees her in the house will praise her, and say, 'There is no woman better than this among all mankind, nor more beautiful.' But on another day she is unbearable to look at or come near to; then she raves so that you can't approach her, like a bitch over her pups, and she shows herself ungentle and contrary to enemies and friends alike. Just so the sea often stands without a tremor, harmless, a great delight to sailors, in the summer season; but often it raves, tossed about by thundering waves. It is the sea that such a woman most resembles in her temper; like the ocean, she has a changeful nature.

Another he made from an ash-grey ass that has suffered many blows; when compelled and scolded she puts up with everything, much against her will, and does her work to satisfaction. But meanwhile she munches in the back room all night and all day, and she munches by the hearth; and likewise when she comes to the act of love, she accepts any partner.

Another he made from a ferret, a miserable, wretched creature; nothing about her is beautiful or desirable, pleasing or lovable. She is mad for the bed of love, but she makes any man she has with her sick. She does great damage to her neighbours by her thieving, and often eats up sacrifices left unburned.

Another was the offspring of a proud mare with a long mane. She pushes servile work and trouble on to others; she would never set her hand to a mill, nor pick up a sieve nor throw the dung out of the house, nor sit over the oven dodging the soot; she makes her husband acquainted with Necessity. She washes the dirt off herself twice, sometimes three times, every day; she rubs herself with scents, and always has her thick hair combed and garlanded with flowers. A woman like her is a fine sight for others, but for the man she belongs to she proves a plague, unless he is some tyrant or king [who takes pride in such objects].

Another is from a monkey; this is the biggest plague of all that Zeus has given to men. Her face is hideous; when a woman like her goes through the town, everyone laughs at her. She is short in the neck; she moves awkwardly; she has no bottom, and is all legs. Hard luck on the poor man who holds such a misery in his arms! She knows every trick and twist, just like a monkey; she does not mind being laughed at, and will do no one a good turn but considers, and spends the whole day planning, how she can do someone the worst possible harm.

Another is from a bee; the man who gets her is fortunate, for on her alone blame does not settle. She causes his property to grow and increase, and she grows old with a husband whom she loves and who loves her, the mother of a handsome and reputable family. She stands out among all women, and a godlike beauty plays about her. She takes no pleasure in sitting among women in places where they tell stories about love. Women like her are the best and most sensible whom Zeus bestows on men.

Zeus has contrived that all these tribes of women are with men and remain with them. Yes, this is the worst plague Zeus has made – women; if they seem to be some use to him who has them, it is to him especially that they prove a plague. The man who lives with a woman never goes through all his day in cheerfulness; he will not be quick to push out of his house Starvation, a housemate who is an enemy, a god who is against us. Just when a man most wishes to enjoy himself at home, through the dispensation of a god or the kindess of a man, she finds a way of finding fault with him and lifts her crest for battle. Yes, where there is a woman, men cannot even give hearty entertainment to a guest who has come to the house; and the very woman who seems most respectable is the one who turns out guilty of the worst atrocity; because while her husband is not looking ... and the neighbours get pleasure in seeing how he too is mistaken. Each man will take care to praise his own wife and find fault with the other's; we do not realise that the fate of all of us is alike. Yes, this is the greatest plague that Zeus has made, and he has bound us to them with a fetter that cannot be broken. Because of this some have gone to Hades fighting for a woman ...

31. *The best days in a woman's life. Ephesus, 6th cent. B.C. (Hipponax, Fr. 68 West. Tr. M.R.L.)*

A famous quotation (the original context is lost) from the work of a poet famed for his vicious satire.

The two best days in a woman's life are when someone marries her and when he carries her dead body to the grave.[8]

In addition to the famous descriptions of women's lives in surviving plays (such as Euripides, *Medea* 244-8, *Andromache* 207-28, or Sophocles, *Trachiniae* 141-52), fragments of lost plays testify to male poets' understanding of the social forces that compelled women to violence.

32. *The lot of women. Athens, mid-5th cent. B.C. (Sophocles, Tereus, Fr. 583 Radt. Tr. M.R.L.)*

Procne's husband, Tereus, has seduced her sister; in revenge she plans to murder their son.

But now outside my father's house, I am nothing, yes often I have looked on women's nature in this regard, that we are nothing. Young women, in my opinion, have the sweetest existence known to mortals in their fathers' homes, for their innocence always keeps children safe and happy. But when we reach puberty and can understand, we are thrust out and sold away from our ancestral gods and from our parents. Some go to strange men's homes, others to foreigners', some to joyless houses, some to hostile. And all this once the first night has yoked us to our husband, we are forced to praise and to say that all is well.

33. *Pasiphae. Athens, mid-5th cent. B.C. (Euripides, Cretans, GLP 11. Tr. H. Lloyd-Jones)*

Pasiphae, condemned to death for having had intercourse with a bull and having given birth to the monster Minotaur, speaks in her own defence. In Euripides' *Trojan Women* 914-51, Helen puts responsibility for her adultery on Paris' mother Hecuba and the goddess Aphrodite.

If I were to deny the fact you would never believe me; it is clear enough. Now if I had prostituted my body in clandestine love to a man, you could have rightly said I was a whore. But as things are, it was a god who drove me mad; I am sorry, but it was not my fault. It makes no sense; what is it about the bull that could have stirred up my feelings with such a shameful passion? Did he look so splendid in his robes? Did his auburn hair and his eyes flash brilliantly? Was it his dark beard? It can hardly have been the symmetry of his form! This is the love for which I got into the skin and went on all fours; and this makes Minos angry! I could hardly wish to make *this* husband the father of children; why was I afflicted with this madness? It was *Minos'* evil genius who afflicted me with his curse; the one human being who bears all the guilt is *Minos!* It was he who broke the promise he had made to sacrifice the bull that came as a portent to the sea god. It was for *this* that Poseidon's vengeance came upon you, and it is on *me* that it descended! And then you cry aloud and call all the gods to witness, when the doer of the act that put me to shame is you yourself! I who gave birth to the creature have done no harm; I kept secret the godsent affliction of the curse. It is you who publish to all your wife's disgrace, handsome as it is and proper to display, as though you had no part in it, maddest of madmen! You are my ruin, because the crime is yours; you are the cause of my affliction! Well, if you wish to drown me, drown me! You are expert in bloody deeds and murder. Or if you lust to eat my flesh, then eat it, feed to your heart's content! I shall perish free and guiltless, for a crime for which *you* are guilty!

34. *Weighing bad women against good. Athens, 4th cent. B.C. (Eubulus, 116, 117 Kock. Tr. M.R.L.)*

As often, the faults of an individual are attributed to the whole 'race', cf. Euripides, *Hippolytus* 616-68.

I wish the second man who took a wife would die an awful death. I don't blame the first man; he had no experience of that evil. The second man knew what kind of evil a wife was! Oh honoured Zeus, shall I ever say something unkind about women. By Zeus, may I perish then. They are the best possessions one can have. Medea was an evil woman, but Penelope was a good thing; some might criticise Clytemnestra, but I'll set Alcestis against her. Maybe someone else will criticise Phaedra – but, by Zeus, there must be another good wife! Who? Oh, poor me, I've run out of good women, and I still have so many more bad ones to talk about.

35. *The price of a wife. Athens, 4th cent. B.C. (Alexis, Fr. 146 Kock Tr. M.R.L.)*

Poor men! We sold away our freedom of speech and our comfort and lead the life of slaves with our wives. We're not free. We can't say we don't pay a price for their dowries: bitterness and women's anger. Compared to that, a man's is honey, for men forgive when someone does them wrong, but women do you wrong and keep on recriminating. They control what doesn't belong to them and neglect what they should control. They break their promises. When there's nothing wrong, they say they're sick every time.[9]

36. *Betrayal. Athens, 4th cent. B.C. (Menander, Fr. 15 P. Antinoop. Tr. M.R.L.)*

In this fragment of a lost comedy, a young husband complains that the wife he loves has betrayed him.

Who in this city has suffered more dreadfully than I? By Demeter and Heaven! I have been married for five months, and since the night I was married – queen Night, I call you as witness to the truth of what I say – I haven't been away from bed a single night, away from my wife. ... I wanted her, honestly ... I was tied to her by her noble character and her unaffected way of life; she loved me and I loved her.[10]

37. *An overbearing wife. Athens, 4th cent. B.C. (Menander, Fr. 333 Koerte. Tr. M.R.L.)*

A husband complains that his wife Crobyle (whom he married for her money)[11] has made him get rid of a pretty female slave that he liked.

Now our beautiful heiress can sleep on both sides. She has accomplished a great and remarkable feat: she has thrown out of the house the girl who was causing her trouble, as she wanted to. So now everyone can look at Crobyle's face and see that she is that famous woman, my wife and ruler. That face she has – 'jackass among apes', as the saying goes. I won't mention the other night that was the beginning of my many problems – poor me, I took Crobyle as wife. She may have brought me ten talents, but she has a nose one cubit long! How can one live with someone so overbearing? By Olympian Zeus and Athena, impossible! The girl is a good servant, and quicker than a word. 'Take her away!' Who can argue with her?[12]

38. *A fragment of a comedy. Athens, 4th/3rd cent. B.C. (Anon., in Menander, ed. Sandbach, p.328 (GLP 185-7).[13] Tr. H. Lloyd-Jones)*

A daughter tries to persuade her father not to make her marry a man richer than her present husband.[14]

Father, you ought to be making the speech that I am now making, because you ought to have more sense than I have and to do any speaking that is needed. But since you have given me permission, maybe all I can do is to say what is right myself, since I must. If my husband has done great wrong I am not the one that ought to punish him. If he has offended against me, I should take note of it. But I know nothing of it; perhaps I am stupid, I couldn't deny that. Yet, father, even if a woman is a silly creature when it comes to judging other matters, about her own affairs perhaps she has some sense.[15] Explain to me how by whatever he has done he has done me wrong. There is a covenant between man and wife; he must love her, always, until the end, and she must never cease to do what gives her husband pleasure. He was all that I wished with regard to me, and my pleasure is his pleasure, father. But suppose he is satisfactory as far as I am concerned but is bankrupt, and you, as you say, now want to give me to a rich man to save me from living out my life in distress. Where does so much money exist, father, that having it can give me more pleasure than my husband can? How can it be just or honourable that I should take a share in any good things he has, but take no share in his poverty? Tell me, if the man you now want me to marry – may that never happen, dear Zeus, nor shall it ever happen, at least if I can help it – if this man in turn loses his property, will you give me to another husband? How long will you go on tempting fortune in the matter of my life, father? When I was a young girl, you had to find a husband to whom to give me. *Then* the choice was yours. But once you had given me to a husband, from that moment this responsibility belonged to me, naturally, because if I make a mistake in judgment, it's my own life that I shall ruin. So in the name of Hestia don't rob me of the husband to whom you have married me; the favour that I ask of you, father, is just and humane. If you refuse it, you will be enforcing your will and I shall try to bear my fate properly and avoid disgrace.

1. Tyrant of Athens, 527-510 B.C., son of Pisistratus.

2. Cf. Sophocles, *Oedipus Tyrannus* 873-80.

3. The mother's name is ordinarily omitted in archaic inscriptions; cf. H. McClees, *A Study of Women in Attic Inscriptions* (New York 1920) 3, 35. But cf. FH 132: 'Her father Cleodamus son of Hyperanor and her mother Corona placed me here as a monument to Thessalia, their daughter' (late 6th cent., Olooson in Thessaly).

4. *Hetaera*.

5. Cf. Euripides, *Alcestis* 304-8.

6. From 'all' (*pantes*) and 'gift' (*doron*).

7. I.e. your neighbours will laugh because she is unfaithful; cf. Semonides, p. 16 and Archilochus, p. 19

8. Cf. also the enigmatic Roman inscription *(CIL* VI. 29149, tr. Lattimore, op. cit., p. 280), 'To my dear wife, with whom I lived two years, six months, three days, ten hours. On the day of her death I gave thanks to god and man'.

9. On conventional attitudes towards women in the fourth century, see K.J. Dover, *Greek Popular Morality* (Oxford 1974) 95-102.

10. Perhaps the only instance in extant Greek literature where the three words for love (*eraō*, denoting sexual passion; *phileō*, love for family and friends; *agapaō*, affection) 'recur at such short intervals, in each case referring to love between a man and a woman, and indeed between a husband and a wife' (H. Lloyd-Jones, *JHS* 84 (1964) 28).

11. The practice was widespread enough to be a good subject for social comedy; see D.M. Schaps, *Economic Rights of Women in Ancient Greece* (Edinburgh 1979) 76. Apuleius in his *Apology* (2nd cent. A.D.) offers a spirited defence of why he married a rich widow, older than himself; cf. also Plutarch's *Amatorius*.

12. In the Latin translation by Caecilius (3rd cent. B.C.) the husband emphasises how badly he will be disgraced if people find out that his wife has such great power over him (Aulus Gellius 2. 23).

13. On authorship and date, see W. Bühler, *Hermes* 91 (1963) 351.

14. Fathers (or guardians) had the right to determine whom their daughters should marry in order to preserve the family property; see below, p.138. The plot of Menander's *Epitrepontes* concerns a similar situation.

15. On the presumption that the male is naturally more intelligent, see Schaps, op. cit., p. 92.

III

Accomplishments

39. *A woman's bravery. Sparta, 5th cent. B.C. (Plutarch, Moralia 245 c-f, 2nd cent. A.D. Tr. F. C Babbitt (LCL))*

Of all the deeds performed by women for the community none is more famous than the struggle against Cleomenes for Argos,[1] which the women carried out at the instigation of Telesilla the poetess. She, as they say, was the daughter of a famous house but sickly in body, and so she sent to the god to ask about health; and when an oracle was given her to cultivate the Muses, she followed the god's advice, and by devoting herself to poetry and music she was quickly relieved of her trouble, and was greatly admired by the women for her poetic art.

But when Cleomenes king of the Spartans, having slain many Argives ... proceeded against the city, an impulsive daring, divinely inspired, came to the younger women to try, for their country's sake, to hold off the enemy. Under the lead of Telesilla they took up arms, and, taking their stand by the battlements, manned the walls all round, so that the enemy were amazed. The result was that they repulsed Cleomenes with great loss, and the other king, Demaratus, who managed to get inside ... they drove out. In this way the city was saved. The women who fell in the battle they buried close by the Argive Road, and to the survivors they granted the privilege of erecting a statue of Ares as a memorial of their surpassing valour. ... On the anniversary of [the battle] they celebrate even to this day the 'Festival of Impudence', at which they clothe the women in men's shirts and cloaks, and the men in women's robes and veils.

To repair the scarcity of men they did not unite the women with slaves, as Herodotus records, but with the best of their neighbouring subjects, whom they made Argive citizens. It was reputed that the women showed disrespect and an intentional indifference to those husbands in their married relations from a feeling that they were underlings. Wherefore the Argives enacted a law, the one which says that married women having a beard must occupy the same bed with their husbands![2]

40. *Artemisia, the sea-captain. Salamis, 480 B.C. (Herodotus, Histories 8. 87–8. Tr. M.R.L.)*

A local legend from Halicarnassus, a city in Asia Minor and Herodotus' home. Halicarnassus was an ally of Persia in the second war with Greece, at the battle of Salamis in 480.

I cannot offer a precise account of how anyone else fought, either on the Greek or the Persian side, but as far as Artemisia is concerned, this is what happened, and as a result of it she rose in King Xerxes' estimation. The king's forces had been thrown into great confusion, and at this point Artemisia's ship was being chased by an Athenian ship. She wasn't able to get away (three friendly ships were in her way, and her own ship happened to be closest to the enemy). So she decided to act as follows, and the plan worked out well for her. As she was being pursued by the Athenian ship, she attacked at full speed a friendly ship, manned by Calyndians and the king of Calynda himself, Damasithymus. Whether she had been involved in a dispute with him while they were at the Hellespont, I can't say; nor whether her action was premeditated or whether the Calyndian ship had the bad luck to get in her way. In any case, she attacked it and sank it, and used her good luck to get herself a double advantage. When the captain of the Athenian ship saw that she was attacking a Persian ship, he thought that Artemisia's ship either was Greek or had defected from the Persians and was fighting on the Athenian side, so he turned away and took off after other ships. That was the first benefit, to be able to get away and not be killed. The second was that by doing damage she rose higher as a result in Xerxes' estimation. The story goes that when the king was watching the battle and saw her ship making its attack, one of the bystanders said: 'Master, do you see how well Artemisia is fighting and that she has sunk an *enemy* ship?' The king asked if this were truly Artemisia's achievement, and they confirmed that it was, because they recognised her ship's insignia; they believed that the ship she had destroyed was the enemy's. In addition to everything else, she had the good luck that there were no survivors from the Calyndian ship to accuse her. Xerxes is said to have remarked on what he had been told: 'My men have turned into women, and my women into men.'

41. *Melosa. Athens, 5th cent. B.C. (FH 177m. Tr. M.R.L.)*

Inscription on a black-figured vase.

I am Melosa's prize. She won a victory in the girls' carding contest.

42. *Praxidice and Dyseris. Thessaly, early 5th cent. B.C. (FH 152. Tr. M.R.L.)*

A dedicatory epigram for an offering.

Praxidice made this garment, Dyseris designed it: the skill of both is united.

43. *A female philosopher.*[3] *Athens, 3rd cent. B.C. (Diogenes Laertius 6. 96-8, 3rd cent. A.D. Tr. M.R.L.)*

Hipparchia fell in love with both Crates' discourses and his way of life. She paid no attention to any of her suitors, their money, their high birth, or their good looks. To her Crates was everything. And in fact she threatened her parents that she would kill herself, if they didn't let her marry him. Her parents begged Crates to dissuade her. He did everything he could, but finally when he couldn't persuade her, he stood up and took off his clothes in front of her and said: 'This is your bridegroom; these are his possessions; plan accordingly!' He didn't think she would be able to be his partner, unless she could share in the same pursuits.

But the girl chose him. She adopted the same dress and went about with him; she made love to him in public; she went to dinner parties with him.[4] Once, when she went to a dinner party at Lysimachus' house, she put down Theodorus called the Atheist by using the following trick of logic: if an action could not be called wrong when done by Theodorus it could not be called wrong when done by Hipparchia. Therefore, if Theodorus does nothing wrong when he hits himself, Hipparchia does nothing wrong if she hits Theodorus. He had no defence against her logic, and started to pull off her cloak.[5] But Hipparchia did not get upset or excited as other women would. Then when he said to her: 'Here I am, Agave, who left behind my shuttles beside my loom',[6] 'Indeed it is I,' said Hipparchia; 'Theodorus – you don't think that I have arranged my life so badly, do you, if I have used the time I would have wasted on weaving for my education?'[7] These and many other stories are told about the woman philosopher.

Women victors in athletic contests all appear to have been sponsored by men and to have had professional charioteers.

44. *A royal victor. Sparta, early 4th cent. B.C. (AP XIII. 16. Tr. M.R.L.)*

My father and brothers were kings of Sparta. I, Cynisca, won a victory

with my swift-running horses[8] and set up this statue. I claim that I am
the only woman from all Greece to have won this crown.

45. *Winner of a four-horse chariot race. Oxyrhynchus, 268/7 B.C. (FGH 257a*
Fr. 6/Oxyrhynchus papyrus 2082. Tr. M.R.L.)

Bilistiche[9] of Magnesia's four-colt chariot. She was the hetaera of
Ptolemy Philadelphus.

46. *Winner of a two-horse chariot race. Larisa, early 2nd cent. B.C. (IG IX. ii.*
526. 19-20. Tr. M.R.L.)

From a list of victors in various competitions from all over the Greek
world.

Aristoclea from Larisa, daughter of Megacles, in the two-horse chariot
race.

47. *From the Panathenaic victor lists.*[10] *Athens, 2nd cent. B.C. (IG II² 2313.*
9-15, 60; 2314. 50, 92-4. Tr. M.R.L.)

(*194/3 B.C.*) Zeuxo of Argos, daughter of Polycrates,[11] in the horse race
... Encrateia of Argos, daughter of Polycrates, in the four-horse chariot
race; Hermione of Argos, daughter of Polycrates ... (*190/89 B.C.*) Zeuxo
of Cyrene, daughter of Ariston, in the four-horse chariot race ... (*182
B.C.*) Zeuxo of Argos from Achaea, daughter of Polycrates, in the four-
horse chariot race ... Hermione of Argos, daughter of Polycrates ...

48. *A benefactress. Priene, 1st cent. B.C. (Pleket 5. Tr. M.R.L.)*

Phile, daughter of Apollonius wife of Thessalus son of Polydeuces; as
the first woman *stephanephorus*[12] she dedicated at her own expense a
receptacle for water and the water pipes in the city.

49. *An accomplished woman. Sardis, 1st cent. B.C. (Peek 1881. Tr. M.R.L.)*

Inscription set up by the municipality, in honour of Menophila, daughter
of Hermagenes.

This stone marks a woman of accomplishment and beauty. Who she is the Muses' inscriptions reveal: Menophila. Why she is honoured is shown by a carved lily and an alpha, a book and a basket, and with these a wreath. The book shows that you were wise, the wreath that you wore on your head shows that you were a leader; the letter alpha[13] that you were an only child; the basket is a sign of your orderly excellence; the flower shows the prime of your life, which Fate stole away. May the dust lie light on you in death. Alas; your parents are childless; to them you have left tears.

1. 494 B.C. Cf. Herodotus 6.77-83.

2. The whole story may be an aetion (or fictional narrative explanation) for this transvestite ritual and the strange law cited below. Cf. Plutarch's account (*Theseus* 7) of the origin of the Athenian transvestite Oschophoria.

3. Her brother Metrocles was also a philosopher; cf. Magnilla (no. 168).

4. Two of Plato's women disciples were said to have worn men's clothing; Diog. Laert. 3. 46. Usually the only women at men's dinner parties were courtesans, e.g. Neaera, below, p. 54

5. Cf. how the prefect sentences the scholarly Irene to a brothel, below, p. 274.

6. Agave's boast to her father in Euripides, *Bacchae* 1326, when she returns from the hunt, thinking she has caught a lion; but the head she is carrying turns out to be her son's.

7. Cf. Antipater of Thessalonica's epigram (*AP* VII, 413): 'I, Hipparchia, have no use for the works of deep-robed women; I have chosen the Cynics' virile life. I don't need capes with brooches or deep-soled slippers; I don't like glossy nets for my hair. My wallet is my staff's travelling companion, and the double cloak that goes with them, the cover for my bed on the ground. I'm much stronger than Atalanta from Maenalus, because my wisdom is better than racing over the mountain.'

8. The wording suggests that she could have owned the horses herself; see below, p. 65.

9. She won again in 264, and was made a goddess as well!

10. None is from Athens.

11. An important Ptolemaic official, governor of Cyprus.

12. A special magistrate who had the right to wear a crown (*stephanos*).

13. The numeral one.

IV

Occupations

All specific information about women in retail trade comes from Athens. Men dominated lucrative trades (armaments, books, animals); women handled only relatively small sums. Prostitution may have been an exception, but we lack data about prices, and fees paid to owners or employers.

50. *A washerwoman. Athens, 6th cent. B.C. (IG I² 473. Tr. M.R.L.)*

Smikythe, a washerwoman, offered a tithe.

51. *A society of launderers. Athens, 4th cent. B.C. (IG II² 2934. Tr. M.R.L.)*

A tablet set up by a society of persons who washed clothes on the banks of the Ilissos river.

To the nymphs and all the gods, fulfilling a vow, the washers set up this tablet: Zoagoras the son of Zocyprus, Socyprus the son of Zoagoras, Thallos, Leuce,[1] Socrates son of Polycrates, Apollopanes, Euporionus, Sosistratus, Manes, Myrrhine,[2] Sosias, Sosigenes, Midas.

52. *A midwife and physician. Athens, 4th cent. B.C. (Kaibel 45/Pleket 1. Tr. M.R.L.)*

The memorial tablet represents two women, one seated, one standing, surrounded by infants of both sexes.

Phanostrate, a midwife and physician,[3] lies here. She caused pain to none, and all lamented her death.

53. *Prostitutes. Athens, 4th cent. B.C. (Alexis, Fr. 18 Pickard-Cambridge. Tr. M.R.L.)*

First of all, they care about making money and robbing their neighbours. Everything else has second priority. They string up traps for everyone. Once they start making money, they take in new prostitutes who are getting their first start in the profession. They remodel these girls immediately, and their manners and looks remain no longer the same. Suppose one of them is small; cork is sewn into her shoes. Tall? she wears thin slippers and goes around with her head pitched toward her shoulder; that reduces her height. No hips? she puts on a bustle, and the onlookers make comments about her nice bottom. They have false breasts for them like the comic actors'; they set them on straight out and pull their dresses forwards as if with punting poles. Eyebrows too light? They paint them with lamp-black. Too dark? she smears on white lead. Skin too white? she rubs on rouge. If a part of her body is pretty, she shows it bare. Nice teeth? then she is forced to keep laughing, so present company can see the mouth she's so proud of. If she doesn't like laughing, she spends the day inside, like the meat at the butcher's, when goats' heads are on sale; she keeps a thin slip of myrtle wood propped up between her lips, so that in time she will grin, whether she wants to or not. They rebuild their bodies with these devices.

54. *A nurse. Athens, after 350 B.C. (Kaibel 48/IG II² 7873. Tr. M.R.L.)*

[Epitaph for] Apollodorus the immigrant's[4] daughter, Melitta, a nurse.[5] Here the earth covers Hippostrate's good nurse; and Hippostrate still misses you. 'I loved you while you were alive, nurse, I love you still now even beneath the earth and now I shall honour you as long as I live. I know that for you beneath the earth also, if there is reward for the good, honours will come first to you, in the realm of Persephone and of Pluto.'

55. *A mother. Athens, after 350 B.C. (Kaibel 776/IG II² 4334. Tr. M.R.L.)*

By her handiwork and skill, and with righteous courage, Melinna raised her children and set up this memorial to you, Athena, goddess of handiwork, a share of the possessions she has won, in honour of your kindness.

56. *A thrifty woman. Athens, after 350 B.C. (IG II² 12254. Tr. M.R.L.)*

I worked with my hands; I was a thrifty woman, I, Nicarete who lie here.

57. *A groceress. Athens, 4th cent. B.C. (IG III. iii. 87. Tr. M.R.L.)*[6]

... Callias the grocer in the neighbour's street and his wife Thraitta ... Glycanthis whom they call Malthace ... Mania the groceress near the spring ...

58. *Professions of freedwomen, from inscriptions recording the completion of the process of manumission. Athens, 4th cent. B.C.*

(i) Lewis, *Hesperia* 28 (1959) 208-38

(A. 221) Onesime, sesame seed-seller ... (255) Lampris, wet-nurse ... (259) Eupeithe, her child, wet-nurse ... (328) Lyde, woolworker[7]... (468) Rhodia, woolworker ... (472) Cordype, her child, woolworker ... (493) Thraitta, groceress ... (497) Itame, woolworker ... (505) Demetria, harpist ... (518) Olympias, woolworker ... (B. 91) ... one,[8] horsetender ... (112) Atta, pulse vendor ... (114) Malthace, woolworker (with her three children) ... (212) ... rityra,[9] *aulos*-player ... (214) Echo, woolworker.

(ii) Lewis, *Hesperia* 37 (1968) 368-80

(49.4-5) Elpis,[10] *aulos*-player ... (50.34) Habrosyne, perfume vendor[11]

(iii) (*IG* II[2] 1561. 22-7) Midas[12] sesame seed-seller and Soteris[13] sesame seed-seller (from the same household) ... (1570. 73) Piloumene, honey-seller ... (1576.15ff) Melitta, frankincense seller ... (1578.5ff) shoe-seller ...[14]

59. *Professions of women, from inscriptions on gravestones. Athens, 4th cent. B.C.*

(*IG* II[2] 11647) Good Theoxene, wet-nurse ... (12387) Good Paideusis, wet-nurse ...(12559) Good Pynete, wet-nurse (11254) Elephantis, cloak-seller ... (11688) Thraitta, unguent-boiler ... (12073) Melitta, salt-vendor ... (12996) Philyra, wet-nurse (13065) Choerile, wet-nurse[15]

60. *A tumbler. Athens, 2nd cent. B.C. (IG II[2] 12583. Tr. M.R.L.)*

Excellent Sanno, a good tumbler.

61. *Menophila. Athens, 1st cent. B.C.? (Agora XVII no. 913. Tr. M.R.L.)*

The tomb of Menophila [connected] with the theatre.

62. *A daughter. Cape Zoster, near Athens, 56/5 B.C. (Kaibel 118. Tr. M.R.L.)*

An epitaph by a mother for a daughter who worked for Cleopatra at the royal court of Alexandria.

Her mother, an Athenian woman, raised her to be an attendant of foreign storerooms. She too rushed for her child's sake to come to the palace of the king who had set her over his rich possessions. Yet still she could not bring her daughter back alive. But the daughter has a tomb in Athens instead of on Libyan sand.[16]

63. *A harpist. Delphi, 86 B.C. (Pleket 6. Tr. M.R.L.)*

An inscription honouring a Theban woman for her services to Delphi. In a succeeding paragraph, similar honours are awarded to her nephew Lycinus, who lived with her.

To the god. With good fortune. During the archonship of Habromachus, in the month Boucatios. Strategos, Cleon, Antiphilus, and Damon were serving as councillors for the first six-month period.

The city of Delphi has decreed: whereas Polygnota, daughter of Socrates, a Theban harpist having come to Delphi, at the appointed time of the Pythian games, which could not be held on account of the present war, began on that very day and gave a day's time and performed at the request of the archons and the citizens for three days, and won the highest degree of respect, deserving the praise of Apollo and of the Theban people and of our city – she is awarded a crown and five hundred drachmas. With good fortune.

Voted: to commend Polygnota, daughter of Socrates, the Theban, for her piety and reverence toward the god and for her dedication to her profession; to bestow on her and on her descendants the guest-friendship of the city, the right to consult the oracle, the privileges of being heard first, of safety, of exemption from taxes, and of front seating at the games held by the city, the right of owning land and a house and all the other honours ordinarily awarded to other benefactors of the city; to invite her to the town hall to the public hearth, and provide her with a victim to sacrifice to Apollo. To the god. With good fortune.

IV. Occupations

1. Woman's name.
2. Woman's name.
3. See S.B. Pomeroy, *AJP*99 (1978) 499-500.
4. Literally, the Isoteles' daughter, referring to a favoured class of metics.
5. Kaibel 47 is a 4th cent. epitaph for a nurse who came from the Peloponnesus.
6. From a bronze curse tablet.
7. All woolworkers listed are female.
8. The word-ending indicates a female name.
9. See note 7.
10. Set free by her master under arrangements similar to those made for Neaera, below, p. 51.
11. Her owner was a resident alien.
12. Male.
13. Female.
14. See note 8.
15. 12812-12816 state only wet-nurse, without proper name.
16. The desirability of burial at home is a common motif in epitaphs. Cf. FH 75 and Peek 927.

V

Law

64. *Laws relating to women, Gortyn, c. 450 B.C. (Gortyn Law Code, Inscr.*
Creticae 4.72, cls II. 45 – III. 49; V. 9-28; VII. 15-29; VIII. 42-3, 12-20. Tr.
C. Fornara and M.R.L.)

The laws recorded on this long inscription differ in many respects from
Athenian practice; in particular, women appear to have more
independence.

The property of divorced women

If a husband and wife divorce, that which is her property she shall keep,
whatever she had when she went to the husband, and [she shall keep], of
the produce, the half, if there is any [derived] from her property, and
[she shall keep] of whatever she weaves [in the household], the [half],
whatever there may be, and five staters, if the husband is responsible for
the separation. But if the husband claims [the guilt] is [not] his own, the
judge shall decide under oath [whether it is]. If anything else is taken by
her from the husband, five staters shall be her payment and whatever she
takes from him and whatever she purloins, she shall return it. But as to
those things she denies, [the judge] shall rule that the woman take oath
by Artemis [by going] to [the] Amyclaean [temple] to the Archeress.
Whatever someone takes away from her when she has taken oath, five
staters shall be his payment and the thing itself. If a stranger helps her
carry [anything] off, ten staters shall be his payment and the thing's
double value, whatever the judge shall swear he carried off.

If a man dies with children left behind, if the wife wishes, with her
property in her possession she shall marry and with [as well] whatever
her husband gave her in accordance with the written agreements, in the
presence of witnesses, three in number, adult, and free. But if she takes
anything away from the children, she shall be subject to trial.

If [the husband] is without issue when he dies, her own possessions
she shall keep and of whatever she weaves the half, and of the produce
from within [the household] she shall together with the heirs have her

share apportioned to her and whatever the husband gave in written agreement. If she takes anything else, she shall be subject to trial.

If the wife is without issue when she dies, her property they shall give to the heirs, and of whatever she weaved the half, and of the produce, if there is any from her property, the half. If [either] wishes to give gifts, man or woman, either clothing or twelve staters or a twelve-stater object [it is permitted] but not more.

If a female serf be separated from a male serf, whether he is alive or dead, her own property she shall keep. If she takes anything else, she shall be subject to trial.

If a woman gives birth when she is divorced, she shall bring it to her husband at his house in the presence of witnesses, three in number. If he does not accept it, it shall be in the power of the mother whether the child shall be raised or exposed.

The inheritance line

If a man dies or a woman, if there are children or, of children, [grand]children, or of these [children, great grand]children, these shall possess the property. If there is none of these, brothers of the dead person and brothers' children or their children, [if they exist,] these shall possess the property. If there is none of these, those to whom it falls by way of the source of the property, these shall take it. If there are no heirs of the household those who make up the *kleros*[1] shall possess the property.

The marriage line for heiresses

The heiress shall marry the brother of the father, of those who are alive, who is the oldest. If there are more heiresses [than one] and brothers of the father, to the next oldest shall she be married. If there are no brothers of the father, but sons of the brothers, [the heiress] shall marry the one who [is son] of the oldest. If there are more heiresses and sons of the brothers, [the additional heiress] shall marry that other who is next [in age] to the oldest. But only one heiress shall be obtained by the heir, and not more.

A woman becomes an heiress if her father is not alive nor a brother from the same father. If there are no claimants for the heiress as prescribed[2] she is to have all the property and to marry whomever of her tribe she might wish. If no one in her tribe wishes to marry her, the relatives of the heiress should announce to the tribe, 'Doesn't anyone want to marry her?' And if someone wants to marry her, he must do so in thirty days from the time of the announcement. If he doesn't, she may marry someone else, whomever she can.[3]

Athens

65. *Funeral law. Ioulis on Keos, late 5th cent. B.C. (Syll. 1218. Tr. N. Lewis)*

Legislation frequently limited the expense, luxury, and amount of mourning at funerals. In practical terms, such laws also effectively restricted women's opportunities for gathering and self-expression. The following, from Ioulis on the island of Keos, dates from the late fifth century B.C. but is a copy of an earlier Athenian law.[4]

The dead shall be buried as follows: in three or fewer white cloths – i.e. a spread, a shroud and a coverlet – the three worth not over a hundred drachmas. They shall carry him out on a simply-wrought bed and shall not cover the bier with the cloths. They shall take to the tomb not more than three measures of wine and not more than one measure of olive oil, and they shall carry away the [empty] jars. They shall carry the corpse, covered, in silence all the way to the tomb. They shall perform the pre-burial sacrifice according to ancestral custom. They shall carry home from the tomb the bed and the spreads.

On the following day a free man shall sprinkle first the house with sea water, and then all the rooms with hyssop. When it has been sprinkled throughout, the house shall be cleansed and they shall offer sacrifices upon the hearth.

The women who go to the funeral shall not go away from the tomb before the men.

They shall not hold monthly services for the dead.

They shall not place a cup beneath the bed, nor pour out the water, nor carry the sweepings to the tomb.

Wherever a person dies, after the bed is carried out no women shall go to the house except those polluted [by the death]; those polluted are mother, wife, sisters and daughters, in addition to these not more than five women, namely children of daughters and cousins, and no one else. The polluted shall be cleansed by washing ... in poured water.

(*The rest is lost.*)

66. *A will giving a man's wife to his freedman. Athens, 4th cent. B.C. (Demosthenes 45. 28. Tr. M.R.L.)*

I, Pasion of Archarnae, have made the following provisions in my will: I leave my wife Archippe to Phormios, and in addition I leave Archippe as dowry a talent from my property in Peparethus,[5] and another talent from here,[6] a household worth one hundred minae, its maidservants and gold, and everything else therein – all this I leave to Archippe.[7]

67. *Aristotle's will. 4th cent. B.C. (Diogenes Laertius 5. 11-16, 3rd cent. A.D. Tr. R.D. Hicks (LCL))*

Restriction of women's rights to own property and to determine the course of their own lives provides vivid illustrations of Athenian male society's estimation of women's capabilities and general value. In this document the speaker is Aristotle himself.

All will be well; but, in case anything should happen, Aristotle has made these dispositions. Antipater is to be executor in all matters and in general; but, until Nicanor shall arrive, Aristomenes, Timarchus, Hipparchus, Dioteles and (if he consent and if circumstances permit him) Theophrastus shall take charge as well of Herpyllis and the children as of the property. And when the girl shall be grown up she shall be given in marriage to Nicanor; but if anything happen to the girl (which heaven forbid – and no such thing will happen) before her marriage, or when she is married but before there are children, Nicanor shall have full powers, both with regard to the child and with regard to everything else, to administer in a manner worthy both of himself and of us. Nicanor shall take charge of the girl and of the boy Nicomachus as he shall think fit in all that concerns them as if he were father and brother. And if anything should happen to Nicanor (which heaven forbid!) either before he marries the girl, or when he has married her but before there are children, any arrangements that he may make shall be valid. And if Theophrastus is willing to live with her, he shall have the same rights as Nicanor. Otherwise, the executors in consultation with Antipater shall administer as regards the daughter and the boy as seems to them to be best. The executors and Nicanor, in memory of me and of the steady affection which Herpyllis has borne towards me, shall take care of her in every other respect and, if she desires to be married, shall see that she be given to one not unworthy; and besides what she has already received they shall give her a talent of silver out of the estate and three handmaids whomsoever she shall choose besides the maid she has at present and the man-servant Pyrrhaeus; and if she chooses to remain at Chaleis, the lodge by the garden, if in Stagira, my father's house. Whichever of these two houses she chooses, the executors shall furnish with such furniture as they think proper and as Herpyllis herself may approve. Nicanor shall take charge of the boy Myrmex, that he be taken to his own friends in a manner worthy of me with the property of his which we received. Ambraeis shall be given her freedom, and on my daughter's marriage shall receive 500 drachmas and the maid whom she now has. And to Thale shall be given, in addition to the maid whom she has and who was bought, 1,000 drachmas and a maid. And Simon, in addition to the money before paid to him towards another servant, shall either have a servant purchased for him or receive a further sum of money. And Tycho, Philo, Olympius and his child shall have their freedom when my daughter is married. None of the servants who waited upon me shall be sold but they shall continue to be employed; and when they arrive at the proper age they shall have their freedom if they deserve it. My executors shall see to it, when the images which Gryllion has been commissioned to execute are finished, that they be set up, namely that of Nicanor, that of Proxenus, which it was my intention to have executed, and that of Nicanor's mother; also they shall set up the bust which has been executed of Arimnestus, to be a memorial of him seeing that he died childless, and shall dedicate my mother's statue to Demeter at Nemea or wherever they think best. And wherever they bury me, there the bones of Pythias shall be laid, in accordance with her own instructions. And to commemorate Nicanor's safe return, as I vowed on his behalf, they shall set up in Stagira stone statues of life size to Zeus and Athena the Saviours.

Nos 68 and 69 are citations of the 'law' from orations representing established custom rather than actual legislation.

68. *Provisions for female children. Athens, 4th cent. B.C (Demosthenes,. Against Macartatus 51, 54. Tr. A. T. Murray (LCL))*

Whenever a man dies without making a will, if he leaves female children his estate shall go with them, but if not, the persons herein mentioned shall be entitled to his property.[8] If there be brothers by the same father, and if there be lawfully born sons of brothers, they shall take the share of the father. But if there are no brothers or sons of brothers, their descendants shall inherit it in like manner; but males and the sons of males shall take precedence, if they are of the same ancestors, even though they be more remote of kin. If there are no relatives on the father's side within the degree of children of cousins, those on the mother's side shall inherit in like manner. But if there shall be no relatives on either side within the degree mentioned, the nearest of kin on the father's side shall inherit. But no illegitimate child of either sex shall have the right of succession either to religious rites or civic privileges, from the time of the archonship of Euclides.[9]

In regard to all heiresses who are classified as Thetes,[10] if the nearest of kin does not wish to marry one, let him give her in marriage with a portion of five hundred drachmas, if he be of the class of Pentacosiomedimni, if of the class of Knights, with a portion of three hundred, and if of the class of Zeugitae, with one hundred and fifty, in addition to what is her own. If there are several kinsmen in the same degree of relationship, each one of them shall contribute to the portion of the heiress according to his due share. And if there be several heiresses, it shall not be necessary for a single kinsman to give in marriage more than one, but the next of kin shall in each case give her in marriage or marry her himself. And if the nearest of kin does not marry her or give her in marriage, the archon shall compel him either to marry her himself or give her in marriage. And if the archon shall not compel him, let him be fined a thousand drachmas, which are to be consecrated to Hera. And let any person who chooses denounce to the archon any person who disobeys this law.

69. *Married heiresses. Athens, 4th cent. B.C. (Isaeus 3. 64. Tr. M.R.L.)*

The law states that women who have been given in marriage by their fathers and who have been living with their husbands (and who could make better provision for them than a father?), that even a woman thus given in marriage, if her father dies without leaving legitimate sons, becomes subject to the legal power of their next of kin; and many men who have already been living with their wives have been deprived of them [in this manner].[11]

70. *Property. Athens, 4th cent. B.C. (Isaeus 10.10. Tr. M.R.L.)*

A child is not permitted to make a will. For the law expressly forbids children and women from being able to make a contract [about anything worth] more than a bushel of barley.[12]

71. *Maintenance. Athens, 4th cent. B.C. (Isaeus 3. 39. Tr. M.R.L.)*

Even men who give their female relatives as concubines make agreements about what will be given to them as concubines.

72. *Payment of a dowry. Athens, 4th cent. B.C. (IG II² 2679. Tr. M.R.L.)*

Renewal of a document in which Pythodorus had assigned a dowry of four thousand drachmas to his daughter.

In the year Euxenippus was archon;[13] boundary of the lands and houses, securities for the dowry of Xenariste daughter of Pythodorus of Gargettus; this is half, with interest accrued [given to] her, of the four thousand drachmas[?], until the year Leostratus was archon.[14]

73. *Proof of marriage. Athens, 4th cent. B.C. (Isaeus 8. 18-20. Tr. E.S. Forster (LCL))*

> Proof of legal marriage, offered by the son of the woman who is making claims to her husband Ciron's estate. Because she is a respectable woman (cf. Neaera, below, no. 77), her name is not mentioned.[15]

Now it is not only from these proofs that our mother is clearly shown to be the legitimate wife of Ciron; but there is also the evidence of our father's conduct and the attitude adopted by the wives of his fellow-demesmen towards her. When our father took her in marriage, he gave a wedding-feast and invited three of his friends as well as his relatives, and he gave a marriage-banquet to the members of his *phratry* according to their statutes. Also the wives of the demesmen afterwards chose our mother, together with the wife of Diocles of Pithus, to preside at the Thesmophoria[16] and to carry out the ceremonies jointly with her. Again, our father at our birth introduced us to the members of his *phratry*, having declared on oath, in accordance with the established laws, that he was introducing the children of an Athenian mother duly married; and none of the members made any objection or disputed the truth of his statements, though they were present in large numbers and always look carefully into such matters. Yet do not for a moment suppose, that, if our mother had been such as our opponents allege, our father would have either given a wedding-feast or provided a marriage-banquet and not rather hushed up the whole matter; or that the wives of the other demesmen would have chosen her to celebrate the festival with the wife of Diocles and given the sacred objects into her hands and not rather entrusted this office to some other woman; or that the members of the *phratry* would have admitted us and not rather objected and justified their objection, if it had not been universally admitted that our mother was a legitimate wife of Ciron. As it was, owing to the notoriety of the fact and its recognition by so many persons, no such question was raised from any quarter. Now call the witnesses to prove the truth of these statements.

74. *Legitimacy. Athens, 4th cent. B.C. (Isaeus 6. 18-24. Tr. E.S. Forster (LCL))*

The sons of Euctemon's mistress, Alce, claim that they were adopted by Euctemon and thus are heirs to his estate. Since his legitimate sons are all dead, his sons-in-law, their successors in line of inheritance, hired Isaeus to protect their interests, alleging that Alce's sons gutted the estate.

It is perhaps painful, gentlemen, to Phanostratus[17] to bring to light the misfortunes of Euctemon; but it is essential that a few facts should be given, so that, knowing the truth, you may more easily give the right verdict. Euctemon lived for ninety-six years, and for most of this period had the reputation of being a fortunate man; he possessed considerable property and had children and a wife, and in all other respects enjoyed a reasonable degree of prosperity. In his old age, however, a serious misfortune befell him, which brought ruin to his house, caused him great financial loss, and set him at variance with his nearest relatives. The cause and manner of it I will set forth in the fewest possible words. He had a freedwoman, gentlemen, who managed a tenement-house of his at the Piraeus and kept prostitutes. As one of these she acquired a woman of the name of Alce, whom I think many of you know. This Alce, after her purchase, lived the life of a prostitute for many years but gave it up when she became too old. While she was still living in the tenement-house, she had relations with a freedman whose name was Dion, whom she declared to be the father of the young men [who are claiming to be his heirs]; and Dion did, in fact, bring them up as his own children. Some time later Dion, having committed a misdemeanour and being afraid of the consequences, withdrew to Sicyon. The woman Alce was then installed by Euctemon to look after his tenement-house in the Cerameicus near the postern gate, where wine is sold. Her establishment there, gentlemen, had many evil consequences. Euctemon, going there constantly to collect the rent, used to spend most of his time in the tenement-house, and sometimes took his meals with the woman, leaving his wife and children and his own home. In spite of the protests of his wife and sons, not only did he not cease to go there but eventually lived there entirely, and was reduced to such a condition by drugs or disease or some other cause, that he was persuaded by the woman to introduce the elder of the two boys to the members of his *phratry* under his own name. When, however, his son Philoctemon refused to agree to this, and the members of his *phratry* would not admit the boy, and the victim for the sacrifice of admission was removed from the altar,[18] Euctemon, being enraged against his son and wishing to insult him, announced his intention of marrying a sister of Democrates of Aphidna and recognising any children who should be born to her and bringing them into the family, unless he consented to allow Alce's son to be introduced. His relatives, knowing that no more children would be born to him at his time of life but that they would be forthcoming in some other manner, and that, as a result, still more serious quarrels would arise, advised Philoctemon, gentlemen, to allow him to introduce this child on the conditions which he demanded, giving him a single farm. And Philoctemon, ashamed at his father's folly but at a loss how to deal with the embarrassment of the moment, made no objection. An agreement having been thus concluded, and the child having been introduced on these terms, Euctemon gave up his project of marriage, proving thereby that the object of his threatened marriage was not to procure children but to obtain the introduction of this child into the *phratry*.

In each of the following three cases only one side's argument survives and the verdict is unknown.

75. *A husband's defence. Athens, c. 400 B.C. (Lysias, On the Murder of Eratosthenes 9-33, 37-50. Tr. K. Freeman)*

A husband who murdered his wife's lover, Eratosthenes, speaks in his own defence.

Members of the jury: when I decided to marry and had brought a wife home, at first my attitude towards her was this: I did not wish to annoy her, but neither was she to have too much of her own way. I watched her as well as I could, and kept an eye on her as was proper. But later, after my child had been born, I came to trust her, and I handed all my possessions over to her, believing that this was the greatest possible proof of affection.

Well, members of the jury, in the beginning she was the best of women. She was a clever housewife, economical and exact in her management of everything. But then, my mother died; and her death has proved to be the source of all my troubles, because it was when my wife went to the funeral that this man Eratosthenes saw her; and as time went on, he was able to seduce her. He kept a look out for our maid who goes to market; and approaching her with his suggestions, he succeeded in corrupting her mistress.

Now first of all, gentlemen, I must explain that I have a small house which is divided into two – the men's quarters and the women's – each having the same space, the women upstairs and the men downstairs.

After the birth of my child, his mother nursed him; but I did not want her to run the risk of going downstairs every time she had to give him a bath, so I myself took over the upper storey, and let the women have the ground floor. And so it came about that by this time it was quite customary for my wife often to go downstairs and sleep with the child, so that she could give him the breast and stop him from crying.

This went on for a long while, and I had not the slightest suspicion. On the contrary, I was in such a fool's paradise that I believed my wife to be the chastest woman in all the city.

Time passed, gentlemen. One day, when I had come home unexpectedly from the country, after dinner, the child began crying and complaining. Actually it was the maid who was pinching him on purpose to make him behave so because – as I found out later – this man was in the house.

Well, I told my wife to go and feed the child, to stop his crying. But at first she refused, pretending that she was glad to see me back after my long absence. At last I began to get annoyed, and I insisted on her going.

'Oh, yes!' she said. 'To leave *you* alone with the maid up here! You mauled her about before, when you were drunk!'

I laughed. She got up, went out, closed the door – pretending that it was a joke – and locked it. As for me, I thought no harm of all this, and I had not the slightest suspicion. I went to sleep, glad to do so after my journey from the country.

Towards morning, she returned and unlocked the door.

I asked her why the doors had been creaking during the night. She explained that the lamp beside the baby had gone out, and that she had then gone to get a light from the neighbours.

I said no more. I thought it really was so. But it did seem to me, members of the jury, that she had done up her face with cosmetics, in spite of the fact that her brother had died only a month before. Still, even so, I said nothing about it. I just went off, without a word.

After this, members of the jury, an interval elapsed, during which my injuries had progressed, leaving me far behind. Then, one day, I was approached by an old hag. She had been sent by a woman – Eratosthenes' previous mistress, as I found out later. This woman, furious because he no longer came to see her as before, had been on the look-out until she had discovered the reason. The old crone, therefore, had come and was lying in wait for me near my house.

'Euphiletus,' she said, 'please don't think that my approaching you is in any way due to a wish to interfere. The fact is, the man who is wronging you and your wife is an enemy of ours. Now if you catch the woman who does your shopping and works for you, and put her through an examination, you will discover all. The culprit,' she added, 'is Eratosthenes from Oea. Your wife is not the only one he has seduced – there are plenty of others. It's his profession.'

With these words, members of the jury, she went off.

At once I was overwhelmed. Everything rushed into my mind, and I was filled with suspicion. I reflected how I had been locked into the bedroom. I remembered how on that night the middle and outer doors had creaked, a thing that had never happened before; and how I had had the idea that my wife's face was rouged. All these things rushed into my mind, and I was filled with suspicion.

I went back home, and told the servant to come with me to market. I took her instead to the house of one of my friends; and there I informed her that I had discovered all that was going on in my house.

'As for you,' I said, 'two courses are open to you: either to be flogged and sent to the tread-mill, and never be released from a life of utter misery; or to confess the whole truth and suffer no punishment, but win pardon from me for your wrongdoing. Tell me no lies. Speak the whole truth.'

At first, she tried denial, and told me that I could do as I pleased – she knew nothing. But when I named Eratosthenes to her face, and said that he was the man who had been visiting my wife, she was dumbfounded, thinking that I had found out everything exactly. And then at last, falling at my feet and exacting a promise from me that no harm should be done to her, she denounced the villain. She described how he had first approached her after the funeral, and then how in the end she had passed the message on, and in course of time my wife had been over-persuaded. She explained the way in which he had contrived to get into the house, and how when I was in the country my wife had gone to a religious service with this man's mother, and everything else that had happened. She recounted it all exactly.

When she had told all, I said: 'See to it that nobody gets to know of this; otherwise the promise I made you will not hold good. And furthermore, I expect you to show me this actually happening. I have no use for words. I want the *fact* to be exhibited, if it really is so.'

She agreed to do this.

Four or five days then elapsed, as I shall prove to you by important evidence. But before I do so, I wish to narrate the events of the last day.

I had a friend and relative named Sostratus. He was coming home from the country after sunset when I met him. I knew that as he had got back so late, he would not find any of his own people at home; so I asked him to dine with me. We went home to my place, and going upstairs to the upper storey, we had dinner there. When he felt restored, he went off; and I went to bed.

Then, members of the jury, Eratosthenes made his entry; and the maid wakened me and told me that he was in the house.

I told her to watch the door; and going downstairs, I slipped out noiselessly.

I went to the houses of one man after another. Some I found at home; others, I was told, were out of town. So collecting as many as I could of those who were there, I went back. We procured torches from the shop

near by, and entered my house. The door had been left open by
arrangement with the maid.

We forced the bedroom door. The first of us to enter saw him still
lying beside my wife. Those who followed saw him standing naked on
the bed.

I knocked him down, members of the jury, with one blow. I then
twisted his hands behind his back and tied them. And then I asked him
why he was committing this crime against me, of breaking into my
house.

He answered that he admitted his guilt; but he begged and besought
me not to kill him – to accept a money-payment instead.

But I replied: 'It is not I who shall be killing you, but the law of the
state, which you, in transgressing, have valued less highly than your own
pleasure. You have preferred to commit this great crime against my wife
and my children, rather than to obey the law and be of decent
behaviour.'

Thus, members of the jury, this man met the fate which the laws
prescribe for wrongdoers of his kind.[19]

Eratosthenes was not seized in the street and carried off, nor had he
taken refuge at the altar, as the prosecution alleges. The facts do not
admit of it: he was struck in the bedroom, he fell at once, and I bound his
hands behind his back. There were so many present that he could not
possibly escape through their midst, since he had neither steel nor wood
nor any other weapon with which he could have defended himself
against all those who had entered the room.

No, members of the jury: you know as well as I do how wrongdoers
will not admit that their adversaries are speaking the truth, and attempt
by lies and trickery of other kinds to excite the anger of the hearers
against those whose acts are in accordance with Justice.

To the Clerk of the Court: Read the law.

*The Law of Solon is read, that an adulterer may be put to death by the man who
catches him.*

He made no denial, members of the jury. He admitted his guilt, and
begged and implored that he should not be put to death, offering to pay
compensation. But I would not accept his estimate. I preferred to accord
a higher authority to the law of the state, and I took that satisfaction
which you, because you thought it the most just, have decreed for those
who commit such offences. Witnesses to the preceding, kindly step up.

*The witnesses come to the front of the court, and the Clerk reads their depositions.
When the Clerk has finished reading, and the witnesses have agreed that the
depositions are correct, the defendant again addresses the Clerk:*

Now please read this further law from the pillar of the Court of the Areopagus:

The Clerk reads another version of Solon's law, as recorded on the pillar of the Areopagus Court.

You hear, members of the jury, how it is expressly decreed by the Court of the Areopagus itself, which both traditionally and in your own day has been granted the right to try cases of murder, that no person shall be found guilty of murder who catches an adulterer with his wife and inflicts this punishment. The lawgiver was so strongly convinced of the justice of these provisions in the case of married women, that he applied them also to concubines, who are of less importance. Yet obviously, if he had known of any greater punishment than this for cases where married women are concerned, he would have provided it. But in fact, as it was impossible for him to invent any more severe penalty for corruption of wives, he decided to provide the same punishment as in the case of concubines.

To the Clerk of the Court: Please read me this law also.

The Clerk reads out further clauses from Solon's laws on rape.

You hear, members of the jury, how the lawgiver ordains that if anyone debauch by force a free man or boy, the fine shall be double that decreed in the case of a slave. If anyone debauch a woman — in which case it is *permitted* to kill him — he shall be liable to the same fine. Thus, members of the jury, the lawgiver considered violators deserving of a lesser penalty than seducers: for the latter he provided the death-penalty; for the former, the doubled fine. His idea was that those who use force are loathed by the persons violated, whereas those who have got their way by persuasion corrupt women's minds, in such a way as to make other men's wives more attached to themselves than to their husbands, so that the whole house is in their power, and it is uncertain who is the children's father, the husband or the lover ...

Consider, members of the jury, their accusation that it was I who on that day told the maid to fetch the young man. In my opinion, gentlemen, I should have been justified in using any means to catch the seducer of my wife. If there had been only words spoken and no actual offence, I should have been doing wrong; but when by that time they had gone to all lengths and he had often gained entry into my house, I consider that I should have been within my rights whatever means I employ to catch him. But observe that this allegation of the prosecution is also false. You can easily convince yourselves by considering the following:

I have already told you how Sostratus, an intimate friend of mine, met me coming in from the country around sunset, and dined with me, and when he felt refreshed, went off. Now in the first place, gentlemen, ask yourselves whether, if on that night I had had designs on Eratosthenes, it would have been better for me that Sostratus should dine elsewhere, or that I should take a guest home with me to dinner. Surely in the latter circumstances Eratosthenes would have been less inclined to venture into the house. Further, does it seem to you probable that I would have let my guest go, and been left alone, without company? Would I not rather have urged him to stay, so that he could help me to punish the adulterer?

Again, gentlemen, does it not seem to you probable that I would have passed the word round among my friends during the daytime, and told them to assemble at the house of one of my friends who lived nearest, rather than have started to run round at night, as soon as I found out, without knowing whom I should find at home and whom away? Actually, I called for Harmodius and certain others who were out of town – I did not know it – and others, I found, were not at home, so I went along taking with me whomever I could. But if I had known beforehand, does it not seem to you probable that I would have arranged for servants and passed the word round to my friends, so that I myself could go in with the maximum of safety – for how did I know whether he too might not have had a dagger or something? – and also in order that I might exact the penalty in the presence of the greatest number of witnesses? But in fact, since I knew nothing of what was going to happen on that night, I took with me whomever I could get.

Witnesses to the preceding, please step up.

Further witnesses come forward, and confirm their evidence as read out by the Clerk.

You have heard the witnesses, members of the jury. Now consider the case further in your own minds, inquiring whether there had ever existed between Eratosthenes and myself any other enmity but this. You will find none. He never brought any malicious charge against me, nor tried to secure my banishment, nor prosecuted me in any private suit. Neither had he knowledge of any crime of which I feared the revelation, so that I desired to kill him; nor by carrying out this act did I hope to gain money. So far from ever having had any dispute with him, or drunken brawl, or any other quarrel, I had never even set eyes on the man before that night. What possible object could I have had, therefore, in running so great a risk, except that I had suffered the greatest of all injuries at his hands? Again, would I myself have called in witnesses to my crime, when it was possible for me, if I desired to murder him without justification, to have had no confidants?

It is my belief, members of the jury, that this punishment was inflicted not in my own interests, but in those of the whole community. Such villains, seeing the rewards which await their crimes, will be less ready to commit offences against others if they see that you too hold the same opinion of them. Otherwise it would be far better to wipe out the existing laws and make different ones, which will penalise those who keep guard over their own wives, and grant full immunity to those who criminally pursue them. This would be a far more just procedure than to set a trap for citizens by means of the laws, which urge the man who catches an adulterer to do with him whatever he will, and yet allow the injured party to undergo a trial far more perilous than that which faces the law-breaker who seduces other men's wives. Of this, I am an example – I, who now stand in danger of losing life, property, everything, because I have obeyed the laws of the state.

76. *The case for the prosecution in a poisoning trial. Athens, c. 420 B.C. (Antiphon, Against a stepmother, on a charge of poisoning (excerpts). Tr. K. Freeman)*

The prosecutor is the deceased's son by his first marriage; the defendant is the deceased's second wife, represented by her sons, the prosecutor's half-brothers.

Members of the jury:

Young as I am, and still without experience of litigation, I am placed by this event in a position of terrible difficulty. Either I have to disobey the injunction laid on me by my father, that I should seek vengeance on his murderers; or if I do seek vengeance, I am driven into a feud with those with whom it is least desirable – my half-brothers and their mother. Events, and my half-brothers themselves, have driven me into bringing this suit against them. They are the very men who ought naturally to have come forward as avengers of the deceased, and allies of the avenger. But in fact, the precise opposite has come about: they have taken their stand here as my adversaries, on the side of murder as I and my indictment declare.

My plea to you, gentlemen, is this: if I prove that their mother did by intention and forethought cause the death of our father, and that she had been caught before, not once but several times, in the very act of plotting his murder, inflict punishment – avenge, in the first instance your laws, which you have received as an inheritance from heaven and your ancestors, and by which you must be guided when considering condemnation as judges in this court; avenge, in the second instance him who is dead and gone, and with him me also, who, alone and deserted,

am left to take his part! You, gentlemen, stand to me now in the place of
my family, because those who should have been his avengers and my
allies have come forward as the dead man's murderers and my
opponents. To whom, then, can anyone turn to for help, or where can he
go to seek sanctuary, except to you and to Justice? ...

There was in our house an upper room, which Philoneus used to
occupy whenever he had business in town. This Philoneus was an
honest, respectable man, a friend of my father's. He had a concubine,
whom he was intending to dispose of to a brothel. My stepmother, having
heard of this, made a friend of this woman; and when she got to know of
the injury Philoneus was proposing to do her, she sent for her. When the
woman came, my stepmother told her that she herself also was being
wrongly treated, by my father; and that if the woman would do as she
said, she was clever enough to restore the love of Philoneus for the
concubine, and my father's love for herself. As she expressed it, hers was
the creative part, the other woman's part was that of obeying orders. She
asked her therefore if she was willing to act as her assistant; and the
woman promised to do so – very readily, I imagine.

Later, it happened that Philoneus had to go down to the Piraeus in
connection with a religious ceremony to Zeus, Guardian of Property;
and at the same time my father was preparing for a voyage to Naxos. It
seemed to Philoneus an excellent idea, therefore, that he should make
the same trip serve a double purpose: that he should accompany my
father, his friend, down to the harbour, and at the same time perform his
religious duty and entertain him at a feast. Philoneus' concubine went
with them, to help them with the sacrifice and the banquet.

When they arrived at the port, they of course performed the sacrifice.
When the religious ceremony was over, the woman began to deliberate
with herself as to how and when she should administer the drug,
whether before dinner or after dinner. The result of her deliberation was
that she decided to do so after dinner, thus carrying out the instructions
of this Clytemnestra, my stepmother.

The whole story of the dinner would be too long for me to tell or you to
hear; but I shall try to narrate the rest to you in the fewest possible
words, that is, how the actual administration of the poison was
accomplished. When they had finished dinner, they naturally – as one of
them was sacrificing to Zeus and entertaining a guest, and the other was
about to set off on a voyage and was dining with his friend – they
naturally were proceeding to pour libations, and accompany them with
an offering of incense. Philoneus' concubine, as she was serving them
with the wine for the libation – a libation that was to accompany prayers
destined, alas! gentlemen, not to be fulfilled – poured in the poison. And
in the belief that she was doing something clever, she gave the bigger
dose to Philoneus, thinking that perhaps the more she gave him, the

more he would love her. She still did not know that she had been deceived by my stepmother, and did not find out until she was already involved in disaster. She poured in a smaller dose for my father. The two men poured out their libation; and then, taking in hand that which was their own destroyer, they drained their last draught.

Philoneus dropped dead instantly. My father was seized with an illness from which he died in three weeks. For this, the woman who had acted under orders has paid the penalty for her offence, in which she was an innocent accomplice: she was handed over to the public executioner after being broken on the wheel. But the woman who was the real cause, who thought out and engineered the deed – she will pay the penalty now, if you and heaven so decree ...

Which is more just – that the murderer should pay the penalty, or not? Which is more just – to pity rather the dead man, or the woman who killed him? The dead man, I would say. That would be the far more just and more righteous course for you in the eyes of god and man. And so at this point I demand that as she destroyed him without pity and without mercy, so she too shall be destroyed by you and by Justice. She acted of her own free will and compassed his death with guile; he died by force, an unwilling victim. Can it be denied, gentlemen, that he died by force – a man who was intending to set out on a voyage from this country, and who was dining with his friend? She it was who sent the poison, who gave the order that it should be given him to drink, and so killed my father. What claim has she to be pitied or to win consideration from you or anyone else? She did not see fit to have pity on her husband – no, but she wickedly and shamefully destroyed him.

Pity, as you know, is more properly bestowed in cases of involuntary suffering than of crime and offences committed voluntarily and with malice aforethought. Even as she, fearing neither gods nor heroes nor her fellow-men, destroyed the dead man, so let her in turn be destroyed by you and by Justice! Let her win neither consideration nor pity nor any sort of compunction from you, and thus meet with the punishment she has so justly earned!

I am amazed at my brother's hardihood, and puzzled as to his object, in declaring on oath, on his mother's behalf, that he 'knows for certain' that she has not committed this crime. How can anyone 'know for certain' about events at which he was not present? Naturally, people who are plotting the murder of their neighbours do not prepare their plans and make their preparations in the presence of witnesses. They do so with the greatest possible secrecy, so that no other human soul may know. But the victims of their machinations know nothing until they are caught in the grip of the menace; not till then do they recognise the destruction that is upon them. And then, if they are able – if they are not forestalled by death – they summon their friends and relatives, and give evidence and tell them the names of their murderers, and enjoin upon them to avenge the crime. Such was the injunction which my father laid on me when I was still a boy, when he was suffering from his last unhappy illness ...

I have now completed my account, and my effort on behalf of the dead man and the law. It rests with you to consider among yourselves what is to be done, and to pass a just verdict. It is my belief that the gods of the nether worlds have at heart the cause of those who are the victims of crime.

77. *The past activities of a courtesan. Athens, 4th cent. B.C. (Apollodorus, Against Neaera (excerpts). Tr. K. Freeman)*

This case, spitefully brought against the courtesan Neaera's pimp-lover Stephanus years after the facts described, when Neaera was in her seventies, concentrates not only on the legal issue of Neaera's citizenship, but on her past sexual activities.

She was one of seven little girls bought when small children by Nicaretê, a freedwoman who had been the slave of Charisius of Elis, and the wife of Charisius' cook Hippias. Nicaretê was a clever judge of beauty in little girls, and moreover she understood the art of rearing and training them skilfully, having made this her profession from which she drew her livelihood. She used to address them as daughters, so that she might exact the largest fee from those who wished to have dealings with them, on the ground that they were freeborn girls; but after she had reaped her profit from the youth of each of them, one by one, she then sold the whole lot of them together, seven in all: Anteia, Stratôla, Aristocleia, Metaneira, Phila, Isthmias, and the defendant Neaera.

Now who were their respective purchasers, and how they were set free by those who bought them from Nicaretê, I will explain in the course of my speech, if you wish to hear, and if I have enough time. But the fact that the defendant Neaera did belong to Nicaretê and worked as a prostitute open to all comers – this is the point to which I wish to return.

Lysias the professor of rhetoric was the lover of Metaneira. He decided that in addition to the other expenses he had incurred for her, he would like to get her initiated. He thought that the rest of his expenditure went to her owner, but whatever he spent on her over the festival and initiation ceremony would be a present for the girl herself. He therefore asked Nicaretê to come to the Mysteries and bring Metaneira so that she could be initiated and he promised to instruct her himself in the Mysteries.

When they arrived, Lysias did not admit them to his house, out of respect for his own wife, who was the daughter of Brachyllus and his own niece, and for his mother, who was somewhat advanced in years and lived in the same house. Instead, he lodged them – that is, Metaneira and Nicaretê – with Philostratus of Celonus, who was still a bachelor and also a friend of his. The women were accompanied by the defendant Neaera, who was already working as a prostitute, though she was not yet of the proper age.

As witness to the truth of my statements, namely that she was the slave of Nicaretê and used to accompany her and was hired out to anyone willing to pay, I now call upon Philostratus himself.

Philostratus testifies ...

On a later occasion, gentlemen, Simos the Thessalian brought Neaera here to the Great Panathenaic Festival. Nicaretê also accompanied them, and they put up at the house of Ctesippus son of Glauconidas. The defendant Neaera drank and dined with them in the presence of a large company, as a courtesan would do.

I now call witnesses to the truth of these statements. Please call Euphiletus son of Simon, and Aristomachus son of Critodemus.

They testify ...

After that, she worked openly at Corinth as a prostitute, and became famous. Among her lovers were Xenoclides the poet and Hipparchus the actor, who had her on hire. For the truth of these statements, I am unable to put before you the deposition of Xenoclides, because he is debarred by law from giving evidence ... But I now call Hipparchus himself, and I shall compel him to give evidence or else take the oath disclaiming knowledge of the facts, according to the law; otherwise I will subpoena him.

He testifies ...

After that, she acquired two lovers, Timanoridas of Corinth and Eucrates of Leucas. These men found Nicaretê's charges excessive, as she expected them to pay all the daily expenses of her household; so they paid down to Nicaretê 30 minas as the purchase-price of Neaera, and bought her outright from her mistress, according to the law of that city, to be their slave. They kept her and made use of her for as long as they wished. Then, being about to get married, they informed her that they did not wish to see the woman who had been their own mistress plying her trade in Corinth nor kept in a brothel: they would be glad to receive less money for her than they had paid, and to see her also reaping some benefit. They therefore offered to allow her, towards the price of her freedom, 1,000 drachmas, that is, 500 each; as for the 20 minas remaining, they told her to find this sum herself and repay it to them.

Neaera, on hearing these propositions from Timanoridas and Eucrates, sent messages to a number of her former lovers, asking them to come to

Corinth. Among these was Phrynion, an Athenian from Paeania, the son of Demon, and the brother of Demochares, a man who was living a dissolute and extravagant life, as the older of you remember. When Phrynion arrived, she told him of the proposition made to her by Eucrates and Timanoridas, and handed him the money which she had collected from her other lovers as a contribution towards the purchase of her freedom, together with her own savings, asking him to make up the amount to the 20 minas, and pay it to Eucrates and Timanoridas, so that she should be free.

Phrynion was delighted to hear this proposition of hers. He took the money which had been contributed by her other lovers, made up the deficit himself, and paid the 20 minas to Eucrates and Timanoridas as the price of her freedom and on condition that she would not practice her profession in Corinth. As a proof of these statements, I will call the man who then witnessed the transaction. Please call Philagrus of the suburb of Melite.

He testifies.

When they arrived here at Athens, he kept her and lived with her in a most dissolute and reckless way. He took her out to dinner with him wherever he went, where there was drinking; and whenever he made an after-dinner excursion, she always went too. He made love to her openly, anywhere and everywhere he chose, to excite the jealousy of the onlookers at his privilege. Among the many houses to which he took her on an after-dinner call was that of Chabrias of the suburb Alexonê, when the latter had won the victory at Delphi with a four-horse chariot team which he had bought from the sons of Mitys the Argive, and on his return from Delphi was celebrating victory down at Colias. On that occasion, many men made love to Neaera when she was drunk and Phrynion was asleep, including even some of Chabrias' servants. In proof of this I shall produce before you the actual eyewitnesses.

Please call Chionidês and Euthetion.

They testify.

However, finding herself treated with the most outrageous brutality by Phrynion, instead of being loved as she had expected, or having attention paid to her wishes, she packed up the goods in his house, including all the clothes and jewellery which he had provided for her personal adornment, and taking with her two servants, Thratta and Coccalina, ran away to Megara.

This happened when Asteius was Chief Magistrate at Athens[20] during your second war against Sparta. Neaera spent two years in Megara; but her profession did not produce sufficient income to run her house, as she was extravagant, and the Megarians are mean and stingy, and there was no great foreign colony there because it was war-time, and the Megarians favoured the Spartan side, but you were in command of the seas. She could not go back to Corinth because the terms of her release by Eucrates and Timanoridas were that she should not practise her profession there.

However, peace came.[21] It was then that our opponent Stephanus visited Megara. He put up at her house, as that of a prostitute, and became her lover. She told him her whole life-story and of her ill-treatment at the hands of Phrynion. She longed to live in Athens, but was afraid of Phrynion, because she had done him wrong and he was furious with her. She knew the violence and arrogance of his character. She therefore made the defendant Stephanus her protector, and while they were still in Megara, he talked encouragingly and filled her with hope, saying that Phrynion would be sorry for it if he laid hands on her, as he himself would take her as his wife, and would introduce the sons she already had to his clansmen as being his own, and would make citizens of them.No one on earth, he said, should do her any harm. And so he arrived here at Athens from Megara with her and her three children, Proxenus, Ariston, and a daughter, who now bears the name of Phano. He took her and the children to the little house which he owned, alongside the Whispering Hermes, between the house of Dorotheus the Eleusinian and the house of Cleinomachus, which now Spintharus has bought from him for 7 minas. Thus, the place was the whole of Stephanus' property at that time – he had nothing else.

He had two reasons for bringing her here: first, that he would have a handsome mistress without expense; secondly, that her profession would provide him with the necessaries of life and keep the household, for he had no other source of income, except what he picked up by occasional blackmail.

When Phrynion heard that she was in Athens and living with the defendant, he took some young men with him and went to Stephanus' house to get her. Stephanus asserted her freedom, according to law, and Phrynion thereupon summoned her before the Polemarch, under surety.[22] In proof of this, I will bring before you the Polemarch of that year ...

Please call Aietes.

He testifies.

When she had thus been bailed out by Stephanus and was living with him, she carried on the same profession no less than before, but she exacted a larger fee from those who wished to consort with her, as having now a certain position to keep up and as being a married woman. Stephanus helped her by blackmail; if he caught any rich unknown stranger making love to her, he used to lock him up in the house as an adulterer caught with his wife, and extract a large sum of money from him – naturally, because neither Stephanus nor Neaera had anything, not even enough to meet their daily expenses, but their establishment was large. There were himself and herself to keep, and three small children – the ones she brought with her to him – and two maids and a man-servant; and above all, she had acquired the habit of good living, as formerly it had been others who had provided her with all necessaries ...

To continue: Phrynion began his law-suit against Stephanus, on the grounds that Stephanus had robbed him of the defendant Neaera and made a free woman of her, and that Stephanus had received the goods of which Neaera had robbed him when she left. However, their friends brought them together and persuaded them to submit the dispute to arbitration. The arbitrator who sat on Phrynion's behalf was Satyrus of Alôpece, the brother of Lacedaemonius, and on Stephanus' behalf, Saurias of Lampra; they chose as umpire Diogeiton of Acharnae. These three met in the temple, and after hearing the facts from both the litigants and also from the woman herself, they gave their judgment, which was accepted by the litigants: namely, that the woman should be free and her own mistress, but that the goods which Neaera had taken from Phrynion when she left should all be returned to Phrynion, except the clothes and jewellery and maid-servants which had been bought for Neaera herself; further, that she should spend the same number of days with each of them; but that if they agreed to any other arrangement, this same arrangement should hold good; that the woman's upkeep should be provided by the person with whom she was living at the time; and that for the future the litigants should be friends and should bear no malice. Such was the settlement brought about by the decision of arbitrators in the case of Phrynion and Stephanus, concerning the defendant Neaera. In proof of this, the Clerk will read you the deposition.

Please call Satyrus of Alôpece, Saurias of Lampra, and Diogeiton of Acharnae.

They testify.

The following were the terms of settlement between Phrynion and Stephanus: that each shall keep at his house and have the enjoyment of Neaera for an equal number of days per month, unless they come to some different agreement.

When the business was over, the friends of each party, those who had assisted them at the arbitration and the rest, did as I believe is usual in such cases, especially when a mistress is in dispute: they went to dine with each of them at the times when he had Neaera with him, and she dined and drank with them as mistresses do ...

I have now outlined the facts about Neaera, and have supported my statements with evidence: that she was originally a slave, was twice sold, and practised the profession of a prostitute; that she ran away from Phrynion to Megara, and on her return to Athens was summoned before the Polemarch under surety. I now desire to prove to you that Stephanus himself has given evidence against her, showing that she is an alien.

The daughter of the defendant Neaera, whom she had brought as a little girl to Stephanus' house, was in those days called Strybele, but now has the name Phano. Stephanus gave this girl in marriage, as being his own daughter, to an Athenian citizen, Phrastor, together with a dowry of 30 minas. When she went to live with Phrastor, who was a hard-working man and who had got together his means by careful living, she was unable to accommodate herself to his ways, but hankered after her mother's habits and the dissolute ways of that household, being, I suppose, brought up to a similar licence. Phrastor observed that she was not well-behaved nor willing to be guided by him, and at the same time he found out for certain that she was not the daughter of Stephanus, but only of Neaera, so that he had been deceived on the first occasion when he was betrothed to her. He had understood that she was the daughter of Stephanus and not Neaera, the child of Stephanus' marriage with a free-born Athenian lady before he began to live with Neaera. Phrastor was most indignant at all this, and considering himself to have been outrageously treated and swindled, he turned the young woman out of his house after having lived with her for a year and when she was pregnant; and he refused to return the dowry.

Stephanus began a suit against him for alimony, lodged at the Odeon, according to the law enacting that if a man divorce his wife, he shall pay back the dowry, or else be liable to pay interest on it at the rate of eighteen per cent per annum; and that her legal guardian is entitled to bring a law-suit for alimony at the Odeon, on the wife's behalf. Phrastor also brought an indictment against Stephanus before the Thesmothetae, that Stephanus had betrothed to him, an Athenian citizen, the daughter of an alien woman, pretending that the girl was his own daughter, contrary to the following law. *To the Clerk*: Please read it.

The Clerk of the Court reads out the following law:

If any person give in marriage an alien woman to an Athenian citizen, pretending that she is related to him, he shall be deprived of his citizen status, and his property shall be confiscated, the third part to go to the person securing the conviction. The indictment shall be brought before the Thesmothetae, by any person so entitled, as in the case of usurpations of citizenship.

Thus the young woman was openly adjudged to be an alien, although Stephanus had dared to pretend to have caught a man in adultery with her.

Greece

Yet the defendants Stephanus and Neaera had reached such a pitch of impudence that they were not content with merely declaring her to be a free-born Athenian woman. They noticed that Theogenes of Cothocidae had been chosen by the lot as King-Archon, a man of good family, but poor and without business experience; so Stephanus supported him at his examination, and helped him out with his expenses. When he entered upon office, Stephanus wormed his way in, and having bought from him the office of assessor, he gave him this woman, Neaera's daughter, as wife, guaranteeing her to be his own daughter: such was his contempt for you and for the laws! So this woman Phano performed for you the secret sacrifice for the safety of the state; she looked upon mysteries which she, as an alien, had no right to behold. This was the sort of woman who entered into the holy place where no other of all the great Athenian people can enter – only the wife of the King-Archon. She administered the oath to the reverend priestesses who officiate at the sacrifices; she went through the ceremony of the Bride of Dionysus, and carried out the ancestral religious duties of the state, fulfilling numerous sacred and mysterious functions. How can it be in accord with piety that things which the rest of the community are not allowed even to hear spoken of should actually be done by any woman chosen by chance, especially such a woman as this, and one who is guilty of such actions? ...

To the Clerk: Now please take the law I have here, which deals with these matters, and read it.

To the jury: You will see from this that it was proper for her [Phano] as a woman of such a character and such activities, not only to keep away from all these rites, from seeing, from sacrificing, from performing any of the ceremonies laid down by ancestral usage for the safety of the state: she should have been debarred from all public occasions at Athens. The law decrees that where a woman is found with an adulterer, she is forbidden to attend any of the public sacrifices, even those which the laws permit an alien woman or slave to attend for the purpose of worship and prayer. The only class of woman forbidden by law to attend the public sacrifices is the woman caught in adultery; if she attends and breaks the law, the law allows any person who wishes to inflict upon her with impunity any punishment short of death, the right of punishment being legally granted to any chance person. The reason why the law permitted the infliction with impunity of any ill-treatment upon her except death, was to avoid any pollution or sacrilege in the temple; it holds out for women a threat terrifying enough to deter them from unrestraint or any sort of misbehaviour, and compel them to carry out their duties at home, teaching them that if anyone misbehaves in this fashion, she will be banished not only from her husband's house but from the public places of worship. That this is so will be clear to you when you hear the law itself read out ...

Law on adultery: If the husband catch the adulterer in the act, he (thè husband) shall not be permitted to continue cohabitation with the wife. If he continues cohabitation, he shall be disfranchised. It shall not be lawful for the woman to be admitted to the public sacrifices, if she has been caught with an adulterer. If she gains entrance, she shall be liable to suffer any ill-treatment whatsoever, short of death, and impunity ...

Each one of you must believe, therefore, that he is giving his vote in defence of his wife, or his daughter, or his mother, or on behalf of the state, the laws, and religion – to prevent respectable women from acquiring the same standing as the prostitute, and to protect those who have been reared by their families in every propriety and with every care, and given in marriage according to law, from having no better position than this woman, who with every sort of licentious behaviour surrendered herself dozens of times a day to dozens of men, whenever anyone asked her. You must not think of me, the speaker, merely as Apollodorus, nor of those who will speak on the side of the defence as merely your fellow-citizens: you must regard this lawsuit as being fought by Neaera against the laws, over the actions done by her. So that while you are considering the case for the prosecution, you must listen to the laws themselves, by which this city-state is governed and in accordance with which you have sworn to give your verdict: you must ask what the laws ordain, and how my opponents have transgressed them. But while you are hearing the defence, bear in mind the accusation put forward by the laws and the proof offered by the prosecution; take a look at the woman's appearance, and ask yourselves one thing only: if she, Neaera, has done the things of which she is accused.

Amorgos[23]

Athenian women are mentioned only in transactions about their dowries; outside Athens women apparently had more control over their property.

78. *A mortgage. Amorgos, 3rd cent. B.C. (Finley 9. Tr. M.R.L.)*

Boundary of the household and garden which Antenor son of Cleodicus mortgaged to Pasariste daughter of Evagoras with Samon as guardian, for ninety drachmas of silver, according to agreements deposited with Evaces son of Critolaus.

79. *Security for a dowry. Amorgos, c. 300 B.C. (Finley 155. Tr. M.R.L.)*

Boundary of the houses and gardens adjoining the houses put up as
security to Nicesarete for her dowry, consecrated and dedicated to
Aphrodite Urania in Aspis by Nicesarete, wife of Naucrates, and her
guardian Naucrates, and according to the wills deposited in the temple
of Aphrodite and with Eunomides the archon and with the official
Ctesiphon.

80. *Transactions with a society. Amorgos, 3rd cent. B.C. (Finley 8. Tr.
M.R.L.)*

Boundary of the lands in ... and of the house and gardens of Xenocles
located in Phylincheia and of the recorded pledges mortgaged, with the
agreement of the woman Eratocrate and her guardian Brychion to the
society and to Aristocratus chief of the society and to his wife Echenice,
for the surety which he had put Xenocles down for on behalf of the
society, which Aristagoras had collected according to the law of the
society members.

81. *Leased property. Amorgos, late 4th cent. B.C. (Finley 130. Tr. M.R.L.)*

The estate of orphans during their minority ordinarily was transferred
from their guardians to lessees, but in Athens girls were never named as
beneficiaries of a will.

Boundary of the leased property of Simone and Demodice, daughters of
Simon, in the [properties] of Dexibios. Lessee Dexibios. Aristotimus son
of Xanthides set the evaluation at one third; he was sent by the archons
Xanthippides son of Xanthippides, Praxiteles son of Theognotus ...

Egypt

The papyrus, a plant which grew abundantly in the Nile, was used by the
Egyptians to produce a writing material which they exported throughout
the Mediterranean. While the damp weather of other countries caused the
papyrus sheets to disintegrate, Egypt's climate preserved them. As a
result, the majority of the hundreds of thousands of papyri which survive
today come from Egypt, and most were discovered in rubbish-piles and town
dumps. Papyri written in Greek, the language of Egypt after its occupation
by Alexander the Great, survive from the late fourth century B.C. to the end
of the ancient world.

While many fragments have provided literary texts, we are concerned
here with the category known as 'documentary papyri', which includes
private letters (often dictated to professional scribes by illiterate
correspondents), public documents, and records of financial transactions,
both public and private. Like inscriptions, papyri can tell us about the
ordinary people whom historians have ignored, but they go further than
the stone remains in giving us priceless, often touching glimpses into the
daily life of the lower classes.

82. *A marriage contract, Alexandria, 92 B.C. (Tebtunis papyrus 104*[24] *Tr.
A.S. Hunt and C.C. Edgar (LCL))*

The year 22, Mecheir 11. Philiscus son of Apollonius, Persian of the
Epigone, acknowledges to Apollonia also called Kellauthis, daughter of
Heraclides, Persian, with her guardian her brother Apollonius, that he
has received from her in copper money two talents and four thousand
drachmas, which is the dowry agreed upon by him for her, Apollonia ...
The keeper of the contract is Dionysius.

In the twenty-second year of the reign of Ptolemy also called
Alexander, the god Philometor, in the priesthood of Alexander's priest
and of the rest as written in Alexandria, in the month Xandikos 11,
Mecheir 11, at Kerkeosiris of the division of Polemon of the Arsinoïte
nome. Philiscus, son of Apollonius, Persian of the Epigone,
acknowledges to Apollonia, also called Kellauthis, daughter of
Heraclides, Persian, with her guardian her brother Apollonius, that he
has received from her in copper money two talents and four thousand
drachmas, the dowry agreed upon by him for her, Apollonia. Apollonia
shall remain with Philiscus, obeying him as a wife should obey her
husband, owning their property jointly with him. Philiscus, whether he
is at home or away from home, shall furnish Apollonia with everything
necessary and clothing and whatsoever is proper for a wedded wife, in
proportion to their means. It shall not be lawful for Philiscus to bring
home another wife in addition to Apollonia or to have a concubine or
boy-lover, nor to beget children by another woman while Apollonia is
alive nor to maintain another house of which Apollonia is not mistress,
nor to eject or insult or illtreat her nor to alienate any of their property
with injustice to Apollonia. If he be shown to be doing any of these
things or do not furnish her with what is necessary or clothing or the rest
as stipulated, Philiscus shall immediately pay back to Apollonia the
dowry of the two talents and four thousand drachmas of copper. In the
same way it shall not be lawful for Apollonia to spend night or day away
from the house of Philiscus without Philiscus' knowledge, or to have
intercourse with another man or to ruin the common household or to
bring shame upon Philiscus in whatever causes a husband shame. If

Apollonia voluntarily wishes to separate from Philiscus, Philiscus shall
pay back to her the bare dowry within ten days from the day it is
demanded. If he does not pay it back as stipulated he shall immediately
forfeit the dowry he has received plus one half. The witnesses are
Dionysius, son of Patron, Dionysius, son of Hermaïscus, Theon, son of
Ptolemaeus, Didymus, son of Ptolemaeus, Dionysius, son of Dionysius,
Heracles, son of Diocles, all six Macedonians of the Epigone. The keeper
of the contract is Dionysius.

I, Philiscus, son of Apollonius, Persian of the Epigone, acknowledge
that I have received the dowry, the two talents and four thousand
drachmas of copper, as written above, and I have deposited the
agreement, which is valid, with Dionysius. Dionysius, son of
Hermaïscus, the aforesaid, wrote for him since he is illiterate.

I, Dionysius, have the contract which is valid.

Registered the year 22, Mecheir 11.

83. *Annulment of a marriage contract. Alexandria, 1st cent. B.C. (Berlin
papyrus 1104. Tr. M.R.L.)*

To Protarchus, from Dionysarion, daughter of Protarchus, with her
brother Protarchus as guardian, and from Hermione, daughter of
Hermias, a citizen, on the authority of her brother's son, Hermias, son of
... Dionysarion agrees that the contract is invalidated which the son of
Hermione, Hermias, made with her, with Hermione serving as
bondsman ... It is agreed, on behalf of her deceased husband, that
Dionysarion take from Hermione's house by hand the dowry which she
brought to Hermias, with Hermione serving as bondsman: a dowry of
clothes to the value of 240 silver pieces, earrings, and a ring ... The
contract is invalidated with all documents sealed by her. Dionysarion is
not to enter suit against Hermione, nor is any man acting on her behalf,
not for any of the deceased Hermias' possessions nor concerning the
dowry or support nor about any other written or unwritten agreement
made in the past up to the present day. Since Dionysarion has become
pregnant, she is not to sue her for childbirth, because she is more
persuasive on that account; she is permitted to expose her baby and to
join herself in marriage to another husband. She agrees that if she breaks
this authorised agreement she is subject to damages and the established
fine ...

84. *Agreement to transfer a concubine. Egypt, 284/3 B.C. (Elephantine papyrus
3.[25] Tr. M.R.L.)*

Elaphion of Syria, with Pantarces as her guardian, herewith pays

Antipatros of Arcadia a fee of 300 drachmas for having maintained her. Antipatros is hereby forbidden to sue her, to demand that he is supporting her or to reduce her to slavery on any condition, and so is anyone acting on his behalf. If he violates this agreement, his action is invalid and his agent and Antipatros must pay a fine of 3000 drachmas to Elaphion or to the men currently maintaining her. This writ shall be in effect from the time Elaphion or someone acting on her behalf serves it on Antipatros, as Elaphion has written it. Witnesses: *signed* Pancrates of Arcadia, Caphisias of Phocis, Diphilus of Phocis, Epinicus of Chalcis, Athenagoras of Alexandria, Xenocles of Rhodes.

85. *Problems over a dowry. Oxyrhyncha, early 2nd cent. B.C. (Tebtunis papyrus 776. Tr. M.R.L.)*

To Ptolemaeus, state official, from Senesis daughter of Menelaus, one of the women living in Oxyrhyncha in the Polemon area. I lived with Didymus son of Peteimouthes from the said village, on the terms of an Egyptian alimentary silver contract for [?] gold pieces in accordance with the laws of the country, and for this money and my maintenance he had pledged all his property, including a house in the aforesaid village. But the accused wished to deprive me of this and went round to one person after another in the said village and wanted to alienate the house from me. But they did not go along with him because I would not give my consent. After that he tried to give it as collateral to the treasury for Heraclides the tax farmer, and accordingly thinks he can exclude me from my rights.

On account of this I beg and beseech you; do not allow me, a defenceless woman,[26] to be deprived of the property pledged for my dowry because of the irresponsibility of the accused, but if you will, order that a letter be written to Ptolemaeus the treasurer asking him not to accept the house from Didymus as collateral. If this is done, I shall have your assistance. Farewell.

1. Possibly other free families, related by kinship or neighbourhood. See R. Meiggs and D. Lewis, *Greek Historical Inscriptions* (Oxford 1969) 98.

2. In the law code.

3. Under these conditions a woman could choose her own husband; this was not possible in Athens. See Schaps, op. cit., pp. 44, 46-7.

4. On political reasons for suppressing mourning, see M. Alexiou, *The Ritual Lament in Greek Tradition* (Cambridge 1974) 21-3.

5. In Euboea.

6. Athens.

7. For interpretation, see G.E.M. de Ste Croix, *CR* 20 (1970) 274-5; A.R.W. Harrison, *The Law of Athens: the Family and Property* (Oxford 1968) 110; Schaps, op. cit., pp. 10-11, 14.

8. The property would, however, be managed by a guardian (*kyrios*); see de Ste Croix, op. cit., pp 273-8; Schaps, op. cit., pp. 48-60.

9. 403 B.C.

10. The four classes of Athenian society at this time were: (1) Pentacosiomedimni, '500-measure men', who had an income of 500 measures of grain or wine. (2) Knights, who were able to bring a horse to the army and had an income of 300 measures. (3) Zeugitae, 'yoke men', who could own a yoke of oxen and had an income of 200 measures. (4) Thetes, 'serfs', who had either no land or an income of less than 200 measures.

11. On this 'law' see Schaps, op. cit., pp. 28-9.

12. On the interpretation of this 'law', see especially de Ste Croix, op. cit., p. 274; Schaps, op. cit., p. 52.

13. 305/4 B.C.

14. 303/2 B.C.

15. D. Schaps, *CQ* 27 (1977) 323-30.

16. See below, p. 117.

17. A son-in-law.

18. Thus deferring the question.

19. Cf. the 'law' cited in Demosthenes 23. 53: 'If a man involuntarily kills another in the course of competing in an athletic contest or in apprehending a thief on a road, or when he does not recognise [him] in war, or if [he catches] him with his wife or mother or sister or daughter or with a concubine whom he keeps for the purpose of begetting legitimate children; in the event of any of these the murderer is not prosecuted.'

20. 373/2 B.C., thirty years or more before the present trial.

21. The next year.

22. Until it could be determined whether she was slave or free. The polemarch was the archon in charge of suits involving foreign residents.

23. On these texts see de Ste Croix, op. cit., pp. 275-6; M.I. Finley, *Studies in Land and Credit in Ancient Athens, 500-200 B.C.* (New Brunswick, N.J. 1952, reissue New York 1973); Schaps, op. cit., p. 85.

24. The document is written in four different hands. The first and last paragraphs are in the same hand; the second, third and fourth paragraphs are each in a different hand.

25. A second papyrus (Elephantine papyrus 4) records in identical language the payment of four hundred drachmas to Pantarces (her master in the preceding agreement) with Dion acting as her new guardian. Violation of the agreement is subject to a fine of ten thousand drachmas, and signatures of six witnesses are appended.

26. Cf. Euripides, *Supplices,* 40-1: 'Women can usually get everything through men, if they are clever.'

VI

Politics

In antiquity the term 'philosopher' described professors of general knowledge, both of how life was and of how life ought to be. Plato's constructions of theories of ideal behaviour were later counterbalanced by his student Aristotle's systematic descriptions of observed existence.

Athens

86. *The female role. Athens, 4th cent. B.C. (Aristotle, Politics 1254b3-1277b25 (excerpts); 1313b33-39; 1335a8-17. Tr. B. Jowett)*

First then we may observe in living creatures both a despotical and a constitutional rule; for the soul rules the body with a despotical rule, whereas the intellect rules the appetites with a constitutional and royal rule. And it is clear that the rule of the soul over the body, and of the mind and the rational element over the passionate is natural and expedient; whereas the equality of the two or the rule of the inferior is always hurtful. The same holds good of animals as well as of men; for tame animals have a better nature than wild and all tame animals are better off when they are ruled by man; for then they are preserved. Again, the male is by nature superior, and the female inferior; and the one rules, and the other is ruled; this principle of necessity, extends to all mankind ...

Of household management we have seen that there are three parts – one is the rule of a master over slaves, which has been discussed already, another of a father, and the third of a husband. A husband and father rules over wife and children, both free, but the rule differs, the rule over his children being a royal, over his wife a constitutional rule. For although there may be exceptions to the order of nature, the male is by nature fitter for command than the female, just as the older and full-grown is superior to the younger and more immature. But in most constitutional states the citizens rule and are ruled by turns, for the idea of a constitutional state implies that the natures of the citizens are equal, and do not differ at all. Nevertheless, when one rules and the other is ruled we endeavour to create a difference of outward forms and names and titles of respect ... The relation of the male to the female is of this kind, but there the inequality is permanent. The rule of a father over his children is royal, for he receives both love and the respect due to age, exercising a kind of royal power. And therefore Homer has appropriately called Zeus 'father of gods and men', because he is the king of them all. For a king is the natural superior of his subjects, but he should be of the same kin or kind with them, and such is the relation of elder and younger, of father and son ...

The freeman rules over the slave after another manner from that in which the male rules over the female, or the man over the child; although the parts of the soul are present in all of them, they are present in different degrees. For the slave has no deliberative faculty at all; the woman has, but it is without authority, and the child has, but it is immature. So it must necessarily be with the moral virtues also; all may be supposed to partake of them, but only in such manner and degree as is required by each for the fulfilment of his duty. Hence the ruler ought to have moral virtue in perfection, for his duty is entirely that of a master artificer, and the master artificer is reason; the subjects, on the other hand, require only that measure of virtue which is proper to each of them. Clearly, then, moral virtue belongs to all of them; but the temperance of a man and of a woman, or the courage and justice of a man and of a woman, are not, as Socrates maintained, the same; the courage of a man is shown in commanding, of a woman in obeying ... All classes must be deemed to have their special attributes; as the poet says of women, 'Silence is a woman's glory',[1] but this is not equally the glory of a man. The child is imperfect, and therefore obviously his virtue is not relative to himself alone, but to the perfect man and to his teacher, and in like manner the virtue of the slave is relative to a master ...

Nor is there any way of preventing brothers and children and fathers and mothers from sometimes recognising one another; for children are born like their parents, and they will necessarily be finding indications of their relationship to one another. Geographers declare such to be the fact; they say that in Upper Libya, where the women are common, nevertheless the children who are born are assigned to their respective fathers on the ground of their likeness. And some women, like the females of other animals – for example mares and cows – have a strong tendency to produce offspring resembling their parents, as was the case with the Pharsalian mare called Dicaea [the Just] ...

The licence of the Lacedaemonian women defeats the intention of the Spartan constitution, and is adverse to the good order of the state. For a husband and a wife, being each a part of every family, the state may be considered as about equally divided into men and women; and, therefore, in those states in which the condition of the woman is bad, half the city may be regarded as having no laws. And this is what has actually happened at Sparta; the legislator wanted to make the whole state hardy and temperate, and he has carried out his intention in the case of the men, but he has neglected the women, who live in every sort of intemperance and luxury. The consequence is that in such a state wealth is too highly valued, especially if the citizens fall under the dominion of their wives, after the manner of all warlike races, except the Celts and a few others who openly approve of male loves. The old mythologer would seem to have been right in uniting Ares and Aphrodite, for all warlike races are prone to the love either of men or of women. This was exemplified among the Spartans in the days of their greatness; many things were managed by their women. But what difference does it make whether women rule, or the rulers are ruled by women? The result is the same. Even in regard to courage, which is of no use in daily life, and is needed only in war, the influence of the Lacedaemonian women has been most mischievous. The evil showed itself in the Theban invasion,[2] when, unlike the women in other cities, they were utterly useless and caused more confusion than the enemy. This licence of the Lacedaemonian women existed from the earliest times, and was only what might be expected. For, during the wars of the Lacedaemonians, first against the Argives, and afterwards against the Arcadians and Messenians, the men were long away from home, and, on the return of peace, they gave themselves into the legislator's hand, already prepared by the discipline of a soldier's life (in which there are many elements of virtue), to receive his enactments. But, when Lycurgus, as tradition says, wanted to bring the women under his laws, they resisted, and he gave up the attempt. They, and not he, are to blame for what then happened, and this defect in the constitution is clearly to be attributed to them. We are not, however, considering what is or is not to be excused, but what is right or wrong, and the disorder of the women, as I have already said, not only of itself gives an air of indecorum to the state, but tends in a measure to foster avarice.

The mention of avarice naturally suggests a criticism of the inequality of property. While some of the Spartan citizens have quite small properties, others have very large ones; hence the land has passed into the hands of a few. And here is another fault in their laws; for, although the legislator rightly holds up to shame the sale or purchase of an inheritance, he allows anybody who likes to give and bequeath it. Yet both practices lead to the same result. And nearly two-fifths of the whole country are held by women; this is owing to the number of heiresses and to the large dowries which are customary.[3] It would surely have been better to have given no dowries at all, or, if any, but small or moderate ones. As the law now stands, a man may bestow his heiress on any one whom he pleases, and, if he die intestate, the privilege of giving her away descends to his heir. Hence, although the country is able to maintain 1500 cavalry and 30,000 hoplites, the whole number of Spartan citizens[4] fell below 1000 ...

The good man, who is free and also a subject, will not have one virtue only, say justice – but he will have distinct kinds of virtue, the one qualifying him to rule, the other to obey, and differing as the temperance and courage of men and women differ. For a man would be thought a coward if he had no more courage than a courageous woman, and a woman would be thought loquacious if she imposed no more restraints on her conversation than the good man; and indeed their part in the management of the household is different, for the duty of the one is to acquire, and of the other to preserve ...

Again, the evil practices of the last and worst form of democracy are all found in tyrannies. Such are the powers given to women in their families in the hope that they will inform against their husbands, and the licence which is allowed to slaves in order that they may betray their masters; for slaves and women do not conspire against tyrants; and they are of course friendly to tyrannies and also to democracies, since under them they have a good time. For the people too would fain be a monarch ...

Since the time of generation is commonly limited within the age of seventy years in the case of a man, and of fifty in the case of a woman, the commencement of the union should conform to these periods. The union of male and female when too young is bad for the procreation of children; in all other animals the offspring of the young are small and ill-developed, and generally of the female sex, and therefore also in man, as is proved by the fact that in those cities in which men and women are accustomed to marry young, the people are small and weak.

87. *More responsibilities for women. Athens, 4th cent. B.C. (Plato, Republic 5. 451c-452c, 455c-456b, 457a, 457c, 458c-d, 459d-461e. Tr. B. Jowett)*

Plans for a new society in which women would share some of the responsibilities for governing. Socrates' suggestions for revised family structure follow the Spartan model.[5]

For men born and educated like our citizens, the only way, in my opinion, of arriving at a right conclusion about the possession and use of women and children is to follow the path on which we originally started, when we said that the men were to be the guardians and watchdogs of the herd.

True.

Let us further suppose the birth and education of our women to be subject to similar or nearly similar regulations; then we shall see whether the result accords with our design.

What do you mean?

What I mean may be put into the form of a question, I said: Are dogs divided into hes and shes, or do they both share equally in hunting and in keeping watch and in the other duties of dogs? or do we entrust to the males the entire and exclusive care of the flocks, while we leave the females at home, under the idea that the bearing and suckling their puppies is labour enough for them?

No, he said, they share alike; the only difference between them is that the males are stronger and the females weaker.

But can you use different animals for the same purpose, unless they are bred and fed in the same way?

You cannot.

Then, if women are to have the same duties as men, they must have the same nurture and education?

Yes.

The education which was assigned to the men was music and gymnastic.

Yes.

Then women must be taught music and gymnastic and also the art of war, which they must practise like the men?

That is the inference, I suppose.

I should rather expect, I said, that several of our proposals, if they are carried out, being unusual, may appear ridiculous.

No doubt of it.

Yes, and the most ridiculous thing of all will be the sight of women naked in the palaestra, exercising with the men,[6] especially when they are no longer young; they certainly will not be a vision of beauty, any more than the enthusiastic old men who in spite of wrinkles and ugliness continue to frequent the gymnasia.

Yes, indeed, he said: according to present notions the proposal would be thought ridiculous.

But then, I said, as we have determined to speak our minds, we must not fear the jests of the wits which will be directed against this sort of innovation; how they will talk of women's attainments both in music and gymnastic, and above all about their wearing armour and riding upon horseback!

And can you mention any pursuit of mankind in which the male sex has not all these gifts and qualities in a higher degree than the female? Need I waste time in speaking of the art of weaving, and the management of pancakes and preserves, in which womankind does really appear to be great, and in which for her to be beaten by a man is of all things the most absurd?

You are quite right, he replied, in maintaining the general inferiority of the female sex: although many women are in many things superior to many men, yet on the whole what you say is true.

And if so, my friend, I said, there is no special faculty of administration in a state which a woman has because she is a woman, or which a man has by virtue of his sex, but the gifts of nature are alike diffused in both; all the pursuits of men are the pursuits of women also, but in all of them a woman is inferior to a man.

Very true.

Then are we to impose all our enactments on men and none of them on women?

That will never do.

One woman has a gift of healing, another not; one is a musician, and another has no music in her nature?

Very true.

And one woman has a turn for gymnastic and military exercises, and another is unwarlike and hates gymnastics?

Certainly.

And one woman is a philosopher, and another is an enemy of philosophy; one has spirit, and another is without spirit?

That is also true.

Then one woman will have the temper of a guardian, and another not. Was not the selection of the male guardians determined by differences of this sort?

Yes.

Men and women alike possess the qualities which make a guardian; they differ only in their comparative strength or weakness.

Obviously.

And those women who have such qualities are to be selected as the companions and colleagues of men who have similar qualities and whom they resemble in capacity and in character?

Very true.

And ought not the same natures to have the same pursuits?

They ought.

Then, as we were saying before, there is nothing unnatural in assigning music and gymnastic to the wives of the guardians – to that point we come round again.

Then let the wives of our guardians strip, for their virtue will be their robe, and let them share in the toils of war and the defence of their country; only in the distribution of labours the lighter are to be assigned to the women, who are the weaker natures, but in other respects their duties are to be the same. And as for the man who laughs at naked women exercising their bodies from the best of motives, in his laughter he is plucking

'A fruit of unripe wisdom',

and he himself is ignorant of what he is laughing at, or what he is about; – for that is, and ever will be, the best of sayings, *That the useful is the noble and the hurtful is the base.*

Very true.

The law, I said, which is the sequel of this and of all that has preceded, is to the following effect, – 'that the wives of our guardians are to be common, and their children are to be common, and no parent is to know his own child, nor any child his parent'.

Yes, he said, that is a much greater way than the other; and the possibility as well as the utility of such a law are far more questionable.

I do not think, I said, that there can be any dispute about the very great utility of having wives and children in common; the possibility is quite another matter, and will be very much disputed.

I think that a good many doubts may be raised about both.

You, I said, who are their legislator, having selected the men, will now select the women and give them to them; – they must be as far as possible of like natures with them; and they must live in common houses and meet at common meals. None of them will have anything specially his or her own; they will be together, and will be brought up together, and will associate at gymnastic exercises. And so they will be drawn by a necessity of their natures to have intercourse with each other – necessity is not too strong a word, I think?

Yes, he said; – necessity, not geometrical, but another sort of necessity which lovers know, and which is far more convincing and constraining to the mass of mankind.

True, I said; and this, Glaucon, like all the rest, must proceed after an orderly fashion; in a city of the blessed, licentiousness is an unholy thing which the rulers will forbid.

Yes, he said, and it ought not to be permitted.

Then clearly the next thing will be to make matrimony sacred in the highest degree, and what is most beneficial will be deemed sacred?

Exactly.

The principle has been already laid down that the best of either sex should be united with the best as often, and the inferior with the inferior, as seldom as possible; and that they should rear the offspring of the one sort of union, but not of the other, if the flock is to be maintained in first-rate condition. Now these goings-on must be a secret which the rulers only know, or there will be a further danger of our herd, as the guardians may be termed, breaking out into rebellion.

Very true.

Had we not better appoint certain festivals at which we will bring together the brides and bridegrooms, and sacrifices will be offered and suitable hymeneal songs composed by our poets: the number of weddings is a matter which must be left to the discretion of the rulers, whose aim will be to preserve the average of population? There are many other things which they will have to consider, such as the effects of wars and diseases and any similar agencies, in order as far as this is possible to prevent the state from becoming either too large or too small.

Certainly, he replied.

We shall have to invent some ingenious kind of lots which the less worthy may draw on each occasion of our bringing them together, and then they will accuse their own ill-luck and not the rulers.

To be sure, he said.

And I think that our braver and better youth, besides their other honours and rewards, might have greater facilities of intercourse with women given them; their bravery will be a reason, and such fathers ought to have as many sons as possible.

True.

And the proper officers, whether male or female or both, for offices are to be held by women as well as by men –

Yes –

The proper officers will take the offspring of the good parents to the pen or fold, and there they will deposit them with certain nurses who dwell in a separate quarter; but the offspring of the inferior, or of the better when they chance to be deformed, will be put away in some mysterious, unknown place, as they should be.

Yes, he said, that must be done if the breed of the guardians is to be kept pure.

They will provide for their nurture, and will bring the mothers to the fold when they are full of milk, taking the greatest possible care that no mother recognises her own child; and other wet-nurses may be engaged if more are required. Care will also be taken that the process of suckling shall not be protracted too long; and the mothers will have no getting up at night or other trouble, but will hand over all this sort of thing to the nurses and attendants.

You suppose the wives of our guardians to have a fine easy time of it when they are having children.

Why, said I, and so they ought. Let us, however, proceed with our scheme. We were saying that the parents should be in the prime of life?

Very true.

And what is the prime of life? May it not be defined as a period of about twenty years in a woman's life, and thirty in a man's?

Which years do you mean to include?

A woman, I said, at twenty years of age may begin to bear children to the state, and continue to bear them until forty; a man may begin at five-and-twenty, when he has passed the point at which the pulse of life beats quickest, and continue to beget children until he be fifty-five.

Certainly, he said, both in men and women those years are the prime of physical as well as of intellectual vigour.

Any one above or below the prescribed ages who takes part in the public hymeneals shall be said to have done an unholy and unrighteous thing; the child of which he is the father, if it steals into life, will have been conceived under auspices very unlike the sacrifices and prayers, which at each hymeneal priestesses and priests and the whole city will offer, that the new generation may be better and more useful than their good and useful parents, whereas his child will be the offspring of darkness and strange lust.

Very true, he replied.

And the same law will apply to any one of those within the prescribed age who forms a connexion with any woman in the prime of life without the sanction of the rulers; for we shall say that he is raising up a bastard to the state, uncertified and unconsecrated.

Very true, he replied.

This applies, however, only to those who are within the specified age: after that we allow them to range at will, except that a man may not marry his daughter or his daughter's daughter, or his mother or his mother's mother; and women, on the other hand, are prohibited from marrying their sons or fathers, or son's son or father's father, and so on in either direction. And we grant all this, accompanying the permission with strict orders to prevent any embryo which may come into being from seeing the light; and if any force a way to the birth, the parents must understand that the offspring of such a union cannot be maintained, and arrange accordingly.

That also, he said, is a reasonable proposition. But how will they know who are fathers and daughters, and so on?

They will never know. The way will be this: – dating from the day of the hymeneal, the bridegroom who was then married will call all the male children who are born in the seventh and tenth month afterwards his sons, and the female children his daughters, and they will call him father, and he will call their children his grandchildren, and they will call the elder generation grandfathers and grandmothers. All who were begotten at the time when their fathers and mothers came together will be called their brothers and sisters, and these, as I was saying, will be forbidden to intermarry. This, however, is not to be understood as an absolute prohibition of the marriage of brothers and sisters; if the lot favours them, and they receive the sanction of the Delphic oracle, the law will allow them.

Quite right, he replied.

Such is the scheme, Glaucon, according to which the guardians of our state are to have their wives and families in common. And now you would have the argument show that this community is consistent with the rest of our polity, and also that nothing can be better – would you not?

Yes, certainly.

88. *Men and women should be treated alike. Athens, 4th cent. B.C. (Plato, Laws
6.780e-781d, 7.804c-806c, 8.838a-839b. Tr. T.J. Saunders)*

Provisions for women to play a more responsible role in society, no longer
attributed directly to Socrates, with more specific commentary than in the
Republic on the problems inherent in traditional Athenian family
structure.

Thanks to some providential necessity, Cleinias and Megillus, you have
a splendid and – as I was saying – astonishing institution: communal
meals for men. But it is entirely wrong of you to have omitted from your
legal code any provision for your women, so that the practice of
communal meals for them has never got under way. On the contrary,
half the human race – the female sex, the half which in any case is
inclined to be secretive and crafty, because of its weakness – has been left
to its own devices because of the misguided indulgence of the legislator.
Because you neglected this sex, you gradually lost control of a great
many things which would be in a far better state today if they had been
regulated by law. You see, leaving women to do what they like is not just
to lose *half* the battle (as it may seem): a woman's natural potential for
virtue is inferior to a man's, so she's proportionately a greater danger,
perhaps even twice as great. So the happiness of the state will be better
served if we reconsider the point and put things right, by providing that
all our arrangements apply to men and women alike. But at present,
unhappily, the human race has not progressed as far as that, and if
you're wise you won't breathe a word about such a practice in other
parts of the world where states do not recognise communal meals as a
public institution at all. So when it comes to the point, how on earth are
you going to avoid being laughed to scorn when you try to force women
to take their food and drink in public? There's nothing the sex is likely to
put up with more reluctantly: women have got used to a life of obscurity
and retirement, and any attempt to force them into the open will provoke
tremendous resistance from them, and they'll be more than a match for
the legislator. Elsewhere, as I said, the very mention of the correct policy
will be met with howls of protest. But perhaps this state will be different.

The education of females

Let me stress that this law of mine will apply just as much to girls as to
boys. The girls must be trained in precisely the same way, and I'd like to
make this proposal without any reservations whatever about horse-
riding or athletics being suitable activities for males but not for females.
You see, although I was already convinced by some ancient stories I
have heard, I now know for sure that there are pretty well countless
numbers of women, generally called Sarmatians, round the Black Sea,

who not only ride horses but use the bow and other weapons. There, men and women have an equal duty to cultivate these skills, so cultivate them equally they do. And while we're on the subject, here's another thought for you. I maintain that if these results can be achieved, the state of affairs in our corner of Greece, where men and women do *not* have a common purpose and do *not* throw all their energies into the same activities, is absolutely stupid. Almost every state, under present conditions, is only half a state, and develops only half its potentialities, whereas with the same cost and effort, it could double its achievement. Yet what a staggering blunder for a legislator to make!

Cleinias: I dare say. But a lot of these proposals, sir, are incompatible with the average state's social structure. However, you were quite right when you said we should give the argument its head, and only make up our minds when it had run its course. You've made me reproach myself for having spoken. So carry on, and say what you like.

Athenian: The point I'd like to make, Cleinias, is the same one as I made a moment ago, that there might have been something to be said against our proposal, if it had not been proved by the facts to be workable. But as things are, an opponent of this law must try other tactics. We are not going to withdraw our recommendation that so far as possible, in education and everything else, the female sex should be on the same footing as the male. Consequently, we should approach the problem rather like this. Look: if women are *not* to follow absolutely the same way of life as men, then surely we shall have to work out some other programme for them?

Cleinias: Inevitably.

Athenian: Well, then, if we deny women this position of equality we're now demanding for them, which of the systems actually in force today shall we adopt instead? What about the practice of the Thracians and many other peoples, who make their women work on the land and mind sheep and cattle, so that they turn into serfs indistinguishable from slaves? Or what about the Athenians and all the other states in that part of the world? Well, here's how we Athenians deal with the problem: we 'concentrate our resources', as the expression is, under one roof and let our women take charge of our stores and the spinning and wool-working in general. Or we could adopt the Spartan system, Megillus, which is a compromise. You make your girls take part in athletics and you give them a compulsory education in the arts; when they grow up, though dispensed from working wool, they have to 'weave' themselves a pretty hard-working sort of life which is by no means despicable or useless: they have to be tolerably efficient at running the home and managing the house and bringing up children – but they *don't* undertake military service. This means that even if some extreme emergency ever led to a battle for their state and the lives of their children, they wouldn't have the expertise to use bows and arrows, like so many Amazons, nor could they join the men in deploying any other missile. They wouldn't be able to take up shield and spear and copy Athena, so as to terrify the enemy (if nothing more) by being seen in some kind of battle-array gallantly resisting the destruction threatening their native land. Living as they do, they'd never be anything like tough enough to imitate the Sarmatian women, who by comparison with such femininity would look like men. Anyone who wants to commend your Spartan legislators for this state of affairs, had better get on with it: I'm not going to change *my* mind. A legislator should go the whole way and not stick at half-measures; he mustn't just regulate the men and allow the women to live as they like and wallow in expensive luxury. That would be to give the state only half the loaf of prosperity instead of the whole of it.

How to discourage unnatural sexual intercourse

Athenian: I want to put the law on this subject on a firm footing, and at the moment I'm thinking of a method which is, in a sense, simplicity itself. But from another point of view, nothing could be harder.

Megillus: What are you getting at?

Athenian: We're aware, of course, that even nowadays most men, in spite of their general disregard for the law, are very effectively prevented from having relations with people they find attractive. And they don't refrain reluctantly, either – they're more than happy to.

Megillus: What circumstances have you in mind?

Athenian: When it's one's brother or sister whom one finds attractive. And the same law, unwritten though it is, is extremely effective in stopping a man sleeping – secretly or otherwise – with his son or daughter, or making any kind of amorous approach to them. Most people feel not the faintest desire for such intercourse.

Megillus: That's perfectly true.

Athenian: So the desire for this sort of pleasure is stifled by a few words?

Megillus: What words do you mean?

Athenian: The doctrine that 'these acts are absolutely unholy, an abomination in the sight of the gods, and at that nothing is more revolting.' We refrain from them because we never hear them spoken of in any other way. From the day of our birth each of us encounters a complete unanimity of opinion wherever we go; we find it not only in comedies but often in the high seriousness of tragedy too, when we see a Thyestes on the stage, or an Oedipus or a Macareus, the clandestine lover of his sister. We watch these characters dying promptly by their own hand as a penalty for their crimes.

Megillus: You're right in this, anyway, that when no one ventures to challenge the law, public opinion works wonders.

Athenian: So we were justified in what we said just now. When the legislator wants to tame one of the desires that dominate mankind so cruelly, it's easy for him to see his method of attack. He must try to make everyone – slave and free, women and children, and the entire state without any exception – believe that this common opinion has the backing of religion. He couldn't put his law on a securer foundation than that.

Megillus: Very true. But how on earth it will ever be possible to produce such spontaneous unanimity –

Athenian: I'm glad you've taken me up on the point. This is just what I was getting at when I said I knew of a way to put into effect this law of ours which permits the sexual act only for its natural purpose, procreation, and forbids not only homosexual relations, in which the human race is deliberately murdered, but also the sowing of seeds on rocks and stones where it will never take root and mature into a new individual and we should also have to keep away from any female 'soil' in which we'd be sorry to have the seed develop. At present however, the law is effective only against intercourse between parent and child, but if it can be put on a permanent footing and made to apply effectively, as it deserves to, in other cases as well, it'll do a power of good. The first point in its favour is that it is a *natural* law. But it also tends to check the raging fury of the sexual instinct that so often leads to adultery; discourages excesses in food and drink, and inspires men with affection for their own wives. And there are a great many other advantages to be gained, if only one could get this law established.

Sparta

The Spartan way of life always intrigued other Greeks, who could never remain neutral on the subject. No other Greek city was like it. Sparta's social institutions and its famous discipline were designed for a single purpose: to protect the state by maintaining the best fighting force in the world. Women were trained to be fitting wives and mothers for these heroes. Their education included rigorous athletic training in which the spirit of competition was encouraged. Every effort was made to extirpate all traces of effeminacy: jewellery, cosmetics, perfumes, and coloured clothing were all prohibited. Among Greek women, only Spartans did no wool work, the traditional female occupation.[7]

Many of the distinctive characteristics of the Spartan system were attributed to the legendary lawgiver Lycurgus. His date was disputed even in antiquity; historians now place the reforms in the late seventh century B.C. The biographer Plutarch provided an account of Spartan laws in his *Life of Lycurgus*, and made a collection of the famous sayings of Spartan women among his numerous ethical treatises.

89. *Regulations of Lycurgus concerning women. Sparta, 7th cent. B.C.?*
(Plutarch, Life of Lycurgus 14-16 (excerpts), 2nd cent. A.D. Tr. J. Dryden)

For the good education of their youth (which, as I said before, Lycurgus
thought the most important and noblest work of a lawgiver), he went so
far back as to take into consideration their very conception and birth, by
regulating their marriages. For Aristotle is wrong in saying, that, after he
had tried all ways to reduce the women to more modesty and sobriety,
he was at last forced to leave them as they were, because that in the
absence of their husbands, who spent the best part of their lives in the
wars, their wives, whom they were obliged to leave absolute mistresses at
home, took great liberties and assumed the superiority; and were treated
with overmuch respect and called by the title of lady or queen. The truth
is, he took in their case, also, all the care that was possible; he ordered
the maidens to exercise themselves with wrestling, running, throwing the
quoit, and casting the dart, to the end that the fruit they conceived
might, in strong and healthy bodies, take firmer root and find better
growth, and withal that they, with this greater vigour, might be the more
able to undergo the pains of childbearing. And to the end he might
take away their overgreat tenderness and fear of exposure to the air, and
all acquired womanishness, he ordered that the young women should go
naked in the processions, as well as the young men, and dance, too, in
that condition, at certain solemn feasts, singing certain songs, whilst the
young men stood around, seeing and hearing them. On these occasions
they now and then made, by jests, a befitting reflection upon those who
had misbehaved themselves in the wars; and again sang encomiums
upon those who had done any gallant action, and by these means
inspired the younger sort with an emulation of their glory. Those that
were thus commended went away proud, elated, and gratified with their
honour among the maidens; and those who were rallied were as sensibly
touched with it as if they had been formally reprimanded; and so much
the more, because the kings and the elders, as well as the rest of the city,
saw and heard all that passed. Nor was there anything shameful in this
nakedness of the young women; modesty attended them, and all
wantonness was excluded. It taught them simplicity and a care for good
health, and gave them some taste of higher feelings, admitted as they
thus were to the field of noble action and glory. Hence it was natural for
them to think and speak as Gorgo, for example, the wife of Leonidas, is
said to have done, when some foreign lady, as it would seem, told her
that the women of Lacedaemon were the only women in the world who
could rule men. 'With good reason,' she said, 'for we are the only women
who bring forth men.'

These public processions of the maidens, and their appearing naked in
their exercises and dancings, were incitements to marriage, operating

upon the young with the rigour and certainty, as Plato says, of love, if not of mathematics.[8] ...

In their marriages, the husband carried off his bride by a sort of force; nor were their brides ever small and of tender years, but in their full bloom and ripeness. After this, she who superintended the wedding comes and clips the hair of the bride close round her head, dresses her up in man's clothes, and leaves her upon a mattress in the dark; afterwards comes the bridegroom, in his everyday clothes, sober and composed, as having supped at the common table, and, entering privately into the room where the bride lies, unties her virgin zone, and takes her to himself; and, after staying some time together, he returns composedly to his own apartment, to sleep as usual with the other young men. And so he continues to do, spending his days, and, indeed, his nights, with them, visiting his bride in fear and shame, and with circumspection, when he thought he should not be observed; she, also, on her part, using her wit to help and find favourable opportunities for their meeting, when company was out of the way. In this manner they lived a long time, insomuch that they sometimes had children by their wives before ever they saw their faces by daylight. Their interviews, being thus difficult and rare, served not only for continual exercise of their self-control, but brought them together with their bodies healthy and vigorous, and their affections fresh and lively, unsated and undulled by easy access and long continuance with each other; while their partings were always early enough to leave behind unextinguished in each of them some remaining fire of longing and mutual delight. After guarding marriage with this modesty and reserve, he was equally careful to banish empty and womanish jealousy. For this object, excluding all licentious disorders, he made it, nevertheless, honourable for men to give the use of their wives to those whom they should think fit, that so they might have children by them; ridiculing those in whose opinion such favours are so unfit for participation as to fight and shed blood and go to war about it. Lycurgus allowed a man who was advanced in years and had a young wife to recommend some virtuous and approved young man, that she might have a child by him, who might inherit the good qualities of the father, and be a son to himself. On the other side, an honest man who had love for a married woman upon account of her modesty and the well-favouredness of her children, might, without formality, beg her company of her husband, that he might raise, as it were, from this plot of good ground, worthy and well-allied children for himself.[9] And indeed, Lycurgus was of a persuasion that children were not so much the property of their parents as of the whole commonwealth, and, therefore, would not have his citizens begot by the first-comers, but by the best men that could be found; the laws of other nations seemed to him very absurd and inconsistent, where people would be so solicitous for their dogs and horses as to exert interest and to pay money to procure fine breeding, and yet kept their wives shut up, to be made mothers only by themselves, who might be foolish, infirm, or diseased; as if it were not apparent that children of a bad breed would prove their bad qualities first upon those who kept and were rearing them, and well-born children, in like manner, their good qualities. These regulations, founded on natural and social grounds, were certainly so far from that scandalous liberty which was afterwards charged upon their women, that they knew not what adultery meant ...

Nor was it in the power of the father to dispose of the child as he thought fit; he was obliged to carry it before certain judges at a place called Lesche,[10] these were some of the elders of the tribe to which the child belonged; their business it was carefully to view the infant, and, if they found it stout and well made, they gave orders for its rearing, and allotted it one of the nine thousand shares of land above mentioned for its maintenance, but if they found it puny and ill-shaped, ordered it to be taken to what was called the Apothetae, a sort of chasm under Mt. Taygetus; as thinking it neither for the good of the child itself, nor for the public interest, that it should be brought up, if it did not, from the very outset, appear made to be healthy and vigorous. Upon the same account, the women did not bathe the newborn children with water, as is the custom in all other countries, but with wine, to prove the temper and complexion of their bodies; from a notion they had that epileptic and weakly children faint and waste away upon their being thus bathed, while, on the contrary, those of a strong and vigorous habit acquire firmness and get a temper by it, like steel. There was much care and art, too, used by the nurses; they had no swaddling bands; the children grew up free and unconstrained in limb and form, and not dainty and fanciful about their food; not afraid in the dark, or of being left alone; and without peevishness, or ill-humour, or crying. Upon this account Spartan nurses were often brought up, or hired by people of other countries; and it is recorded that she who suckled Alcibiades was a Spartan.

90. *Spartan women. Sparta, 5th cent. B.C.? (Plutarch, Moralia 240c-242d (excerpts), 2nd cent. A.D. Tr. F.C. Babbitt (LCL)*

Being asked by a woman from Attica, 'Why is it that you Spartan women are the only women that lord it over your men?' [one woman] said, 'Because we are the only women that are mothers of men.'

As she was encouraging her husband Leonidas, when he was about to set out for Thermopylae, to show himself worthy of Sparta, she asked what she should do; and he said, 'Marry a good man, and bear good children.'

Another was burying her son, when a commonplace old woman came up to her and said, 'Ah the bad luck of it, you poor woman.' 'No, by heaven,' said she, 'but good luck, for I bore him that he might die for Sparta, and this is the very thing that has come to pass for me.'

When a woman from Ionia showed vast pride in a bit of her own weaving, which was very valuable, a Spartan woman pointed to her four sons, who were most well-behaved, and said, 'Such should be the employments of the good and honourable woman, and it is over these that she should be elated and boastful.'

A girl had secret relations with a man, and, after bringing on an abortion, she bore up so bravely, not uttering a single sound, that her delivery took place without the knowledge of her father and others who were near. For the confronting of her indecorum with decorum gained the victory over the poignant distress of her pains.

A Spartan woman who was being sold as a slave, when asked what she knew how to do, said, 'To be faithful.'

Another, taken captive, and asked a similar question, said, 'To manage a house well.'

Another, asked by a man if she would be good if he bought her, said, 'Yes, and if you do not buy me.'

Another who was being sold as a slave, when the crier inquired of her what she knew how to do, said, 'To be free.' And when the purchaser ordered her to do something not fitting for a free woman, she said, 'You will be sorry that your meanness has cost you such a possession', and committed suicide.

1. Sophocles, *Ajax* 293.
2. 369 B.C.
3. The contrast with Athenian women is striking; see Schaps, op. cit., p. 88.
4. At the time of the Theban invasion.
5. On Plato's reforms, see J. Annas, *Philosophy* 51 (1976) 307-21.
6. But women ran races naked also at Brauron (in 4th cent.) and in Argos (in 3rd cent.) and on the island of Chios in the Roman period (Athenaeus 13. 566).
7. For a detailed discussion of women in Sparta and the ancient sources, see P. Cartledge, *CQ* 31 (1981) 84-105.
8. *Republic* 458d, see above, p. 69
9. According to Diogenes Laertius (7. 33), the philosopher Zeno (333-261 B.C.), founder of Stoicism, suggested in his Utopia that wives should be shared and that men and women dress alike, covering no part of the body completely.
10. A *leschē* is a public building or meeting-place. Here it may be the tribe's headquarters.

VII

Medicine

Observable phenomena and deduction by analogy, not human dissection and clinical study, formed the premises on which ancient anatomical theories are based. Hence social norms, such as men's superiority over women, could provide acceptable 'data' about human reproductive systems.

Study of the human cadaver made Hellenistic doctors, like Herophilus of Alexandria, better able to understand female anatomy; the results of such scientific advance is represented in the work of Soranus in the first century A.D. (below, nos 213, 214, 217).[1]

91. *Origins of the desire for procreation. Athens, 4th cent. B.C. (Plato, Timaeus 91 (excerpts). Tr. B. Jowett)*

Of the men who came into the world, those who were cowards or led unrighteous lives may with reason be supposed to have changed into the nature of women in the second generation. And this was the reason why at that time the gods created in us the desire of sexual intercourse, contriving in man one animated substance, and in woman another, which they formed respectively in the following manner. The outlet for drink by which liquids pass through the lung under the kidneys and into the bladder, which receives and then by the pressure of the air emits them, was so fashioned by them as to penetrate also into the body of the marrow, which passes from the head along the neck and through the back, and which in the preceding discourse we have named the seed. And the seed having life, and becoming endowed with respiration, produces in that part in which it respires a lively desire of emission, and thus creates in us the love of procreation. Wherefore also in men the organ of generation becoming rebellious and masterful, like an animal disobedient to reason, and maddened with the sting of lust, seeks to gain absolute sway; and the same is the case with the so-called womb or matrix of women; the animal within them is desirous of procreating children, and when remaining unfruitful long beyond its proper time, gets discontented and angry, and wandering in every direction through the body, closes up the passages of the breath, and, by obstructing respiration, drives them to extremity, causing all varieties of disease, until at length the desire and love of the man and the woman, bringing them together and as it were plucking the fruit from the tree, sow in the womb, as in a field, animals unseen by reason of their smallness and without form; these again are separated and matured within; they are then finally brought out into the light, and thus the generation of animals is completed. Thus were created women and the female sex in general.

92. *The female role in generation. Athens, 4th cent. B.C. (Aristotle, On the Generation of Animals, 716a5-23, 727a2-30, 727b31-33, 728b18-31, 765b8-20, 766a17-30, 783b26-784a12. Tr. A.L. Peck (LCL))*

Explanation of the process of conception is deduced from external secretions: male semen has primary generative importance, female semen (i.e. menstrual fluid, which also sustains the developing embryo) purely nutritive value.

As far as animals are concerned, we must describe their generation just as we find the theme requires for each several kind as we go along, linking our account on to what has already been said. As we mentioned, we may safely set down as the chief principles of generation the male [factor] and the female [factor]; the male as possessing the principle of movement and of generation, the female as possessing that of matter. One is most likely to be convinced of this by considering how the semen is formed and whence it comes; for although the things that are formed in the course of Nature no doubt take their rise out of semen, we must not fail to notice how the semen itself is formed from the male and the female, since it is because this part is secreted from the male and the female, and because its secretion takes place in them and out of them, that the male and the female are the principles of generation. By a 'male' animal we mean one which generates in another, by 'female' one which generates in itself. This is why in cosmology too they speak of the nature of the earth as something female and call it 'mother', while they give to the heaven and the sun and anything else of that kind the title of 'generator', and 'father'.

Now male and female differ in respect of their *logos* in that the power or faculty possessed by the one differs from that possessed by the other; but they differ also to bodily sense, in respect of certain physical parts. They differ in their *logos*, because the male is that which has the power to generate in another (as was stated above), while the female is that which can generate in itself, i.e. it is that out of which the generated offspring, which is present in the generator, comes into being ...[2]

This much is evident: the menstrual fluid is a residue, and it is the analogous thing in females to the semen in males. Its behaviour shows that this statement is correct. At the same time of life that semen begins to appear in males and is emitted, the menstrual discharge begins to flow in females, their voice changes and their breasts begin to become conspicuous; and similarly, in the decline of life the power to generate ceases in males and the menstrual discharge ceases in females. Here are still further indications that this secretion which females produce is a residue. Speaking generally, unless the menstrual discharge is suspended, women are not troubled by haemorrhoids or bleeding from the nose or any other such discharge, and if it happens that they are, then the evacuations fall off in quantity, which suggests that the substance secreted is being drawn off to the other discharges. Again, their blood vessels are not so prominent as those of males; and females are more neatly made and smoother than males, because the residue which goes to produce those characteristics in males is in females discharged together with the menstrual fluid. We are bound to hold, in addition, that for the same cause the bulk of the body in female vivipara is smaller than that of the males, as of course it is only in vivipara that the menstrual discharge flows externally, and most conspicuously of all in women, who discharge a greater amount than any other female animals. On this account it is always very noticeable that the female is pale, and the blood-vessels are not prominent, and there is an obvious deficiency in physique as compared with males.

Now it is impossible that any creature should produce two seminal secretions at once, and as the secretion in females which answers to semen in males is the menstrual fluid, it obviously follows that the female does not contribute any semen to generation; for if there were semen, there would be no menstrual fluid; but as menstrual fluid is in fact formed, therefore there is no semen ...

There are some who think that the female contributes semen during coition because women sometimes derive pleasure from it comparable to that of the male and also produce a fluid secretion. This fluid, however, is not seminal; it is peculiar to the part from which it comes in each several individual; there is a discharge from the uterus, which though it happens in some women does not in others. Speaking generally, this happens in fair-skinned women who are typically feminine, and not in dark women of a masculine appearance. Where it occurs, this discharge is sometimes on quite a different scale from the semen discharged by the male, and greatly exceeds it in bulk. Furthermore, differences of food cause a great difference in the amount of this discharge which is produced: e.g. some pungent foods cause a noticeable increase in the amount ...

Further, a boy actually resembles a woman in physique, and a woman is as it were an infertile male; the female, in fact, is female on account of inability of a sort, viz. it lacks the power to concoct semen out of the final state of the nourishment (this is either blood, or its counterpart in bloodless animals) because of the coldness of its nature. Thus, just as lack of concoction produces in the bowels diarrhoea, so in the blood vessels it produces discharge of blood of various sorts, and especially the menstrual discharge (which has to be classed as a discharge of blood, though it is a natural discharge, and the rest are morbid ones).

Hence, plainly, it is reasonable to hold that generation takes place from this process; for, as we see, the menstrual fluid is semen, not indeed semen in a pure concoction, but needing still to be acted upon. It is the same with fruit when it is forming. The nourishment is present right enough, even before it has been strained off, but it stands in need of being acted upon in order to purify it. That is why when the former is mixed with the semen, and when the latter is mixed with pure nourishment the one effects generation, and the other effects nutrition ...

Now the opinion that the cause of male and female is heat and cold, and that the difference depends upon whether the secretion comes from the right side or from the left, has a modicum of reason in it, because the right side of the body is hotter than the left; hotter semen is semen which has been concocted; the fact that it has been cococted means that it has been set and compacted, and the more compacted semen is, the more fertile it is. All the same, to state the matter in this way is attempting to lay hold of the cause from too great a distance, and we ought to come as closely to grips as we possibly can with the primary causes.

We have dealt already elsewhere with the body as a whole and with its several parts, and have stated what each one is, and on account of what cause it is so. But that is not all, for (1) the male and the female are distinguished by a certain ability and inability. Male is that which is able to concoct, to cause to take shape, and to discharge, semen possessing the 'principle' of the 'form'; and by 'principle' I do not mean that sort of principle out of which, as out of matter, offspring is formed belonging to the same kind as its parent, but I mean the *proximate motive principle*, whether it is able to act thus in itself or in something else. Female is that which receives the semen, but is unable to cause semen to take shape or to discharge it. And (2) all concoction works by means of heat. Assuming the truth of these two statements, it follows of necessity that (3) male animals are hotter than female ones, since it is on account of coldness and inability that the female is more abundant in blood in certain regions of the body. And this abundance of blood is a piece of evidence which goes to prove the opposite of the view held by some people, who suppose that the female must be hotter than the male, on account of the discharge of menstrual fluid.

When the 'principle' is failing to gain the mastery and is unable to effect concoction owing to deficiency of heat, and does not succeed in reducing the material into its own proper form, but instead is worsted in the attempt, then of necessity the material must change over into its opposite condition. Now the opposite of the male is the female, and it is opposite in respect of that whereby one is male and the other female. And since it differs in the ability it possesses, so also it differs in the instrument which it possesses. Hence this is the condition into which the material changes over. And when one vital part changes, the whole make-up of the animal differs greatly in appearance and form. This may be observed in the case of eunuchs; the mutilation of just one part of them results in such a great alteration of their old semblance, and in close approximation to the appearance of the female. The reason for this is that some of the body's parts are 'principles', and once a principle has been 'moved' (i.e. changed), many of the parts which cohere with it must of necessity change as well ...

Also, the fact that the menstrual discharge in the natural course tends to take place when the moon is waning is due to the same cause. That time of month is colder and more fluid on account of the waning and failure of the moon (since the moon makes a summer and winter in the course of a month just as the sun does in the course of the whole year) ...

So that if you reckon up (a) that the brain itself has very little heat, (b) that the skin surrounding it must of necessity have even less, and (c) that the hair, being the furthest off of the three, must have even less still, you will expect persons who are plentiful in semen to go bald at about this time of life.[3] And it is owing to the same cause that it is on the front part of the head only that human beings go bald, and that they are the only animals which do so at all; i.e. they go bald in front because the brain is there, and they alone do so, because they have by far the largest brain of all and the most fluid. Women do not go bald because their nature is similar to that of children: both are incapable of producing seminal secretion. Eunuchs, too, do not go bald, because of their transition into the female state, and the hair that comes at a later stage they fail to grow at all, or if they already have it, they lose it, except for the pubic hair: similarly women do not have the later hair, though they do grow the pubic hair. This deformity constitutes a change from the male state to the female.

93. *Intercourse, conception and pregnancy. Cos, 4th cent. B.C. (Hippocrates, On the Generating Seed and the Nature of the Child 4-7, 13, 30.[4] Tr. I.M. Lonie)*

Doctors, who were throughout antiquity with very few exceptions male (see below, p. 161), concerned themselves only with *diseases*. The normal female functions of menstruation, childbirth, nursing, menopause, were dealt with by women – midwives and wet-nurses. Hence few records exist of normal procedures and reactions.

4. In the case of women, it is my contention that when during intercourse the vagina is rubbed and the womb is disturbed, an irritation is set up in the womb which produces pleasure and heat in the rest of the body. A woman also releases something from her body, sometimes into the womb, which then becomes moist, and sometimes externally as well, if the womb is open wider than normal. Once intercourse has begun, she experiences pleasure throughout the whole time, until the man ejaculates. If her desire for intercourse is excited, she emits before the man, and for the remainder of the time she does not feel pleasure to the same extent; but if she is not in a state of excitement, then her pleasure terminates along with that of the man. What happens is like this: if into boiling water you pour another quantity of water which is cold, the water stops boiling. In the same way, the man's sperm arriving in the womb extinguishes both the heat and the pleasure of the woman. Both the pleasure and the heat reach their peak simultaneously with the arrival of the sperm in the womb, and then they cease. If, for example, you pour wine on a flame, first of all the flame flares up and increases for a short period when you pour the wine on, then it dies away. In the same way the woman's heat flares up in response to the man's sperm, and then dies away. The pleasure experienced by the woman during intercourse is considerably less than the man's, although it lasts longer. The reason that the man feels more pleasure is that the secretion from the bodily fluid in his case occurs suddenly, and as the result of a more violent disturbance than in the woman's case.

Another point about women: if they have intercourse with men their health is better than if they do not. For in the first place, the womb is moistened by intercourse, whereas when the womb is drier than it should be it becomes extremely contracted, and this extreme contraction causes pain to the body. In the second place, intercourse by heating the blood and rendering it more fluid gives an easier passage to the menses; whereas if the menses do not flow, women's bodies become prone to sickness.

5. When a woman has intercourse, if she is not going to conceive, then it is her practice to expel the sperm produced by both partners whenever she wishes to do so. If however she is going to conceive, the sperm is not expelled, but remains in the womb. For when the womb has received the sperm it closes up and retains it, because the moisture causes the womb's orifice to contract. Then both what is provided by the man and what is provided by the woman is mixed together. If the woman is experienced in matters of childbirth, and takes note when the sperm is retained, she will know the precise day on which she has conceived.

6. Now here is a further point. What the woman emits is sometimes stronger, and sometimes weaker; and this applies also to what the man emits. In fact both partners alike contain both male and female sperm

(the male being stronger than the female must of course originate from a stronger sperm). Here is a further point: if (a) both partners produce a stronger sperm, then a male is the result, whereas if (b) they produce a weak form, then a female is the result. But if (c) one partner produces one kind of sperm, and the other another, then the resultant sex is determined by whichever sperm prevails in quantity. For suppose that the weak sperm is much greater in quantity than the stronger sperm: then the stronger sperm is overwhelmed and, being mixed with the weak, results in a female. If on the contrary the strong sperm is greater in quantity than the weak, and the weak is overwhelmed, it results in a male. It is just as though one were to mix together beeswax with suet, using a larger quantity of suet than of the beeswax, and melt them together over a fire. While the mixture is still fluid, the prevailing character of the mixture is not apparent: only after it solidifies can it be seen that the suet prevails quantitatively over the wax. And it is just the same with the male and female forms of sperm.

7. Now that both male and female sperm exist in both partners is an inference which can be drawn from observation. Many women have borne daughters to their husbands and then, going with other men, have produced sons. And the original husbands – those, that is, to whom their wives bore daughters – have as the result of intercourse with other women produced male offspring; whereas the second group of men, who produced male offspring, have with yet other women produced female offspring. Now this consideration shows that both the man and the woman have male and female sperm. For in the partnership in which the women produced daughters, the stronger sperm was overwhelmed by the larger quantity of the weaker sperm, and females were produced; while in the partnership in which these same women produced sons, it was the weak which was overwhelmed, and males were produced. Hence the same man does not invariably emit the strong variety of sperm, nor the weak invariably, but sometimes the one and sometimes the other; the same is true in the woman's case. There is therefore nothing anomalous about the fact that the same women and the same men produce both male and female sperm: indeed, these facts about male and female sperm are also true in the case of animals.

13. As a matter of fact I myself have seen an embryo which was aborted after remaining in the womb for six days. It is upon its nature, as I observed it then, that I base the rest of my inferences. It was in the following way that I came to see a six-day-old embryo. A kinswoman of mine owned a very valuable danseuse, whom she employed as a prostitute. It was important that this girl should not become pregnant and thereby lose her value. Now this girl had heard the sort of thing women say to each other – that when a women is going to conceive, the seed remains inside her and does not fall out. She digested this

information, and kept a watch. One day she noticed that the seed had not come out again. She told her mistress, and the story came to me. When I heard it, I told her to jump up and down, touching her buttocks with her heels at each leap. After she had done this no more than seven times, there was a noise, the seed fell out on the ground, and the girl looked at it in great surprise.[5] It looked like this: it was as though someone had removed the shell from a raw egg, so that the fluid inside showed through the inner membrane – a reasonably good description of its appearance. It was round, and red; and within the membrane could be seen thick white fibres, surrounded by a thick red serum; while on the outer surface of the membrane were clots of blood. In the middle of the membrane was a small projection: it looked to me like an umbilicus, and I considered that it was through this that the embryo first breathed in and out. From it, the membrane stretched all around the seed. Such then was the six-day embryo that I saw, and a little further on I intend to describe a second observation which will give a clear insight into the subject. It will also serve as evidence for the truth of my whole argument – so far as is humanly possible in such a matter.

30. ... In fact it is impossible for pregnancy to last longer than ten months, and I shall explain why. The nutriment for growth which the mother's body provides is no longer sufficient for the child after ten months are up and it is fully grown. It is nurtured by drawing the sweetest part of the blood towards itself, although it is fed to some extent from the milk as well. Once these are no longer sufficient and the child is already big, in its desire for more nutriment than is there it tosses about and so ruptures the membranes. This occurs more frequently in women who are bearing their first child; with them, the supply of nutriment for the child tends to give out before the ten months are up. This is the reason; the menstrual flow of some women is sufficiently abundant, while with other women the flow is less. (If this is always the case it is the result of the constitution which the woman has inherited from her mother.) Now it is the women whose menses are small in quantity who also provide their infants with insufficient nutriment towards the end of their term when the infant is already large, and so cause it to toss about and bring on birth before ten months are up. The reason is their small flow of blood. Usually too these women cannot give milk; this is because they have a dry constitution and their flesh is densely packed.

94. *Contraception. Cos, 4th cent. B.C. (Hippocrates, Nature of Women 98. Tr. M.R.L.)*

If a woman does not want to become pregnant, make as thick a mixture of beans and water as you can, make her drink it, and she will not become pregnant for a year.[6]

95. *Menstruation. Athens, 4th cent. B.C. (Aristotle, On Dreams 459b-460a. Tr. M.R.L.)*

An illustration of how the eye affects what it sees.

In the case of very clean mirrors, if a woman who is menstruating looks into the mirror, the mirror's surface becomes bloody-dark, like a cloud. It isn't easy to wipe off the stain if the mirror is new, but if it is old it is easier. The reason for this is that vision, as we have said, is not only affected by the air, but indeed it also affects and does something to it ... Eyes are affected like any other part of the body when the monthly period occurs, since by nature they happen to be full of blood vessels. Accordingly during the monthly period, there is a difference [in the eyes] because of the disturbance and inflammation of the blood – invisible to us, but none the less there, for that is the effect of the seed and the menstrual period; the air is disturbed by them, and it has an effect on the air on the surface of the mirror, similar to how it itself has been affected, and the mirror's surface is affected accordingly ...

96. *Women's illnesses. Cos, 4th cent. B.C. (Hippocrates, Diseases of Women 1. Tr. A. Hanson)*

Problems with the female organs affect the functioning of the entire organism. Cures are based on the premise that the sexual act and pregnancy (or simulation thereof, such as digital manipulation or the insertion of pessaries) can restore health.

1. The following concerns women's diseases. I say that a woman who has never given birth suffers more intensely and more readily from menstruation than a woman who has given birth to a child. For whenever a woman does give birth, her small vessels become more easy-flowing for menstruation (because the birth process stretches the vessels and so makes menstruation easier.) ...

I say that a woman's flesh is more sponge-like and softer than a man's: since this is so, the woman's body draws moisture both with more speed and in greater quantity from the belly than does the body of a man ...

And when the body of a woman – whose flesh is soft – happens to be full of blood and if that blood does not go off from her body, pain occurs, whenever her flesh is full and becomes heated. A woman has warmer blood and therefore she is warmer than a man. If the existing surplus of blood should go off, no pain results from the blood. Because a man has more solid flesh than a woman, he is never so totally overfilled with blood that pain results if some of his blood does not exit each month. He draws whatever quantity of blood is needed for his body's nourishment; since his body is not soft, it does not become overstrained nor is it heated up by fullness, as in the case of a woman. The fact that a man works harder than a woman contributes greatly to this; for hard work draws off some of the fluid.

2. Whenever in a woman who has never given birth the menses are suppressed and cannot find a way out, illness results. This happens if the mouth of the womb is closed or if some part of her vagina is prolapsed. For if one of these things happens, the menses will not be able to find a way out until the womb returns to a healthy state. This disease occurs more frequently in women who have a womb narrow at the mouth or who have a cervix which lies far away from the vagina. For if either of these conditions exists and if the woman in question does not have intercourse and if her belly is more emptied than usual from some suffering, the womb is displaced.[7] The womb is not damp of its own accord (as, for example, in the case of a woman who does not have coitus) and there is empty space for the womb (as, for example, when the belly is more empty than usual) so that the womb is displaced when the woman is drier and emptier than normal.

There are also occasions when, after the womb is displaced, the mouth happens to be turned too far, such as in a case where the cervix lies far away from the vagina. But if her womb is damp from coitus and her belly is not empty, her womb is not easily displaced.

The following things also happen. For some women, when two months' menses are accumulated in quantity in the womb, they move off into the lungs whenever they are prevented from exiting. The woman suffers all the symptons which have been mentioned in the discussion of phthisis and she cannot survive.

6. If a woman is healthy, her blood flows like that from a sacrificial animal and it speedily coagulates. Those women who habitually menstruate for longer than four days and whose menses flow in great abundance, are delicate and their embryos are delicate and waste away. But those women whose menstruation is less than three days or is meagre, are robust, with a healthy complexion and a masculine appearance; yet they are not concerned about bearing children nor do they become pregnant.

7. If suffocation occurs suddenly, it will happen especially to women who do not have intercourse and to older women rather than to young ones, for their wombs are lighter. It usually occurs because of the following: when a woman is empty and works harder than in her previous experience, her womb, becoming heated from the hard work, turns because it is empty and light. There is, in fact, empty space for it to turn in because the belly is empty. Now when the womb turns, it hits the liver and they go together and strike against the abdomen – for the womb rushes and goes upward toward the moisture, because it has been

dried out by hard work, and the liver is, after all, moist. When the womb hits the liver, it produces sudden suffocation as it occupies the breathing passage around the belly.

Sometimes, at the same time the womb begins to go toward the liver, phlegm flows down from the head to the abdomen (that is, when the woman is experiencing the suffocation) and sometimes, simultaneously with the flow of phlegm, the womb goes away from the liver to its normal place and the suffocation ceases. The womb goes back, then, when it has taken on moisture and has become heavy ... Sometimes, if a woman is empty and she overworks, her womb turns and falls toward the neck of her bladder and produces strangury – but no other malady seizes her. When such a woman is treated, she speedily becomes healthy; sometimes recovery is even spontaneous.

In some women the womb falls toward the lower back or toward the hips because of hard work or lack of food, and produces pain.

21. Now I shall discuss the diseases of pregnant women. Some women conceive a child easily, but are not able to carry it full term; the children are lost through miscarriage in the third or fourth month – even though the woman has suffered no physical injury nor eaten the wrong kind of food. In such women the cause of the circumstances mentioned is especially when the womb releases matter which would make the embryo grow. The woman's bowels become upset: weakness, high fever, and lack of appetite affect them during the time in which they are aborting their children. The following is also a cause, namely if the womb is smooth – either naturally or due to the presence of lacerations in the womb. Now if the womb is smooth, sometimes the membranes which envelop the child are detached from the womb when the child begins to move – because these membranes are less a part of the womb than they ought to be, due to the fact that the womb is smooth. Anyone would know all these details if he would carefully ask about them. Insofar as the smoothness of the womb is concerned, let another woman touch the womb when it is empty, for the smoothness is not immediately distinguishable. If the menses flow in these women, they come copiously. Occasionally some of these women carry their embryos to full term, and when such women are cared for, they have hope of a normal birth.

25. I say that if menses flow each month for a woman who is two or three months pregnant or more, she is necessarily thin and weak. Occasionally a fever grips her during the days until the menses flow. When the menstrual blood flows, she becomes pale, yet very little flows out. Her womb has come to gape open more than it ought to and it releases matter which would make the embryo grow. Blood comes down from all the body when a woman is pregnant and gradually enters the womb, encircling that which is inside it; the blood makes it grow. But if the womb gapes open more than it should, it releases the blood each

month just as it has been accustomed to do in the past, and that which is in the womb becomes thin and weak. When such a woman is cared for, the embryo also is better and the woman herself is healthy. If she is not cared for, she loses her child and, in addition, she runs the risk of having a long-lasting disease ...

There are also many other dangers by which embryos are aborted; if, for example, a pregnant woman is sick and weak, and if she picks up a burden with all her bodily strength, or if she is beaten, or leaps into the air, or goes without food, or has a fainting spell, or takes too much or too little nourishment, or becomes frightened and scared, or shouts violently. Nurture is a cause of miscarriage, and so is an excessive drink. Wombs by themselves also have natural dispositions by which miscarriage can occur: wombs that are flatulent, for example, or tightly packed, loose, over large, over small, and other types which are similar.

If a pregnant woman feels distressed in her belly or in her lower back, one must fear lest the embryo bring on a miscarriage, since the membranes which surround it have been broken.

There are also women who lose their children if they eat or drink something pungent or something bitter contrary to their usual habits – if the child is in an early stage of its development. For whenever something happens to a child contrary to its usual habits, it will die when it is little, especially if the mother drinks or eats the kind of thing that strongly upsets her stomach when the child is in an early stage of development. For the womb perceives when a diarrhoetic flux comes down from the belly.

33. If in the case of a pregnant woman the time for birth is already past, if labour pains are present, and if for a long time the woman has been unable to bring forth the child without injury to herself, usually the child is coming in lateral or breech position – yet it is better for it to come out head-first. The pain involved is of the following sort: as if, for example, someone would throw an olive pit into a small-mouthed oil flask, the pit is not naturally suited to be taken out when it is turned on its side. In this way, then, the birth of the embryo laterally presented is also a very painful experience for the woman; it just doesn't go out. The pains are even more difficult if the embryo proceeds feet-first; many times the women die, or the children, or even both. A major cause of the embryo not going out easily is if it is dead, or paralysed, or if there are two of them.

62. All these diseases, then, happen more frequently to women who have not borne a child; yet they also happen to those who have. These diseases are dangerous, as has been said, and for the most part they are both acute and serious, and difficult to understand because of the fact that women are the ones who share these sicknesses. Sometimes women do not know what sickness they have, until they have experienced the diseases which come from menses and they become older. Then both

necessity and time teach them the cause of their sicknesses. Sometimes diseases become incurable for women who do not learn why they are sick before the doctor has been correctly taught by the sick woman why she is sick. For women are ashamed to tell even of their inexperience and lack of knowledge. At the same time the doctors also make mistakes by not learning the apparent cause through accurate questioning, but they proceed to heal as though they were dealing with men's diseases. I have already seen many women die from just this kind of suffering. But at the outset one must ask accurate questions about the cause. For the healing of the diseases of women differs greatly from the healing of men's diseases.

97. *Hysterical suffocation. Cos, 4th cent. B.C. (Hippocrates, Diseases of Women 2. 126, 123. Tr. M.R.L.)*

When the womb remains in the upper abdomen, the suffocation is similar to that caused by the purgative hellebore, with stiff breathing and sharp pains in the heart. Some women spit up acid saliva, and their mouths are full of fluid, and their legs become cold. In such cases, if the womb does not leave the upper abdomen directly, the women lose their voices, and their head and tongue are overcome by drowsiness. If you find such women unable to speak and with their teeth chattering, insert a pessary of wool, twisting it round the shaft of a feather in order to get it in as far as possible – dip it either in white Egyptian perfume or myrtle or bacchar or marjoram. Use a spatula to apply black medicine (the kind you use for the head) to her nostrils. If this is not available, wipe the inside of her nostrils with silphium, or insert a feather that you have dipped in vinegar, or induce sneezing. If her mouth is closed tight and she is unable to speak, make her drink castoreum in wine. Dip your finger in seal oil and wipe inside her nostrils. Insert a wool pessary, until the womb returns, and remove it when the symptoms disappear. But if, when you take the pessary out, the womb returns to the upper abdomen, insert the pessary as you did before, and apply beneath her nostrils fumigations of ground-up goat or deer horn, to which you have added hot ashes, so that they make as much smoke as possible, and have her inhale the vapour up through her nose as long as she can stand it. It is best to use a fumigation of seal oil: put the coals in a pot and wrap the woman up – except for her head. So that as much vapour as possible is emitted, drip a little fat on it, and have her inhale the vapour. She should keep her mouth shut. This is the procedure if the womb has fallen upward out of place ...

When the womb moves toward her head and suffocation occurs in that region, the woman's head becomes heavy, though there are different symptoms in some cases. One symptom: the woman says the veins in her nose hurt her and beneath her eyes, and she becomes sleepy, and when this condition is alleviated, she foams at the mouth.

You should wash her thoroughly with hot water, and if she does not respond, with cold, from her head on down, using cool water in which you have previously boiled laurel and myrtle. Rub her head with rose perfume, and use sweet-scented fumigations beneath her vagina, but foul-scented ones at her nose. She should eat cabbage, and drink cabbage juice.

98. *Dislocation of the womb. Cos, 4th cent. B.C. (Hippocrates, Nature of Women 8, 3. Tr. M.R.L.)*

If her womb moves towards her hips, her periods stop coming, and pain develops in her lower stomach and abdomen. If you touch her with your finger, you will see the mouth of the womb turned toward her hip.[8]

When this condition occurs, wash the woman with warm water, make her eat as much garlic as she can, and have her drink undiluted sheep's milk after her meals. Then fumigate her and give her a laxative. After the laxative has taken effect, fumigate the womb once again, using a preparation of fennel and absinthe mixed together. Right after the fumigation, pull the mouth of the womb with your finger. Then insert a pessary made with squills; leave it in for a while, and then insert a pessary made with opium poppies. If you think the condition has been corrected, insert a pessary of bitter almond oil, and on the next day, a pessary of rose perfume. She should stop inserting pessaries on the first day of her period, and start again the day after it stops. The blood during the period provides a normal interruption. If there is no flow, she should drink four cantharid beetles with their legs, wings and heads removed, four dark peony seeds, cuttlefish eggs, and a little parsley seed in wine. If she has a pain and irregular flow, she should sit in warm water, and drink honey mixed with water. If she is not cured by the first procedure, she should drink it again, until her period comes. When it comes, she should abstain from food and have intercourse with her husband. During her period she should eat mercury plant, and boiled squid, and keep to soft foods. If she becomes pregnant she will be cured of this disease ...

When her womb moves towards her liver, she suddenly loses her voice and her teeth chatter and her colouring turns dark. This condition can occur suddenly, while she is in good health. The problem particularly affects old maids and widows – young women who have been widowed after having had children.

When this condition occurs, push your hand down below her liver, and tie a bandage below her ribs. Open her mouth and pour in very sweet-scented wine; put applications on her nostrils and burn foul-scented vapours below her womb ...

99. *Dropsy in the womb. Cos, 4th cent. B.C. (Hippocrates, Nature of Women 2. Tr. M.R.L.)*

When there is a dropsy ɪ ɪ her womb, her monthly periods become smaller and weaker, and then stop suddenly, and her stomach bloats up, and her breasts dry out, and everything else suffers, and she seems to be pregnant – this is how you know she has dropsy. A further indication is the condition of the mouth of the womb: when she touches it, it seems withered. Fever and swelling attack her. As time goes on, pain develops in her lower stomach and loins and abdomen. This disease is usually brought on by miscarriage, but there are other causes.

When swelling in the womb occurs, one should wash the woman with warm water and apply warm poultices where she has pain. One should make her drink a laxative. After the laxative, put her in a vapour bath made with cow dung, then insert a pessary made with cantharid beetle, and after three days a pessary made of bile. Leave this in for one day, and then after three days give her a vinegar douche. Then if her stomach becomes soft and her fever goes away, and her period comes, have her sleep with her husband. If not, follow the previous procedure over again, until her period comes, and have her use some suppositories. In the days between suppositories have her drink samphire bark and dark peony berries, and eat as much mercury plant as possible, and garlic both raw and cooked. Have her eat soft foods such as squid and other soft animals. If she gives birth, she will be cured.

100. *Hysteria in virgins. Cos, 4th cent. B.C. (Hippocrates, On Virgins. Tr. M.R.L.)*

As a result of visions, many people choke to death, more women than men, for the nature of women is less courageous and is weaker. And virgins who do not take a husband at the appropriate time for marriage experience these visions more frequently, especially at the time of their first monthly period, although previously they have had no such bad dreams of this sort. For after the first period the blood collects in the womb in preparation to flow out; but when the mouth of the egress is not opened up, and more blood flows into the womb on account of the body's nourishment of it and its growth, then the blood which has no place to flow out, because of its abundance, rushes up to the heart and to the lungs; and when these are filled with blood, the heart becomes sluggish, and then, because of the sluggishness, numb, and then, because of the numbness, insanity takes hold of the woman. Just as when one has been sitting for a long time the blood that has been forced away from the hips and the thighs collects in one's lower legs and feet, it brings numbness, and as a result of the numbness, one's feet are useless for movement, until the blood goes back where it belongs. It returns most quickly when one stands in cold water and wets the tops of one's ankles. This numbness presents no complications, since the blood flows back quickly because the veins in that part of the body are straight, and the legs are not a critical part of the body. But blood flows slowly from the heart and from the *phrenes*.[9] There the veins are slanted, and it is a critical place for insanity, and suited for madness.

When these places[10] are filled with blood, shivering sets in with fevers. They call these 'erratic fevers'. When this is the state of affairs, the girl goes crazy because of the violent inflammation, and she becomes murderous because of the decay and is afraid and fearful because of the darkness. The girls try to choke themselves because of the pressure on their hearts; their will, distraught and anguished because of the bad condition of the blood, forces evil on itself. In some cases the girl says dreadful things: [the visions] order her to jump up and throw herself into wells and drown, as if this were good for her and served some useful purpose.[11] When a girl does not have visions, a desire sets in which compels her to love death as if it were a form of good. When this person returns to her right mind, women give to Artemis various offerings, especially the most valuable of women's robes, following the orders of oracles, but they are deceived. The fact is that the disorder is cured when nothing impedes the downward flow of blood. My prescription is that when virgins experience this trouble, they should cohabit with a man as quickly as possible. If they become pregnant, they will be cured. If they don't do this, either they will succumb at the onset of puberty or a little later, unless they catch another disease. Among married women, those who are sterile are more likely to suffer what I have described.

101. *Case histories. Cos, 4th cent. B.C. (Hippocrates, Epidemics 5. 12 and 25. Tr. M.R.L.)*

In Pheres a woman for a long time had headaches and no one could help her at all, not even when she had her head drained. It was easier for her when her period passed easily. When she had a headache, scented pessaries in her womb were helpful, and she was drained [of the fluid in her head] somewhat. But when she became pregnant, her headaches disappeared.

In Larissa a servant in Dyseris' household, when she was young, suffered severe labour pains whenever she had intercourse – otherwise she had no pains. She had never been pregnant. When she was sixty, she felt labour pains in the middle of the day, as severe as if in childbirth. Before that she had eaten a large number of leeks. When a pain came that was more severe than any she had had before, she stood up and felt something rough in the mouth of her womb. Then, after she had fainted, another woman inserted her hand and squeezed out a rough stone, like the whorl of a spindle. And the woman recovered immediately and stayed well thereafter.

102. *Epitaph for a woman who died while pregnant. Egypt, 2nd/1st cent. B.C. (Peek 1233. Tr. M.R.L.)*

Dosithea, daughter of ——. Look at these letters on the polished rock. Thallus' son Chaeremon married me in his great house. I die in pain, escaping the pangs of childbirth, leaving the breath of life when I was twenty-five years old; from a disease which he died of before, I succumbed after. I lie here in Schedia. Wayfarers, as you go by, all of you, say: 'Beloved Dosithea, stay well, also among the dead.'

103. *The women of Miletus (a traditional story). (Plutarch, Moralia 249d, Boeotia, 2nd cent. A.D. Tr. F.C. Babbitt (LCL))*

Once upon a time a dire and strange trouble took possession of the young women in Miletus for some unknown cause. The most popular conjecture was that the air had acquired a distracting and infectious constitution, and that this operated to produce in them an alteration and derangement of mind. At any rate, a yearning for death and an insane impulse toward hanging suddenly fell upon all of them, and many managed to steal away and hang themselves. Arguments and tears of parents and comforting words of friends availed nothing, but they circumvented every device and cunning effort of their watchers in making away with themselves. The malady seemed to be of divine origin and beyond human help, until, on the advice of a man of sense, an ordinance was proposed that the women who hanged themselves should be carried naked through the market-place to their burial. And when this ordinance was passed it not only checked, but stopped completely, the young women from killing themselves. Plainly a high testimony to natural goodness and to virtue as the desire to guard against ill repute, and the fact that the women who had no deterrent sense of shame when facing the most terrible of all things in the world, death and pain, yet could not abide nor bear the thought of disgrace which would come after death.

1. See especially H. von Staden, *BICS* 22 (1975) 184.

2. Cf. Apollo's argument in Aeschylus, *Eumenides* 658-61, which helps win the case for Orestes: 'She who is called the child's mother is not its begetter, but the nurse of the newly sown conception. The begetter is the male, and she as a stranger for a stranger preserves the offspring, if no god blights its birth' (tr. H. Lloyd-Jones).

3. In the Hippocratic Corpus (*On the Nature of the Child* 20), baldness is also attributed to excess fluid.

4. The authorship of the writings collected in the Hippocratic Corpus is uncertain, to say the least. It is unlikely that Hippocrates himself wrote any of them. See G.E.R. Lloyd, *Hippocrates* (Baltimore 1978) 10-11.

5. The flute-girl's gymnastics would not have aborted a healthy pregnancy, but they helped eject more quickly an early defective embryo (or 'blood mole') that would soon have been miscarried in the normal course of events. The embryo was of course much older than six days. See A. Guttmacher's note in T. H. Ellinger, *Hippocrates on Intercourse and Pregnancy* (New York 1952) 113-17.

6. The idea is to induce a substitute pregnancy, by using the Egyptian beans the Pythagoreans would not eat, because they believed that they could house human souls.

7. Womb here translates the plural in Greek. Since human dissection was not practised, doctors inferred that the human uterus was similar to the bicornuate uterus of domestic animals. See A. Guttmacher's note in T.H. Ellinger, *Hippocrates on Intercourse and Pregnancy* (New York 1952) 113-17.

8. Cf. the modern notion of a 'tipped uterus', a disease which mainly afflicts older married women and whose cure involves frequent manual examination by a physician (usually, of course, male). See B. Simon, *Mind and Madness in Ancient Greece* (Ithaca 1978) 242-4.

9. The 'mind', located in or near the lungs.

10. The heart and the *phrenes*.

11. Cf. Io's behaviour in Aeschylus, *Prometheus* 645-9; Simon, op. cit., pp. 563-608.

VIII

Daily Life

104. *'Birth control', Paros, 7th cent. B.C. (Archilochus, P. Colon. 7511. Tr. M.R.L.)*

A poem representing conversation between a girl and a young man who wants to make love to her. She suggests he ask another girl. He promises instead not to get her pregnant.

'But if you are in a hurry and desire drives you on, there is in our house a girl who is eager ... young and delicate. I think she has a perfect figure. You ... her.' So she spoke, and I answered: 'Daughter of Amphimedo (she was a good woman, though now she lies beneath the broad earth), there are many other pleasures for young men besides the Sacred Act. One of those will do. The rest you and I will discuss at leisure when ... I'll follow your orders: beneath the lintel and below the gate – don't begrudge me, dear; I'll put ashore at your garden's grass.[1] But realise this: another man can have Neobule.[2] Alas, she's overripe; her girlhood's flower has fallen, and the charm she had before; [she can't get] enough – a mad-woman who shows no measure ... she can go to hell ... If I had such a wife I'd give my neighbours pleasure.[3] I much prefer you. You aren't faithless or two-faced; she's more bitter and takes on too many. I'm afraid that in my haste I'd hurry to produce blind and premature offspring, like a bitch.' Those were my words. I took the girl and laid her down among the flowers. I covered her with my soft cloak and held my arm around her neck. She stopped trembling like a fawn; I touched her breasts gently with my hand; she revealed her new young skin. I touched her fair body everywhere and sent my white force aside, touching her blonde hair.

105. *Disadvantages of a liberal education. Athens, 4th cent. B.C. (Xenophon, Memoirs of Socrates 2. 7. Tr. M.R.L.)*

Xenophon, a pupil of Socrates, applied his teacher's philosophy to every aspect of life. Here he portrays Socrates using deductive reasoning on a practical problem: his friend Aristarchus finds himself with a household of female relatives to maintain; Socrates offers the revolutionary advice that they should be put to work making cloth, likes slaves, so that they can pay for their upkeep.

'Yes, Socrates, indeed I don't know where to turn. After the civil war began,[4] many people fled to the Piraeus. My female relatives were left behind and all collected at my house – sisters and nieces and cousins, so that there are fourteen freeborn persons in the household. Now we can get no food or income from our land because the enemy has control of it, and we get no rents from the houses we own because of the depopulation in Athens. No one is buying our furniture and one can't borrow money anywhere – a man could find more money looking in the street than he could trying to raise a loan. It's hard, Socrates, to look on and see my relatives dying, but it is impossible to support them in hard times like these.'

After Socrates heard this he asked, 'How is it that Ceramon manages to provide for so many people, not just for himself and his family, but to save enough in addition that he is able to be a rich man? Meanwhile you with your many people to take care of are afraid that all of you will die from want of the necessities of life.' Aristarchus replied, 'The reason is, by Zeus, that he has slaves to provide for, while my people are free-born.' 'Which do you think are better, your free-born people or Ceramus' slaves? 'I think the freeborn people at my house!' 'But,' said Socrates, 'isn't it shocking that Ceramon should live well off the work of people of a lower order, while you who have far better people are in want?' 'Indeed,' said Aristarchus, 'he is supporting technicians but mine have been educated like free persons.'

106. *On training a wife. Athens, 4th cent. B.C. (Xenophon, Oeconomicus 7-10 (excerpts). Tr. C. Lord)*

In this dialogue Xenophon has Socrates discuss the ideal arrangement of a household in the way he might describe order in the soul or in the state.[5]

Seeing him then one day sitting in the colonnade of Zeus the Deliverer, I [Socrates] went over to him, and as he seemed to be at leisure, I sat down with him and spoke. 'Why are you sitting like this, Ischomachos, you who are so unaccustomed to leisure? For I mostly see you either doing something or at least hardly at leisure in the market place.'

'Nor would you see me now, Socrates,' said Ischomachos, 'if I hadn't made an appointment to meet some foreigners here.'

'When you aren't doing this sort of thing,' I said, 'by the gods, how do you spend your time and what do you do?' ...

'As to what you asked me, Socrates,' he said, 'I never spend time indoors. Indeed,' he said, 'my wife is quite able by herself to manage the things within the house.'

'It would please me very much, Ischomachos,' I said, 'if I might also inquire about this – whether you yourself educated your wife to be the way she ought to be, or whether, when you took her from her mother and father, she already knew how to manage the things that are appropriate to her.'

'How, Socrates,' he said, 'could she have known anything when I took her, since she came to me when she was not yet fifteen, and had lived previously under diligent supervision in order that she might see and hear as little as possible and ask the fewest possible questions? Doesn't it seem to you that one should be content if she came knowing only how to take the wool and make clothes, and had seen how the spinning work is distributed among the female attendants? For as to matters of the stomach, Socrates,' he said, 'she came to me very finely educated; and to me, at any rate, that seems to be an education of the greatest importance both for a man and a woman.'

'And in other respects, Ischomachos,' I said, 'did you yourself educate your wife to be capable of concerning herself with what's appropriate to her?' ...

And Ischomachos replied: 'Well, Socrates,' he said, 'when she had got accustomed to me and had been domesticated to the extent that we could have discussions, I questioned her somewhat as follows. "Tell me, woman, have you thought yet why it was that I took you and your parents gave you to me? That it was not for want of someone else to spend the night with – this is obvious, I know, to you too. Rather, when I considered for myself, and your parents for you, whom we might take as the best partner for the household and children, I chose you, and your parents, as it appears, from among the possibilities chose me. Should a god grant us children, we will then consider, with respect to them, how we may best educate them; for this too is a good common to us – to obtain the best allies and the best supporters in old age; but for the present this household is what is common to us. As to myself, everything of mine I declare to be in common, and as for you, everything you've brought you have deposited in common. It's not necessary to calculate which of us has contributed the greater number of things, but it is necessary to know this well, that whichever of us is the better partner will be the one to contribute the things of greater worth."...'

Since work and diligence are needed both for the indoor and for the outdoor things, it seems to me that the god directly prepared the woman's nature for indoor works and indoor concerns. For he equipped the man, in body and in soul, with a greater capacity to endure cold and heat, journeys and expeditions, and so has ordered him to the outdoor works; but in bringing forth, for the woman, a body that is less capable in these respects, the god has, it seems to me, ordered her to the indoor works. But knowing that he had implanted in the woman, and ordered her to, the nourishment of newborn children, he also gave her a greater affection for the newborn infants than he gave to the man. Since he had also ordered the woman to the guarding of the things brought in, the god, understanding that a fearful soul is not worse at guarding, also gave the woman a greater share of fear than the man. And knowing too that the one who had the outdoor works would need to defend himself should someone act unjustly, to him he gave a greater share of boldness. But because it's necessary for both to give and to take, he endowed both with memory and diligence in like degree, so that you can't distinguish whether the male or the female kind has the greater share of these things. As for self-control in the necessary things, he endowed both with this too in like degree; and the god allowed the one who proved the better, whether the man or the woman, to derive more from this good. Since, then, the nature of each has not been brought forth to be naturally apt for all of the same things, each has need of the other, and their pairing is more beneficial to each, for where one falls short the other is capable. ...

'"It will be necessary," I said, "for you to remain indoors and to send out those of the servants whose work is outside; as for those whose work is to be done inside, these are to be in your charge; you must receive what is brought in and distribute what needs to be expended, and as for what needs to be set aside, you must use forethought and guard against expending in a month what was intended to last a year. When wool is brought to you, it must be your concern that clothes be made for whoever needs them. And it must be your concern that the dry grain be fine and fit for eating. There is one thing, however," I said, "among the concerns appropriate to you, that will perhaps seem less agreeable: whenever any of the servants become ill, it must be your concern that all be attended." "By Zeus," said my wife, "that will be most agreeable, at least if those who have been well tended are going to be grateful and feel more good will than before." I admired her reply,' said Ischomachos, 'and spoke: "Isn't it through this kind of forethought that the leader of the hive so disposes the other bees to her that when she leaves the hive, not one of the bees supposes they must let her go, but rather they all follow?"...

'And yet once, Socrates,' he said, 'I saw she had applied a good deal of white lead to her face, that she might seem to be fairer than she was, and some dye, so that she would look more flushed than was the truth, and she also wore high shoes, that she might seem taller than she naturally was. "Tell me, woman," I said, "would you judge me more worthy to be loved as a partner in wealth if I showed you our substance itself, didn't boast of having more substance than is really mine, and didn't hide any part of our substance, or if instead I tried to deceive you by saying I have more substance than is really mine and by displaying to you counterfeit money, necklaces of gilt wood, and purple robes that lose their colour, and asserting they are genuine?" She broke in straightway. "Hush," she said; "don't you become like that; if you did, I could never love you from my soul." "Haven't we also come together, woman," I said, "as partners in one another's bodies?" "Human beings say so, at least," she said. "Would I then seem more worthy to be loved," I said, "as a partner in the body, if I tried to offer you my body after concerning myself that it be healthy and strong, so that I would really be well complexioned, or if instead I smeared myself with vermilion, applied flesh colour beneath the eyes, and then displayed myself to you and embraced you, all the while deceiving you and offering you vermilion to see and touch instead of my own skin?" "I wouldn't touch vermilion with as much pleasure as I would you," she said, "or see flesh colour with as much pleasure as your own, or see painted eyes with as much pleasure as your healthy ones." "You must believe, woman, that I too am not more pleased by the colour of white lead or dye than by your colour, but just as the gods have made horses most pleasant to horses, oxen to oxen, and sheep to sheep, so human beings suppose the pure body of a human being is most pleasant. Such deceits may in some way deceive outsiders and go undetected, but when those who are always together try to deceive one another they are necessarily found out. For either they are found out when they rise from their beds and before they have prepared themselves, or they are detected by their sweat or exposed by tears, or they genuinely are revealed in bathing." '

'By the gods,' I said, 'what did she reply to this?'

'What else,' he said, 'was her reply, if not that she never did anything of the sort again and tried always to display herself suitably and in a pure state. At the same time she asked me if I could not advise her how she might really come to sight as fine and not merely seem to be. I advised her, Socrates,' he said, 'not always to sit about like a slave but to try, with the gods' help, to stand at the loom like a mistress, to teach others what she knew better than they, and to learn what she did not know as well; and also to examine the breadmaker, to watch over the housekeeper in her distribution of things and to go about and investigate whether each kind of thing is in the place it should be. In this way, it seemed to me, she could both attend to her concerns and have the opportunity to walk about. And I said it would be good exercise to moisten and knead the bread and to shake out and fold the clothes and bedcovers. I said that if she exercised in this way, she would take more pleasure in eating, would become healthier, and so would come to sight as better complexioned in truth. And a wife's looks, when in contrast to a waiting maid she is purer and more suitably dressed, become attractive, especially when she gratifies her husband willingly instead of serving him under compulsion. On the other hand, women who always sit about in pretentious solemnity lend themselves to comparison with those who use adornments and deceit. And now, Socrates,' he said, 'know well, my wife still arranges her life as I taught her then and as I tell you now.'

107. *Chastity, Italy, 3rd/2nd cent. B.C. (Thesleff, pp. 151-4. Tr. M.R.L.)*

Treatise attributed to members of the Pythagorean community in Italy.[6]

In general a woman must be good and orderly – and this no one can become without virtue ... A woman's greatest virtue is chastity. Because of this quality she is able to honour and to cherish her own particular husband.

Now some people think that it is not appropriate for a woman to be a philosopher, just as a woman should not be a cavalry officer or a politician ... I agree that *men* should be generals and city officials and politicians, and *women* should keep house and stay inside and receive and take care of their husbands. But I believe that courage, justice and intelligence are qualities that men and women have in common ... Courage and intelligence are more appropriately male qualities because of the strength of men's bodies and the power of their minds. Chastity is more appropriately female.

Accordingly a woman must learn about chastity and realise what she must do quantitatively and qualitatively to be able to obtain this womanly virtue. I believe that there are five qualifications: (1) the sanctity of her marriage bed (2) the cleanliness of her body (3) the manner in which she chooses to leave her house (4) her refusal to participate in secret cults or Cybeline rituals (5) her readiness and moderation in sacrificing to the gods.

Of these the most important quality for chastity is to be pure in respect to her marriage bed, and for her not to have affairs with men from other households. If she breaks the law in this way she wrongs the gods of her family and provides her family and home not with its own offspring but with bastards. She wrongs the true gods, the gods to whom she swore to join with her own ancestors and her relatives in the sharing of life and the begetting of children according to law. She wrongs her own fatherland, because she does not abide by its established rules ... She should also consider the following: that there is no means of atoning for this sin; no way she can approach the shrines or the altars of the gods as a pure woman, beloved of god ... The greatest glory a free-born woman can have – her foremost honour – is the witness her own children will give to her chastity towards her husband, the stamp of likeness they bear to the father whose seed produced them ...[7]

As far as adornment of her body is concerned, the same arguments apply. She should be dressed in white, natural, plain. Her clothes should not be transparent or ornate. She should not put on silken material, but moderate, white-coloured clothes. In this way she will avoid being over-dressed or luxurious or made-up, and not give other women cause to be uncomfortably envious. She should not wear gold or emeralds at all; these are expensive and arrogant towards other women in the village.[8] She should not apply imported or artificial colouring to her face – with her own natural colouring, by washing only with water, she can ornament herself with modesty ...

Women of importance leave the house to sacrifice to the leading divinity of the community on behalf of themselves and their husbands and their households. They do not leave home at night nor in the evening, but at midday, to attend a religious festival or to make some purchase, accompanied by a single female servant or decorously escorted by two servants at most.[9] They make modest sacrifices to the gods also, according to their means. They keep away from secret cults and Cybeline orgies in their homes. For public law prevents women from participating in these rites, particularly because these forms of worship encourage drunkenness and ecstasy.[10] The mistress of the house and head of the household should be chaste and untouched in all respects.

108. *The go-between or procuress. Egypt, 3rd cent. B.C.? (Herodas, Mime 1. Tr. M.R.L.)*

A conversation between a hetaera, Metriche, whose man has been away in Egypt, and her old 'nurse' Gyllis (cf. Neaera's household arrangements in Megara, above, no. 77).

Metriche (to her slave Threissa): Someone is making a noise at the door. See which of the farm workers has come in from the fields.
Threissa: Who's at the door?
Gyllis: It's me.
Threissa: Who are you? Are you afraid to come closer?
Gyllis: Look, here I am. I've come closer.
Threissa: Who are you?
Gyllis: Gyllis, Philaenis' mother.[11] Go inside and tell Metriche I'm here.
Threissa (to Metriche): You're being called by ...
Metriche: Who?
Threissa: Gyllis.
Metriche: Old ma Gyllis. Go away for a bit, slave. What Fate sent you to come to us, Gyllis? *(With ironic exaggeration)* Why have you come like a

god to mortals, for it's already five months, I think, since anyone has seen you – I swear by the Fates, coming to the door of this house.

Gyllis: I live far off,[12] child, and the mud in the back alleys comes up to my knees. I've only the strength of a fly. My old age drags me down. It stands like a shadow beside me.

Metriche: Quiet! Don't bring false charges against your age. You're still able, Gyllis, to use your arms to throttle your adversaries.

Gyllis: Yes, joke away. Just like women *your* age. But joking won't keep you warm. Why, dear child, how long have you been a widow, tossing alone on your lonely bed? It has been ten months since Mandris went off to Egypt. He hasn't even sent you a letter. He has forgotten you, and drunk from a new cup. Egypt is the House of Aphrodite. Everything that exists anywhere in the world is in Egypt, money, gymnasia, power, tranquillity, fame, sights, philosophers, gold, young men, the shrine of the Sibling Gods Ptolemy and Arsinoe, a good king, the Museum, wine, all the good things Mandris could want, and women, more of them, I swear by the Maiden who is Hades' wife, than the stars which the heaven boasts that it holds, and their looks – like the goddesses who once set out to be judged for their beauty by Paris (may they not hear what I am saying). Well, poor thing, what are you thinking of, as you warm your chair? You'll find out you have grown old and the ashes will gulp down your life's prime. Look elsewhere and for two or three days, change your mind and be happy and find a new man. A ship isn't safe in port with only one anchor. If Death comes, there will be no one to resurrect us. A cruel winter ... no one knows ... Mortals' life is uncertain. But now – no one is standing near us?

Metriche: Not a soul.

Gyllis: Then listen. This is what I wanted to come here to tell you. There is Gryllus,[13] son of Matacine, Pataicius' wife; he has won five prizes in Games: as a boy in Delphi, and twice in Corinth when he was first getting a beard, and then he beat his opponents in boxing twice at Olympia. He's nicely rich; he doesn't stir a straw on the ground; he's an untouched sea as far as sex is concerned. When he saw you at the festival of the Descent of Mise,[14] his passions were inflamed, his heart was stung by desire, and, my child, he won't leave my house by night or by day, but weeps over me and wheedles me and says he is dying of passion. So my dear child Metriche, grant the Goddess this one misdemeanour. Dedicate yourself, before you find that age has looked upon you. You will profit in two ways ... and you will be given more than you imagine. Think it over. Do what I say. I am your friend. I swear by the Fates.

Metriche: Gyllis, your white hair has made your wits dull. I swear by Mandris' safe return home and beloved Demeter I wouldn't have listened calmly to any other woman. I would have taught her to limp to her lame song and to have considered my door's threshold an enemy.

My friend, don't you come ever again to my house with one more message like this, but bring me the kind of message that ought to be brought to young girls by old women. You let Pytheas' daughter Metriche warm her chair. No one laughs at Mandris. But those aren't the words Gyllis needs to hear, as the saying goes. Threissa, wipe out the cup and pour her three sixth-parts of straight wine, drop some water into it and give it to her to drink.

Gyllis: No, thank you.

Metriche: Here, Gyllis, drink it.

Gyllis: No thank you. I didn't come here to lead you astray, but because of the Holy Rites.

Metriche: On account of them, Gyllis.

Gyllis (she takes the wine): ... Well, my child, it is sweet. I swear by Demeter, Gyllis has never drunk sweeter wine than this. Good luck to you, child, take care of yourself. May my Myrtale and Sime stay young,[15] while Gyllis is still alive and breathing.

109. *Dildoes. Egypt, 3rd cent. B.C.? (Herodas, Mime 6. Tr. M.R.L.)*

A poem representing a discussion between two middle-class women about the virtues of a particular dildo, referred to here not by its generic name *olisbos* ('slipper'), but euphemistically as a 'pacifier' (*baubon*, from *baubao*, 'sleep'), made by a shoemaker named *Kerdon*, 'Greedy'. The poet manages to imply that the two famous women poets Nossis and Erinna are collaborators in their activities.

Koritto: Metro, sit down. (*To her slave*) Get up and give the lady your chair — I have to *tell* her to do everything — you couldn't do anything on your own, could you? Bah, she's a stone, sitting in the house, not a slave. But when I measure out your barley ration you count the crumbs, and if even a little bit falls off the top you complain for the entire day — the walls fall in with your shouting. Oh, now you're polishing and making it shine, you pirate, just when we need it. Offer a prayer to my friend, since without her here you'd have had a taste of my hands.

Metro: Dear Koritto, our necks are worn out by the same yoke: I bark like a dog yelling at these unmentionable creatures day and night. But the reason I've come to your house — get the hell out of the way, you smart-arses, all ears and tongues, and days-off the rest of the time — please, don't hold back, dear Koritto, who was the man that made the red Pacifier for you?

Koritto: Metro — you haven't seen it have you?

Metro: Nossis, Erinna's daughter, had it a couple of days ago, Mm, nice gift.

Koritto: Nossis? Where'd she get it?

Metro: Will you tell on me if I tell you?

Koritto: By your sweet eyes, dear Metro, nothing you say will be heard escaping from Koritto's mouth.

Metro: Bitas' wife Euboule gave it to her and told her no one should find out about it.

Koritto: Women. That woman will wear me out. She begged me and I took pity on her and gave it to her, Metro, before I could even get to use it myself. And she snatches it away like some hidden treasure and gives it to people who shouldn't get it. A fond farewell to friends like that. She can look for somebody else instead of me to lend my things to Nossis – in case you think that for her (if I'm complaining more than is right, forgive me, Nemesis). If I had a thousand, I wouldn't give her one, not even a rotten one.

Metro: No, Koritto, don't let anger flare in your nostrils, when you hear of some silly story. It's a respectable woman's duty to put up with anything. I'm the one who's responsible, because I chatter so much, and I ought to have my tongue cut out. But what I particularly wanted to find out from you, who made it for you? If you love me, tell me. Why are you looking at me and laughing? Is this the first time you've ever seen me, Metro? Why are you behaving in such an affected way? Please, Koritto, don't hold back, and tell me who made it.

Koritto: Oh, why plead with me? Kerdon made it.

Metro: Who? Tell me! Kerdon? There are two Kerdons. One has grey eyes, Myrtaline's neighbour (Kylaethis' daughter). But he couldn't sew a plectrum for a lyre. The other one lives near Hermodorus' tenement houses, as you go out from Main Street. He was somebody once, but now he's got old. The old lady, Kylaethis, used to use him. (*Piously*) May her friends and family remember her in death.

Koritto: As you say, Metro, it isn't either of *them.* He is – I don't know, either from Chios or Erythrae, bald, a little man. You'd say he was Prexinus – they're as alike as fig and fig, except when he talks, then you know it's Kerdon and not Prexinus. He works at home and sells undercover – every door these days fears the tax collectors. But his workmanship – what workmanship. You'd think Athena's hands, not Kerdon's went into it. I – he came bringing *two* of them, Metro. When I saw them, my eyes swam at the sight – men don't have such firm pricks! Not only that, but its *smoothness* is sleep, and its straps are like wool, not leather. You couldn't find a kinder woman's shoemaker.

Metro: Why did you let the other one go?

Koritto: Metro, what didn't I do to get it? What sort of charm didn't I use to besiege him? I kissed him, and rubbed his bald head, and gave him something sweet to drink, and called him 'Daddy' – the only thing I didn't give him to use was my body.

Metro: Well, you should have given him that if he'd asked for it.

Koritto: Yes, I would have. But it's not a good idea to talk about what's not becoming a lady. Bitas' wife Euboule was there grinding. She has worn down my millstone night and day and turned it into trash, just so she wouldn't need to spend four obols to have her own sharpened.

Metro: How did he manage to come to your house, all this long way, dear Koritto? Don't hold back from me.

Koritto: Artemeis sent him, the wife of Kandas the tanner – she pointed my house out.

Metro: Artemeis always finds out about new discoveries – she can outdrink ... But since you couldn't rescue the two of them you ought to have found out who ordered the other one.

Koritto: I begged him, but he swore that he wouldn't tell me.

Metro: What you're telling me means that I must take a trip. I'm going now, to Artemeis' house, so I can find out who this Kerdon is. Stay well, Koritto dear. (*Ambiguously*) *Someone* is hungry, and it's time for me ...

Koritto: Close the door. You – count the hens, give them some darnel seed. You can be sure bird-snatchers will steal them, unless you hold them in your lap.

110. *Visit to a festival. Egypt, 3rd cent. B.C. (Theocritus, Idyll 15 (excerpt). Tr. M.R.L.)*

Gorgo, a housewife, visits her friend Praxinoa on the day of the festival of Adonis in Alexandria.

Gorgo: Is Praxinoa in?

Praxinoa: Gorgo dear – how long it's been – yes, I'm in. I'm amazed that you've come at last. See that she has a chair, Eunoa; put a cushion on it.

Gorgo: Thank you.

Praxinoa: Sit down.

Gorgo: I'm so incompetent. I barely got here in one piece, Praxinoa, there was such a crowd, so many chariots, everywhere boots, everywhere men wearing cloaks. And the road is endless. Every time you move further away.

Praxinoa: It's that crazy man. He brings me here to the ends of the earth, and gets me a hovel, not a house, so that we can't be neighbours, out of spite, envious brute; he never changes.

Gorgo: Don't talk about your husband that way, dear, when the little boy is around. You see, Praxinoa, how he's looking at you. Don't worry, Zopyrion, sweet baby – she isn't talking about Daddy.

Praxinoa: The child understands, by the great goddess.

Gorgo: Nice daddy.

Praxinoa: Daddy (that man) the other day – just the other day I said to him: 'Daddy, go and buy some soap and rouge at the booth,' and he came back with *salt*, the big ox.

Gorgo: Mine's like that too. He's a spendthrift, Diocleidas. For seven drachmas he bought dog skins, pluckings of old wallets – five fleeces, yesterday, all of it dirt, work and more work. But come on, get your dress and your cloak. Let's go to the house of the king, rich Ptolemy, to see Adonis. I hear the queen has done a beautiful job of decorating it.

Praxinoa: In fine homes everything's fine.

Gorgo: When you've seen it, what won't you be able to say to someone who hasn't. It must be time to go.

Praxinoa: Every day is a holiday if you don't work. Eunoa – you lazy – pick up that spinning and put it back in the centre again. Weasels like to sleep on soft beds. Move, bring me some water, right now. She was supposed to bring water; she brought soap. Give it to me anyway. Not so much, you pirate. Pour on the water. Stupid – why are you getting my cloak wet? Now stop. I've washed as well as the gods permit it. Where is the key to the big chest? Then bring it.

Gorgo: Praxinoa, that pleated dress suits you. Tell me – how much did the cloth cost off of the loom?

Praxinoa: Don't remind me, Gorgo. More than two minas of pure silver. I put my heart into the handwork.

Gorgo: Well, it lives up to your expectations. You can say that.

Praxinoa: Bring me my cloak and my hat. Put them on right. I'm not taking you, baby. Mormo Bogy; horse will bite you. Cry as much as you like, I won't let you be lame. Let's go. Phrygia, take the baby and play with him, call the dog inside, and lock the front door.

111. *Hiring a wet-nurse. Italy, 3rd/2nd cent. B.C. (Thesleff, pp. 123-4. Tr. M.R.L.)*

A letter on how to hire a wet-nurse, with a characteristically Pythagorean emphasis on measure and balance in all things.

Myia to Phyllis, greetings. Here is my advice to you now that you have become a mother. Choose a proper and clean wet-nurse, a modest woman who is inclined neither to drowsiness nor to drunkenness. Such a woman can make the best judgments about how to care for children appropriately, particularly if she has milk to nourish them and is not easily persuaded to sleep with her husband, for it is in this that she has an important part, foremost and prefatory to the whole of the child's life, in her nursing, as concerns his being raised well, for he will do everything well, at the proper time. The nurse will give him the nipple and breast not at his whim, but after due consideration. In this way she will encourage the baby's health. She will not succumb to sleep when she is tired, but when the newborn wants to rest. She will offer the child no small relief.

The wet-nurse should not be temperamental or talkative or uncontrolled in her appetite for food, but orderly and temperate, practical, not a foreigner, but a Greek.[16] It is best, if the baby is put down to sleep when it is well filled with milk. Such rest is sweet for little ones and such feeding most effective. If other food is given, it should be as simple as possible. One should stay away from wine completely because it has such a powerful effect or mix it sparingly with its evening meal of milk. She should not give him continual baths; it is better to have occasional temperate ones. Along the same lines, the atmosphere around the baby should have an even balance of hot and cold, and his housing should be neither too airy nor too close. Moreover, his water should not be too hard nor too soft, nor his bed too rough – rather, it should fall comfortably on his skin. In each of these areas Nature desires what is rightfully hers, not luxuries.

This much then I think it is useful to write at present – my hopes based on Nursing according to Plan. With the god's help, I shall in the future provide the possible and appropriate reminders about the child's upbringing.

112. *A brother to his sister. Egypt, 1 B.C. (Oxyrhynchus papyrus 744. Tr. G. Milligan)*

Hilarion to Alis his sister,[17] heartiest greetings, and to my dear Berous and Apollonarion. Know that we are still even now in Alexandria. Do not worry if when all the others return I remain in Alexandria. I beg and beseech of you to take care of the little child, and as soon as we receive wages I will send them to you. If – good luck to you! – you bear offspring, if it is a male, let it live; if it is a female, expose it. You told Aphrodisias, 'Do not forget me.' How can I forget you? I beg you therefore not to worry.

The 29th year of Caesar, Pauni 23.

1. Apparently the blonde (pubic) hair mentioned in the last line; he suggests that he will penetrate but then withdraw before ejaculation.
2. Since Neobule was said to have been Archilochus' fiancé, the 'I' of the poem may represent the poet.
3. Cf. the cuckold who is a joy to his neighbours in Semonides' poem, 110-11, above, p. 16 and Hesiod above, p. 14.

4. The revolt against the Thirty in 403 B.C.

5. Cf. W.E. Higgins, *Xenophon the Athenian* (Albany 1976) 28-30.

6. Cf. also the letter of Perictione on the 'harmonious woman', quoted in S. Pomeroy, *Goddesses, Whores, Wives, and Slaves* (New York 1975) 134-6.

7. The ultimate proof; cf. Glycon's praise for his wife Panthia (below, p. 162), 'You bore me children completely like myself': Lattimore, op. cit., p. 277.

8. Cf. Cicero's emphasis on the luxury of Clodia's household, below, no. 155.

9. But even religious festivals could provide opportunity for misconduct. Thus Simaetha, below, no. 130 meets Delphis at the Thesmophoria of Artemis.

10. Cf. the Athenian law against excessive mourning (above, no. 65) and the public reaction to Dionysiac ritual (below, no. 243).

11. A clear indication of her profession – Philaenis was a noted courtesan, who is said to have written pornographic books (see below, p. 160 n. 4).

12. Testimony to the problems of getting round growing suburbs; cf. Theocritus, *Idyll* 15, below, no. 110.

13. Also the name of Xenophon's son, who was a war hero.

14. In the Eleusinian myth of the Hellenistic period, the name of the hostess, otherwise called Iambe or Baubo, who persuaded Demeter to break her fast of mourning for Persephone (cf. *Homeric Hymn to Demeter*, 198-204).

15. Other *hetaerae*, for whom she will now try to get offers.

16. Cf. the similar advice in Plutarch, *Moralia* 3e.

17. Also his wife, following an Egyptian custom.

IX

Religion

The politically oppressed often turn to ecstasy as a temporary means of possessing the power they otherwise lack: orgiastic ritual, secret cults, trances, and magic provided such outlets, especially for women, who could not justify meeting together for any other purpose.[1]

Dionysus

113. *Rules of ritual. Miletus, 276/5 B.C. (Sokolowski, LSAM 48. Tr. A. Henrichs)*

Whenever the priestess performs the holy rites on behalf of the city ..., it is not permitted for anyone to throw pieces of raw meat [anywhere], before the priestess has thrown them on behalf of the city, nor is it permitted for anyone to assemble a band of maenads [*thiasos*] before the public *thiasos* [has been assembled] ...
... to provide [for the women] the implements for initiation in all the orgies ...
And whenever a woman wishes to perform an initiation for Dionysus Bacchius in the city, in the countryside, or on the islands, she must pay a piece of gold to the priestess at each biennial celebration.

114. *Epitaph for a priestess. Miletus, 3rd/2nd cent. B.C. (HSCP 82 (1978) 148. Tr. A. Henrichs)*

Bacchae of the City, say 'Farewell you holy priestess.' This is what a good woman deserves. She led you to the mountain and carried all the sacred objects and implements, marching in procession before the whole city. Should some stranger ask for her name: Alcmeonis, daughter of Rhodius, who knew her share of the blessings.

115. *Authorisation by the Delphic oracle to establish a temple in Ionian Magnesia.[2] Delphi, Hellenistic. (I. Magn. 215 (a). 24-40. Tr. A. Henrichs)*

Go to the holy plain of Thebes to fetch maenads from the race of

Cadmean Ino. They will bring you maenadic rites and noble customs and will establish troops of Bacchus in your city.[3]

'In accordance with the oracle, and through the agency of the envoys, three maenads were brought from Thebes: Cosco, Baubo and Thettale. And Cosco organised the thiasus named after the plane tree, Baubo the thiasus outside the city, and Thettale the thiasus named after Cataebates. After their death they were buried by the Magnesians, and Cosco lies buried in the area called Hillock of Cosco, Baubo in the area called Tabarnis, and Thettale near the theatre.'

116. *Equipment for women's orgiastic rites. Egypt, c. 245 B.C. (Hibeh papyrus 54. Tr. M.R.L.)*

Demophon to Ptolemaeus, greetings. Send us at your earliest opportunity the flautist Petoun with the Phrygian flutes, plus the other flutes. If it's necessary to pay him, do so, and we will reimburse you. Also send us the eunuch Zenobius with a drum, cymbals and castanets. The women need them for their festival. Be sure he is wearing his most elegant clothing. Get the special goat from Aristion and send it to us ... Send us also as many cheeses as you can, a new jug, and vegetables of all kinds, and fish if you have it. Your health! Throw in some policemen at the same time to accompany the boat.

Demeter

117. *The story of Persephone. 7th cent. B.C.? (Homeric Hymn to Demeter (verses 370-495). Tr. M.R.L.)*

Secret rites at Eleusis celebrated the return to her mother, Demeter, of Persephone from Hades. Though no one knows exactly what happened at the Mysteries, the possibility of rebirth suggested by the story was represented also in the notion of the dead grain's becoming the live seed of the next year's crop. The *Homeric Hymn to Demeter* describes in detail how Hades, god of the underworld, stole Persephone, how her mother searched for her and hid the seed within the earth until she got her daughter back again. This excerpt describes how Persephone returns, but only for part of the year, because she ate seeds in the underworld and must now forever return to spend four months of the year with her husband.

So Aidoneus spoke, and wise Persephone was delighted, and in her joy swiftly rose up from the bed; but Aidoneus gave her to eat the sweet seed of a pomegranate, furtively, looking out for himself to keep her from spending all of her days here on earth with revered black-robed Demeter. And before them Aidoneus, ruler of many, got ready his immortal horses in his golden chariot. Persephone got into the chariot, and beside her strong Hermes took the reins and whip in his hands and drove out of the palace. The two horses flew on eagerly; they easily completed the long journey – neither the sea nor the water of rivers nor grassy valleys nor mountain peaks held back the horses' speed, but as they went they cut the steep air beneath them. Hermes stopped and brought her where fair-crowned Demeter was waiting beside her fragrant temple [at Eleusis]. And when Demeter saw Persephone, she rushed like a maenad along the mountain shaded in forest; and Persephone opposite ... leaped down ... [Demeter asked ...] ... 'Child ...? [You have not tasted food in the Underworld?] Tell me! Because if you refused it, you could live with me and your father, Zeus of the black clouds, honoured by all the immortals ... But if you have tasted food you must live for a third part of the seasons [below] and for two parts with me and the other immortals. When the earth blooms with all kinds of fragrant spring flowers, then from the murky darkness you will come up once again and be a great wonder to gods and to mortal men. And with what trick did the strong Receiver of Many deceive you?'

Then beautiful Persephone addressed her in return: 'Then, Mother, I will tell you everything truthfully. When Hermes came as a messenger from my father Zeus and the other gods of Heaven to say I was to come from the Underworld, so you could see me with your own eyes and end your anger and cruel rage against the immortals, then in my joy I got up from the bed and he furtively put into me the seed of a pomegranate, sweet food; he compelled me to taste it by force, against my will. And I will tell you how Aidoneus carried me off because of my father's clever plan, and went and took me beneath the depths of the earth; I will relate everything in detail, as you request. We were playing, all of us, in the lovely meadow: Leuippe and Phaeno and Electre and Ianthe and Melite and Iache and Rhodeia and Callirhoe and Melobrosis and Tyche and pretty Ocyrhoe and Chryseis and Ianeira and Acaste and Rhodope and Plouto and lovely Calypso and Styx and Urania and lovely Galaxaure and Pallas rouser of battles and Artemis shooter of arrows; and we were gathering lovely flowers in our arms, soft crocuses mingled with irises and hyacinths and rose blossoms and lilies, wondrous to see; and the narcissus which the broad earth made grow like a crocus. This I picked in my joy, and the earth parted beneath me, and there the strong lord, the Receiver of Many, leaped out. He came and took me away beneath the earth in his golden chariot, much against my will, and I cried out in a shrill voice. This, in my sorrow, is the whole truth that I tell you.'

So then with their hearts in agreement they cheered their souls and hearts by embracing each other, and their hearts had respite from their sorrows. They took and gave joyousness to one another. And Hecate with her bright headband came near them, and embraced many times the daughter of holy Demeter; since then she has been her guardian and attendant queen. And then far-seeing Zeus of the loud thunder sent them a messenger, fair-haired Rhea, to bring black-robed Demeter back to the family of the gods, and he promised to give her honours that she could choose for herself among the immortals. He agreed that her daughter should spend the third part of the circling year beneath the murky darkness, but two parts with her mother and the other immortals. This was what Zeus said, and Demeter did not disobey his message. But she rushed swiftly to the peaks of Olympus, and she came to the Rharian plain, which before had been the nourishing breast of the land, but now no longer nourishing, since it stood fallow and leafless; it hid the white barley because of slim-ankled Demeter's devising. But then as spring grew strong, she began to adorn the field with long stalks of grain, and the plain's rich furrows were laden with grain stalks, which were bound into sheaves. Here she went first of all from the barren air. And the goddesses were happy to see one another and rejoiced in their hearts.

Then Rhea of the shining headband spoke to her thus: 'Come here, my child; far-seeing Zeus of the loud thunder is calling you to come to the family of the gods, and he has promised to give you honours, which you could choose from among the immortals. He has agreed that your daughter should spend the third part of the year beneath the murky darkness, but two with you and the other immortals ... He has nodded his head in confirmation. But come, my child, and obey them, and do not any longer be relentlessly angry at Zeus of the black clouds. Make a nourishing harvest grow for mortal men directly.'

So she spoke, and fair-crowned Demeter did not disobey her. Directly she sent up a harvest for the fields with their dark loam. And all the broad earth was laden with leaves and with flowers. And she came and showed the just kings Triptolemus and Diocles smiter of horses and mighty Eumolpus and Celeus leader of people the performance of her ritual and instructed them in his sacred mysteries, which one must never transgress or hear of or speak of, for great reverence for the gods holds back one's tongue. Happy the man who has seen these mysteries; but he who has not been initiated, and has not taken part in the ritual, does not share in the same rewards when he goes down beneath the broad darkness.

But when the bright goddess had taught them all her rituals, she went to Olympus to the company of the other goddesses. And there the two goddesses live beside Zeus who delights in thunder, awful and revered. Happy the man whom the goddesses willingly love; for directly they send as a guest to his great house Wealth who gives men riches. But now goddesses who protect the city of fragrant Eleusis, and sea-girt Paros and rocky Andron, queen Deo with your shining gifts, bringer of harvests, Mistress, you and your daughter beautiful Persephone willingly give me a good living in return for my song; and I shall remember you and another song also.

118. *Thesmophoria. Alexandria, 3rd cent. B.C. (Callimachus, Hymn 6. 119-33. Tr. M.R.L.)*

Women celebrated the annual festival of Demeter Thesmophoria (Lawgiver) to ensure the continued fertility of the earth. In this hymn the poet Callimachus tells how Demeter punished young Erysichthon when he cut down her sacred tree by giving him an insatiable appetite. The hymn concludes with a prescription for appropriate tribute to the goddess.

Sing, virgins, and mothers join the chorus: 'Demeter, all hail, nurse of many, giver of full measure.' And as four white horses pull the basket, so will the great goddess, the wide-ruler, come to us bringing white spring, and white summer, and winter and the season of withering. She will protect us through another year. As we walk through the city without sandals and with our hair unbound, so we shall have our feet and hands unharmed forever. And as the basket-bearers bring baskets full of gold, so may we taste boundless gold. The uninitiated women may process as far as the city hall; the initiated right to the goddess's temple – all who are younger than sixty. But women who are heavy, who stretch their hands to Eileithuia goddess of childbirth, or who are in pain – it's enough that they go as far as their legs can carry them. For these Deo (Demeter) will give all things full to the brim and let them come to her temple. Hail goddess, and keep this city safe in harmony and in prosperity. Bring all things from the fields in abundance. Nourish the cattle, bring us sheep, bring us grain, bring in the harvest, nourish peace also, so that he who sows may reap. Have mercy on me, thrice-prayed to, great queen among goddesses.

Athena

119. *Inscribed monument dedicated by a woman (only three others exist).*[4] *Athens, 520 B.C. (Raubitschek, DAA 348/IG I² 756. Tr. M.R.L.)*

Callicrate placed me here as a dedication to Athena.

120. *The priestess and temple of Athena Nike. Athens, 450-445 or c. 427 B.C. (IG I² 24/GHI 44. Tr. C. Fornara)*

An inscription on a marble stele, telling of the appointment of the priestess and the building of the temple of Athena Nike on the Acropolis of Athens.

[man's name] made the motion. For Athena Nike a priestess who ... from *all* Athenian women shall be [appointed], and the sanctuary shall be furnished with doors as Callicrates shall prescribe. The Poletai shall let the contract out for hire in the prytany of [the tribe] Leontis. Payment to the priestess shall be fifty drachmas [per year] and the legs and hides from public [sacrifices]. A temple shall be constructed as Callicrates shall prescribe and an altar of marble.

Hestiaeus made a motion. Three men shall be elected from the Boulē. They, together with Callicrates, after making the specifications, shall [indicate to the Boulē] the manner in which (*The rest is lost.*)

121. *A procession. Delphi, 2nd cent. B.C. (IG II² 1136. Tr. M.R.L.)*

Inscription in the form of a letter from the people of Delphi to the people of Athens.

... Greetings. Whereas the people of Athens led a Pythian procession to Pythian Apollo in a grand manner worthy of the god and their particular excellence: the priestess of Athena, Chrysis daughter of Nicetes, also was present with the procession; she made the journey out and the return well, appropriately, and worthily of the people of Athens and of our own city. With good fortune, it was voted by the city of Delphi to praise Chrysis, daughter of Nicetes, and to crown her with the god's crown that is customary among the Delphians. It was voted also to give *proxenia* to her and to her descendants from the city, and the right to consult the oracle, priority of trial, safe conduct, freedom from taxes, and a front seat at all the contests held by the city, the right to own land and a house and all the other honours customary for *proxenoi* and benefactors of the city.

Artemis

Women of all ages were concerned to appease the goddess Artemis, killer of women; but young women reaching the age of puberty and women bearing children were particularly vulnerable. There may be a correspondence between the shedding of blood requisite for those stages of female life and the sacrifice of ritual victims on the altar.

122. *A puberty ritual. Sparta, 7th cent. B.C. (Alcman, Fr. 1.5-101. Tr. M.R.L.)*

A chorus of young girls describe themselves and their ceremonial role in a special song. They appear to be offering a robe to a goddess, possibly Helen, who was worshipped in Sparta. Their erotic attraction to their leaders, Hagesichora and her friend Agido, recalls Sappho's world; perhaps Aenesimbrota was their teacher and trainer. Emphasis on the beauty of face and hair suggests that they are involved in a ritual that marks the transition (hence perhaps the references to battle) from girlhood to womanhood: the running of races is also a feature of puberty rites for Athena in Argos and Artemis in Brauron. Comparison to horses may suggest the imminence of marriage, which is often described in metaphors of taming and yoking. Doves frequently represent women's vulnerability.[5] The girls readily accept their leaders' preeminence. But in men's competition, success is ordinarily accompanied by strong expressions of envy and resentment.

I sing of Agido's light. I see her as the sun; Agido calls him to testify to us that he is shining. But our famous leader will not let me either praise or criticise her; for our leader seems to us to be supreme, as if one set a horse among the herds, strong, prize-winning, with thundering hooves – a horse of the world of dreams. And don't you see: the race-horse is Venetic; but my cousin[6] Hagesichora's hair blooms like unmixed gold. And her silver face – why should I spell it out? Here is Hagesichora. And she who is second to Agido in looks, runs like a Colaxian horse to an Ibenian. For the Doves bring the robe to the Goddess of the Dawn for us; they rise like the dog star through the immortal night and fight for us. There is not enough purple to protect us, nor jewelled snake of solid gold, nor Lydian cap – adornment of girls with their dark eyes; nor Nanno's hair, no nor Areta who is like the gods; not Sylakis and Cleeisera. You wouldn't go to Aenesimbrota's house and say: let me have Astaphis; may Philylla look at me, and lovely Damareta and Vianthemis – no, it's Hagesichora who excites me. For Hagesichora of the fair ankles is near her; close to Agido ... she praises our festival. Yes, gods, receive [their prayer]. From the gods [comes] accomplishment and fulfilment. Leader, I could say – a young girl that I am; I shriek in vain from my roof like an owl, and I will say what will please Dawn most, for she has been healer of our troubles; but it is through Hagesichora that girls have reached the peace they long for ...

123. *Excerpts from records of offerings to Artemis at Brauron. Brauron, Attica, 4th cent. B.C. (IG II² 1514. Tr. M.R.L.)*

The women's names indicate aristocratic rank; the list gives an idea of the variety of decoration and colour in their clothing.[7]

Archippe [dedicated] a dotted, sleeved tunic in a box during the year Callimachus was archon.[8] Callippe a short tunic, scalloped and embroidered; it has letters woven in. Chaerippe and Eucoline, a dotted tunic in a box. Philumene a silken tunic, in the year Theophilus was archon.[9] Pythias a dotted robe in the year Themistocles was archon.[10] There is an embroidered purple tunic; Thyaene and Malthace dedicated it. Phile [dedicated] a woman's girdle; Pheidylla a white woman's cloak[11] in a box. Mneso a frog-green garment. Nausis a woman's cloak, with a broad purple border in a wave design.[12]

124. *Records of dedications to Artemis Brauronia. Athens, early 4th cent. B.C. (IG II² 1388. 78-80, 82-3; 1400. 41-2, 46, 47. Tr. M.R.L.)*

Five perforated earrings: these Thaumarete the wife of Timonides dedicated, in a wooden box ... An ivory lyre and wooden pick inlaid with ivory in a carved box, which Cleito daughter of Aristocrates, Cimon's wife, dedicated ... A seal with a gold ring; Dexilla dedicated it ... To Artemis Brauronia a punctured golden ornament with a golden chain, which Callion dedicated, weight two drachmas ... a silver bowl which Aristola dedicated ... A gold ring which Dorcas who lives in Peiraeus[13] dedicated to Artemis Brauronia ...

125. *Ritual procedures. Cyrene, 4th cent B.C. (SEG IX.72. 13-16/Sokolowski, LSCG Supp. 115 (excerpts). Tr. M.R.L.)*

13. [If a bride comes to the dormi]tory,[14] she must sacrifice as a penalty to Artemis. She must not share a roof with her husband and must not be polluted; she must purify the temple of Artemis and as penalty sacrifice a full-grown victim, and then she should go to the dormitory. If she pollutes involuntarily, she must purify the temple.

14. A bride must make a ceremonial visit to the bride-room at the temple of Artemis at the festival of Artemis, whenever she wishes, but the sooner the better. If she does not make her ceremonial visit, she must make the regular sacrifice to Artemis at the festival of Artemis as one who has made no visit, and she must purify the temple and sacrifice a victim as penalty.

15. [A pregnant woman] shall make a ceremonial visit [before birth] to the bride-room in the precinct of Artemis and give the Bear priestess feet and head and skin of the sacrifice. If she does not make a ceremonial visit before giving birth she must make a visit afterwards with a full-grown victim. If she makes a ceremonial visit to the temple she must observe ritual purity on the seventh, eighth, and ninth day, and if she does not make a visit, she must perform the rites on these days. If she is polluted, she must purify herself and the temple and sacrifice a full-grown victim as penalty.

16. If a woman miscarries, if the foetus is fully formed, they are polluted as if by a death; if it is not fully formed, the household is polluted as if from childbirth.[15]

Aphrodite

126. *Dedication of statues of women. Corinth, 5th cent. B.C. (Kaibel 129-32. Tr. M.R.L.)*

Several versions of this epigram survive, explaining the dedication of statues of women in the temple of Aphrodite on Acrocorinth, the Acropolis of Corinth, after the war against Xerxes. The text does not make clear whether the supplication was made by cult prostitutes in the temple or by Corinthian wives (cf. Fornara, no. 53).

These women stand here on behalf of the Hellenes and the courageous soldiers of their own city, after they made their sacred vows to the goddess Cypris. For divine Aphrodite contrived not to betray the acropolis of the Hellenes to the bow-carrying Medes.

Asclepius

127. *Cures of sterility and pregnancy. Epidaurus, 4th cent. B.C. (IG IV² 121-2. Tr. N. Lewis)*

Incubation was a 'treatment' associated with the god Asclepius. The patient would sleep within a temple precinct, see the god in a dream and be miraculously cured. The following case histories were inscribed on the shrine of Asclepius at Epidaurus.

Cleo was pregnant for five years. After she had been pregnant for five years she came as a suppliant to the god and slept in the adytum. As soon as she left it and was outside the sanctuary, she gave birth to a son, and he, immediately after birth, washed himself at the fountain and walked about with his mother. After obtaining these results she had the following inscribed on her votive tablet: 'Wondrous the greatness, not of this tablet but of the god, seeing that Cleo bore for five years the weight in her womb until she slept in the shrine and he made her sound.'

A three-year pregnancy. Ithmonice of Pellene came to the sanctuary for offspring. After going to sleep here she saw a vision. She dreamt she asked of the god that she conceive a daughter and Asclepius said she would become pregnant and if she asked for something else he would bring that about too, but she said she didn't need anything more. She became pregnant and carried in her womb for three years, until she approached the god as a suppliant regarding the birth. She went to sleep here and saw [another] vision. She dreamt the god asked her whether she had not obtained all that she had asked for, since she was now pregnant; she hadn't said a word about birth even though he had asked her if she needed anything else she should say so and he would do that too; since she had now come to him as a suppliant for that, he said he would accomplish that too for her. After that she quickly left the adytum, and when she was outside the sanctuary she gave birth to a daughter.

Arata, a Spartan woman, a case of dropsy. She remained in Sparta and her mother slept here for her and had a dream. She dreamt the god cut off her daughter's head and hung her body with the neck down; then after a copious effusion he took down the body and put the head back on the neck. After having this dream she went back to Sparta and found that her daughter had had the same dream and was now well.

Aristagora of Troezen. Suffering from a tapeworm in her belly, she slept in the precinct of Asclepius in Troezen and had a dream. She dreamt that when the god was not there but away in Epidaurus his sons cut off her head and, finding themselves unable to put it back again, sent someone to ask Asclepius to come; meanwhile daylight overtakes them and the priest sees the head severed from the body; with the coming of night Aristagora saw a vision; she dreamt the god arrived from Epidaurus and put her head back on her neck, then cut open her belly, removed the tapeworm and stitched her up again. After that she was well.

Sostrata, of Pherae, had a false pregnancy. In fear and trembling she came in a litter to the sanctuary and slept here. But she had no clear dream and started for home again. Then, near Curni she dreamt that a man, comely in appearance, fell in with her and her companions; when he learned about their bad luck he bade them set down the litter on which they were carrying Sostrata; then he cut open her belly, removed an enormous quantity of worms – two full basins; then he stitched up her belly and made the woman well; then Asclepius revealed his presence and bade her send thank-offerings for the cure to Epidaurus.

Andromache, an Epeirote, for offspring. In her sleep here she had a dream: she dreamt that a blooming young boy uncovered her and then the god touched her with his hand. After that Andromache bore a son tò Arybbas.

A woman of Troezen, for offspring. In her sleep here she had a dream: she dreamt the god said she would give birth and asked if she wanted a boy or a girl and she said a boy. Within a year a son was born to her.

Agameda of Ceus. She came for offspring and in her sleep here had a dream: she dreamt in her sleep that a snake lay on her belly. Thereafter she gave birth to five children.

Nicasiboula, a Messenian, for offspring. In her sleep here she had a dream: she dreamt the god approached her carrying a snake, and she had intercourse with it. Within a year she gave birth to twin sons.

Serapis

128. *A petition to Ptolemy and Cleopatra. Memphis, 163/2 B.C. (UPZ 19. Tr. G. Milligan)*

The cult of the Egyptian god Serapis grew out of the worship, at Memphis, of Apis, the sacred bull. Beginning under the first Ptolemy and continuing through the Roman Empire, Serapis came to combine features of Egyptian, Greek and Roman gods, namely, Osiris, Zeus-Jupiter, Hades-Pluto, Asclepius, Helios and Dionysus. Incubation was associated with his cult as well as with that of Asclepius.

To King Ptolemy and Queen Cleopatra the sister, gods Philometores, greeting. We, Thaues and Taous are twins, who minister in the great Serapeum at Memphis. On a former occasion when you were in residence at Memphis and had gone up to the temple to sacrifice, we petitioned you, and gave in a petition, bringing before you our plea that we are not receiving the contribution of necessaries which it is fitting should be given to us both from the Serapeum and the Asclepeum. And having failed to receive them up to the present time in full, we have been compelled, under pressure of necessity, wasting away as we are through starvation, to petition you again, and in a few words to set before you the selfishness of those who are injuring us. For although you already from former times have proclaimed a contribution for the Serapeum and Asclepeum, and in consequence of this the twins who were there before us daily received what they required, to us also when we first went up to the temple straightway for a few days the impression was conveyed as if everything fitting would be done for us in good order, but for the remainder of the time this was not carried out. Wherefore we both sent repeatedly to the supervisors persons to petition on our behalf, and laid information on these matters before you, on the occasion of your visits to Memphis. And when those who had been appointed to the administration in the Serapeum and Asclepeum had insolently maltreated us, and were removing the privileges conferred on you by us, and were paying no regard to religious scruple, and when we were being crushed by our wants, we often made representations even to Achomarres the supervisor of the temple to give us [our rights]. And we approached the son of Psintaes the supervisor of the sacrifices, when we went up to the temple the day before yesterday, and gave him detailed information. And having called Achomarres to him, he strictly commanded him to give what was owing to us. And he, being by nature the most unfeeling of all mankind, promised us that he would perform what he had been directed to do, but no sooner had the son of Psintaes departed from Memphis than he took no further account of the matter. And not only this man, but also others connected with the Serapeum, and others connected with the Asclepeum in the administration, from whom it is usual for us to receive what we need, are defrauding, whose names and obligations, because they are numerous, we have decided not to record.

We beg you therefore, having as our one hope the assistance that lies in your power, to send away our petition to Dionysius Privy Councillor and strategus, that he may write to Apollonius the supervisor to compel them to render to us [what is owing], when he has received from us the written list of the necessaries owing to us and what further debts are due us along with the periods for which they have been owing and the persons who owe them, so that, when we have everything in order, we may be much better able to perform our regular duties to Serapis and to Isis, both for your own sakes and for the sake of your children. May it be given you to hold fast all the territory you desire. Farewell.

Witchcraft

129. *Medea. (Apollonius of Rhodes, Argonautica 3. 838-67. Alexandria, 3rd cent. B.C. Tr. M.R.L.)*

A poet's account of how the young Medea found the drug she needed to protect Jason.

Medea called to her maidservants – there were twelve in all; they slept in the porch of her fragrant bedchamber, of the same age as she; they had not yet shared their beds with husbands – swiftly to yoke the mules to the wagon, so they might bring her to the beautiful temple of Hecate. Then the maidens got the chariot ready. And meanwhile Medea took from a hollow casket the drug that men say is called Prometheian. If a man should wet his body with this drug and appease Persephone with sacrificial offerings by night, he would not be wounded by blows from bronze weapons nor would he yield to blazing fire, but on that day he would be superior in valour and power. The drug first sprang up when the savage eagle let drop to earth in the valleys of Caucasus bloody ichor from Prometheus in his agony.[16] Its flower came out as high as a cubit above the ground, in colour like the Corycian crocus, rising on twin stems. In the ground its root was like new-cut flesh. Its juice, dark like a beech tree in the mountains, Medea collected in a shell from the Caspian sea to use as a drug; she washed it seven times in flowing water, and seven times called on Brimo protectress of children. Brimo who travels by night, from the underworld, queen of the dead, in the murky night, in black clothes. And the dark earth shook beneath and groaned as the root of the Titan god was cut, and Prometheus himself cried out in pain in his heart's agony. Medea now took out this drug and put it underneath the fragrant band that was fastened below her divine breasts.

130. *A love potion. Alexandria, 3rd cent. B.C. (Theocritus, Idyll 2 (excerpt). Tr. M.R.L.)*

A dramatic representation of a courtesan's attempt to win back a handsome lover.

Where are my bay-leaves? Go get them, Thestylis. And where are my drugs? Put a wreath of crimson wool round the bowl, so I can bind my dear lover, who is cruel to me. It's now the twelfth day that the beast hasn't even come near me and he doesn't know if I'm dead or alive; cruel man, he hasn't knocked on my door. I'm sure that Love has gone off with his fickle heart elsewhere, and so has Aphrodite. I'll go to Timagetus' wrestling-ring tomorrow, so I can see him, and I'll complain about how he is treating me.

But today I will bind him with what I burn here. Now, Moon, shine brightly, and I will sing to you softly, goddess, and to Hecate underground, before whom even dogs tremble as she comes from the graves of the dead and their black blood. Hail, Hecate unapproachable, and guide me until I am finished; make these drugs of mine in no way inferior to Circe's or Medea's or blonde Perimede's. *Magic wheel, draw that man to my house.*

First barley melts on the fire. Sprinkle them on, Thestylis. Fool, where have your wits flown to? You curse, do you also think you can make fun of me? Sprinkle it on and say as follows: 'I sprinkle the bones of Delphis.' *Magic wheel, draw that man to my house.*

Delphis has hurt me. So I burn this bay on Delphis. As they catch fire, crackle loudly and are consumed in an instant and I can't even see their ashes, so may Delphis' flesh be consumed in flames. *Magic wheel, draw that man to my house.*

Now I'll burn the bran. Artemis, you can move the power of Death and anything else that is immovable – Thestylis, dogs all round the city are barking; the goddess is at the crossroads. As quick as you can, clash the cymbals. *Magic wheel, draw that man to my house.*

Now the sea is still; the winds are still, but the pain in my heart is not still, but the whole of me burns for him; instead of a wife, he has made me miserable, a fallen woman, no longer a virgin. *Magic wheel, draw that man to my house.*

As I melt this wax with the goddess's assistance, so may Delphis from Myndus melt with desire. As this bronze wheel of Aphrodite's spins, so may Delphis spin in front of my door. *Magic wheel, draw that man to my house.*

I shall pour three libations and say three times as follows, 'O goddess: whether a woman lies beside him or whether a man does, let him forget that person as fast as they say Theseus once forgot fair-haired Ariadne on Naxos.' *Magic wheel, draw that man to my house.*

Coltsfoot is an herb that grows in Arcadia, and for it all the swift mares and colts run mad through the mountains, swift mares. May I see Delphis like that; may he rush to this house like a madman, from the glistening wrestling-ring. *Magic wheel, draw that man to my house.*

Delphis lost this, the fringe of his cloak. I now shred it and throw it in the wild fire. *Ai ai*, painful Desire, why have you drunk the black blood from my flesh, all of it, like a marsh leech stuck to me?

I'll grind up a lizard and bring it tomorrow for him to drink. Now, Thestylis, take these flowers and knead them over his threshold, while it's still night, and say in a whisper, 'I knead the bones of Delphis.' *Magic wheel, draw that man to my house.*

131. *Bitto's curse. Athens, 3rd/2nd cent. B.C. (Kaibel 1136. Tr. M.R.L.)*

A curse inscribed on a leaden tablet; at the end of the name of the author Bitto and her victim Sosiclea are written upside-down.

I shall bind Sosiclea and her possessions and her actions and her thoughts. May she become hateful to her friends. I shall bind her beneath empty Tartarus in cruel bonds, and, with the aid of Hecate under the earth. Sosiclea. Bitto. Dedicated to the Maddener[17] Furies.

---

1. See especially I.M. Lewis, *Ecstatic Religion* (Harmondsworth 1971) 101.

2. The verse inscription is followed by a prose postscript confirming the transfer.

3. *HSCP* 82 (1978) 123-4; considered 'legendary' by J. Fontenrose, *The Delphic Oracle* (Berkeley 1978) 409-10.

4. *IG* I² 745/DAA 369; 582/DAA 232; *IG* I² 425.

5. See especially C. Calame, *Les Choers de jeunes filles en Grèce archaïque II: Alcman* (Rome 1977).

6. Perhaps the term is metaphorical, signifying only that they are members of the same social group; Calame, op. cit., pp. 84-5.

7. On offerings to Artemis, see T. Linders, *Studies in the Treasure Records at Artemis Brauronia* (Stockholm 1972).

8. 349/8 B.C.

9. 348/7 B.C.

10. 347/6 B.C.

11. Cf. the offering referred to in the Hippocratic treatise, *On Virgins*, above, no. 100.

12. Cf. the Pythagorean admonition that women should wear white, above, no. 107.

13. A resident alien.

14. The restoration is uncertain. Apparently Cyrenaean girls were required before marriage to spend a night in a dormitory in the precinct of Artemis.

15. A woman in childbirth pollutes everyone who enters the house for three days.

16. Prometheus was punished by Zeus for disobedience by having his liver eaten each day by Zeus' eagle.

17. A word used only here; cf. Aeschylus, *Eumenides* 326.

PART TWO

ROME

X

A Poet, Sulpicia

(Rome, 1st cent. B.C.)

Though other Roman women are known to have written poetry – Melinno (2nd cent. A.D.) composed sapphic stanzas (in Greek) in praise of Rome – Sulpicia is the only Roman woman of whose work we possess more than fragments. She was the ward of M. Valerius Messala Corvinus, writer, politician and patron of the arts during the Augustan age. Among his circle was the poet Albius Tibullus, who seems to have befriended the young Sulpicia. The identity of her love, whom she calls 'Cerinthus', is unknown. The poems are preserved in Book 3 of Tibullus' works.

132. *To Messala. (Tibullus 3. 14. Tr. M.B.F.)*

My hated birthday approaches, and I will have to spend it in sorrow in the nasty country and without Cerinthus. What is nicer than the city? Or is a farmhouse a fit place for a girl – or a freezing river around Arezzo? Now, Messala, calm yourself; you take too good care of me, and a trip can often come at an awkward moment. Here I leave my heart and soul – while I am carried unwilling away – though you will not let me make my own decision about them.

133. *To Cerinthus. (Tibullus, 3. 15, 17, 18, 16, 13. Tr. M.B.F.)*

You know that that tiresome trip now has been lifted from your sweetheart's shoulders? I am now allowed to have my birthday in Rome. Everybody should celebrate that birthday, which now by chance catches you unawares.

Have you no solicitude, Cerinthus, for your sweetheart, because a fever is tormenting my exhausted body? Oh, I would never want to conquer the miserable disease unless I thought you wanted me to. After all, what good would it do me to vanquish my illness if you could bear my woes with a steady heart?

Light of my life, may I be no longer your love's fire – as I seem to have
been a few days ago – if I ever again do such a stupid girlish thing that
would make me sorrier than leaving you alone last night, in my desire to
keep from you my desire.

It is a fine thing this – that you are so sure of me now that you take
liberties, lest I, incapable, should suddenly take a foolish spill. Let a
toga'd whore and her wool-basket be of more importance to you than is
Sulpicia, Servius' daughter. There are those who care about me, and
their greatest worry is that I might lose my place to a nobody's bed.

At last a love has come of such a kind that my shame, Gossip, would be
greater if I kept it covered than if I laid it bare. Cythera, implored by my
verses, brought that man to me and gave him into my embrace. Venus
kept her promise: let anyone talk about my joy who – it's said – never
had any of his own. I would not want to send anything to him on sealed
tablets, lest anyone should read it before my own love does; but my sin is
a joy, though it's tiresome to keep a straight face for gossip's sake. Let it
be said that I was a worthy woman, with a worthy man.

XI
Wives, Mothers, Daughters

Praise

While most Roman epitaphs are short and simple, containing only a dedication to the gods of the underworld and the name and age of the deceased, some contain a eulogy and brief biography. In some texts the survivor who dedicated the tomb speaks directly to the soul of the deceased or to the passer-by. Many inscriptions give the impression that the soul is living inside the tomb and wishes to maintain a friendly relationship with the living. As cemeteries were most frequently situated along the main roads to and from towns, strangers constantly passed the tombs during the course of their daily business. For this reason, benches and gardens were often provided in tomb plots, where the passer-by might stop and rest and feel grateful to the dead. He was expected to show proper respect for the tomb, legally a sanctified place, and was sometimes cursed or fined if he did not.

134. *Claudia. Rome, 2nd cent. B.C. (ILLRP 973/ILS 8403. Tr. R. Lattimore)*

Friend, I have not much to say; stop and read it. This tomb, which is not fair, is for a fair woman. Her parents gave her the name Claudia. She loved her husband in her heart. She bore two sons, one of whom she left on earth, the other beneath it. She was pleasant to talk with, and she walked with grace. She kept the house and worked in wool. That is all. You may go.

135. *Eucharis. Rome, 1st cent. B.C. (ILLRP 803/ILS 5213. Tr. M.R.L.)*

[The grave] of Eucharis, freedwoman of Licinia, an unmarried girl who was educated and learned in every skill. She lived fourteen years.
  Ah, as you look with wandering eye at the house of death, stay your foot and read what is inscribed here. This is what a father's love gave his daughter, where the remains of her body lie gathered. 'Just as my life with its young skills and growing years brought me fame, the sad hour of

death rushed on me and forbade me to draw another breath in life. I was educated and taught as if by the Muses' hands. I adorned the nobility's festivals with my dancing, and first appeared before the common people in a Greek play.

'But now here in this tomb my enemies the Fates have placed my body's ashes. The patrons of learning – devotion, passion, praise, honour, are silenced by my burnt corpse and by my death.

'His child, I left lamentation to my father, though born after him, I preceded him in the day of my death. Now I observe my fourteenth birthday here among the shadows in Death's ageless home.

'I beg you when you leave, ask that the earth lie light upon me.'

136. *Posilla Senenia. Monteleone Sabino, 1st cent. B.C. (ILLRP 971. Tr. M.B.F.)*

Posilla Senenia, daughter of Quartus, and Quarta Senenia, freedwoman of Gaius.

Stranger, stop and, while you are here, read what is written: that a mother was not permitted to enjoy her only daughter, whose life, I believe, was envied by some god.

Since her mother was not allowed to adorn her while she was alive, she does so just the same after death; at the end of her time, [her mother] with this monument honours her whom she loved.

137. *A butcher and his wife. Rome, 1st cent. B.C. (ILLRP 793/ILS 7472. Tr. M.B.F.)*

A man and a woman, hands joined, are shown in relief on this tombstone.

(*On the left*)
Lucius Aurelius Hermia, freedman of Lucius, a butcher from the Viminal Hill.

My wife, who died before me, chaste in body, my one and only, a loving woman who possessed my heart, she lived as a faithful wife to a faithful husband with affection equal to my own, since she never let avarice keep her from her duty. Aurelia Philmatio, freedwoman of Lucius.

(*On the right*)
Aurelia Philmatio, freedwoman of Lucius.

When I was alive I was called Aurelia Philematium. I was chaste and modest; I did not know the crowd; I was faithful to my husband. He whom, alas, I have lost was my fellow-freedman and was truly more than a father to me. When I was seven years old, he took me to his bosom; now at forty, I am possessed by violent death. He, through my diligent performance of duty, flourished at all [times ...]. (*The rest is lost.*)

138. *The household of P. Larcius Nicia. Rome, 1st cent. B.C. (ILLRP 977. Tr. M.B.F.)*

Publius Larcius Nicia, freedman of Publius; Saufeia Thalea, freedwoman of Aulus; Lucius Larcius Rufus, son of Publius; Publius Larcius Brocchus, son of Publius; Larcia Horaea, freedwoman of Publius [and Saufeia].[1]

I was respected by good people and was envied by no woman of character. I was obedient to my old master and mistress, and to this man, my husband, I was dutiful. They honoured me with my freedom, he with a [matron's] robe. I kept the house for twenty years, beginning as a little girl. My last day made its judgment; death snatched away my soul but did not take my life's honour.

Lucius Eprius Chilo, messenger of the tribune of the people, Epria Cri ... (*The rest is lost.*)

139. *Murdia. Rome, c. 27 B.C./A.D. 14 (CIL VI. 10230/ILS 8394. Tr. M.R.L.)*

Funeral eulogy for Murdia, spoken by her son by her first marriage.

(The first part of the inscription is lost.)
She made all her sons equal heirs, after she gave a bequest to her daughter. Her love as a mother is formed from affection for her children and her fairness to each. She willed her husband [the speaker's stepfather] a fixed sum, so that his dower right would be increased by the honour of her deliberate choice.

Recalling my father's memory and taking account of it and of the trust she owed him she bequeathed certain property to me. She did so not in order to wound my brothers by preferring me to them, but remembering my father's generosity, she decided that I should have returned to me the part of my inheritance which she had received by the decision of her husband, so that what had been taken care of by his orders should be restored to my ownership.

In such action she determined to maintain the marriages given to her by her parents to worthy men, with obedience and propriety, and as a bride to become more beloved because of her merits, to be thought dearer because of her honour, to be considered more dedicated because of her discretion, and after her death to be praised in the judgment of her fellow citizens, since the division of her estate indicated her grateful and honourable intentions towards her husbands, her fairness to her children, and the justice shown by her sincerity.

For these reasons praise for all good women is simple and similar, since their native goodness and the trust they have maintained do not require a diversity of words. Sufficient is the fact that they have all done the same good deeds with the fine reputation they deserve, and since it is hard to find new forms of praise for a woman, since their lives fluctuate with less diversity, by necessity we pay tribute to values they hold in common, so that nothing may be lost from fair precepts and harm what remains.

Still, my dearest mother deserved greater praise than all others, since in modesty, propriety, chastity, obedience, woolworking, industry and honour she was on an equal level with other good women, nor did she take second place to any woman in virtue, work and wisdom in times of danger. (*The rest is lost.*)

140. *Pythion and Epicydilla. Thasos, 1st cent. A.D. (Pleket 10. Tr. M.R.L.)*

Pythion son of Hicesius set up this common memorial to himself and to his wife Epicydilla daughter of Epicydes. He was married at eighteen and she at fifteen, and for fifty years of life together they shared agreement unbroken, and were fathers of fathers [*sic*], twice archons of their city, happy among the living and blessed among the dead. If anyone places another body here, he must pay to the city 12,000 minae.

141. *Socratea. Paros, 2nd cent. A.D. (Kaibel 218. Tr. M.R.L.)*

... Nicander was my father, my country was Paros, and my name Socratea. My husband Parmenion buried me when I died, granting me that favour so that my good conduct in life might be remembered also by future generations.

The cruel Fury of the new-born,[2] implacable, with a haemorrhage took me from my happy life. In my third decade of life I reached the sixth year. I left my husband male offspring: two for my father and for my spouse; for myself, because of the third, I got this grave.

142. *Epitaph for a little girl, Politta. Memphis, 2nd/3rd cent. A.D. (Peek 1243. Tr. M.R.L.)*

A good plant from a holy root – citizens, weep for me. I was pleasing to all, blameless in my mother's eyes, faultless in my father's. I lived five years.

143. *Allia Potestas. Rome, 3rd cent. A.D. (CIL VI. 37965. Tr. M.R.L.)*

Scholars have found this unusual inscription difficult to classify. It may have been intended as a serious encomium, but parts of it, at least, may have been meant deliberately to be amusing.

To the gods of the dead, [the tomb] of Aulus' freedwoman, Allia Potestas.

Here lies a woman from Perugia. None was more precious than she in the world. One so diligent as she has never been seen before. Great as you were you are now held in a small urn. Cruel arbiter of fate, and harsh Persephone, why do you deprive us of good, and why does evil triumph, everyone asks. I am tired of answering. They give me their tears, tokens of their good will.

She was courageous, chaste, resolute, honest, a trustworthy guardian. Clean at home, sufficiently clean when she went out, famous among the populace. She alone could confront whatever happened. She would speak briefly and so was never reproached. She was first to rise from her bed, and last to return to her bed to rest after she had put each thing in its place. Her yarn never left her hands without good reason. Out of respect she yielded place to all; her habits were healthy. She was never self-satisfied, and never took liberties.

Her skin was white, she had beautiful eyes, and her hair was gold. An ivory glow always shone from her face – no mortal (so they say) ever possessed a face like it. The curve of her breasts was small on her snow-white bosom. And her legs? Such is the figure of Atalanta upon the stage.

In her anxiety she never stayed still, but moved her smooth limbs, beautiful with her generous body; she sought out every hair. Perhaps one may find fault with her hard hands. She was content with nothing but what she did for herself. There was never a topic she thought she knew well enough. She remained virtuous because she never committed any crime.

While she lived she so guided her two young lovers that they became like the example of Pylades and Orestes – one house would hold them both and one spirit. But now that she is dead, they will separate, and each is growing old by himself. Now instants damage what such a woman built up; look at Troy, to see what a woman once did. I pray that it be right to use such grand comparisons for this lesser event.

In your place I have only your image as solace;[3] this we cherish with reverence and lavish with flowers. When I come with you, it follows in attendance. But to whom in my visiting can I trust a thing so venerable? If there ever is anyone to whom I can entrust it, I shall be fortunate in this alone now that I have lost you. But – woe is me – you have won the contest – my fate and yours are the same.

These verses for you your patron – whose tears never end – writes in tribute. You are lost, but never will be taken from his heart. These are the gifts he believes the lost will enjoy. After you no woman can seem good. A man who has lived without you has seen his own death while alive. He carries your name in gold back and forth on his arm, where he can keep it, possessing Potestas.[4] As long as these published words of ours survive, so long will you live in these little verses of mine.

The man who tries to harm this tomb, dares to harm the gods: this tomb, distinguished by its inscription, believe me, has divinity.

144. *Athenodora. Athens, Christian period. (Kaibel 176. Tr. M.R.L.)*

Good Athenodora of Attica, wife of Thaumasius, filled with God's influence. She bore children and nursed them when they were infants. Earth took this young mother and keeps her, though the children need her milk.

145. *An anecdote about Cornelia, mother of the Gracchi. Rome, 2nd cent. B.C. (Valerius Maximus, Memorable Deeds and Sayings 4.4pr., 1st cent A.D. Tr. M.B.F.)*

Daughter of a hero, wife of an aristocrat and mother of champions of the Roman people, Cornelia was admired for her virtue, fidelity and, not least, her intelligence. She was the standard by which Roman matrons were measured and has been remembered as the ideal of Roman womanhood for two millennia. This familiar anecdote illustrates the perfection to which a Roman mother might aspire.

When a Campanian matron who was staying with Cornelia, mother of the Gracchi, was showing off her jewels – the most beautiful of that period, Cornelia managed to prolong the conversation until her children got home from school. Then she said, 'These are *my* jewels.'

146. *Tiberius chooses to die for Cornelia. Rome, 2nd cent. B.C. (Plutarch, Life of Tiberius Gracchus 1.2-2, 2nd cent. A.D. Tr. J. Dryden)*

After the death of Scipio who overthrew Hannibal, [Tiberius Gracchus, the elder] was thought worthy to match with his daughter Cornelia, though there had been no friendship or familiarity between Scipio and him, but rather the contrary. There is a story told, that he once found in his bedchamber a couple of snakes, and that the soothsayers, being consulted concerning the prodigy, advised that he should neither kill them both nor let them both escape; adding, that if the male serpent was killed, Tiberius should die, and if the female, Cornelia. And that, therefore, Tiberius, who extremely loved his wife, and thought, besides, that it was much more his part, who was an old man, to die, than it was hers, who as yet was but a young woman, killed the male serpent, and let the female escape; and soon after himself died, leaving behind him twelve children borne to him by Cornelia.[5]

Cornelia, taking upon herself all the care of the household and the education of her children, proved herself so discreet a matron, so affectionate a mother, and so constant and noble-spirited a widow, that Tiberius seemed to all men to have done nothing unreasonable, in choosing to die for such a woman; who, when king Ptolemy himself proffered her his crown, and would have married her, refused it, and chose rather to live a widow. In this state she continued, and lost all her children, except one daughter, who was married to Scipio the younger, and two sons, Tiberius and Gaius, whose lives we are now writing.

These she brought up with such care, that though they were without dispute in natural endowments and dispositions the first among the Romans of their time, yet they seemed to owe their virtues even more to their education than to their birth.

147. *Cornelia's noble nature. Misenum, 2nd cent. B.C. (Plutarch, Life of Gaius Gracchus 19, 2nd cent. A.D. Tr. J. Dryden)*

It is reported, that as Cornelia, their mother, bore the loss of her two sons[6] with a noble and undaunted spirit, so, in reference to the holy places in which they were slain, she said, their dead bodies were well worthy of such sepulchres. She removed afterwards, and dwelt near the place called Misenum,[7] not at all altering her former way of living. She had many friends, and hospitably received many strangers at her house; many Greeks and learned men were continually about her; nor was there any foreign prince but received gifts from her and presented her again. Those who were conversant with her, were much interested, when she pleased to entertain them with her recollections of her father Scipio Africanus, and of his habits and way of living. But it was most admirable to hear her make mention of her sons, without any tears or sign of grief, and give the full account of all their deeds and misfortunes, as if she had been relating the history of some ancient heroes. This made some imagine, that age, or the greatness of her afflictions, had made her senseless and devoid of natural feelings. But they who so thought, were themselves more truly insensible, not to see how much a noble nature and education avail to conquer any affliction; and though fortune may often be more successful, and may defeat the efforts of virtue to avert misfortunes, it cannot, when we incur them, prevent our bearing them reasonably.

148. *Seneca to his mother, Corsica, A.D. 41/9. (Seneca, On Consolation 16. Tr. J. Basore (LCL))*

L. Annaeus Seneca, Stoic philosopher, politician, and tutor to the young Nero, spent eight years (A.D. 41-9) in Corsica, exiled because the empress Messallina had accused him of adultery with Julia Livilla, Caligula's sister. During this period he wrote the essay, *To Helvia on Consolation*, to comfort his mother, Helvia.

It is not for you to avail yourself of the excuse of being a woman, who, in a way, has been granted the right to inordinate, yet not unlimited, tears. And so our ancestors, seeking to compromise with the stubbornness of a woman's grief by a public ordinance, granted the space of ten months as the limit of mourning for a husband. They did not forbid their mourning, but limited it; for when you lose one who is most dear, to be filled with endless sorrow is foolish fondness, and to feel none is inhuman hardness. The best course is the mean between affection and reason – both to have a sense of loss and to crush it. There is no need for you to regard certain women, whose sorrow once assumed ended only with their death – some you know, who, having put on mourning for sons they had lost, never laid the garb aside. From you life, that was sterner from the start, requires more; the excuse of being a woman can be of no avail to one who has always lacked all the weaknesses of a woman.

Unchastity, the greatest evil of our time, has never classed you with the great majority of women; jewels have not moved you, nor pearls; to your eyes the glitter of riches has not seemed the greatest boon of the human race; you, who were soundly trained in an old-fashioned and strict household, have not been perverted by the imitation of worse women that leads even the virtuous into pitfalls; you have never blushed for the number of your children, as if it taunted you with your years, never have you, in the manner of other women whose only recommendation lies in their beauty, tried to conceal your pregnancy as if an unseemly burden, nor have you ever crushed the hope of children that were being nurtured in your body; you have not defiled your face with paints and cosmetics; never have you fancied the kind of dress that exposed no greater nakedness by being removed. In you has been seen that peerless ornament, that fairest beauty on which time lays no hand, the chiefest glory which is modesty. You cannot, therefore, allege your womanhood as an excuse for persistent grief, for your very virtues set you apart; you must be as far removed from woman's tears as from her vices. But even women will not allow you to pine away from your wound, but will bid you finish quickly with necessary sorrow, and then rise with lighter heart – I mean, if you are willing to turn your gaze upon the women whose conspicuous bravery has placed them in the rank of mighty heroes.

Cornelia bore twelve children, but Fortune had reduced their number to two; if you wished to count Cornelia's losses, she had lost ten, if to appraise them, she had lost the two Gracchi. Nevertheless, when her friends were weeping around her and cursing her fate, she forbade them to make any indictment against Fortune, since it was Fortune who had allowed the Gracchi to be her sons. Such a woman had right to be the mother of him who exclaimed in the public assembly: 'Do you dare to revile the mother who gave birth to me?' But to me his mother's utterance seems more spirited by far; the son set great value on the birthday of the Gracchi, but the mother on their funerals as well.

Rutilia followed her son Cotta[8] into exile, and was so wrapped up in her love for him that she preferred exile to losing him; and only her son's return brought her back to her native land. But when, after he had been restored and now had risen to honour in the state, he died, she let him go just as bravely as she had clung to him; and after her son was buried no one saw her shed any tears. When he was exiled, she showed courage, when she lost him, wisdom; for in the one case she did not desist from her devotion, and in the other did not persist in useless and foolish sorrow. In the number of such women as these I wish you to be counted. In your effort to restrain and suppress your sorrow your best course will be to follow the example of those women whose life you have always copied.

149. *Tacitus on mothers. Rome, late 1st cent. A.D. (Dialogue 28 (excerpt). Tr. Church and Brodribb)*

The historian Tacitus looks back on the time when mothers played a role in their sons' education and thus, directly or indirectly, had a share in Rome's greatness.

Every citizen's son, the child of a chaste mother, was from the beginning reared, not in the chamber of a purchased nurse, but in that mother's bosom and embrace, and it was her special glory to study her home and devote herself to her children. It was usual to select an elderly kinswoman of approved and esteemed character to have the entire charge of all the children of the household. In her presence it was the last offence to utter an unseemly word or to do a disgraceful act. With scrupulous piety and modesty she regulated not only the boy's studies and occupations, but even his recreations and games. Thus it was, as tradition says, that the mothers of the Gracchi, of Caesar, of Augustus, Cornelia, Aurelia, Atia, directed their children's education and reared the greatest of sons.

Whether writing to advise a young protégé or to a female relative about domestic concerns, Pliny intended his letters to be published, and nine of ten books were published during his lifetime.

150. *Arria. A.D. 97/107. (Pliny the Younger, Letters 3.16. Tr. B. Radice)*

I think I have remarked that the more famous words and deeds of men and women are not necessarily their greatest. I was strengthened in this opinion by a conversation I had yesterday with Fannia, granddaughter of the famous Arria who sustained and encouraged her husband by her example at the time of his death. She told me several things about her grandmother which were quite as heroic though less well known, and I think they will make the same impression on you as you read them as they did on me during their telling.

Arria's husband, Caecina Paetus, was ill; so was their son, and it was thought that neither could recover. The son died, a most beautiful boy with an unassuming manner no less remarkable, and dear to his parents for reasons beyond the fact that he was their son. Arria made all the preparations for his funeral and took her place at the ceremony without her husband knowing; in fact whenever she entered his room she pretended that their son was alive and even rather better, and when Paetus kept asking how the boy was, she would answer that he had had a good sleep and was willing to take some food. Then when the tears she had held back for so long could no longer be kept from breaking out, she left the room; not till then did she give way to her grief. Her weeping over, she dried her eyes, composed her face, and returned as if she had left the loss of her child outside the room. It was a glorious deed, I know, to draw a sword, plunge it into her breast, pull it out, and hand it to her husband with the immortal, almost divine words: 'It does not hurt, Paetus.' [9] But on that well-known occasion she had fame and immortality before her eyes. It was surely even more heroic when she had no hope of any such reward, to stifle her tears, hide her grief, and continue to act the mother after she had lost her son.

At the time of the revolt against Claudius raised by Scribonianus in Illyricum,[10] Paetus had joined his party, and after Scribonianus' death was being brought as a prisoner to Rome. He was about to board ship when Arria begged the soldiers to take her with him. 'This is a senator of consular rank,' she insisted, 'and of course you will allow him a few slaves to serve his meals, dress him and put on his shoes; all of which I can do for him myself.' Her request was refused. She then hired a small fishing smack, and the great ship sailed with her following in her tiny boat.

Again, when she came before Claudius and found the wife of Scribonianus volunteering to give evidence of the revolt, 'Am I to listen to you,' she cried, 'who could go on living after Scribonianus died in your arms?' This proves that her determination to die a glorious death was not a sudden impulse. Indeed, when her son-in-law Thrasea was trying to persuade her not to carry out her resolve, in the course of his argument he asked her whether if he ever had to die she would wish her daughter to die with him.[11] 'If she lives as long and happily with you,' she said, 'as I have with Paetus – yes.' This answer increased the anxiety felt for her by her family and she was watched even more carefully. Perceiving this, 'It is no good,' she said. 'You can make me choose a painful death, but you cannot make it impossible.' With these words she leaped out of her chair and dashed her head against the wall opposite, so that she fell senseless from the violent blow. When she came round, 'I told you,' she said, 'that I should find a hard way to die if you denied me an easy one.'

Surely you think these words greater than the well-known 'It does not hurt, Paetus' which was their culmination? And yet this is widely famous, while the earlier sayings are not known at all. Hence the inference with which I began this letter, that the words and deeds which win fame are not always the greatest.[12]

151. *The death of Helvidius' daughters. A.D. 104/5. (Pliny the Younger, Letters 4.21. Tr. B. Radice)*

This premature death of Helvidius' daughters is tragic[13] – both sisters giving birth to girls and dying in labour. I am deeply distressed, and not unduly, that these were noble young women in the flower of their youth and I must mourn to see them the victims of their motherhood. I grieve too for the plight of their infants left motherless at birth, and for their excellent husbands, and I grieve no less on my own account; for my love for their father has remained constant since his death, as my defence of him and my published speeches bear witness. Now only one of his three children survives, left as the sole prop and stay of a family which not so long ago had many members to support it. But if Fortune will keep him at least safe and sound, and make him as fine a man as his father and his grandfather, I can take comfort in my sorrow. I am all the more anxious for his safety and character now that he is the last of his line. You know my nervous apprehensions for anyone I love, so you must not be surprised at my fears being worst where my hopes are highest.

152. *Minicia Marcella. A.D. 105/6. (Pliny the Younger, Letters 5.16. Tr. B. Radice)*

I am writing to you in great distress: our friend Fundanus has lost his younger daughter.[14] I never saw a girl so gay and lovable, so deserving of a longer life or even a life to last for ever. She had not yet reached the age of fourteen, and yet she combined the wisdom of age and dignity of womanhood with the sweetness and modesty of youth and innocence. She would cling to her father's neck, and embrace us, his friends, with modest affection; she loved her nurses, her attendants and her teachers, each one for the service given her; she applied herself intelligently to her books and was moderate and restrained in her play. She bore her last illness with patient resignation and, indeed, with courage; she obeyed her doctor's orders, cheered her sister and father, and by sheer force of will carried on after her physical strength had failed her. This will-power remained with her to the end, and neither the length of her illness nor fear of death could break it. So she has left us all the more sad reasons for lamenting our loss. Hers is a truly tragic and untimely end – death itself was not so cruel as the moment of its coming. She was already engaged to marry a distinguished young man, the day for the wedding was fixed, and we had received our invitations. Such joy, and now such sorrow! No words can express my grief when I heard Fundanus giving his own orders (for one heart-rending detail leads to another) for the money he had intended for clothing, pearls and jewels to be spent on incense, ointment and spices.[15] He is indeed a cultivated man and a philosopher who has devoted himself from youth to higher thought and the arts, but at the moment he rejects everything he has so often heard and professed himself: he has cast off all his other virtues and is wholly absorbed by his love for his child. You will forgive and even admire him if you think of what he has lost – a daughter who resembled him in character no less than in face and expression, and was her father's living image in every way.

If then you write anything to him in his very natural sorrow, be careful not to offer any crude form of consolation which might suggest reproof; be gentle and sympathetic. Passage of time will make him readier to accept this; a raw wound shrinks from a healing hand but later permits and even seeks help, and so the mind rejects and repels any consolation in its first pangs of grief, then feels the need of comfort and is calmed if this is kindly offered.

153. *Womanly virtue. 1st cent. A.D. (Valerius Maximus, Memorable Deeds and Sayings 6. 7.1-3. Tr. M.B.F.)*

The following three women were chosen by the historian Valerius

Maximus as examples of womanly virtue; loyalty to a husband appears to have been the highest excellence a woman could attain (cf. Arria, above, no. 150 and Fannia, below, no. 209).

Tertia Aemilia, the wife of Scipio Africanus and the mother of Cornelia,[16] was a woman of such kindness and patience that, although she knew that her husband was carrying on with a little serving girl, she looked the other way, [as she thought it unseemly for] a woman to prosecute her great husband, Africanus, a conqueror of the world, for a dalliance. So little was she interested in revenge that, after Scipio's death, she freed the girl and gave her in marriage to one of her own freedmen.[17]

When Quintus Lucretius [Vespillo] was proscribed by the triumvirs, his wife Thuria[18] hid him in her bedroom above the rafters. A single maidservant knew the secret. At great risk to herself, she kept him safe from imminent death. So rare was her loyalty that, while the other men who had been proscribed found themselves in foreign, hostile places, barely managing to escape the worst tortures of body and soul, Lucretius was safe in that bedroom in the arms of his wife.[19]

Sulpicia, despite the very close watch her mother Julia was keeping on her so that she would not follow her husband to Sicily (he was Lentulus Cruscellio, proscribed by the triumvirs), nevertheless put on slave's clothing and, taking two maids and the same number of manservants, fled secretly and went to him. She was not afraid to risk proscription herself, and her fidelity to her proscribed spouse was firm.[20]

154. *The family of Julia Domna. Rome, 3rd cent. A.D. (Dio Cassius, History of Rome 78.2, 18 (excerpts). 79.23 (excerpts). Tr. E. Cary (LCL))*

Julia Domna, born in Syria, was the wife of the emperor Septimius Severus and mother of Caracalla (Antoninus). She was known for her love of learning and her wit. After her husband's death, she supported her younger son, Geta, in his unsuccessful claim to the throne against Caracalla.

Antoninus [Caracalla] wished to murder his brother at the Saturnalia, but was unable to do so; for his evil purpose had already become too manifest to remain concealed, and so there now ensued many sharp encounters between the two, each of whom felt that the other was plotting against him, and many defensive measures were taken on both sides. Since many soldiers and athletes, therefore, were guarding Geta, both abroad and at home, day and night alike, Antoninus induced his mother to summon them both, unattended, to her apartment, with a view to reconciling them. Thus Geta was persuaded, and went in with him; but when they were inside, some centurions, previously instructed by Antoninus, rushed in in a body and struck down Geta, who at sight of them had run to his mother, hung about her neck and clung to her bosom and breasts, lamenting and crying: 'Mother that didst bear me, mother that didst bear me, help! I am being murdered.' And so she, tricked in this way, saw her son perishing in most impious fashion in her arms, and received him at his death into the very womb, as it were, whence he had been born; for she was all covered with his blood, so that she took no note of the wound she had received on her hand. But she was not permitted to mourn or weep for her son, though he had met so miserable an end before his time (he was only twenty-two years and nine months old), but, on the contrary, she was compelled to rejoice and laugh as though at some great good fortune; so closely were all her words, gestures, and changes of colour observed. Thus she alone, the Augusta, wife of the emperor and mother of the emperors, was not permitted to shed tears even in private over so great a sorrow ...

Neither in these matters nor in any others did [Antoninus] heed his mother, who gave him much excellent advice. And yet he had appointed her to receive petitions and to have charge of his correspondence in both languages, except in very important cases, and used to include her name, in terms of high praise, together with his own and that of the legions, in his letters to the senate, stating that she was well. Need I add that she held public receptions for all the most prominent men, precisely as did the emperor? But, while she devoted herself more and more to the study of philosophy with these men, he kept declaring that he needed nothing beyond the necessaries of life and plumed himself over his pretended ability to live on the cheapest kind of fare; yet there was nothing on land or sea or in the air that we did not regularly supply to him both by private gifts and by public grants ...

Now Julia, the mother of Tarautas [Caracalla], chanced to be in Antioch, and at the first information of her son's [Caracalla's] death she was so affected that she dealt herself a violent blow and tried to starve herself to death. Thus she mourned, now that he was dead, the very man whom she had hated while he lived; yet it was not because she wished that he were alive, but because she was vexed at having to return to private life. This led her to indulge in much bitter abuse of [his successor] Macrinus. Then, as no change was made in her royal retinue or in the guard of Pretorians in attendance upon her, and the new emperor sent her a kindly message, although he had heard what she had said, she took courage, put aside her desire for death, and without writing him any reply, began intriguing with the soldiers she had about her, who [were mutinous] to begin with, [were very fond of] her, and were [angry] with Macrinus, and [consequently] held her son in [pleasant]er remembrance; for she hoped to become sole ruler and make herself the equal of Semiramis and Nitocris, inasmuch as she came in a sense from the same part [of the world] as they ...

She heard, moreover, what was said in Rome about her son, she no longer cared to live, but hastened her death by refusing food, though one might say that she was already in a dying condition by reason of the cancer of the breast that she had had for a very long time; it had, however, been quiescent until, on the occasion referred to, she had inflamed it by the blow with which she had smitten her breast on hearing of her son's death.

And so this woman, sprung from the people and raised to a high station, who had lived during her husband's reign in great unhappiness because of Plautianus,[21] who had beheld her younger son slain in her own bosom and had always from first to last borne ill will toward her elder son while he lived, and finally had received such tidings of his assassination, fell from power during her lifetime and thereupon destroyed herself.

Blame

155. *Cicero on Clodia. Rome, 56 B.C. (Pro Caelio 13-16.*[22] *Tr. R.Y. Hathorn)*

Speaking last in the defence of Marcus Caelius Rufus, a former protégé, Cicero deliberately blurred the formal charges under the law against riot and diverted the jury, restive because it had been empanelled on a holiday, with a sarcastic and witty character assassination. Cicero argued that the notorious Clodia had sponsored the prosecution for personal reasons. In obliterating her as a presence in society, Cicero in fact paid off an old grudge of his own against her brother Clodius (p. 254.)

Our whole concern in this case, jurors, is with Clodia,[23] a woman not only noble but also notorious. Of her I will say no more than is necessary to refute the charges. And you too, Gnaeus Domitius,[24] sensible man that you are, you understand that our whole business here is with her and her only. If she does not admit that she obliged Caelius with the loan of the gold, if she does not accuse him of preparing poison for her, then my behaviour is ungentlemanly in dragging in a matron's name otherwise than the respect due to ladies requires. But if on the contrary aside from that woman their case against Caelius is deprived of all strength and foundation, what else can I do as an advocate but repel those who press the assault? Which I would do all the more vehemently if I did not have cause for ill-feeling towards that woman's lover – I am sorry; I meant to say 'brother'. I am always making that slip. But now I will handle her with moderation, and proceed no further than my honour and the case itself demand. I have never thought it right to take up arms against a lady, especially against one whose arms are so open to all.

First I would like to ask her: 'Shall I deal with you severely and strictly and as they would have done in the good old days? Or would you prefer something more indulgent, bland, sophisticated?' If in that austere mode and manner, I shall have to call up someone from the dead, one of those old gentlemen bearded not with the modern style of fringe that so titillates her, but with one of those bristly bushes we see on antique statues and portrait-busts. And he will scold the woman and speak for me and keep her from getting angry with me as she might otherwise do. So let us call up some ancestor of hers, preferably old blind Appius Claudius himself.[25] He will be the least likely to be grieved, since he won't have to look at her. Doubtless if he rose among us he would say something like this:

'Woman, what business did you have with Caelius, a man scarce out of his teens, a man not your husband? Why were you so friendly with him as to lend him gold? Or how did you grow so unfriendly as to fear his poison? Did you never hear that your father, uncle, grandfather, great-grandfather, great-great-grandfather, and great-great-great-grandfather were consuls? Did you forget that only recently you were the wife of Quintus Metellus, a gentleman of the highest type, a distinguished patriot who had only to show his face to eclipse almost all other citizens in character, reputation, dignity? Born of a high-ranking family, married into a prominent family, how did it happen that you admitted Caelius to such familiarity? Was he a relative or friend of your husband? Not at all. What was it then but hot and headstrong passion? If the portraits of us male ancestors meant nothing to you, how could my granddaughter, Quinta Claudia, have failed to inspire you to emulate her domestic virtue and womanly glory? Or that vestal virgin of our name who kept her arms around her father throughout his triumph and foiled the tribune's attempt to drag him from his chariot? Why choose to imitate your brother's vices in preference to the good qualities of your father and grandfather and of men and women of our line back to myself? Did I break the agreement with King Pyrrhus that you might every day enter into disgusting agreements with your paramours? Did I bring in the Appian Aqueduct that you might put its waters to your dirty uses? Did I build the Appian Way that you might ride up and down with other women's husbands?'

But perhaps it was a mistake for me to introduce such an august personage, gentlemen. He might suddenly turn on Caelius and make him feel the weight of his censorial powers. Though I will see to this later, I am convinced I can justify Marcus Caelius' behaviour to the most captious of critics. But as for you, woman — I am not speaking to you now through the mouth of another – if you have in mind to make good what you are doing, saying, pretending, plotting, and alleging, you had better do some explaining as well, and account for this extraordinarily intimate association. The prosecutors have been lavish with their tales of affairs, amours, adulteries, Baiae,[26] beach-picnics, banquets, drinking-bouts, songfests, musical ensembles, and yachting-parties. And they indicate that they are describing all this with your full permission. Since for some rash, mad purpose you have been willing to have all these stories come out at a trial in the Forum, you must either tone down their effect by showing they are groundless, or else admit that no one need believe your charges and your testimony.

But if you would rather I dealt with you more suavely, I will take this tack: I will whisk that old fellow off the scene, unfeeling rustic that he is, and will bring on someone of your own day, your younger brother, say, the most sophisticated of all that crew. He loves you dearly. When he was a young sprout he used to sleep with big sister because, I am told, he was subject to mysterious nervousness and fanciful fears at night. Suppose we let him talk to you: 'Why are you making such a fuss, sister? Why are you behaving like an insane woman?

> Why, with shout and speech, inflate
> A little thing into a great?[27]

You saw a young man living nearby. He had a fresh complexion. He was tall. He was handsome. His eyes were attractive. You were much taken with all this. You wanted to see him more often. You met sometimes on the same suburban estates. A woman of means, you thought to bind the young man with fetters of gold, still dependent on a tightfisted father. But you can't. He kicks, he spits, he bucks. He doesn't set much value on your presents. Well, go somewhere else. You have gardens on the Tiber. You deliberately chose them for their location, since they are at the very place where all the young men go in swimming. You can pick your bargains there any day. Why do you bother with this fellow who spurns you?'

[Caelius] will have no trouble defending all his conduct. I am not saying anything against that woman now; but if there were someone – not the same as her, you understand – some woman who made herself cheap and easy to approach, who always had some man or other hanging about openly acknowledged as her current interest, in whose gardens and home and place at Baiae anybody and everybody could arrange assignations with her permission, who even boarded young men and made up deficiencies in their allowances out of her own purse, if this person, being widowed, lived loosely, being forward, lived wantonly, being rich, lived extravagantly, being prurient, lived like a harlot, am I to think a man an adulterer if he does not address her exactly like a lady?

156. *Plutarch on Cleopatra. Egypt, 1st cent. B.C. (Life of Mark Antony 25-9, 2nd cent. A.D. Tr. J. Dryden)*

'For Rome, who had never condescended to fear any nation or people, did in her time fear two human beings; one was Hannibal, and the other was a woman.'[28]

In Roman literature during her lifetime and just after her death (e.g. Horace, *Odes* 1.37), Cleopatra represented the dangerous appeal of decadence and corruption; a highly educated Greek, with the wealth of Egypt at her disposal, she was mistress of both Caesar and Mark Antony. In Plutarch's account traditional anecdotes are related with considerable sympathy and admiration.

[Caesar and Pompey were acquainted with Cleopatra when she was] a girl, young and ignorant of the world, but she was to meet Antony in the time of life[29] when women's beauty is most splendid and their intellects are in full maturity. She made great preparation for her journey, of money, gifts and ornaments of value, such as so wealthy a kingdom might afford, but she brought with her her surest hopes in her own magic arts and charms.

She received several letters, both from Antony and from his friends, to summon her, but she took no account of these orders[30] and at last, as if in mockery of them, she came sailing up the river Cydnus, in a barge with gilded stern and outspread sails of purple, while oars of silver beat time to the music of flutes and fifes and harps. She herself lay all alone under a canopy of cloth of gold, dressed as Venus in a picture, and beautiful young boys, like painted Cupids, stood on each side to fan her. Her maids were dressed like sea nymphs and graces, some steering at the rudder, some working at the ropes. The perfumes diffused themselves from the vessel to the shore, which was covered with multitudes, part following the galley up the river on either bank, part running out of the city to see the sight. The market-place was quite emptied, and Antony at last was left alone sitting upon the tribunal; while the word went through all the multitude that Venus was come to feast with Bacchus, for the common good of Asia ...

The next day Antony invited her to supper, and was very desirous to outdo her as well in magnificence as contrivance; but he found he was altogether beaten in both, and was so well convinced of it that he was himself the first to jest and mock at his poverty of wit and his rustic awkwardness. She, perceiving that his raillery was broad and gross and savoured more of the soldier than the courtier, rejoined in the same taste and fell into it at once, without any sort of reluctance or reserve. For her actual beauty, it is said, was not in itself so remarkable that none could be compared with her, or that no one could see her without being struck by it, but the contact of her presence, if you lived with her, was irresistible; the attraction of her person, joining with the charm of her conversation, and the character that attended all she said or did, was something bewitching. It was a pleasure merely to hear the sound of her voice, with which, like an instrument of many strings, she could pass from one language to another; so that there were few of the barbarian nations that she answered by an interpreter; to most of them she spoke herself, as to the Ethiopians, Troglodytes, Hebrews, Arabians, Syrians, Medes, Parthians, and many others, whose language she had learnt; which was all the more surprising because most of the kings, her predecessors, scarcely gave themselves the trouble to acquire the Egyptian tongue, and several of them quite abandoned the Macedonian.

Antony was so captivated by her that, while Fulvia his wife maintained his quarrels in Rome against Caesar by actual force of arms, and the Parthian troops were assembled in Mesopotamia and ready to enter Syria, he could yet suffer himself to be carried away by her to Alexandria, there to keep holiday, like a boy, in play and diversion, squandering and fooling away in enjoyments that most costly (as Antiphon says) of all valuables, time ...

Plato admits four sorts of flattery, but she had a thousand. Were Antony serious or disposed to mirth, she had at any moment some new delight or charm to meet his wishes; at every turn she was upon him, and let him escape her neither by day nor by night. She played at dice with him, drank with him, hunted with him; and when he exercised in arms, she was there to see. At night she would go rambling with him to disturb and torment people at their doors and windows, dressed like a servant-woman, for Antony also went in servant's disguise, and from these expeditions he often came home very scurvily answered and sometimes even beaten severely, though most people guessed who it was. However, the Alexandrians in general liked it all well enough, and joined good-humouredly and kindly in his frolic and play, saying they were much obliged to Antony for acting his tragic parts at Rome and keeping his comedy for them. It would be trifling without end to be particular in his follies, but his fishing must not be forgotten. He went out one day to angle with Cleopatra, and, being so unfortunate as to catch nothing in the presence of his mistress, he gave secret orders to the fishermen to dive under water, and put fishes that had been already taken upon his hooks; and these he drew so fast that the Egyptian[31] perceived it. But, feigning great admiration, she told everybody how dexterous Antony was, and invited them next day to come and see him again. So, when a number of them had come on board the fishing-boats, as soon as he had let down his hook, one of her servants was beforehand with his divers, and fixed upon his hook a salted fish from Pontus. Antony, feeling his line give, drew up the prey, and when, as may be imagined, great laughter ensued, 'Leave,' said Cleopatra, 'the fishing-rod, general, to us poor sovereigns of Pharos and Canopus; your game is cities, provinces, and kingdoms.'

157. *Juvenal on women in general. Rome, 2nd cent. A.D. (Satire 6 (excerpts). Tr. M.R.L.)*

Ancient biographers, characteristically confusing poet and poetry, regarded this famous satire as factual evidence that Juvenal hated women. Stories of the same type were attributed to Lucretius (1st cent. B.C.), because of his caustic statements about marriage in Book 4 of his *De Rerum Natura*.

Eppia, though the wife of a senator, went off with a gladiator to Pharos and the Nile on the notorious walls of Alexandria (though even Egypt condemns Rome's disgusting morals). Forgetting her home, her husband, and her sister, she showed no concern whatever for her homeland (she *was* shameless) and her children in tears, and (you'll be dumbfounded by this) she left the theatre and Paris the actor behind. Even though when she was a baby she was pillowed in great luxury, in the down of her father's mansion, in a cradle of the finest workmanship, she didn't worry about the dangers of sea travel (she had long since stopped worrying about her reputation, the loss of which among rich ladies' soft cushions does not matter much). Therefore with heart undaunted she braved the waves of the Adriatic and the wide-resounding Ionian Sea (to get to Egypt she had to change seas frequently).

You see, if there's a good reason for undertaking a dangerous voyage, then women are fearful; their cowardly breasts are chilled with icy dread; they cannot stand on their trembling feet. But they show courageous spirit in affairs they're determined to enter illicitly. If it's their *husband* who wants them to go, then it's a problem to get on board ship. They can't stand the bilgewater; the skies spin around them. The woman who goes off with her *lover* of course has no qualms. She eats dinner with the sailors, walks the quarter-deck, and enjoys hauling rough ropes. Meanwhile the first woman gets sick all over her husband.

And yet what was the glamour that set her on fire, what was the prime manhood that captured Eppia's heart? What was it she saw in him, that would compensate for her being called *Gladiatrix*? Note that her lover, dear Sergius, had now started shaving his neck, and was hoping to be released from duty because of a bad wound on his arm. Moreover, his face was deformed in a number of ways: he had a mark where his helmet rubbed him, and a big wart between his nostrils, and a smelly discharge always dripping from his eye. But he was a *gladiator*. That made him look as beautiful as Apollo's friend Hyacinth. This is what she preferred to her children and her homeland, her sister and her husband. It's the *sword* they're in love with: this same Sergius, once released from service, would begin to seem like her husband Veiento.

Do you care about a private citizen's house, about Eppia's doings? Turn your eyes to the gods' rivals. Hear what the Emperor Claudius had to put up with. As soon as his wife thought that he was asleep, this imperial whore[32] put on the hood she wore at night, determined to prefer a cheap pad to the royal bed, and left the house with one female slave only. No, hiding her black hair in a yellow wig she entered the brothel, warm with its old patchwork quilts and her empty cell, her very own. Then she took her stand, naked, her nipples gilded, assuming the name of Lycisca, and displayed the stomach you came from, noble Brittanicus. She obligingly received customers and asked for her money, and lay there through the night taking in the thrusts of all comers. Then when the pimp sent the girls home, at last she went away sadly, and (it was all she could do) was the last to close up her cell – she was still burning, her vagina stiff and erected; tired by men, but not yet satisfied, she left, her face dirty and bruised, grimy with lampsmoke, she brought back to her pillow the smell of the brothel.

Isn't there anyone then in such large herds of women that's worth marrying? Let her be beautiful, graceful, rich, fertile, let her place on her porticoes her ancestors' statues; let her be more virginal than the Sabine women (the ones that with their dishevelled hair brought the war with Rome to an end); let her be a phoenix on earth, something like a black swan – but who could stand a wife who has every virtue? I'd rather have (much rather) a gal from Venusia than you, Cornelia, mother of the Gracchi, if along with your great excellence you bring a snob's brow and count your family's triumphs as part of your dowry.[33]

All chance of domestic harmony is lost while your wife's mother is living. She gets her to rejoice in despoiling her husband, stripping him naked. She gets her to write back politely and with sophistication when her seducer sends letters. She tricks your spies or bribes them. Then when your daughter is feeling perfectly well she calls in the doctor Archigenes and says that the blankets are too heavy. Meanwhile, her lover, in hiding shut off from her, impatient at the delay, waits in silence and stretches his foreskin. Maybe you think that her mother will teach her virtuous ways – ones different from her own? It's much more productive for a dirty old lady to bring up a dirty little girl.

There's hardly a case in court where the litigation wasn't begun by a female. If Manilia can't be defendant, she'll be the plaintiff.[34] They'll draw up indictments without assistance, and are ready to tell Celsus the lawyer how to begin his speech and what arguments he should use.

Who doesn't know about the Tyrian wrappers and the ointment for women's athletics? Who hasn't seen the wounds in the dummy, which she drills with continual stabbings and hits with her shield and works through the whole course of exercise – a matron, the sort you'd expect to blow the trumpet at the Floralia[35] – unless in her heart she is plotting something deeper still, and seriously training for the actual games? How can a woman who wears a helmet be chaste? She's denying her sex, and likes a man's strength. But she wouldn't want to turn into a man, since we men get so little pleasure.

Yet what a show there would be, if there were an auction of your wife's stuff – her belt and gauntlets and helmet and half-armour for her left leg. Or she can try the other style of battle – lucky you, when she sells her greaves. Yet these same girls sweat even in muslin, even the thinnest little netting burns their delicacies. Look at the noise she makes when she drives home the blows her trainer showed her, at the weight of her helmet, how solidly she sits on her haunches (like the binding around a thick tree), and laugh when she puts her armour aside to pick up her chamber-pot.

You ask where these monsters come from, the source that they spring from? Poverty made Latin women chaste in the old days, hard work and a short time to sleep and hands calloused and hardened with wool-working, and Hannibal close to the city,[36] and their husbands standing guard at the Colline Gate – that kept their humble homes from being corrupted by vice. But now we are suffering from the evils of a long peace. Luxury, more ruthless than war, broods over Rome and takes revenge for the world she has conquered. No cause for guilt or deed of lust is missing, now that Roman poverty has vanished. Money, nurse of promiscuity, first brought in foreigners' ways, and effete riches weakened the sinews of succeeding generations. What does Venus care when she's drunk? She can't tell head from tail when she eats big oysters at midnight, and when her perfume foams with undiluted wine, when she drinks her conch-shell cup dry, and when in her dizziness the roof turns round and the table rises up to meet two sets of lights.

An even worse pain is the female who, as soon as she sits down to dinner, praises Vergil and excuses Dido's suicide:[37] matches and compares poets, weighing Vergil on one side of the scale and Homer in the other. Schoolmasters yield; professors are vanquished; everyone in the party is silenced. No one can speak, not a lawyer, not an auctioneer, not even another woman. Such an avalanche of words falls, that you'd say it's like pans and bells being beaten. Now no one needs trumpets or bronzes: this woman by herself can come help the Moon when she's suffering from an eclipse.[38] As a philosopher she sets definitions on moral behaviour. Since she wants to seem so learned and eloquent she ought to shorten her tunic up to her knees[39] and bring a pig to Sylvanus[40] and go to the penny bath with the philosophers. Don't let the woman who shares your marriage bed adhere to a set style of speaking or hurl in well-rounded sentences the enthymeme shorn of its premise. Don't let her know all the histories. Let there be something in books she does not understand. I hate the woman who is continually poring over and studying Palaemon's[41] treatise, who never breaks the rules or principles of grammar, and who quotes verses I never heard of, ancient stuff that men ought not to worry about. Let her correct her girl-friend's verses – she ought to allow her husband to commit a solecism.

Pauper women endure the trials of childbirth and endure the burdens of nursing, when fortune demands it. But virtually no gilded bed is laid out for childbirth – so great is her skill, so easily can she produce drugs that make her sterile or induce her to kill *human beings* in her womb. You fool, enjoy it, and give her the potion to drink, whatever it's going to be, because, if she wants to get bloated and to trouble her womb with a live baby's kicking, you might end up being the father of an Ethiopian – soon a wrong-coloured heir will complete your accounts, a person whom it's bad luck to see first thing in the morning.

1. The parents/masters of this household are P. Larcius Nicia and Saufeia Thalea, both former slaves themselves. They had two sons, L. Larcius Rufus and P. Larcius Brocchus. Horaea, a former slave in the household, married Brocchus. She took the family name Larcia, not when she married, but when she received her freedom.

2. In revenge, as if murdered by his next-of-kin, cf. Euripides, *Medea* 1389.

3. In Aeschylus' *Agamemnon* (416-19) the chorus comments on the inadequacy of a statue as substitute for Menelaus' real wife Helen. Admetus, in Euripides' *Alcestis*, promises his dying wife that he will put a likeness of her in his bed, so that he can embrace and caress it and hold it in his arms, 'so that I will seem to hold my dear wife in my arms even though I am not holding her' (348-54), a speech that illustrates how much emphasis he places on her physical presence. Compare Anyte's epitaph for Thersis, above, no. 13.

4. A play on the word *potestas* which means 'power'.

5. The story also appears in Pliny, *NH* 7.122.

6. The Gracchi, champions of popular reform, were killed as a result of political violence in 133 and 122 B.C.

7. On the Bay of Naples.

8. Gaius Aurelius Cotta was an orator. He was exiled from Rome but returned with Sulla (the dictator) and became consul in 75 B.C.

9. Martial 1.13 also records these words: 'When chaste Arria handed to Paetus the sword which she had drawn from her own breast, she said, "If you believe me, the wound which I have made does not hurt, but, the wound which you are going to make, that one, Paetus, hurts me."'

10. A.D. 42.

11. This, in fact, happened. Thrasea Paetus was a member of the 'Stoic opposition' to Nero and was condemned to death in A.D. 66. He persuaded his wife, the younger Arria, not to follow her mother's example, but to live for their daughter Fannia. See Tacitus, *Annals* 16. 34 for the story.

12. It would appear that Arria was given a sort of divine status in popular belief. Cf. for example, this verse from a woman's epitaph from Anagnia in Latium (*CIL* X. 5920/*ILS* 6261):

A paragon has died; mourn, maidens!
Oppia is no more, Oppia has been taken from Firmus.
Receive this soul and, Arria, increase it by the
Roman sacred number, and you, Laodamia, by the Greek.

The mythical Laodamia, like the historical Arria, took her own life for her husband.

13. This Helvidius was Fannia's stepson, her husband's son by his first wife. An ex-consul, he was condemned to death, possibly for his associations, in A.D. 93 by the Emperor Domitian.

14. Minicius Fundanus, consul in A.D. 107. The girl's epitaph was found in the family tomb outside Rome (*CIL* VI. 16631/*ILS* 1030): 'To the gods of the dead. The tomb of Minicia Marcella, daughter of Fundanus. She lived twelve years, eleven months, seven days.'

156   *Rome*

15. For the funeral.

16. Mother of the Gracchi, above, pp. 138-40.

17. 191 B.C. Cf. Plutarch's suggestion that a wife should see respect for herself in her husband's turning to another woman for debauchery (*Moralia* 140b).

18. Cf. below, no. 207.

19. 42 B.C.

20. 42 B.C.

21. Because of his influence over her husband. Confidant of his fellow African, the Emperor Septimius Severus, Plautianus became Prefect of the Praetorian Guard and, in 202, the father-in-law of Caracalla. In 203 he became Geta's colleague in the consulship. In 205, an unhappily married Caracalla arranged his fall from grace.

22. See K.A. Geffcken, *Comedy in the Pro Caelio* (Leiden 1973) on Cicero's use of ridicule to discredit Clodia.

23. This is the 'Lesbia' of Catullus. She was the sister of Publius Clodius Pulcher, Cicero's bitter enemy. Her husband was Quintus Caecilius Metellus Celer (consul in 60 B.C.)

24. Gnaeus Domitius Calvinus, the praetor who presided over the trial.

25. Appius Claudius Caecus ('blind'), consul in 307 and 296 B.C. An aristocrat, he championed the lower classes and built the first aqueduct in Rome and the major highway, the Via Appia.

26. A spa on the Bay of Naples known for luxury and loose living. 'The mere mention of Baiae [in the *Pro Caelio*] contributed effectively to the impression of Clodia's immorality which Cicero was striving to establish.' J.H. D'Arms, *Romans on the Bay of Naples* (Cambridge, Mass. 1970) 43.

27. From a comic playwright, perhaps Caecilius Statius (d. 168 B.C.).

28. W.W. Tarn, *Cambridge Ancient History*, vol. 10, p. 111.

29. She was 29.

30. 41 B.C. Antony summoned her to Tarsus in Asia Minor, accusing her of aiding Cassius, one of the murderers of Caesar.

31. Plutarch probably uses this term in derogation. Cleopatra was of Macedonian descent and had no Egyptian blood.

32. The infamous Empress Messalina, mother of Octavia and Brittanicus. She was later put to death for conspiracy against Claudius.

33. The 'triumphs' are those of her father Scipio Africanus, the hero of the Second Punic War. Cf. above, p. 138.

34. Cf. below, p. 206, Valerius Maximus on Gaia Afrania.

35. At the Floralia, a particularly joyous festival in honour of the goddess Flora, celebrated from April 28 to May 3. See Ovid, *Fasti* 5. 331 ff.

36. Cf. below, p. 179.

37. Queen of Carthage, lover of Aeneas. She committed suicide when he abandoned her.

38. Eclipses of the moon, thought by some to be caused by witchcraft, were met with loud noises to dispel the accompanying evil spirits.

39. A reference to the short tunic worn by men.

40. Forbidden to women.

41. Palaemon, a freedman, was a grammarian of the early 1st cent. A.D.

XII

Accomplishments

Inscriptions, which have been found by the thousands throughout the Roman Empire, are our principal source of information about people not important or influential enough to be mentioned by the historical writers. Public benefactors often recorded their good deeds on stone, or grateful recipients did it for them. Outstanding citizens were frequently immortalised in a statue accompanied by an explanatory inscription.

158. *Junia Theodora. Corinth, c. A.D. 43 (Pleket 8 (excerpt). Tr. M.R.L.)*

The people of Patara[1] have decreed: Whereas Junia Theodora, a Roman resident in Corinth, a woman held in highest honour … who copiously supplied from her own means many of our citizens with generosity, and received them in her home and in particular never ceased acting on behalf of our citizens in regard to any favour asked – the majority of citizens have gathered in assembly to offer testimony on her behalf. Our people in gratitude agreed to vote: to commend Junia and to offer testimony of her generosity to our native city and of her good will, and declares that it urges her to increase her generosity toward the city in the knowledge that our people also would not cease in their good will and gratitude to her and would do everything for the excellence and the glory that she deserved. For this reason (with good fortune), it was decreed to commend her for all that she had done.

159. *The priestess Lalla. Lycia, 1st cent. A.D. (Pleket 13. Tr. M.R.L.)*

The people of Arneae and vicinity, to Lalla daughter of Timarchus son of Diotimus, their fellow citizen, wife of Diotimus son of Vassus; priestess of the Emperor's cult and gymnasiarch out of her own resources, honoured five times, chaste, cultivated, devoted to her husband and a model of all virtue, surpassing in every respect. She has glorified her ancestors' virtues with the example of her own character. [Erected] in recognition of her virtue and good will.

160. *Lalla of Arneae. Lycia, c. A.D. 100 (Pleket 14. Tr. M.R.L.)*

To Lalla of Arneae, daughter of Timarchus son of Diotimus, Masas, because she had set him free, in accordance with her will.

161. *The chaste Asë. Lycia, A.D. 100 (Pleket 15. Tr. M.R.L.)*

Timarchus of Arneae son of Diotimus, to Asë (who was also called Dimanthis), his daughter and daughter also of Pinnarma, daughter of Diodotus, in loving remembrance. She has also been honoured by the people: the people of Arneae and the entire vicinity honoured with a gold wreath and a bronze statue Asë (who was also called Dimanthis, daughter of Timarchus of Arneae son of Diotimus), a woman who was chaste, and cultivated and who glorifies both her city and her family with praise won for her conduct, in recognition of her virtue and the incomparable and enviable manner in which she exemplifies every admirable quality of womanhood.

162. *Flavia Publica Nicomachis. Phocaea in Asia Minor, 2nd cent. A.D.*
    (Pleket 9. Tr. M.R.L.)

The council and the people, to Flavia Publicia Nicomachis, daughter of Dinomachus and Procle ... their benefactor, and benefactor through her ancestors, founder of our city, president for life, in recognition of her complete virtue.

163. *Modia Quintia. Africa Proconsularis, 2nd/3rd cent. A.D. (CIL VIII.*
    23888. Tr. M.B.F.)

The town council decreed a statue of Modia Quintia, daughter of Quintus Modius Felix, perpetual priestess, who, on account of the honour of the priesthood, adorned the portico with marble paving, coffered ceilings and columns, exceeding in cost her original estimate with an additional contribution and quite apart from the statutory entry fee [for the priesthood] and also [built] an aqueduct. By decree of the town council, [erected] with public funds.

164. *Aurelia Leite. Paros, c. A.D. 300 (Pleket 31. Tr. M.R.L.)*

A monument set up by the husband of a benefactress, recording the honours given her by her city.

To the most renowned and in all respects excellent Aurelia Leite, daughter of Theodotus, wife of the foremost man in the city, Marcus Aurelius Faustus, hereditary high priest for life of the cult of Diocletian and his co-rulers, priest of Demeter and gymnasiarch. She was gymnasiarch[2] of the gymnasium which she repaired and renewed when it had been dilapidated for many years. The glorious city of the Parians, her native city, in return for her many great benefactions, receiving honour rather than giving it, in accordance with many decrees, has set up a marble statue of her. She loved wisdom, her husband, her children, her native city: (*in verse*) this woman, with her wisdom, best of mothers, his wife Leite, renowned Faustus glorifies.

165. *Scholasticia. Ephesus, Christian period. (JÖAI 43 (1956) 22-3. Tr. M.R.L.)*

Epigram for the statue of a woman who restored two public baths.

You see here, stranger, the statue of a woman who was pious and very wise, Scholasticia. She provided the great sum of gold for constructing the part of the [buildings] here that had fallen down.

166. *A learned woman. 1st cent. A.D. (The Suda (an ancient encyclopaedia) FHG 3. 520ff. Tr. M.R.L.)*

Pamphile was an Epidaurian, a learned woman, the daughter of Soterides, who is also said to have been an author of books,[3] according to Dionysius in the thirteenth book of his *History of Learning*; or, as others have written, it was Socratides her husband. She wrote historical memoirs in thirty-three books, an epitome of Ctesias' history in three books, many epitomes of histories and other books, about controversies, sex,[4] and many other things.

167. *An author. Rome, A.D. 26. (Tacitus, Annals 4.53. Tr. Church and Brodribb)*

Agrippina the Younger, known to history as the murdered mother of the Emperor Nero, wrote the story of her life and her family in sufficient detail for it to have been of use to the historian Tacitus, who cites the work.

Agrippina in stubborn rage, with the grasp of disease yet on her, when the emperor came to see her, wept long and silently, and then began to mingle reproach and supplication. She begged him to relieve her loneliness and provide her with a husband; her youth still fitted her for marriage, which was a virtuous woman's only solace, and there were citizens in Rome who would not disdain to receive the wife of Germanicus and his children. But the emperor, who perceived the political aims of her request, but did not wish to show displeasure or apprehension, left her, notwithstanding her urgency, without an answer. This incident, not mentioned by any historian, I have found in the memoirs of the younger Agrippina, the mother of the Emperor Nero, who handed down to posterity the story of her life and of the misfortunes of her family.

168. *A philosopher. Apollonia, Mysia, 2nd/3rd cent. A.D. (Pleket 30. Tr. M.R.L.)*

For Magnilla the philosopher, daughter of Magnus the philosopher, wife of Menius the philosopher.

169. *Women athletes. Delphi, c. A.D. 45 (Pleket 9. Tr. M.R.L.)*

Hermesianax, son of Dionysius, of Caesaria in Tralles (also from Corinth), for his daughters, who themselves have the same citizenships.

(1) Tryphosa, at the Pythian Games with Antigonus and Cleomachis as judges, and at the Isthmian Games, with Juventius Proclus as president, each time placed first in the girls' single-course race.

(2) Hedea, at the Isthmian Games with Cornelius Pulcher as judge, won the race in armour, and the chariot race; at the Nemean Games she won the single-course race with Antigonus as president and also in Sicyon with Menoites as president. She also won the children's lyre contest at the Augustan Games in Athens with Nuvius son of Philinus as president. She was first in her age group ... citizen ... a girl.

(3) Dionysia won at ... with Antigonus as president, the single-course race at the Asclepian Games at the sanctuary of Epidaurus with Nicoteles as president.

To Pythian Apollo.

1. In Lycia.
2. Technically, a magistrate who supervised the town gymnasia; but by this period the office had become honorific, providing an opportunity for financial contribution to the municipality.
3. Demo, a woman grammarian, is said to have written an allegorical commentary on Homer (Cramer, *Anec. Graeca* iii, p. 189); Agallis, daughter of Agallias of Corcyra, a pupil of Aristophanes of Byzantium (3rd cent. B.C.) also wrote on Homer (*Suda*, s.v.).
4. Pornographic works are also attributed to the courtesans Astyanassa and Elephantine. A fragment survives of a manual by Philaenis of Samos (4th cent. B.C., above, p. 105), with advice on how to flatter women (Oxyrhynchus papyrus 2891; see K. Tsantsanoglou, *ZPE* 12 (1973) 183-95). But it was claimed in antiquity that her work was written by a man (Aeschrion, *AP* IX. 518); see M. West, *ZPE* 25 (1977) 118.

XIII

Occupations

170. *Antiochis. Tlos, Lycia, 1st cent. A.D. (Pleket 12. Tr. M.R.L.)*

Antiochis, daughter of Diodotus of Tlos, awarded special recognition by
the council and the people of Tlos for her experience in the healing art,
has set up this statue of herself.

171. *Domnina. Neoclaudopolis, Asia, 2nd/3rd cent. A.D. (Pleket 26. Tr.
M.R.L.)*

You rush off to be with the gods, Domnina, and forget your husband.
You have raised your body to the heavenly stars. Men will say that you
have not died but that the gods stole you away because you saved your
native fatherland from disease. Goodbye, and rejoice in the Elysian
fields. But you have left pain and eternal lamentations behind for your
loved ones.

172. *Primilla. Rome, 1st/2nd cent. A.D. (CIL VI. 7581/ILS 7804. Tr.
M.B.F.)*

To my holy goddess. To Primilla, a physician, daughter of Lucius Vibius
Melito. She lived forty-four years, of which thirty were spent with Lucius
Cocceius Apthorus without a quarrel. Apthorus built this monument for
his best, chaste wife and for himself.

173. *Terentia Prima. Rome, 1st/2nd cent. A.D. (CIL VI. 9619. Tr.
M.B.F.)*

To Terentia Nice, freedwoman of Terentia Prima the physician.
Mussius Antiochus and Mussia Dionysia, her children, put this up for
their well-deserving mother.

174. *Four doctors. Rome, 1st/2nd cent. A.D. (CIL VI. 9614, 9615, 9617, 6851. Tr. M.B.F.)*

9614. Julia Pye, a doctor.

9615. Minucia Asste, a doctor, freedwoman of Gaia.[1]

9617. Venuleia Sosis, a doctor, freedwoman of Gaia.

6851. Melitine, a doctor, [slave] of Appuleius.

175. *Panthia. Pergamum, 2nd cent. A.D. (Pleket 20, Tr. M.R.L.)*

Farewell, lady Panthia, from your husband. After your departure, I keep up my lasting grief for your cruel death. Hera, goddess of marriage, never saw such a wife: your beauty, your wisdom, your chastity. You bore me children completely like myself; you cared for your bridegroom and your children; you guided straight the rudder of life in our home and raised high our common fame in healing – though you were a woman you were not behind me in skill. In recognition of this your bridegroom Glycon built this tomb for you. I also buried here the body of [my father] immortal Philadelphus, and I myself will lie here when I die, since with you alone I shared my bed when I was alive, so may I cover myself in ground that we share.[2]

Midwives

176. *Qualities and training. Rome, 2nd cent. A.D. (Soranus, Gynaecology 1 (abridged). Tr. O. Temkin)*

A unique account of the elaborate professional skill involved in an exclusively female profession.

A suitable person ... must be literate in order to be able to comprehend the art through theory too: she must have her wits about her so that she may easily follow what is said and what is happening: she must have a good memory to retain the imparted instructions (for knowledge arises from memory of what has been grasped). She must love work in order to persevere through all vicissitudes (for a woman who wishes to acquire such vast knowledge needs manly patience). She must be respectable since people will have to trust their household and the secrets of their lives to her and because to women of bad character the semblance of medical instruction is a cover for evil scheming. She must not be handicapped as regards her senses since there are things which she must see, answers which she must hear when questioning, and objects which she must grasp by her sense of touch. She needs sound limbs so as not to be handicapped in the performances of her work and she must be robust, for she takes a double task upon herself during the hardship of her professional visits. Long and slim fingers and short nails are necessary to touch a deep lying inflammation without causing too much pain. This skill, however, can also be acquired through zealous endeavour and practice in her work ...

We call a person the best midwife if she is trained in all branches of therapy (for some cases must be treated by diet, others by surgery, while still others must be cured by drugs); if she is moreover able to prescribe hygienic regulations for her patients, to observe the general and the individual features of the case, and from this to find out what is expedient, not from the causes or from the repeated observations of what usually occurs or something of the kind. Now to go into detail: she will not change her methods when the symptoms change, but will give her advice in accordance with the course of the disease: she will be unperturbed, unafraid in danger, able to state clearly the reasons for her measures, she will bring reassurance to her patients, and be sympathetic. And it is not absolutely essential for her to have borne children, as some people contend, in order that she may sympathise with the mother, because of her experience with pain; for [to have sympathy] is not more characteristic of a person who has given birth to a child. She must be robust on account of her duties but not necessarily young as some people maintain, for sometimes young persons are weak whereas on the contrary older persons may be robust. She will be well disciplined and always sober, since it is uncertain when she may be summoned to those in danger. She will have a quiet disposition, for she will have to share many secrets of life. She must not be greedy for money, lest she give an abortive wickedly for payment; she will be free from superstition so as not to overlook salutary measures on account of a dream or omen or some customary rite or vulgar superstition. She must also keep her hands soft, abstaining from such wool-working as may make them hard, and she must acquire softness by means of ointments if it is not present naturally. Such persons will be the best midwives.

177. *Epitaphs of midwives. Rome, 1st/2nd cent. A.D. (CIL VI. 6325, 6647, 8192, 9720-9723. Tr. M.B.F.)*

The nomenclature and status-indications of midwives in the inscriptions suggest that they began their careers in slavery, but continued to practise, and to own slaves themselves, after receiving their freedom. Some of the stones were dedicated by the midwives' slaves.

6325. Secunda, the midwife, [slave] of Statilia the Elder.

6647. To Hygia [goddess of health]. [The tomb] of Flavia Sabina, midwife. She lived thirty years. Marius Orthrus and Apollonius [put this up] to [Apollonius'] dearest wife.

8192. Quintus Sallustius Dioges, freedman of Dioga. Sallustia Athenais, midwife, freedwoman of Artemidorus.

9720. To Claudia Trophima, midwife. Titus Cassius Trophimus, her son, to his most gentle mother, and Tiberius Cassius Trophimianus to his grandmother, and to their descendants, [put this up]. She lived seventy-five years and five months.

9721. Gaius Grattius Plocamus, freedman of Hilara, the midwife from the Esquiline Hill.

9722. To the gods of the dead. To Julia Veneria, the midwife, well-deserving. Julius He ... put this up.

9723. Poblicia Aphe, midwife, freedwoman of Gaia.³ May your bones rest peacefully. She lived twenty-one years.

Wet-nurses

178. *Advice on hiring a wet-nurse. Rome, 1st cent. A.D. (Soranus, Gynaecology 1. 19-20. Tr. O. Temkin)*

A physician's advice; as in the pseudo-Pythagorean treatise on this subject, the nurse is thought to pass her character on with her milk.

To be sure, other things being equal, it is better to feed the child with maternal milk, for this is more suited to it, and the mothers become more sympathetic towards the offspring, and it is more natural to be fed from the mother after parturition just as before parturition. But if anything prevents it one must choose the best wet-nurse, lest the mother grows prematurely old, having spent herself through the daily suckling.⁴

One should choose a wet-nurse not younger than twenty nor older than forty years, who has already given birth twice or thrice, who is healthy, of good constitution, of large frame, and of a good colour. Her breasts should be of medium size, lax, soft and unwrinkled, the nipples neither big nor too small and neither too compact nor too porous and discharging milk overabundantly. She should be self-controlled, sympathetic and not ill-tempered, a Greek, and tidy. And for each of these points the reasons are as follows:

She should be in her prime because younger women are ignorant in the rearing of children and their minds are still somewhat careless and childish; while older ones yield a more watery milk because of the atony of the body. In women in their prime, however, every natural function is at its highest. She should already have given birth twice or thrice, because women with their first child are as yet unpractised in the rearing of children and have breasts whose structure is still infantile, small and too compact; while those who have delivered often have nursed children often and, being wrinkled, produce thick milk which is not at its best. [She should be healthy because healthful] and nourishing milk comes from a healthy body, unwholesome and worthless milk from a sickly one; just as water which flows through worthless soil is itself rendered worthless, spoiled by the qualities of its basin. And she should be of good constitution, that is, fleshy and strong, not only for the same reason, but also lest she easily become too weak for hard work and nightly duties with the result that the milk also deteriorates. Of large frame: for everything else being equal, milk from large bodies is more nourishing. Of a good colour: for in such women bigger vessels carry the material up to the breasts so that there is more milk. And her breasts should be of medium size: for small ones have little milk, whereas excessively large ones have more than is necessary so that if after nursing the surplus is retained it will be drawn out by the newborn when no longer fresh, and in some way already spoiled. If, on the other hand, it is all sucked out by other children or even other animals, the wet-nurse will be completely exhausted ...

The wet-nurse should be self-controlled so as to abstain from coitus, drinking, lewdness, and any other such pleasure and incontinence. For coitus cools the affection towards the nursling by the diversion of sexual pleasure and moreover spoils and diminishes the milk or suppresses it entirely by stimulating menstrual catharsis through the uterus or by bringing about conception. In regard to drinking, first the wet-nurse is harmed in soul as well as in body and for this reason the milk also is spoiled. Secondly, seized by a sleep from which she is hard to awaken, she leaves the newborn untended or even falls down upon it in a dangerous way. Thirdly, too much wine passes its quality to the milk and therefore the nursling becomes sluggish and comatose and sometimes even afflicted with tremor, apoplexy, and convulsions, just as suckling pigs become comatose and stupefied when the sow has eaten drugs. [She should be] sympathetic and affectionate, that she may fulfill her duties without hesitation and without murmuring. For some wet-nurses are so lacking in sympathy towards the nursling that they not only pay no heed when it cries for a long time, but do not even arrange its position when it lies still; rather, they leave it in one position so that often because of the pressure the sinewy parts suffer and consequently become numb and bad. Not ill-tempered: since by nature the nursling becomes similar to the nurse and accordingly grows sullen if the nurse is ill-tempered, but of mild disposition if she is even-tempered. Besides, angry women are like maniacs and sometimes when the newborn cries from fear and they are unable to restrain it, they let it drop from their hands or overturn it dangerously. For the same reason the wet-nurse should not be superstitious and prone to ecstatic states so that she may not expose the infant to danger when led astray by fallacious reasoning, sometimes even trembling like mad. And the wet nurse should be tidy-minded lest the odour of the swaddling clothes cause the child's stomach to become weak and it lie awake on account of itching or suffer some ulceration subsequently. And she should be a Greek so that the infant nursed by her may become accustomed to the best speech.

At the most she should have had milk for two or three months. For very early milk, as we have said, is thick of particles and is hard to digest, while late milk is not nutritious, and is thin. But some people say that a woman who is going to feed a male must have given birth to a male, if a female, on the other hand, to a female. One should pay no heed to these people, for they do not consider that mothers of twins, the one being male and the other female, feed both with one and the same milk. And in general, each kind of animal makes use of the same nourishment, male as well as female; and this is [no] reason at all for the male to become more feminine or for the female to become more masculine. One should, on the other hand, provide several wet-nurses for children who are to be nursed safely and successfully. For it is precarious for the nursling to become accustomed to one nurse who might become ill or die, and then, because of the chage of milk, the child sometimes suffers from the strange milk and is distressed, while sometimes it rejects it altogether and succumbs to hunger.

179. *Engagement of a wet-nurse. Egypt, 13 B.C. (Berlin papyrus 1107. Tr. A.S. Hunt and C.C. Edgar (LCL))*

To Protarchus from Isidora daughter of ..., having with her as guardian her brother Eutychides son of ..., and from Didyma daughter of Apollonius, Persian, having with her as guardian her brother Ischyrion son of Apollonius, Persian of the Epigone. Didyma agrees to nurse and suckle, outside at her own home in the city, with her own milk pure and untainted, for a period of sixteen months from Pharmouthi of the current 17th year of Caesar, the foundling infant slave child ... called ... which Isidora has given out to her, receiving from her, Isidora, as wages for milk and nursing ten silver drachmas and two cotyls of oil every month. So long as she is duly paid she shall take proper care both of herself and of the child, not injuring her milk nor sleeping with a man nor becoming pregnant nor suckling another child, and whatever things of the child she receives or is entrusted with she shall keep safe and shall give back when demanded or else forfeit the value of each except in the case of manifest loss, on proof of which she shall be exempted. Didyma has forthwith received from Isidora by hand from the house oil for the first three months, Pharmouthi, Pachon, and Pauni. She shall not cease nursing before the end of the time, and if she breaks the agreement in any way she shall forfeit the wages which she has already received and those which she may have received besides, increased by one half, with damages and expenses, and shall moreover pay 500 drachmas and the prescribed fine, Isidora having the right of execution upon the person of Didyma and all her property as if by legal decision, all assurances which she may produce and all resort to protection being invalid. If she fulfils every condition, Isidora shall deliver to her the monthly wages as stated above for the remaining thirteen months and shall not remove the child before the end of the time, or she herself shall pay the like penalty. Didyma shall visit Isidora every month regularly on four separate days bringing the child to be inspected by her. We request [ratification]. (*Signed*) I, Isidora, agree on the above terms. I, Eutychides, have professed myself guardian of my sister and have written for her as she is illiterate. I, Didyma, agree on the above terms. I, Ischyrion, have professed myself guardian of my sister and have written for her, as she is illiterate. (*Docketed*) Isidora's [agreement]. The 17th year of Caesar ...

180. *Receipt for wages for nursing. Oxyrhynchus, A.D. 187. (Oxyrhynchus papyrus 91. Tr. A.S. Hunt and C.C. Edgar (LCL))*

Chosion son of Sarapion of Harpocration, his mother being Sarapias, of Oxyrhynchus, to Tanenteris daughter of Thonis son of Thonis, her mother being Zoilous, of the said city, with her guardian Demetrius son of Horion and Arisone, of the said city, greeting. I acknowledge that I have received from you through Heliodorus and his fellow supervisors of the bank at the Serapeum by Oxyrhynchus, for which Epimachus issued the promise of payment, 400 silver drachmas of Imperial coin for nurse's wages, oil, clothing, and all other expenses of the two years for which my slave Sarapias nursed your daughter Helena, styled as daughter of her male parent, whom you have received back after having been weaned and treated with every attention, and that I neither make nor will make any claim upon you nor will take any proceedings about this or about any other matter whatsoever up to the present day. This receipt is valid. The 28th year of the Emperor Caesar Marcus Aurelius Commodus Antoninus Pius Felix Augustus Armeniacus Medicus Parthicus Sarmaticus Germanicus Maximus Britannicus, Phaophi 15. (*Signed*) I,

Chosion son of Sarapion, have received the 400 drachmas forming the nurse's wages, and I make no claim as stated above. I, Tanenteris daughter of Thonis, with my guardian Demetrius son of Horion, assent, and I have received back my daughter as stated above. I, Plution son of Hermes, have written for them, as they are illiterate.

Other occupations

181. *Women painters. 1st cent. A.D. (Pliny the Elder, Natural History 35. 40. Tr. M.B.F.)*

Women, too, have been painters. Timarete, the daughter of Micon, painted a Diana on a panel of the very archaic painting in Ephesus. Irene, daughter and student of Cratinus, painted a girl at Eleusis, a Calypso, the old juggler Theodorus, and the dancer Alcisthenes. Aristarete, daughter and pupil of Nearchus, painted an Asclepius. Iaia of Cyzicus, who never married, worked in Rome during the youth of Marcus Varro.[5] She used both the painter's brush and, on ivory, the graving tool. She painted women most frequently, including a panel picture of an old woman in Naples, and even a self-portrait for which she used a mirror. No one's hand was quicker to paint a picture than hers; so great was her talent that her prices far exceeded those of the most celebrated painters of her day, Sopolis and Dionysius, whose works fill the galleries. A certain Olympias, too, was a painter. About her we know only that Autobulus was her student.

182. *Women in the service of the imperial household[6] (epitaphs). Rome, 1st cent. A.D. (CIL VI. 8947, 8949, 5201/ILS 1837, 4352, 9037/ILS 1788, 8958/ILS 1784, 5539/ILS 1786, 8959/ILS 1786a, 8957. Tr. M.B.F.)*

8947. [The tomb] of Antonia Thallusa, freedwoman of the emperor, a midwife.

8949. To Julia ...sia, freedwoman of the deified empress,[7] a midwife.

5201. Gaius Papius Asclepiades, Papia, freedwoman of Eros, Julia Jucunda, nurse of Drusus and Drusilla.[8]

4352. Prima, freedwoman of the emperor [Tiberius] and empress [Livia], nurse of Julia [Livilla], daughter of Germanicus.

9037. Extricata, seamstress of Octavia, daughter of [Claudius] Augustus, lived twenty years.

8958. To Juno. [The tomb] of Dorcas, hairdresser of Julia Augusta,[9] born a slave on Capri [in the imperial house]. Lycastus, polling-clerk, her fellow freedman, [put this up] for his dearest wife and for himself.

5539. To Paezusa, hairdresser of Octavia, daughter of Caesar Augustus [Claudius], who lived eighteen years. Philetus, silver-slave of Octavia, daughter of Caesar Augustus [Claudius], put this up for his dearest wife and for himself.

8959. To the gods of the dead. To Telesphoris, who lived twenty-five years, three months, and eleven days, hairdresser of Domitia [wife] of the emperor Domitian. Theopompus [put this up] for his wife.

8957. To the gods of the dead. Claudia Parata, freedwoman of the emperor, hairdresser. She lived twenty-seven years. Tiberius Julius Romanus, Tiberius Claudius Priscus, and Nedimus, slave of the emperor,[10] her husbands,[11] put up [this altar] at their own expense.

183. *Occupations of slaves and freedwomen at Rome*[12] *(epitaphs). Rome, 1st cent. B.C./2nd cent. A.D. (CIL VI. 9754, 6331, 9758, 33892/ILS 7760, 9523/ILS 7397, 9496, 9497, 9498, 6350, 9884/ILS 7567, 6357/ILS 7435b, 9980/ILS 7428, 6362, 9727/ILS 7420, 9730/ILS 7419, 9732/ILS 7420a, 9801/ILS 7500, 9683/ILS 7488, 6326, 6336, 6395. Tr. M.B.F.)*

Unless freed status is particularly noted, it should be assumed that the women are slaves. It was generally more common to name the occupation of the deceased in the case of slaves than of freedmen and women.

9754. Gaius Sulpicius Venustus, freedman of Gaius, Sulpicia Ammia, freedwoman of Gaius. Sulpicia Galbilla daughter of Gaius, [put this up] for her pedagogues.

6331. Statilia Tyrannis, freedwoman of Titus, pedagogue of Statilia.

9758. Urbana, pedagogue. She lived twenty-five years.

33892. Sacred to the gods of the dead. To Hapate, a Greek stenographer, who lived twenty-five years. Pittosus put this up for his sweetest wife.

9523. Grapte, secretary of Egnatia Maximilla.[13] Gaius Egnatius Arogus [dedicated this] to his dearest wife.

9496. Crecusa, the wool-weigher.

9497. To the gods of the dead. [The tomb] of Irene the wool-weigher. She lived twenty-eight years. Olympus put this up for his well-deserving wife.

9498.[14] To the gods of the dead. [The tomb] of Julia Soter, a wool-weigher. She lived eighty years. Marcus Julius Primus, Julia Musa, Julia Thisbe, Julia Ampliata, and Julia Romana put this up.

6350. Here lies Musa the seamstress.

9884. Titus Thoranius Savius, freedman of Titus, [erected this monument] for himself and for Matia Prima, freedwoman of Gaia,[15] his wife, a seamstress from Six Altars.[16] She lived forty-six years.

6357. Phyllis, Statilia's seamstress, [dedicated this stone] to Sophrus, her deserving husband.

9980. To Italia, dressmaker of Cocceia Phyllis. She lived twenty years. Acastus, her fellow slave, put this up because she was poor.

6362. The bones of Italia, the little weaver.

9727.[17] To the gods of the dead. Polydeuces dedicated this to the well-deserving Cypare, a hairdresser.

9730. Gnome, handmaiden and hairdresser of Pieris, was buried on January 28 of the year of Caesar [Augustus'] thirteenth consulship,[18] when Marcus Plautius Silvanus was his colleague.[19]

9732. Psamate, Furia's hairdresser, lived nineteen years. Mithridates, baker of Thorius Flaccus, put up [this stone].[20]

9801.[21] Aurelia Nais, freedwoman of Gaius, fishmonger in the warehouses of Galba. Gaius Aurelius Phileros, freedman of Gaius, and Lucius Valerius Secundus, freedman of Lucius, [dedicated this altar].

9683. To the gods of the dead. To Abudia Megiste, freedwoman of Marcus, most kindly, Marcus Abudius Luminaris, her patron and husband, built [this tomb] for the well-deserving dealer in grains and vegetables from the middle staircase,[22] and for himself and for his freedmen and freedwomen and descendants and for Marcus Abudius Saturninus his son, of the senior body of the Esquiline tribe. He lived eight years.

6326. Optata Pasa, portress. Her friends put this up.

6336. Posis, Statilia's attendant.

6395. Hilara, slave of Hermia.[23] Fourteen years old.

184. *Occupations in Roman Athens. Athens, 2nd/3rd cent. A.D. (IG II² 11244/ Kaibel 121, IG II² 11205, IG II² 11496/Kaibel 102. Tr. M.R.L.)*

11244. Irene, salt vendor.

11205. Dmois, worn out by her work; beloved by the household that raised her. When she died she received this tomb.

11496. Eutychousa and Nais, unfortunate; sisters, both musical, both eloquent, both trained to play the harp and the lyre, here the earth covers them gently, O stranger.

185. *From leaden curse tablets (cf. no. 350). (IG III. iii. 68, 69 (excerpts). Tr. M.R.L.)*

Parthenia the groceress (her hands, feet) ... Arescusa the procuress (her hands, feet, tongue) ... Anyte the groceress (hands, feet, shop and everything in the shop) ... Lacaina Melanus' concubine (her hands and feet) ... Dionysius the helmet maker and his wife Artemis the gilder (their household and workshop and work and livelihood) ...

186. *An actress. Theatre at Aquileia, 3rd cent. A.D. (Kaibel 609. Tr. M.R.L.)*

In the past she won resounding fame in many towns and many cities for her various accomplishments in plays,[24] mimes, and choruses, and (often) dances. But she did not die on the stage, this tenth Muse.

To Bassilla the actress Heracleides, the skilled speaker and biographer, set up this stone. Even though she is dead, she will have the same honour she had in life, when she made her body 'die' on the floor of the stage. This is what her fellow actors are saying to her: 'Bassilla farewell, no one lives forever.'

---

1. The designation Gaia (abbreviated Ɔ) refers to any woman, regardless of her actual name. This might be translated 'freedwoman of a woman'.
2. Kaibel 590 expresses many of the same sentiments of affection, but without so much self-praise.
3. See above, note 1.

4. Cf. the similar advice in Plutarch, *Moralia* 3c-d.

5. 116-27 B.C. A scholar and politician whose extant writings were on agriculture and the Latin language. On women artists, see B. Baldwin, *Classical News and Views* 25 (1981) 18-21.

6. On this subject, see S. Treggiari, 'Women in domestic service in the early Roman empire,' paper delivered at the Berkshire Conference on the History of Women, 26 October 1974, Cambridge, Mass; *Proc. Brit. School Rome* 43 (1975) 48-77; *AJAH* 1 (1976) 76-104.

7. Livia. She was deified by Claudius in A.D. 41.

8. Children of Germanicus and Agrippina. Drusus was born in A.D. 7, Drusilla about ten years later.

9. Again Livia. She received the name Julia Augusta by order of Augustus' will in A.D. 14, so this inscription must date from between 14 and 41.

10. Probably Claudius.

11. See Treggiari, op. cit., p. 6, who suggests that the three men are Claudia's divorced husbands, evidently friendly enough, listed in order of manumission.

12. On this subject, see S. Treggiari, 'Libertine ladies,' *Classical World* 64 (1971) 196-8; 'Domestic staff at Rome in the Julio-Claudian period, 27 B.C. to A.D. 68,' *Histoire sociale; revue canadienne* 6 (1973) 241-55; *Roman Freedmen During the Late Republic* (Oxford 1969).

13. Grapte's mistress is herself noteworthy. According to Tacitus (*Ann.* 15.71), she accompanied her husband, Glitius Gallus, into the exile imposed on him by Nero. She was possessed of a large personal fortune, which was subsequently taken away from her, both of which circumstances, Tacitus says, 'increased her glory'.

14. Everyone mentioned in this inscription is freed.

15. See above, n. 1.

16. An unspecified area of the city.

17. This marble plaque is decorated with a roughly carved comb and hairpin.

18. A consular date on the tombstone of a slave is extremely rare.

19. 2 B.C.

20. The stone is Augustan. Thorius Flaccus was proconsul of the province of Bithynia under Augustus.

21. An altar carved with a laurel wreath.

22. Another obscure topographical reference.

23. Hilara is called *vicaria*, a general term for a slave of a slave.

24. The talents of actors and actresses may have been admired, but their low social status was enforced by law; see p. 133.

XIV

Law

The Kings and the Republic

187. *The Laws of the Kings. Rome, 8th/7th cent. B.C. (FIRA, p. 3. Tr. ARS)*

Although the history of Rome's regal period is based in large part on legend, and was so in antiquity, tradition was strong, and many of Rome's laws and customs, committed to writing much later, have their roots in the distant past.

Laws attributed to Romulus, the founder; traditional dates, 753-716 B.C.

4. Romulus compelled the citizens ... to rear every male child and the first-born of the females, and he forbade them to put to death any child under three years of age, unless it was a cripple or a monster from birth. He did not prevent the parents from exposing such children, provided that they had displayed them first to their five nearest neighbours and had secured their approval. For those who disobeyed the law he prescribed the confiscation of half of their property as well as other penalties.

6. By the enactment of a single ... law ... Romulus brought the women to great prudence and orderly conduct ... The law was as follows: A woman united with her husband by a sacred marriage[1] shall share in all his possessions and in his sacred rites.

7. The cognates sitting in judgment with the husband ... were given power to pass sentence in cases of adultery and ... if any wife was found drinking wine Romulus allowed the death penalty for both crimes.

9. He also made certain laws, one of which is severe, namely, that which does not permit a wife to divorce her husband, but gives him power to divorce her for the use of drugs or magic on account of children[2] or for counterfeiting the keys or for adultery. The law ordered that if he should divorce her for any other cause part of his estate should go to the wife and that part should be dedicated to Ceres. Anyone who sold his wife was sacrificed to the gods of the underworld.

10. It is strange, ... when he established no penalty against patricides, that he called all homicide patricide.

11. If a daughter-in-law strikes her father-in-law she shall be dedicated as a sacrifice to his ancestral deities.

Laws attributed to Numa Pompilius; traditional dates, 716-673 B.C.

9. On the vestal virgins he conferred high honours, among which was the right of making a will while their fathers lived and of doing all other juristic acts without a guardian.

12. A royal law forbids the burial of a pregnant woman before the child is extracted from the womb. Whoever violates this law is deemed to have destroyed the child's expectancy of life along with the mother.

13. A concubine shall not touch the Altar of Juno. If she touches it she shall sacrifice, with her hair unbound, a ewe lamb to Juno.

188. *The Twelve Tables (excerpts). Rome, 450 B.C. (traditional date). (FIRA, p. 23. Tr. ARS)*

These laws, the basis of Roman civil law, have their origins in what the Romans called *mos maiorum*, the tradition of their ancestors. The codification and publication of the ancestral laws on twelve bronze tablets in the Roman Forum represented a victory for the plebeian class, which hitherto had been subject to prejudiced legal interpretations by the patricians. Though some of the laws became outdated, the code was never abolished.

Table IV. Paternal power

1. A notably deformed child shall be killed immediately.
3. To repudiate his wife her husband shall order her ... to have her own property for herself, shall take the keys, shall expel her.[3]
4. A child born within ten months of the father's death shall enter into the inheritance ...

Table V. Inheritance and guardianship

1. ... Women, even though they are of full age, because of their levity of mind shall be under guardianship ... except vestal virgins, who ... shall be free from guardianship.[4]
2. The conveyable possessions of a woman who is under guardianship of male agnates[5] shall not be acquired by prescriptive right unless they are transferred by the woman herself with the authorisation of her guardian ...
4. If anyone who has no direct heir dies intestate the nearest male agnate shall have the estate.

5. If there is not a male agnate the male clansmen shall have the estate.

6. Persons for whom[6] by will ... a guardian is not given, for them ... their male agnates shall be guardians.

Table VI. *Ownership and possession*

5. ... If any woman is unwilling to be subjected in this manner to her husband's marital control, she shall absent herself for three successive nights in every year and by this means shall interrupt his prescriptive right of each year.

Table X. *Sacred law*

4. Women shall not tear their cheeks or shall not make a sorrowful outcry on account of a funeral.

189. *Punishment for adultery. Rome, 2nd cent. B.C. (Aulus Gellius, Attic Nights 10. 23, 2nd cent. A.D. Tr. J.C. Rolfe (LCL))*

A passage from a speech of Marcus Cato[7] on the mode of life and manners of women of the olden time; and also that the husband had the right to kill his wife, if she were taken in adultery.

Those who have written about the life and civilisation of the Roman people say that the women of Rome and Latium 'lived an abstemious life,' that is, that they abstained altogether from wine, which in the early language was called *temetum*; that it was an established custom for them to kiss their kinsfolk for the purpose of detection, so that, if they had been drinking, the odour might betray them. But they say that the women were accustomed to drink the second brewing, raisin wine, spiced wine and other sweet-tasting drinks of that kind. And these things are indeed made known in those books which I have mentioned, but Marcus Cato declares that women were not only censured but also punished by a judge no less severely if they had drunk wine than if they had disgraced themselves by adultery.

I have copied Marcus Cato's words from the oration entitled *On the Dowry*, in which it is also stated that husbands had the right to kill wives taken in adultery: 'When a husband puts away his wife,' says he, 'he judges the woman as a censor[8] would, and has full powers if she has been guilty of any wrong or shameful act; she is severely punished if she has drunk wine; if she has done wrong with another man, she is condemned to death.' Further, as to the right to put her to death it was thus written: 'If you should take your wife in adultery, you may with impunity put her to death without a trial; but if you should commit adultery or indecency, she must not presume to lay a finger on you, nor does the law allow it.'

190. *Punishment of wives in early Rome. (Valerius Maximus, Memorable Deeds and Sayings 6. 3. 9-12, 1st cent. A.D. Tr. M.B.F.)*

Egnatius Metellus[9] ... took a cudgel and beat his wife to death because she had drunk some wine. Not only did no one charge him with a crime, but no one even blamed him. Everyone considered this an excellent example of one who had justly paid the penalty for violating the laws of sobriety. Indeed, any woman who immoderately seeks the use of wine closes the door on all virtues and opens it to vices.

There was also the harsh marital severity of Gaius Sulpicius Gallus.[10] He divorced his wife because he had caught her outdoors with her head uncovered: a stiff penalty, but not without a certain logic. 'The law,' he said, 'prescribes for you my eyes alone to which you may prove your beauty. For these eyes you should provide the ornaments of beauty, for these be lovely: entrust yourself to their more certain knowledge. If you, with needless provocation, invite the look of anyone else, you must be suspected of wrongdoing.'

Quintus Antistius Vetus felt no differently when he divorced his wife because he had seen her in public having a private conversation with a common freedwoman. For, moved not by an actual crime but, so to speak, by the birth and nourishment of one, he punished her before the sin could be committed, so that he might prevent the deed's being done at all, rather than punish it afterwards.

To these we should add the case of Publius Sempronius Sophus[11] who disgraced his wife with divorce merely because she dared attend the games without his knowledge. And so, long ago, when the misdeeds of women were thus forestalled, their minds stayed far from wrongdoing.

191. *Repeal of the Oppian law. Rome, 195 B.C. (Livy, History of Rome 34. 1-8 (abridged), 1st cent. A.D. Tr. M.B.F.)*

In 215 B.C., after its disastrous defeat by Hannibal at Cannae, Rome passed the Oppian law, an emergency measure which limited women's use of expensive goods. Twenty years later, the crisis having long since passed, the law was repealed against the objections of many conservatives, here represented by the consul and champion of traditional values, Marcus Porcius Cato. Livy's reconstruction of the debate over the law's repeal devotes considerable space to ethical issues raised in legislation initiated in his own time by the Emperor Augustus (see pp.180 ff.).

Among the troubles of great wars, either scarcely over or yet to come, something intervened which, while it can be told briefly, stirred up enough excitement to become a great battle. Marcus Fundanius and Lucius Valerius, the tribunes of the people, brought a motion to repeal the Oppian law before the people. Gaius Oppius had carried this law as tribune at the height of the Punic War, during the consulship of Quintus Fabius and Tiberius Sempronius. The law said that no woman might own more than half an ounce of gold nor wear a multicoloured[12] dress nor ride in a carriage in the city or in a town within a mile of it, unless there was a religious festival. The tribunes, Marcus and Publius Junius Brutus, were in favour of the Oppian law and said that they would not allow its repeal. Many noble men came forward hoping to persuade or dissuade them; a crowd of men, both supporters and opponents, filled the Capitoline Hill. The matrons, whom neither counsel nor shame nor their husbands' orders could keep at home, blockaded every street in the city and every entrance to the Forum. As the men came down to the Forum, the matrons besought them to let them, too, have back the luxuries they had enjoyed before, giving as their reason that the republic was thriving and that everyone's private wealth was increasing with every day. This crowd of women was growing daily, for now they were even gathering from the towns and villages. Before long they dared go up and solicit the consuls, praetors, and other magistrates; but one of the consuls could not be moved in the least, Marcus Porcius Cato,[13] who spoke in favour of the law:

'If each man of us, fellow citizens, had established that the right and authority of the husband should be held over the mother of his own family, we should have less difficulty with women in general; now, at home our freedom is conquered by female fury, here in the Forum it is bruised and trampled upon, and, because we have not contained the individuals, we fear the lot ...

'Indeed, I blushed when, a short while ago, I walked through the midst of a band of women. Had not respect for the dignity and modesty of certain ones (not them all!) restrained me (so they would not be seen being scolded by a consul), I should have said, "What kind of behaviour is this? Running around in public, blocking streets, and speaking to other women's husbands! Could you not have asked your own husbands the same thing at home? Are you more charming in public with others' husbands than at home with your own? And yet, it is not fitting even at home (if modesty were to keep married women within the bounds of their rights) for you to concern yourselves with what laws are passed or repealed here." Our ancestors did not want women to conduct any – not even private – business without a guardian; they wanted them to be under the authority of parents, brothers, or husbands; we (the gods help us!) even now let them snatch at the government and meddle in the Forum and our assemblies. What are they doing now on the streets and crossroads, if they are not persuading the tribunes to vote for repeal? Give the reins to their unbridled nature and this unmastered creature, and hope that they will put limits on their own freedom; unless you do something yourselves, this is the least of the things imposed upon them either by custom or by law which they endure with hurt feelings. They want freedom, nay licence (if we are to speak the truth), in all things.

'If they are victorious now, what will they not attempt? ... As soon as they begin to be your equals, they will have become your superiors ...

'What honest excuse is offered, pray, for this womanish rebellion? "That we might shine with gold and purple," says one of them, "that we might ride through the city in coaches on holidays and working-days, as though triumphant over the conquered law and the votes which we captured by tearing them from you; that there should be no limit to our expenses and our luxury." ...

'The woman who can spend her own money will do so; the one who cannot will ask her husband. Pity that husband – the one who gives in and the one who stands firm! What he refuses, he will see given by another man. Now they publicly solicit other women's husbands, and, what is worse, they ask for a law and votes, and certain men give them what they want. You there, *you*, are easily moved about things which concern yourself, your estate, and your children; once the law no longer limits your wife's spending, you will never do it by yourself. Fellow citizens, do not imagine that the state which existed before the law was passed will return. A dishonest man is safer never accused than acquitted, and luxury, left alone, would have been more acceptable than it will be now, as when wild animals are first chafed by their chains and then released. I vote that the Oppian law should not, in the smallest measure, be repealed; whatever course you take, may all the gods make you happy with it.'

After this, when the tribunes of the people, who had declared that they would oppose the motion to repeal, had added a few remarks along the same lines, Lucius Valerius spoke on behalf of the motion which he himself had brought:

'[Cato] used up more words castigating the women than he did opposing the motion, and he left in some uncertainty whether the women had done the deeds which he reproached on their own or at our instigation. I shall defend the motion, not ourselves, against whom the consul has hurled this charge, more for the words than for the reality of the accusation. He has called this assemblage "secession" and sometimes "womanish rebellion", because the matrons have publicly asked you, in peacetime when the state is happy and prosperous, to repeal a law passed against them during the straits of war ...

'What, may I ask, are the women doing that is new, having gathered and come forth publicly in a case which concerns them directly? Have they never appeared in public before this? Allow me to unroll your own *Origines*[14] before you. Listen to how often they have done so – always for the public good. From the very beginning – the reign of Romulus – when the Capitoline had been taken by the Sabines and there was fighting in the middle of the Forum, was not the battle halted by the women's intervention between the two lines? How about this? After the kings had been expelled, when the Volscian legions and their general, Marcius Coriolanus, had pitched camp at the fifth milestone, did not the matrons turn away the forces which would have buried the city? When Rome was in the hands of the Gauls, who ransomed it? Indeed the matrons agreed unanimously to turn their gold over to the public need. Not to go too far back in history, in the most recent war, when we needed funds, did not the widows' money assist the treasury? And when new gods were summoned to bring their power to our difficulties, was it not all the matrons who went to the sea to meet the Idaean Mother? You say these cases are different. I am not here to say they are the same; it is enough to prove that nothing new has been done. Indeed, as no one is amazed that they acted in situations affecting men and women alike, why should we wonder that they have taken action in a case which concerns themselves? What, after all, have they done? We have proud ears indeed, if, while masters do not scorn the appeals of slaves, we are angry when honourable women ask something of us ...

'Who then does not know that this is a recent law, passed twenty years ago? Since our matrons lived for so long by the highest standards of behaviour without any law, what risk is there that, once it is repealed, they will yield to luxury? For if the law were an old one, or if it had been passed to restrain feminine licence, there might be reason to fear that repeal would incite them. The times themselves will show you why the law was passed. Hannibal was in Italy, victorious at Cannae. Already he held Tarentum, Arpi, and Capua. He seemed on the verge of moving against Rome. Our allies had gone over to him. We had no reserve troops, no allies at sea to protect the fleet, no funds in the treasury. Slaves were being bought and armed, on condition that the price be paid their owners when the war was over. The contractors had declared that they would provide, on that same day of payment (after the war), the grain and other supplies the needs of war demanded. We were giving our slaves as rowers at our own expense, in proportion to our property rating. We were giving all our gold and silver for public use, as the senators had done first. Widows and children were donating their funds to the treasury. We were ordered to keep at home no more than a certain amount of wrought and stamped gold and silver. At a time like that were the matrons so taken up with luxury and fancy trappings that the Oppian law was needed to restrain them, when, since the rites of Ceres had been suspended because all the women were in mourning, the senate ordered mourning limited to thirty days? To whom is it not clear that poverty and misfortune were the authors of that law of yours, since all private wealth had to be turned over to public use, and that it was to remain in effect only as long as the reason for its writing did? ...

'Shall it be our wives alone to whom the fruits of peace and tranquillity of the state do not come? ... Shall we forbid only women to wear purple? When you, a man, may use purple on your clothes, will you not allow the mother of your family to have a purple cloak, and will your horse be more beautifully saddled than your wife is garbed? ...

'[Cato] has said that, if none of them had anything, there would be no rivalry among individual women. By Hercules! All are unhappy and indignant when they see the finery denied them permitted to the wives of the Latin allies, when they see them adorned with gold and purple, when those other women ride through the city and they follow on foot, as though the power belonged to the other women's cities, not to their own. This could wound the spirits of men; what do you think it could do the spirits of women, whom even little things disturb? They cannot partake of magistracies, priesthoods, triumphs, badges of office, gifts, or spoils of war; elegance, finery, and beautiful clothes are women's badges, in these they find joy and take pride, this our forebears called the women's world. When they are in mourning, what, other than purple and gold, do they take off? What do they put on again when they have completed the period of mourning? What do they add for public prayer and thanksgiving other than still greater ornament? Of course, if you repeal the Oppian law, you will not have the power to prohibit that which the law now forbids; daughters, wives, even some men's sisters will be less under your authority – never, while her men are well, is a woman's slavery cast off; and even they hate the freedom created by widowhood and orphanage. They prefer their adornment to be subject to *your* judgment, not the law's; and you ought to hold them in *manus*[15] and guardianship, not slavery; you should prefer to be called fathers and husbands to masters. The consul just now used odious terms when he said "womanish rebellion" and "secession". For there is danger – he would have us believe – that they will seize the Sacred Hill as once the angry plebeians did, or the Aventine. It is for the weaker sex to submit to whatever you advise. The more power you possess, all the more moderately should you exercise your authority.'

When these speeches for and against the law had been made, a considerably larger crowd of women poured forth in public the next day; as a single body they besieged the doors of the Brutuses, who were vetoing their colleagues' motion, and they did not stop until the tribunes took back their veto. After that there was no doubt but that all the tribes would repeal the law. Twenty years after it was passed, the law was repealed.

The Empire

In 18 B.C., the Emperor Augustus turned his attention to social problems at Rome. Luxury and adultery were widespread. Among the upper classes, marriage was increasingly infrequent and, for couples who did marry, childlessness was common. Augustus was interested in raising both the morals and the numbers of the upper classes in Rome, and in increasing the population of native Italians in Italy. He enacted sumptuary laws, laws against adultery, and laws which encouraged marriage and having children.

The law against adultery (*lex Iulia de adulteriis coercendis*) made the offence a crime punishable by exile and confiscation of property. Fathers were permitted to kill daughters and their partners in adultery. Husbands could kill the partners under certain circumstances and were required to divorce adulterous wives. It is ironic that Augustus was eventually obliged to invoke this law against his own daughter, Julia, and to relegate her to the island of Pandateria.[16]

The Augustan social laws were badly received, and the emperor, years later, modified them. The *lex Papia Poppaea*, enacted in A.D. 9, softened slightly the rigidity of the earlier legislation (*lex Iulia de maritandis ordinibus*). It takes its name from the two consuls of that year – both bachelors. While the laws were never formally repealed, they were never fully successful.

The texts which follow are taken from handbooks and post-classical collections of legal writings. They contain many late interpolations, some based on readers' marginal notes.

192. *Prizes for marriage and children. Rome, 1st cent. A.D. (Dio Cassius, History of Rome 54. 16. 1-2, 3rd cent. A.D. Tr. E. Cary (LCL))*

He [Augustus] laid heavier assessments upon the unmarried men and women and on the other hand offered prizes for marriage and the begetting of children. And since among the nobility there were far more males than females, he allowed all [free men] who wished, except senators, to marry freedwomen, and ordered that their offspring should be held legitimate.

193. *Laws relating to adultery, fornication, prostitution and concubinage.*

(i) Paulus, *Opinions* 2. 26. 1-17. Rome, 3rd cent. A.D. Tr. S.P. Scott.

In the second chapter of the *lex Julia* concerning adultery, either an adoptive or a natural father is permitted to kill an adulterer caught in the act with his daughter in his own house or in that of his son-in-law, no matter what his rank may be.

If a son under paternal control, who is the father, should surprise his daughter in the act of adultery, while it is inferred from the terms of the law that he cannot kill her, still, he ought to be permitted to do so.

Again, it is provided in the fifth chapter of the *lex Julia* that it is permitted to detain witnesses for twenty hours, in order to convict an adulterer taken in the act.

A husband cannot kill anyone taken in adultery except persons who are infamous, and those who sell their bodies for gain, as well as slaves, and the freedmen of his wife, and those of his parents and children; his wife, however, is excepted, and he is forbidden to kill her.

It has been decided that a husband who kills his wife when caught with an adulterer, should be punished more leniently, for the reason that he committed the act through impatience caused by just suffering.

After having killed the adulterer, the husband should at once dismiss his wife, and publicly declare within the next three days with what adulterer, and in what place he found his wife.

An angry husband who surprises his wife in adultery can only kill the adulterer when he finds him in his own house.

It has been decided that a husband who does not at once dismiss his wife whom he has taken in adultery can be prosecuted as a pander.

It should be noted that two adulterers can be accused at the same time with the wife, but more than that number cannot be.

It has been decided that adultery cannot be committed with women who have charge of any business or shop.

Anyone who debauches a male who is free, against his consent, shall be punished with death.

It has been held that women convicted of adultery shall be punished with the loss of half of their dowry and the third of their estates, and by relegation to an island. The adulterer, however, shall be deprived of half his property, and shall also be punished by relegation to an island; provided the parties are exiled to different islands.

It has been decided that the penalty for incest, which in case of a man is deportation to an island, shall not be inflicted upon the woman; that is to say when she has not been convicted under the *lex Julia* concerning adultery.

Fornication committed with female slaves, unless they are deteriorated in value or an attempt is made against their mistress through them, is not considered an injury.

If a delay is demanded in a case of adultery it cannot be obtained.

(ii) Justinian, *Codex* 9.1, 8, 11, 17, 18, 20, 22-5, 27, 29, 6th cent. A.D. Tr. S. P. Scott.

The *lex Julia* declares that wives have no right to bring criminal accusations for adultery against their husbands, even though they may desire to complain of the violation of the marriage vow, for while the law grants this privilege to men it does not concede it to women ...

The *lex Julia* relating to chastity forbids the two parties guilty of adultery, that is to say, the man and the woman, to be prosecuted at the same time, and in the same case, but they can both be prosecuted in succession ...

No one doubts that a husband cannot accuse his wife of adultery if he continues to retain her in marriage ... Under the new law, however, he can do so, and if the accusation is proved to be true, he can then repudiate her, and he should file a written accusation against her. If, however, the husband should not be able to establish the accusation of adultery which he brought, he will be liable to the same punishment which his wife would have undergone if the accusation had been proved ...

You can resume marital relations with your wife without fear of being liable to the penalty prescribed by the *lex Julia* for the suppression of adultery, as you did nothing more than file the written accusation, for the reason that you assert that you afterwards ascertained that you were impelled by groundless indignation to accuse her; for he alone will be liable to the penalty specifically mentioned by the law who is aware that his wife has been publicly convicted of adultery, or that she is an adulteress, as he cannot simulate ignorance of the fact, and retain her as his wife ...

There is no doubt that he who has two wives at once is branded with infamy, for, in a case of this kind, not the operation of the law by which our citizens are forbidden to contract more than one marriage at a time, but the intention, should be considered; and therefore he who pretended to be unmarried, but had another wife in the province, and asked you to marry him, can lawfully be accused of the crime of fornication, for which you are not liable, for the reason that you thought that you were his wife. You can obtain from the governor of the province the return of all your property of which you deplore the loss on account of the fraudulent marriage, and which should be restored to you without delay. But how can you recover what he promised to give you as his betrothed? ...

The laws punish the detestable wickedness of women who prostitute their chastity to the lusts of others, but do not hold those liable who are compelled to commit fornication through force, and against their will. And, moreover, it has very properly been decided that their reputations are not lost, and that their marriage with others should not be prohibited on this account ...

If a woman whom you have carnally known indiscriminately sold herself for money, and prostituted herself everywhere as a harlot, you did not commit the crime of adultery with her ...

Slaves cannot accuse their wives of adultery for violation of conjugal faith.

If you should be accused of adultery by her with whom you have lived in violation of law, you can defend yourself by an innumerable number of expedients.

Although it is established by the contents of certain documents that you are consumed with the lust of immoderate desire, still, as it has been ascertained that you confined yourself to female slaves, and did not have intercourse with free women, it is clear that by a sentence of this kind your reputation suffers, rather than that you become infamous ...

Adultery committed with a man whom a woman afterwards married is not extinguished by the fact of the marriage ...

It should be ascertained whether the woman who committed adultery was the owner of the inn, or only a servant; and if, by employing herself in servile duties (which frequently happens), she gave occasion for intemperance, since if she were the mistress of the inn, she will not be exempt from liability under the law. Where, however, she served liquor to the men who were drinking, she would not be liable to accusation as having committed the offence, on account of her inferior rank, and any freemen who have been accused shall be discharged, as the same degree of modesty is required of these women as of those who are legally married, and bear the name of mothers of families. Those, also, are not subject to judicial severity who are guilty of fornication or adultery, and the vileness of whose lives does not render them worthy of the attention of the laws.

(iii) Justinian, *Digest* 48. 5. 1. pr., 48. 2.2, 2.8 (Ulpian); 48. 5. 8. pr., 10. pr.-2, 11. 8-9, 11. 12-13 (Papinian); 48. 5. 13. pr., 3, 8; 19. 3 (Ulpian); 48. 5. 20 (Papinian); 48. 5. 21 (Ulpian); 48. 5. 22. pr., 1, 2, 4 (Papinian); 48. 5. 23 (Ulpian); 48. 5. 24 (Macer); 48. 5. 25. pr., 26. pr.-1 (Ulpian); 23. 2. 43. pr.-6 (Ulpian); 23. 2.. 41. pr.-1 (Marcellus); 23. 2. 44. pr.-1, 6-8 (Paulus); 23. 2. 45. pr. (Ulpian); 26. 7. 1. pr.-1, 4 (Ulpian); 26. 7. 2. pr. (Paulus). 6th cent. A.D. Tr. S.P. Scott.

This law was introduced by the Divine Augustus ... The crime of pandering is included in the Julian law of adultery, as a penalty has been prescribed against a husband who profits pecuniarily by the adultery of his wife; as well as against one who retains his wife after she has been taken in adultery ...

If the husband and the father of the woman appear at the same time for the purpose of accusing her, the question arises, which of them should be given the preference by the Praetor? The better opinion is, that the husband should be entitled to the preference, for it may well be believed that he will prosecute the accusation with greater anger and vexation ...

Anyone who knowingly lends his house to enable debauchery or adultery to be committed there with a matron who is not his wife, or with a male, or who pecuniarily profits by the adultery of his wife, no matter what may be his status, is punished as an adulterer ... A matron means not only a married woman, but also a widow. Women who lend their houses, or have received any compensation for debauchery which they have committed, are also liable under this section of the law. A woman who gratuitously acts as a bawd for the purpose of avoiding the penalty for adultery, or hires her services to appear in the theatre, can be accused and convicted of adultery under the decree of the senate.

A woman can be prosecuted for adultery after the death of her husband. Should a woman who asks for delay on account of the youth of her son obtain it from the accuser, or ought she to be heard? I answered: This woman does not seem to have a just defence who offers the age of her son as a pretext for evading a legal accusation. For the charge of adultery brought against her does not prejudice the child, since she herself may be an adulteress, and the child still have the deceased for his father ...

A woman, having heard that her absent husband was dead, married another, and her first husband afterwards returned. I ask, what should be decided with reference to this woman? The answer was that the question is one of law and not of fact; for if a long time had elapsed without any proof of debauchery having been made, and the woman, having been induced by false rumours, and, as it were, released from her former tie, married a second time in accordance with law, as it is probable that she was deceived, and she can be held to have done nothing deserving of punishment. If, however, it is established that the supposed death of her husband furnished an inducement for her marrying a second time, as her chastity is affected by this fact, she should be punished in proportion to the character of the offence.

I married a woman accused of adultery, and, as soon as she was convicted, I repudiated her. I ask whether I should be considered to have furnished the cause of the separation. The answer was that, since by the Julian law you are prohibited from keeping a wife of this kind, it is clear that you should not be considered to have furnished the cause for the separation. Therefore, the law will be applied just as if a divorce had taken place through the fault of the woman.

Where a wife did not commit adultery, but a concubine did, the husband cannot accuse her as such, because she is not his wife; still, he is not prohibited by law from bringing an accusation as a stranger, provided that she, in giving herself as a concubine, did not forfeit the name of a matron, as, for instance, a woman who had been the concubine of her patron ... The Divine Severus and Antoninus stated in a rescript, that this offence could even be prosecuted in the case of a woman who was betrothed, because she is not permitted to violate any marriage whatever, nor even the hope of matrimony ...

Where a girl, less than twelve years old, brought into the house of her husband, commits adultery, and afterwards remains with him until she has passed that age, and begins to be his wife, she cannot be accused of adultery by her husband, for the reason that she committed it before reaching the marriageable age; but, according to a rescript of the Divine Severus, which is mentioned above, she can be accused as having been betrothed ...

If the adulterer should be acquitted, a married woman cannot be accused, even by the person who prosecuted the adulterer and was defeated, nor can she be accused if she should cease to be married, for the law only protects a woman as long as she is married.

The right is granted to the father to kill a man who commits adultery with his daughter while she is under his control. Therefore no other relative can legally do this, nor can a son under paternal control, who is a father, do so with impunity.

Hence it happens that neither the father nor the grandfather can kill the adulterer. This is not unreasonable, for he cannot be considered to have anyone under his control who has not control of himself.

In this law, the natural father is not distinguished from the adoptive father. In the accusation of his daughter, who is a widow, the father is not entitled to the preference. The right to kill the adulterer is granted to the father in his own house, even though his daughter does not live there, or in the house of his son-in-law ... Hence the father, and not the husband, has the right to kill the woman and every adulterer; for the reason that, in general, paternal affection is solicitous for the interests of the children, but the heat and impetuosity of the husband, who decides too quickly, should be restrained.

What the law says, that is, 'if he finds a man committing adultery with his daughter,' does not seem to be superfluous; for it signifies that the father shall have this power only when he surprises his daughter in the very act of adultery. Labeo also adopts this opinion; and Pomponius says that the man must be killed while in the very performance of the sexual act. This is what Solon and Dracho mean by the word '*eryō*'.

It is sufficient for the father for his daughter to be subject to his authority at the time when he kills the adulterer, although she may not have been at the time when he gave her in marriage; for suppose that she had afterwards come under his control.

Therefore the father shall not be permitted to kill the parties wherever he surprises them, but only in his own house, or in that of his son-in-law. The reason for this is, that the legislator thought that the injury was greater where the daughter caused the adulterer to be introduced into the house of her father or her husband.

If, however, her father lives elsewhere, and has another house in which he does not reside, and surprises his daughter there, he cannot kill her.

Where the law says, 'He may kill his daughter at once,' this must be understood to mean that having today killed the adulterer he cannot reserve his daughter to be killed subsequently; for he should kill both of them with one blow and one attack, and be inflamed by the same resentment against both. But if, without any connivance on his part, his daughter should take to flight, while he is killing the adulterer, and she should be caught and put to death some hours afterwards by her father, who pursued her, he will be considered to have killed her immediately.

A husband is also permitted to kill a man who commits adultery with his wife, but not everyone without distinction, as the father is; for it is provided by this law that the husband can kill the adulterer if he surprises him in his own house, but not if he surprises him in the house of his father-in-law; nor if he was formerly a pander; or had exercised the profession of a mountebank, by dancing or singing on the stage; or had been convicted in a criminal prosecution and not been restored to his civil rights; or is the freedman of the husband or the wife, or of the father or mother, or of the son or the daughter of any of them; nor does it make any difference whether he belonged exclusively to one of the persons above mentioned, or owed services to two patrons in common, or was a slave.

It is also provided that a husband who has killed any one of these must dismiss his wife without delay.

It is held by many authorities to make no difference whether the husband is his own master, or a son under paternal control.

With reference to both parties, the question arises, in accordance with the spirit of the law, whether the father can kill a magistrate; and also where his daughter is of bad reputation, or has been illegally married, whether the father or the husband will still retain his right; and what should be done if the husband is a pander, or is branded with ignominy for some reason or other. It may properly be held that those have a right to kill who can bring an accusation as a father or a husband.

It is provided as follows in the fifth section of the Julian law: 'That where a husband has surprised an adulterer with his wife, and is either unwilling or unable to kill him, he can hold him for not more than twenty consecutive hours of the day and night, in order to obtain evidence of the crime, and make use of his right without endangering it.'...

A woman cannot be accused of adultery during marriage by anyone who, in addition to the husband, is permitted to bring the accusation; for a stranger should not annoy a wife who is approved by her husband, and disturb a quiet marriage, unless he has previously accused the husband of being a pander.

When, however, the charge has been abandoned by the husband, it is proper for it to be prosecuted by another.

We hold that a woman openly practises prostitution, not only where she does so in a house of ill-fame, but also if she is accustomed to do this in taverns, or in other places where she manifests no regard for her modesty.

We understand the word 'openly' to mean indiscriminately, that is to say, without choice, and not if she commits adultery or fornication, but where she sustains the role of a prostitute. Moreover, where a woman, having accepted money, has intercourse with only one or two persons, she is not considered to have openly prostituted herself. Octavenus, however, says very properly that where a woman publicly prostitutes herself without doing so for money, she should be classed as a harlot. The law brands with infamy not only a woman who practises prostitution, but also one who has formerly done so, even though she has ceased to act in this manner; for the disgrace is not removed even if the practice is subsequently discontinued. A woman is not to be excused who leads a vicious life under the pretext of poverty. The occupation of a pander is not less disgraceful than the practice of prostitution.

It is understood that disgrace attaches to those women who live unchastely, and earn money by prostitution, even if they do not do so openly.

If a woman should live in concubinage with someone besides her patron, I say that she does not possess the virtue of the mother of a family.

It is provided by the *lex Julia* that: 'A senator, or his son, or his grandson, or his great-grandson by his son, or grandson, shall not knowingly or with malicious intent become betrothed to, or marry a freedwoman, or a woman whose father or mother practises, or has practised the profession of an actor. Nor shall the daughter of a senator, or a granddaughter by his son, or a great-granddaughter by his grandson marry a freedman, or a man whose father or mother practises, or has practised the profession of an actor, whether they do so knowingly, or with malicious intent. Nor can any one of these parties knowingly, or with malicious intent become betrothed to, or marry the daughter of a senator.'

Under this head a senator is forbidden to marry a freedwoman whose father or mother has, at any time, exercised the profession of an actor. A freedman is also forbidden to marry the daughter of a senator ...

If the father or mother of a freeborn woman, after the marriage of the latter should begin to exercise the profession of the stage, it would be most unjust for the daughter to be repudiated by her husband, as the marriage was honourably contracted, and children may already have been born. It is evident that if the woman herself becomes a member of the theatrical profession, she should be repudiated by her husband.

Senators cannot marry women whom other freeborn men are forbidden to take as wives.

In that law which provides that where a freedwoman has been married to her patron, after separation from him she cannot marry another without his consent; we understand the patron to be one who has bought a female slave under the condition of manumitting her (as is stated in the rescript of our Emperor and his father), because, after having been manumitted, she becomes the freedwoman of the purchaser.

Where a freedwoman is living in concubinage with her patron, she can leave him without his consent, and unite with another man, either in matrimony or in concubinage. I think, however, that a concubine should not have the right to marry if she leaves her patron without his consent, since it is more honourable for a freedwoman to be the concubine of a patron than to become the mother of a family. I hold with Atilicinus, that only those women who are not disgraced by such a connection can be kept in concubinage without the fear of committing a crime ... It is clear that anyone can keep a concubine of any age unless she is less than twelve years old.

Where a patron, who has a freedwoman as his concubine, becomes insane, it is more equitable to hold that she remains in concubinage.

194. *Adoption and manus. Rome, 2nd cent. A.D. (Gaius, Institutes 1. 97-117 and 136-7a. Tr. F. de Zulueta)*

The jurists Gaius and Justinian give later interpretations of the concept of *patria potestas*, the power of the father over his own family, which was a fundamental principle of Roman law. Compare the laws given in the Twelve Tables (above, no. 188).

Not only are the children of our bodies in our *potestas* according as we have stated, but also those whom we adopt. Adoption takes place in two ways, either by authority of the people or by the *imperium* of a magistrate, such as a praetor ... The former kind of adoption, that by authority of the people, can be performed nowhere but at Rome, whereas the latter kind is regularly performed in the provinces before the provincial governors. Further, females cannot be adopted by authority of the people, for this opinion has prevailed; but before a praetor or, in the provinces, before the proconsul or legate, females are regularly adopted ... But women cannot adopt by any method, for they do not hold even the children of their bodies in their *potestas* ...

Let us proceed to consider persons who are in *manus*, [17] which is another right peculiar to Roman citizens. Now, while both males and females are found in *potestas*, only females can come under *manus*. Of old, women passed into *manus* in three ways, by *usus*, *confarreatio*, and *coemptio*. [18] A woman used to pass into *manus* by *usus* if she cohabited with her husband for a year without interruption, being as it were acquired by a usucapion of one year and so passing into her husband's family and ranking as a daughter. Hence it was provided by the Twelve Tables that any woman wishing not to come under her husband's *manus* in this way should stay away from him for three nights in each year and thus interrupt the *usus* of each year. But the whole of this institution has been in part abolished by statutes and in part obliterated by simple disuse. Entry of a woman into *manus* by *confarreatio* is effected by a kind of sacrifice offered to Jupiter Farreus, in which the spelt cake is employed, whence the name *confarreatio*. In the performance of this ceremony a number of acts and things are done, accompanied by special formal words, in the presence of ten witnesses. This institution still exists at the present day. For the higher flamens, that is those of Jupiter, Mars, and Quirinus, and also the *rex sacrorum*, can only be chosen from those born of parents married by *confarreatio*; indeed, no person can hold the priesthood without being himself so married. Entry of a woman into *manus* by *coemptio* takes the form of a mancipation, that is a sort of imaginary sale: in the presence of not less than five witnesses, being Roman citizens above puberty, and of a scale-holder, the woman is bought by him into whose *manus* she is passing. It is, however, possible for a woman to make a *coemptio* not only with her husband, but also with a stranger; in other words, *coemptio* may be performed for either matrimonial or fiduciary purposes. A woman who makes a *coemptio* with her husband with the object of ranking as a daughter in his household is said to have made a *coemptio* for matrimonial purposes, while one who makes, whether with her husband or a stranger, a *coemptio* for some other object, such as that of evading a tutorship, is said to have done so for fiduciary purposes. What happens is as follows: a woman wishing to get rid of her existing tutors and to get another makes a *coemptio* with the *auctoritas* of her existing tutors; after that she is remancipated by her *coemptionator* to the person of her own choice and, having been manumitted *uindicta* by him, comes to have as her tutor the man by whom she has been manumitted. This person is called a fiduciary tutor, as will appear below. Formerly too fiduciary *coemptio* used to be performed for the purpose of making a will. This was at a time when women, with certain exceptions, had not the right to make a will unless they had made a *coemptio* and had been remancipatèd and manumitted. But the senate on the authority of the late emperor Hadrian has dispensed from this requirement of a *coemptio* ... But if a woman makes a fiduciary *coemptio* with her husband, she nevertheless acquires the position of his daughter. For it is the accepted view that, if for any reason whatever a wife be in her husband's *manus*, she acquires a daughter's rights.

We have still to explain what persons are *in mancipio*.[19] All children, male or female, who are in a parent's *potestas* can be mancipated by him in just the same manner as slaves ...

Also, women cease to be in their father's *potestas* by passing into *manus*. But in the case of the confarreate marriage of the wife of a flamen of Jupiter a decree of the senate passed on the proposal of Maximus and Tubero has provided that she is to be considered to be in *manus* only for sacral purposes, while for all other purposes she is to be treated as though she had not entered *manus*. On the other hand, a woman who enters *manus* by *coemptio* is freed from her father's *potestas*, and it makes no difference whether she be in her husband's or a stranger's *manus*, although only women who are in their husband's *manus* rank as daughters.

Women cease to be in *manus* in the same ways as those by which daughters are freed from their father's *potestas*. Thus, just as daughters pass out of their father's *potestas* by a single mancipation, so women in *manus* cease by a single mancipation to be in *manus*, and if manumitted from that mancipation become *sui iuris*. Between a woman who has made a *coemptio* with a stranger and one who has done so with her husband there is, however, this difference, that the former can compel her *coemptio* to remancipate her to the person of her choice, whereas the latter can no more compel her husband to do this than a daughter can compel her father. But, while a daughter, even if adoptive, is absolutely incapable of compelling her father, a woman in the *manus* of her husband can, if she has sent him notice of divorce, compel him to release her, just as though she had never been his wife.

195. *Patria potestas and guardianship*

(i) Justinian, *Institutes* 1. 9; 1.11. pr., 10; *Codex* 9. 10. 1: *Digest* 23. 2. 36 (Paulus); 48. 5. 7. pr. (Marcianus). 6th cent. A.D. Tr. D.C. Munro, S.P.Scott.

Our children whom we have begotten in lawful wedlock are in our power. Wedlock or matrimony is the union of male and female, involving the habitual intercourse of daily life. The power which we have over our children is peculiar to Roman citizens and is found in no other nation. The offspring then of you and your wife is in your power, and so too is that of your son and his wife, that is to say, your grandson and granddaughter, and so on. But the offspring of your daughter is not in your power, but in that of its own father.

Not only our natural children under our authority as we have already stated, but those whom we adopt as well ... Women also cannot adopt because they have not even control over their own children, but by the indulgence of the Emperor they can do so by way of consolation for the children they have lost.

When a guardian violates the chastity of his female ward, he shall be sentenced to deportation, and all his property shall be confiscated to the treasury, although he must still suffer the penalty which the laws inflict upon ravishers.

A guardian or a curator cannot marry a grown woman who is committed to his care, unless she has been betrothed to, or intended for him by her father, or where the marriage takes place in accordance with some condition mentioned in his will.

A man who contracts matrimony with his own female ward in violation of the decree of the senate is not legally married; and he who was her guardian or curator can be prosecuted for adultery if he marries a girl under twenty-six years of age who has not been betrothed to him, or destined for him, or mentioned for this purpose in a will.

(ii) Ulpian, *Rules* 5. 8-10; 11.1. Rome, 3rd cent. A.D. Tr. S.P. Scott.

When legal marriage takes place, the children always follow the father, but if it does not take place, they follow the condition of the mother; except where a child is born of an alien father, and a mother who is a Roman citizen, as the *lex Minicia* directs that where a child is born of parents one of whom is an alien, it shall follow the condition of the inferior parent.

A child born of a father who is a Roman citizen and a Latin mother is a Latin; one born of a freeman and a female slave is a slave; since the child follows the mother as in cases where there is no legal marriage.

In the case of children who are the issue of a legally contracted marriage, the time of conception is considered; in the case of those who were not legitimately conceived, the time of their birth is considered; for instance, if a female slave conceives and brings forth a child after having been manumitted, the child will be free; for while she did not lawfully conceive, as she was free at the time the child was born the latter will also be free.

Guardians are appointed for males as well as for females, but only for males under puberty, on account of their infirmity of age; for females, however, both under and over puberty, on account of the weakness of their sex as well as their ignorance of business matters.

196. *Marriage and property*

(i) Paulus, *Opinions* 2. 1-9; 2. 20. 1; 3. 10. 1-2; 2. 22. 1. Rome, 3rd cent. A.D. Tr. S. P. Scott.

Betrothal can take place between persons over or under the age of puberty. Marriage cannot legally be contracted by persons who are subject to the control of their father, without their consent; such contracts, however, are not dissolved, for the consideration of the public welfare is preferred to the convenience of private individuals. Marriage cannot be contracted, but cohabitation can exist between slaves and persons who are free. An insane person of either sex cannot contract marriage, but where marriage has been contracted it is not annulled by insanity. An absent man can marry a wife; an absent woman, however, cannot marry. It has been decided that a freedman who aspires to marry his patroness, or the daughter of the wife of his patron, shall be sentenced to the mines, or to labour on the public works, according to the dignity of the person in question.

A man cannot keep a concubine at the same time that he has a wife. Hence a concubine differs from a wife only in the fact that she is entertained for pleasure.

On the Orphitian decree of the senate:

Children born of promiscuous intercourse are not prevented from claiming the estate of their mother, if she died intestate; because, as their estates pass to their mother, so the estate of their mother should vest in them.

Through the operation of the Claudian decree of the senate, the estate of a mother who died intestate cannot pass to a daughter who is either a female slave, or a freedwoman; because neither slaves nor freedmen are understood to have mothers under the civil law.

The crops of dotal land are gathered for the benefit of the husband during the existence of the marriage, and also proportionately during the year in which a divorce takes place.

(ii) Justinian, *Institutes* 1. 10. pr. (excerpt); *Codex* 9. 12. 1; *Digest* 23. 2. 34. 1, 3 (Papinian); 23. 2. 42. pr.-1 (Modestinus); 24. 2. 1, 3 (Paulus); 23. 2. 70 (Paulus); 24. 1. 31. pr.-1 (Pomponius); 12. 4. 9. pr. (Paulus). 6th cent. A.D. Tr. S.P. Scott.

Roman citizens unite in legal marriage when they are joined according to the precepts of the law, and the males have attained the age of puberty and the females are capable of childbirth, whether they are the heads of families or the children of families; if the latter have also the consent of the relatives under whose authority they may be, for this should be obtained and both civil and natural law require that it should previously be secured.

Those who seize the property of a wife on account of a debt of her husband, or because of some public civil liability which he has incurred, are considered to have been guilty of violence.

Where a man has accused his wife of adultery in accordance with his right as a husband, he is not forbidden, after the annulment of the marriage, to marry again. If, however, he does not accuse his wife as her husband, it will be held that the marriage which has been contracted will remain valid.
   Where the daughter of a senator marries a freedman, this unfortunate act of her father does not render her a wife, for children should not be deprived of their rank on account of an offence of their parent.

In unions of the sexes, it should always be considered not only what is legal, but also what is decent. If the daughter, granddaughter, or great-granddaughter of a senator should marry a freedman, or a man who practises the profession of an actor, or whose father or mother did so, the marriage will be void.

Marriage is dissolved by divorce, death, captivity, or by any other kind of servitude which may happen to be imposed upon either of the parties ...
   It is not a true or actual divorce unless the purpose is to establish a perpetual separation. Therefore, whatever is done or said in the heat of anger is not valid, unless the determination becomes apparent by the parties persevering in their intention, and hence where repudiation takes place in the heat of anger and the wife returns in a short time, she is not held to have been divorced.

Where doubtful questions arise, it is better to decide in favour of the dowry.

Where a husband makes clothing for his wife out of his own wool, although this is done for his wife and through solicitude for her, the clothing, nevertheless, will belong to the husband; nor does it make any difference whether the wife assisted in preparing the wool, and attended to the matter for her husband.

Where a wife uses her own wool, but makes garments for herself with the aid of female slaves belonging to her husband, it will belong to him, if he paid his wife the value of the wool.

If I intend to give money to a woman, and pay it to her betrothed as dowry by her direction but the marriage does not take place, the woman has a right of action for its recovery ...

(iii) Ulpian, *Rules* 6. 1, 2, 4, 6, 7, 9, 10, 12; 7. 2. Rome, 3rd cent. A.D. Tr. S.P. Scott.

A dowry is either given, expressly stated, or promised.

A woman who is about to be married can state her dowry, and her debtor can do so, at her direction; a male ascendant of the woman related to her through the male sex, such as her father or paternal grandfather, can likewise so do. Any person can give or promise a dowry ...

When a woman dies during marriage, her dowry given by her father reverts to him, a fifth of the same for each child she leaves being retained by the husband, no matter what the number may be. If her father is not living, the dowry remains in the hands of the husband ...

When a divorce takes place, if the woman is her own mistress, she herself has the right to sue for the recovery of the dowry. If, however, she is under the control of her father, he having been joined with her daughter, can bring the action for the recovery of the dowry; nor does it make any difference whether it is adventitious or profectitious.

If the woman dies after the divorce, no right of action will be granted to her heir, unless her husband has been in default in restoring her dowry ...

Portions of a dowry are retained either on account of children, on account of bad morals, on account of expenses, on account of donations, or on account of articles which have been abstracted.

A portion is retained on account of children, when the divorce took place either through the fault of the wife, or her father; for then a sixth part of the dowry shall be retained in the name of each child, but not more than three-sixths altogether ...

A sixth of the dowry is also retained on the ground of a flagrant breach of morals; an eighth, where the offence is not so serious. Adultery alone comes under the head of a flagrant breach of morals; all other improper acts are classed as less serious.

If a husband in anticipation of divorce abstracts anything belonging to his wife, he will be liable to an action for the clandestine removal of property.

197. *Children and slaves*

(i) Paulus, *Opinions* 2. 24. 1-9; 2. 21. 1-4, 9-13, 16. Rome, 3rd cent. A.D. Tr. S.P. Scott.

If a female slave conceives, and has a child after she has been manumitted, the child will be free.

If a free woman conceives and has a child after having become a slave, the child will be free; for this is demanded by the favour conceded to freedom.

If a female slave conceives, and in the meantime is manumitted, but, having subsequently again become a slave, has a child, it will be free; for the intermediate time can benefit, but not injure freedom.

A child born to a woman who should have been manumitted under the terms of a trust, is born free, if it comes into the world after the grant of freedom is in default.

If, after a divorce has taken place, a woman finds herself to be pregnant, she should within three hundred days notify either her husband, or his father to send witnesses for the purpose of making an examination of her condition: and if this is not done, they shall, by all means, be compelled to recognise the child of the woman.

If the woman should not announce that she is pregnant, and should not permit the witnesses sent to make an examination of her, neither the father nor the grandfather will be compelled to support the child; but the neglect of the mother will not offer any impediment to the child being considered the proper heir of his father.

Where a woman denies that she is pregnant by her husband, the latter is permitted to make an examination of her, and appoint persons to watch her.

The physical examination of the woman is made by five midwives, and the decision of the majority shall be held to be true.

It has been decided that a midwife who introduces the child of another in order that it may be substituted shall be punished with death.

If a freeborn woman, who is also a Roman citizen or a Latin, forms a union with the slave belonging to another, and continues to cohabit with him against the consent and protest of the owner of the slave, she becomes a female slave.

If a freeborn woman forms a union with a slave who is a ward, she becomes a female slave by the denunciation of the guardian.

Although a woman cannot permit her freedwoman to cohabit with the slave of another without the permission of her guardian, still, by denouncing her who has formed such a union with her slave, she will acquire the woman as her slave.

An attorney, a son under paternal control, and a slave, by the order of his father, master, or principal, makes a woman a female slave under such circumstances by denouncing her.

If a daughter under paternal control, without the consent or knowledge of her father, forms a union with a slave belonging to another she will retain her position, even after being denounced; for the reason that the condition of a parent cannot become worse through any act of his children.

If a daughter under paternal control, by order of her father, and against the will of his master, forms a union with the slave of another she becomes a female slave; because parents can render the condition of their children worse.

A freedwoman who forms a union with the slave of her patron will remain in the same condition after having been denounced, because she is considered to have been unwilling to abandon the house of her patron.

Any woman who erroneously thinks that she is a female slave, and on this account forms a union with the slave of another, and, after having ascertained that she is free, continues in the same relation with him, becomes a female slave.

If a patroness forms a union with the slave of her freedman, it has been decided that she does not become a female slave by his denunciation ...

If a mother forms a union with the slave of her son, the Claudian decree of the senate does not abolish the filial reverence which should be entertained for a mother; even though she should blush on account of her disgrace, as in the case of her who cohabits with the slave of her freedman.

(ii) Justinian, *Codex* 11. 11. pr.; *Digest* 23. 2. 13 (Ulpian); 5. 3. 27. pr.-1 (Ulpian). 6th cent. A.D. Tr. S.P. Scott.

When a woman is convicted of having secretly had sexual intercourse with her slave, she shall be sentenced to death, and the rascally slave shall perish by fire ...

Where a patroness is so degraded that she even thinks that marriage with her freedman is honourable, it should not be prohibited by a judge to whom application is made to prevent it.

The issue of female slaves and the offspring of their female children are not considered to be profits, because it is not customary for female slaves to be acquired for breeding purposes; their offspring are, nevertheless, an increase of the estate; and since all these form part of the estate, there is no doubt that the possessor should surrender them, whether he is the actual possessor, or, after suit was brought, he acted fraudulently to avoid being in possession. Moreover, rents which have been collected from persons who leased buildings, are included in the action; even though they may have been collected from a brothel, for brothels are kept on the premises of many reputable persons.

198. *Marriage and inheritance in Egypt. Alexandria, 2nd cent. A.D. (Berlin Papyrus 1210. Tr. J.G. Winter)*

> The *idiologus*, the chief financial officer of Roman Egypt, administered the imperial account, which consisted of funds acquired from means other than taxation (fines and confiscations, for example). The papyrus from which these extracts are taken contains a summary of the rules by which the *idiologus* carried out his duties. This document reveals fiscal oppression not only of women but of an entire province.

6. An Alexandrian, having no children by his wife, may not bequeath to her more than one quarter of his estate; if he does have children by her, her share may not exceed those of each son.

23. It is not permitted to Romans to marry their sisters or their aunts; it is permitted in the case of the daughter of brothers. Pardalas, however, confiscated the property when brothers and sisters married.

24. After death, the *fiscus*[20] takes the dowry given by a Roman woman over fifty to a Roman man under sixty.

26. And when a *Latina*[21] over fifty gives something to one over sixty it is likewise confiscated.

27. What is inherited by a Roman of sixty years, who has neither child nor wife, is confiscated. If he have a wife but no children and register himself, the half is conceded to him.

29. A free-born Roman woman who has an estate of 20,000 sesterces, so long as she is unmarried, pays a hundredth part annually; and a freedwoman who has an estate of 20,000 sesterces pays the same until she marries.

30. The inheritances left to Roman women possessing 50,000 sesterces, who are unmarried and childless, are confiscated.

31. It is permitted a Roman woman to leave her husband a tenth of her property; if she leaves more, it is confiscated.

32. Romans who have more than 100,000 sesterces, and are unmarried and childless, do not inherit; those who have less, do.

33. It is not permitted to a Roman woman to dispose of her property by will without a stipulated clause of the so-called *coemptio fiduciaria*.[22] A legacy by a Roman woman to a Roman woman who is a minor is confiscated.

38. The children of a woman who is a citizen of Alexandria and an Egyptian man remain Egyptians but inherit from both parents.

39. When a Roman man or a Roman woman marries a citizen of Alexandria or an Egyptian, without knowledge [of the true status], the children follow the lower class.

46. To Roman men and citizens of Alexandria who married Egyptian women without knowledge [of their true status] it was granted, in addition to freedom from responsibility, also that the children follow the father's station.

52. It is permitted Roman men to marry Egyptian women.

53. Egyptian women married to ex-soldiers come under the clause of misrepresentation if they characterise themselves in business transactions as Roman women.

54. Ursus did not allow an ex-soldier's daughter who had become a Roman citizen to inherit from her mother if the latter was an Egyptian.

199. *A final dowry payment. Egypt, A.D. 122. (P. Fam. Tebt. 21. Tr. M.R.L.)*

Affidavits about the receipt of a final dowry payment, made fifteen years after a first instalment of 500 drachmas. The text of the actual agreement[23] specifies that the woman is now 48, her cousin 52, her brothers 44 and 38, and her mother 75.

I, Didymarion, daughter of Heraclides, with my cousin Cronion son of Lusanius as guardian, agree that I have received from my brothers Valerius and Lysimachus 600 silver drachmas described under the terms of an agreement my father [made with them on my behalf], under the terms of which (a) I shall not bring suit against them for any transaction whatever made before the present day; (b) I have received the set of earrings (gold with genuine pearls weighing four quarters) and the cloak as specified. I, Cronion have written this on her behalf since she does not know letters.

I, Lysimachus son of Heraclides, and my mother Didyme daughter of Lysimachus on my authority testify that a receipt has been made out to me, Lysimachus, and to Valerius for 600 drachmas, and that my mother Didyme has made a present to her daughter Didymarion of earrings and a purple cloak, and that she guarantees that she will keep unassigned and unencumbered the half share of the house and courtyard in Tebtunis which she turned over to her. I, Lysimachus, have written this for her since she does not know letters.

200. *Dowry payment through a bank. Egypt, A.D. 143. (P. Mich. 6551. Tr. M.R.L.)*

The receipt of the dowry became the most important aspect of the marriage contract; hence the conclusion of the present agreement through the bank.[24]

Copy of a draft of the [bank at ...]. Year 7 of Imperator Caesar Titus Aelius Hadrianus Antoninus Augustus Pius, Hathyr 8, Chaeremonis daughter of N.N. granddaughter of Socrates with as guardian her relative Sarapion son of Seuthes to Pasion son of N.N.; [it is acknowledged] that he has received from Chaeremonis a dowry upon herself of forty silver drachmas and twenty drachmas of a white chiton. And they will live together with each other, Pasion supplying her with all that is necessary and with clothing as befits a married woman in proportion to his means; and when a separation takes place, Pasion will return to Chaeremonis the aforementioned dowry and the chiton in the same valuation.

201. *Legitimacy. Alexandria, 2nd cent. A.D. (P. Cattaoui 3, 4. Tr. M.R.L.)*

When Crotis argued through her lawyer Philoxenus that she was a citizen when she was living with Isidorus (who was a citizen) and that afterwards, when he had gone off to his regiment on campaign, she had by him a son Theodorus, who is the subject of her petition, that she neglected to file a birth certificate but that it was clear that the son was his because of his testament that he wrote down in which he made him heir of his estate. After the will of Julius Martial, [25] a soldier in the first Theban unit, was read, the judge Lupus conferred with his colleagues and stated: 'It is impossible for Martial to have a legitimate son while he was a soldier on campaign, but he was within the law when he made him an heir in his will.'

When Octavius Valens and Cassia Secunda came before the court in regard to one of the cases that had been postponed, the prefect Eudaemon, conferring with his court, stated: 'Yesterday also, the moment the transcript of the honourable Heliodorus was read and the reason why the case had been postponed had been explained, it was evident that the mother of this child was pleading about a forbidden matter, and today also I declare that I have reviewed the facts bearing on this issue and confirm what I maintained yesterday. When a man has entered the army, whether in a regiment or a tactical unit or in a company, a son born to him cannot be legitimate. Since he is not the lawful son of his father, who is an Alexandrian, he cannot be an

Alexandrian. This child was born to Valens when he was on campaign with his unit. He is his bastard son. He cannot be enrolled in the citizenry of Alexandria.' And he added: 'Yesterday you said that you had other children. How old are they? When were they born?' Octavius Valens answered: 'One was just born, the other is older.' Eudaemon said: 'The older one was born some time while you were in the army?' Valens answered: 'While I was with my regiments and so also was the younger child.' Eudaemon said: 'Realise that these children are in the same condition as your other son. Some things cannot be changed.' Valens said: 'But if it were necessary for me to be out of town on business, you yourself would order that I would receive justice through a trustee. How have these children behaved unjustly?' Eudaemon said: 'It was foolish of me to explain at length what I could have said briefly. Since you are attempting the impossible, neither this boy nor your other sons can be citizens of Alexandria.'

202. *A mother's last will and testament. Oxyrhynchus, A.D. 133. (SB X. 10756 (excerpts). Tr. M.R.L.)*

This is the will of Taarpaesis, being of sound mind, also called Isidora, daughter of Apollonius (son of Apollonius) and of Tsenamounis from the city of Oxyrhynchus, with her half-brother Apollon, son of Apollonius and Diogenis from the same city as guardian,[26] a public document ... I, Taarpaesis, also called Isidora, daughter of Apollonius, make my will as follows and leave after my death my children as executors, Ptolemaeus, Berenice, and Isidora (also called Apollonarion).

To Ptolemaeus: from my property in the city of Oxyrhynchus in the South Colonnade district, the house, atrium, courtyard, furnishings, entrances and exits; in the village of Phoboou, the walled lands in the sections from the west to the north, a fourth share of the garden, with the palm trees therein and plans and the well built of baked brick, with its furnishings and everything that belongs to it, and entrances and exits; and in the middle sections of that village my father's walled land, where there is a house and a hall, with entrances and exits, and near the same village. [*Here follow details of parcels of land, one of which she had inherited from her mother.*]

To Berenice and Isidora (also called Apollonarion), because of the agreement each of them has with her husband under the terms of which each keeps her own possessions; also under my will, share and share alike, from my property in front of Herais Teos and other places in the city of Oxyrhynchus in the same South Colonnade district, and half share of the house, atrium, and furnishings, entrances and exits; and in the village of Phoboou in the east section of my father's property a half share of the house and hall, with entrances and exits.

I leave to the son of my aforesaid first daughter Berenice, Eision son of Heraclides, one field, the property that I own near Ophis ...

All other property that I leave, furniture, equipment, household goods, accounts receivable, etc., go to Psenesis[27] who is also called Eision Ptolemaeus, if he survives me; if he does not, then to my aforesaid son Ptolemaeus. This aforesaid Psenesis (also called Eision) will have from the time that I die as long as he lives the income from and habitation of all property remaining to me after taxes, and when Psenesis (also called Eision) dies my daughter Berenice will have the income after taxes and the assignment of the one field to her son Eision. If Ptolemaeus and Isidora die without issue, it is my wish that whatever they leave of my possessions in Ptolemaeus' estate go to my two daughters Berenice and Isidora (also called Apollonarion) equally, and what is left in Isidora's (also called Apollonarion) estate go to Berenice if she survives, who should allow Psenesis (also called Eision) as long as he lives the income, habitation rights and furnishings previously assigned to him. I am satisfied with the preceding terms.

I am fifty-nine years of age, with a scar on the instep of my right foot, and my seal is Aphrodite's. I, Apollon, son of Apollonius and Diogenis, her half-brother, authorise my signature to the aforewritten ... I, Onnophrius son of Thonis, have written out the will on their behalf, since they do not know letters; I am about fifty-three years of age with a scar on my left foot. (*Witnesses.*)

1. This sacred marriage, known as *confarreatio*, was exclusively for patricians. The *pontifex maximus* and the chief priest of Jupiter (*flamen dialis*) were present along with ten witnesses. Only a very elaborate ceremony (*diffarreatio*) could dissolve the marriage. Other types of marriage, *conventio in manum* or *coemptio* and *usus*, existed in the early period. *Coemptio* placed the wife under the husband's power (*manus*, literally 'hand'), by a mock sale, as his chattel. Under *usus*, a wife could free herself from her husband's power by leaving his house for three nights of the year.

2. This most likely refers to contraception and abortion. Divorce for sterility appears to have been first allowed in 235 B.C. (Aulus Gellius, *Attic Nights* 17.21.44). During the Empire, when marriage by *usus* was the norm, divorce required only notification of one party by the other. Complex laws concerning the disposition of the dowry operated to prevent ill-considered divorce.

3. Repudiation (*repudium*, different from *divortium* which required mutual consent) involved a formula which included the words, 'Handle your own property for yourself' (*tuas res tibi habeto* or *agito*). Either the husband or the wife could repudiate the other. The dowry, managed by the husband during the marriage, returned to the wife when the marriage ended, whether by repudiation or divorce.

4. Twenty-five was a woman's age of majority, but not of independence. She remained under either her father's power (*potestas*) or her husband's (*manus*), or, lacking both, under that of a tutor (*tutela*). On vestal virgins, see below, no. 242.

5. In Roman civil law at this time the family is the agnatic, the father's side; the mother's side is called the cognate.

6. Boys 7-14, girls 7-12, and women who were not under a father's or husband's power.

7. Marcus Porcius Cato 'Censorius' – Cato the Elder (234-149 B.C.). He was the quintessential conservative and champion of traditional morality. Among his acts as censor in 184 B.C. was the taxation of luxury. He deplored and fought vainly against the acceptance of anything Greek into Roman life.

8. The magistrate whose jurisdiction included public morals and the leasing of public buildings and spaces.

9. In Romulus' day.

10. Consul in 166 B.C.

11. Consul in 268 B.C.

12. This refers particularly to purple, a very expensive dye obtained from certain shellfish. It was a sign of luxury. The togas of magistrates and wealthy youths (*togae praetextae*) were adorned with a purple stripe.

13. See above, note 7.

14. Cato's history of early Rome.

15. See above, notes 1, 4.

16. On the jurists and their writings, see A. Berger, *Encyclopedic Dictionary of Roman Law* (Trans. Am. Philos. Soc. n. s. 43. 2, Philadelphia 1953). For an interesting fictional account of Julia's exile and the events which led to it, see John Williams, *Augustus* (New York 1972).

17. Hand, marital power.

18. See above, note 1.

19. Bondage.

20. I.e. the exchequer.

21. I.e. a woman possessing Latin rights, halfway between those of aliens and those of citizens.

22. 'As to making a will ... women not only had to have guardian's authorisation but, until Hadrian, also had to go through a complicated rigmarole of changing guardians by *coemptio*.' J.A. Crook, *Law and Life of Rome* (London and Ithaca 1967), p. 120, Cf. above, p. 61 n. 8.

23. For a translation of the formal legal agreement, see *P. Fam. Tebt.* 22, pp. 76-7.

24. See P.J. Sijpesteijn, *ZPE* 34 (1979) 119-22.

25. The Latin name of Isidorus.

26. The name of a male guardian was regularly given in Greek-language contracts made by women, but not consistently in documents written in Egyptian demotic, at least in the Hellenistic age (cf. e.g., *P.Adl.* Gk. 7, 8 with *P.Adl.* dem. 3 in the late 2nd cent. B.C., but guardians in both the demotic text and Greek subscription in *P.Mich.* 253 in A.D. 30).

27. A close friend of the family.

XV

Politics

203. *Sempronia, a revolutionary. Rome, 1st cent. B.C. (Sallust, The Conspiracy of Catiline, 24-5. Tr. S.A. Handford)*

The historian Sallust regarded the conspiracy led by Catiline as a result of moral decline; in his account Catiline's supporter Sempronia egregiously lacks the qualities for which virtuous Roman matrons are celebrated, but possesses others.

Catiline is said to have gained many adherents of every condition, including a number of women who in their earlier days had lived extravagantly on money that they obtained by prostituting themselves, and then, when advancing age reduced their incomes without changing their luxurious tastes, had run headlong into debt. These women, he thought, would do good service by acting as agitators among the city slaves and organising acts of incendiarism; their husbands, too, could either be induced to join his cause, or be murdered.

Among their number was Sempronia, a woman who had committed many crimes that showed her to have the reckless daring of a man. Fortune had favoured her abundantly, not only with birth and beauty, but with a good husband and children.[1] Well educated in Greek and Latin literature, she had greater skill in lyre-playing and dancing than there is any need for a respectable woman to acquire, besides many other accomplishments such as minister to dissipation. There was nothing that she set a smaller value on than seemliness and chastity, and she was as careless of her reputation as she was of her money. Her passions were so ardent that she more often made advances to men than they did to her. Many times already she had broken a solemn promise, repudiated a debt by perjury, and been an accessory to murder. At once self-indulgent and impecunious, she had gone headlong from bad to worse. Yet her abilities were not to be despised. She could write poetry, crack a joke, and converse at will with decorum, tender feeling, or wantonness; she was in fact a woman of ready wit and considerable charm.

204. *Women's eloquence. Rome, 46 B.C. (Cicero, Brutus 58.211. Tr. M.B.F.)*

We have read the letters of Cornelia, mother of the Gracchi; it appears that her sons were brought up not so much at their mother's breast as by her speech. I often heard the speech of Laelia, Gaius' daughter; we saw that she was touched by her father's refinement and so were her two daughters, the Muciae, whose speech is also known to me, and I have heard both her granddaughters, the Liciniae, one of whom, the wife of Scipio, you, Brutus, I believe, have heard speak.

205. *Women advocates. 1st cent. A.D. (Valerius Maximus, Memorable Deeds and Sayings 8.3. Tr. M.B.F.)*

We must be silent no longer about those women whom neither the condition of their nature nor the cloak of modesty could keep silent in the Forum or the courts.

Amasia Sentia, a defendant, pled her case before a great crowd of people and Lucius Titius, the praetor who presided over the court.[2] She pursued every aspect of her defence diligently and boldly and was acquitted, almost unanimously, in a single hearing. Because she bore a man's spirit under the appearance of a woman, they called her *Androgyne*.

Gaia Afrania, the wife of the senator Licinius Buccio, a woman disposed to bring suits, always represented herself before the praetor: not because she had no advocates, but because her impudence was abundant. And so, by constantly plaguing the tribunals with such barking as the Forum had seldom heard, she became the best-known example of women's litigiousness. As a result, to charge a woman with low morals, it is enough to call her 'Gaia Afrania'. She prolonged her life until Caesar's second consulship[3] with Publius Servilius as his colleague; for it is better to record when such a monster died, rather than when it was born.

Hortensia, the daughter of Quintus Hortensius,[4] when the triumvirs burdened the matrons with a heavy tribute[5] and no man dared take their defence, pled their case before the triumvirs, both firmly and successfully. For by bringing back her father's eloquence, she brought about the remission of the greater part of the tax. Quintus Hortensius lived again in the female line and breathed in his daughter's words. If any of her male descendants had wished to follow her strength, the great heritage of Hortensian eloquence would not have come to an end in a woman's action.

206. *Hortensia's speech. Rome, 42 B.C. (Appian, Civil Wars 4. 32-4, 2nd cent. A.D. Tr. H. White (LCL))*

Appian wrote in Greek during the second century A.D. Thus, what follows is his own version of what Hortensia said, though it is known (see p. 235) that her speech was preserved and read many years after it was delivered.

Unable to raise enough money by selling the seized goods of the proscribed, the triumvirs, Octavian, Antony, and Lepidus, decided to take a different approach.

The triumvirs addressed the people on this subject and published an edict requiring 1,400 of the richest women to make a valuation of their property, and to furnish for the service of the war such portion as the triumvirs should require from each. It was provided further that if any should conceal their property or make a false valuation they should be fined, and that rewards should be given to informers, whether free persons or slaves. The women resolved to beseech the womenfolk of the triumvirs. With the sister of Octavian and the mother of Antony they did not fail, but they were repulsed from the doors of Fulvia, the wife of Antony, whose rudeness they could scarce endure. They then forced their way to the tribunal of the triumvirs in the Forum, the people and the guards dividing to let them pass. There, through the mouth of Hortensia, whom they had selected to speak, they spoke as follows:

'As befitted women of our rank addressing a petition to you, we had recourse to the ladies of your households; but having been treated as did not befit us, at the hands of Fulvia, we have been driven by her to the Forum. You have already deprived us of our fathers, our sons, our husbands, and our brothers, whom you accused of having wronged you; if you take away our property also, you reduce us to a condition unbecoming our birth, our manners, our sex. If we have done you wrong, as you say our husbands have, proscribe us as you do them. But if we women have not voted any of you public enemies, have not torn down your houses, destroyed your army, or led another one against you; if we have not hindered you in obtaining offices and honours, why do we share the penalty when we did not share the guilt?

'Why should we pay taxes when we have no part in the honours, the commands, the statecraft, for which you contend against each other with such harmful results? "Because this is a time of war," do you say? When have there not been wars, and when have taxes ever been imposed on women, who are exempted by their sex among all mankind? Our mothers did once rise superior to their sex and made contributions when you were in danger of losing the whole empire and the city itself through the conflict with the Carthaginians. But then they contributed voluntarily, not from their landed property, their fields, their dowries, or their houses, without which life is not possible to free women, but only from their own jewellery, and even these not according to fixed valuation, not under fear of informers or accusers, not by force and violence, but what they themselves were willing to give. What alarm is there now for the empire or the country? Let war with the Gauls or the Parthians come, and we shall not be inferior to our mothers in zeal for the common safety; but for civil wars may we never contribute, nor ever assist you against each other! We did not contribute to Caesar or to Pompey. Neither Marius nor Cinna imposed taxes upon us. Nor did Sulla, who held despotic power in the state, do so, whereas you say that you are re-establishing the commonwealth.'

While Hortensia thus spoke the triumvirs were angry that women should dare to hold a public meeting when the men were silent; that they should demand from magistrates the reasons for their acts, and themselves not so much as furnish money while the men were serving in the army. They ordered the lictors to drive them away from the tribunal, which they proceeded to do until cries were raised by the multitude outside, when the lictors desisted and the triumvirs said they would postpone till the next day the consideration of the matter. On the following day they reduced the number of women, who were to present a valuation of their property, from 1,400 to 400, and decreed that all men who possessed more than 100,000 denarii, both citizens and strangers, freedmen and priests, and men of all nationalities without a single exception, should (under the same dread of penalty and also of informers) lend them at interest a fiftieth part of their property and contribute one year's income to the war expenses.

In the following three texts, women admired for the traditional virtues of Roman matrons are credited with acts of moral and physical courage in the political arena.

207. *A funeral eulogy. Rome, 9 or 10 B.C. (CIL VI. 1527/ILS 8393 (abridged). Tr. D.C. Munro)*

A funeral eulogy by a husband for his wife of forty-one years, who saved him from proscription in 42 B.C. Attempts have been made to identify the woman with the Thuria described on p. 145, but her identity must remain unknown.

Before the day fixed for our marriage, you were suddenly left an orphan, by the murder of your parents in the solitude of the country ... Through your efforts chiefly, their death did not remain unavenged. For I had departed for Macedonia and C. Cluvius, your sister's husband, into the province of Africa.

So active were you in the performance of this pious duty, in searching out and insistently demanding the punishment [of the guilty] that, had we ourselves been present, we could not have done more. You share the credit for this with that pious woman, your sister.

While you were busy with these matters, to shield your honour, immediately after the punishment of the assassins you retired from your father's house to the home of your mother's sister, where you awaited my return ...

In our day, marriages of such long duration, not dissolved by divorce, but terminated by death alone, are indeed rare. For our union was prolonged in unclouded happiness for forty-one years. Would that it had been my lot to put an end to this our good fortune and that I as the older – which was more just – had yielded to fate.

Why recall your inestimable qualities, your modesty, deference, affability, your amiable disposition, your faithful attendance to the household duties, your enlightened religion, your unassuming elegance, the modest simplicity and refinement of your manners? Need I speak of your attachment to your kindred, your affection for your family – when you respected my mother as you did your own parents and cared for her tomb as you did for that of your own mother and father – you who share countless other virtues with Roman ladies most jealous of their fair name? These qualities which I claim for you are your own, equalled or excelled by but few; for the experience of men teaches us how rare they are.

With common prudence we have preserved all the patrimony which you received from your parents. Entrusting it all to me, you were not troubled with the care of increasing it; thus did we share the task of administering it, that I undertook to protect your fortune, and you to guard mine. On this point, I pass by many things in silence, for fear of attributing to myself a portion of your own deserts. Suffice it for me to indicate your sentiments.

You gave proof of your generosity not only towards several of your kin, but especially in your filial devotion ... You brought up in your own home, in the enjoyment of mutual benefits, some young girls of your kinship. And that these might attain to a station in life worthy of our family, you provided them with dowries. C. Cluvius and myself, by common accord, executed your intentions, and, approving of your generosity, in order that your patrimony might suffer no diminution, offered our own family possessions instead and gave up our personal property to provide the dowries, settled upon by you. This I relate, not to sing my own praises, but to show the unanimity of our counsels, that we held ourselves in honour bound to execute those obligations, incurred by you out of the fulness of your heart.

I owe you no less a debt than to Caesar Augustus himself, for this my return from exile to my native land. For unless you had prepared the way for my safety, even Caesar's promises of assistance had been of no avail. So I owe no less a debt to your loyal devotion than to the clemency of Caesar.

Why shall I now conjure up the memory of our domestic counsels and plans stored away in the hidden recesses of the heart? That, aroused by the sudden arrival of messages from you to a realisation of the present and imminent perils, I was saved by your counsel? That you suffered me not to be recklessly carried away by a foolish rashness, or that, when bent on more temperate plans, you provided for me a safe retreat, having as sharers in your plans for my safety, when an exile – fraught with danger as they were for you all – your sister and her husband, C. Cluvius. But I should not finish, were I to attempt to touch on all these matters. Suffice it for me, and for your memory, that the retreat provided by you ensured my safety.

I should confess, however, that on this occasion I suffered one of the bitterest experiences of my life, in the fate that befell you, much against my will. When the favour and permission of Caesar Augustus, then absent [from Rome], had restored me to my country, still a useful citizen perhaps, M. Lepidus, his colleague, then present in the city, interposed objections. Then prostrating yourself at his feet, he not only did not raise you up, but, dragged along and abused as though a common slave, your body all covered with bruises, yet with unflinching steadfastness of purpose, you recalled to him Caesar's edict [of pardon] and the letter of felicitation on my return, that accompanied it. Braving his taunts and suffering the most brutal treatment, you denounced these cruelties publicly so that he [Lepidus] was branded as the author of all my perils and misfortunes. And his punishment was not long delayed.

Could such courage remain without effect? Your unexampled patience furnished the occasion for Caesar's clemency, and, by guarding my life, he branded the infamous and savage cruelty [of the tyrant Lepidus] ...

When all the world was again at peace and the Republic re-established, peaceful and happy days followed. We longed for children, which an envious fate denied us. Had Fortune smiled on us in this, what had been lacking to complete our happiness? But an adverse destiny put an end to our hopes ... Disconsolate to see me without children ... you wished to put an end to my chagrin by proposing to me a divorce, offering to yield the place to another spouse more fertile, with the only intention of searching for and providing for me a spouse worthy of our mutual affection, whose children you assured me you would have treated as your own ... Nothing would have been changed, only you would have rendered to me henceforth the services of a devoted sister or mother-in-law.

I will admit that I was so irritated and shocked by such a proposition that I had difficulty in restraining my anger and remaining master of myself. You spoke of divorce before the decree of fate had forced us to separate, and I could not comprehend how you could conceive of any reason why you, still living, should not be my wife, you who during my exile had always remained most faithful and loyal ...

Would that our time of life had permitted our union to have endured until I, the older, had passed away, which was more just – and that you might perform for me the last sad rites and that I might have departed, leaving you behind, with a daughter to replace me at your side.

By fate's decree your course was run before mine. You left me the grief, the heartache, the longing for you, the sad fate to live alone ...

The conclusion of this discourse will be that you have deserved all, and that I remain with the chagrin of not being able to give you all. Your wishes have always been my supreme law; and whatever it will be permitted me to accord them still, in this I shall not fail.

May the gods, the Manes,[6] assure and protect your repose!

208. *Some examples of bravery. Rome, 1st cent. B.C. (Appian, Civil War 4. 39-40, 2nd cent. A.D. Tr. H. White. (LCL))*

According to Appian, the proscriptions of 43 B.C. – widespread judicial murders for political revenge and financial gain – produced remarkable examples of wives' love for their husbands.

Acilius fled from the city secretly. His hiding-place was disclosed by a slave to the soldiers, but he prevailed upon them, by the hope of a larger reward, to send some of their number to his wife with a private token that he gave them. When they came she gave them all of her jewellery, saying that she gave it in return for what they had promised, although she did not know whether they would keep their agreement. But her fidelity to her husband was not disappointed, for the soldiers hired a ship for Acilius and saw him off to Sicily. The wife of Lentulus asked that she might accompany him in his flight and kept watch upon his movements for that purpose, but he was not willing that she should share his danger, and fled secretly to Sicily. Being appointed praetor there by Pompeius he sent word to her that he was saved and elevated to office. When she learned in what part of the earth her husband was she escaped with two slaves from her mother, who was keeping watch over her. With these she travelled in the guise of a slave, with great hardship and the meanest fare, until she was able to make the passage from Rhegium to Messana about nightfall. She learned without difficulty where the praetor's tent was, and there she found Lentulus, not in the

attitude of a praetor, but on a low pallet with unkempt hair and
wretched food, mourning for his wife.

The wife of Apuleius threatened that if he should fly without her,
she would give information against him. So he took her with him
unwillingly, and he succeeded in avoiding suspicion in his flight by
travelling with his wife and his male and female slaves in a public
manner. The wife of Antius wrapped him up in a clothes-bag and gave
the bundle to some porters to carry from the house to the sea-shore,
whence he made his escape to Sicily. The wife of Rheginus concealed
him by night in a sewer, into which the soldiers were not willing to enter
in the daytime, on account of the foul odour. The next night she
disguised him as a charcoal dealer, and furnished him an ass to drive,
carrying coals. She led the way at a short distance, borne in a litter. One
of the soldiers at the city gates suspected the litter and searched it.
Rheginus was alarmed and hastened his steps, and as if he were a
passer-by admonished the soldier not to give trouble to women. The
latter, who took him for a charcoal dealer, answered him angrily, but
suddenly recognising him (for he had served under him in Syria), said,
'Go on your way rejoicing, general, for such I ought still to call you.' The
wife of Coponius purchased his safety from Antony, although she had
previously been chaste, thus curing one evil with another.

209. *Fannia. A.D. 107 (Pliny the Younger, Letters 7. 19. Tr. B. Radice)*

I am very worried about Fannia's illness. She contracted it while nursing
Junia, one of the vestal virgins, a duty she undertook voluntarily at first
(Junia being a relative of hers) and then by order of the priests. (For
when sickness compels the virgins to leave the hall of Vesta, they are
always committed to the care of some married women.) This service
Fannia was faithfully performing when she fell a victim to her present
illness. Her fever never leaves her, her cough grows worse, and she is
painfully thin and weak. There remain only the courage and the spirit
worthy of her husband Helvidius and her father Thrasea.[7] In every other
way she is failing, and my anxiety on her behalf is coupled with grief,
grief that so great a woman will be lost to the sight of her country when
her like may not be seen again: such are her purity and integrity, her
nobility and loyal heart. Twice she followed her husband into exile, and
a third time was banished herself on his account.[8] For when Senecio was
on trial for having written a life of Helvidius, and said in his defence that
he had done so at Fannia's request, Mettius Carus then demanded in a
threatening tone if this was true. She replied that it was. Had she lent
Senecio her husband's diaries? 'Yes.' Did her mother know of this?[9]
'No.' Not a word in fact did she utter through fear of danger. Moreover,

although the senate was driven through fear of the times to order the destruction of the books in question, she managed to save them when her possessions were confiscated, and took them with her into the exile they had caused.

At the same time she has such friendliness and charm, the rare gift, in fact, of being able to inspire affection as well as respect. Will there be anyone now whom we can hold up as a model to our wives, from whose courage even our own sex can take example, and whom we can admire as much as the heroines of history while she is still in our midst? To me it seems as though her whole house is shaken to its very foundations and is tottering to its fall, even though she may leave descendants; for how can their deeds and merits be sufficient to assure that the last of her line has not perished in her?

A further and more personal pain and grief for me is my feeling that I am losing her mother again – to whom I can pay no higher tribute than by calling her the famous mother of a great woman. The mother was restored to us in her daughter, but soon will be taken away with her, leaving me the pain of a re-opened wound to bear as well as this fresh blow. I honoured and loved them both – I cannot say which the more, nor did they wish a distinction to be drawn. My services were at their command alike in prosperity and adversity; I was their comfort in exile and their champion after their return. I could never make them an adequate return, and so I am all the more anxious for Fannia's life to be spared to give me time to pay my debt. These are my troubles at the time of writing to you; but, if one of the gods will turn them to joy, I shall make no complaint about my present fears.

210. *Electioneering. Pompeii, 1st cent. A.D. (CIL IV. 207; 171/ILS 6431a; 913; 3291/ILS 6415; 1083; 6610; 3678/ILS 6414; 3684; 3527/ILS 6408a. Tr. J.C. Fant)*

> Although women, of course, could not vote, the frequency with which their names appear in the electoral graffiti of Pompeii indicates that they took a lively interest in local politics, endorsing candidates publicly with or without husbands or male associates.

207. Nymphodotus, along with Caprasia, asks you to vote for Marcus Cerrinius Vatia for the aedileship.

171. Caprasia along with Nymphius – her neighbours too – ask you to vote for Aulus Vettius Firmus for the aedileship; he is worthy of the office.

> Caprasia was probably the proprietor of the wine shop on which the second *programma* was painted. Nymphodotus was most likely a retainer of the Helvian family, on whose house the first notice appeared.

913. Amandio, along with his wife, asks you to vote for Gnaeus Helvius Sabinus for aedile; he is worthy of public office.

3291. Pyramus, Olympionica and Calvus ask your support for Marcus Casellius Marcellus.

A notice put up by Pyramus for the same candidate has been found in another part of the city. Were these three partisans campaign workers, or did they just work at the same bakery around the corner?

1083. Recepta, not without Thalamus, asks that you make Gnaeus Helvius Sabinus aedile and Lucius Ceius Secundus duovir.

6610. Epidia, not without Cosmus, asks you to vote for Marcus Samellius for aedile.

3678. Statia and Petronia ask you to vote for Marcus Casellius and Lucius Alfucius for aediles. May our colony always have such citizens!

3684. Statia asks you to vote for Herennius and Suettius for the aedileship.

We cannot know whether the Statias are one and the same woman.

3527. Appuleia and Narcissus, along with their neighbour Mustius, ask you to vote for Pupius for the aedileship.

1. Her husband was Decimus Junius Brutus, consul in 77 B.C. Her son, Decimus Brutus, was one of the assassins of Julius Caesar.
2. In 77 B.C.
3. 48 B.C.
4. Quintus Hortensius Hortalus (114-50 B.C.) was one of the Republic's most famous orators. He was consul in 69 B.C., and was a great forensic rival of Cicero.
5. 42 B.C. The triumvirs, Octavian, Antony and Lepidus, levied this tax to help pay for the war against Brutus and Cassius.
6. Spirits of the dead or gods of the underworld.
7. Fannia was the second wife of Helvidius Priscus, a fervent Stoic and a member, along with Thrasea Paetus, of the 'Stoic opposition' to Nero. Cf. p. 143.
8. The first occasion was in A.D. 66 because of his association with Thrasea. He was able to return after Nero died, and he became praetor in 70. Vespasian relegated him for his opposition, and he was killed outside Italy, possibly by order of the Emperor Titus. See A. N. Sherwin-White, *The Letters of Pliny* (Oxford 1966) 424-5.
9. None the less did Arria accompany her daughter into exile.

XVI

Medicine

211. *Comparison of male and female anatomy. Pergamum, 2nd cent. A.D.*
(Galen, On the Usefulness of the Parts of the Body 14. 6-7 (excerpts). Tr.
M.T. May)

Galen, born and educated in Pergamum, the great Hellenistic seat of
learning in Asia Minor, was philosopher, physician and eclectic dogmatist.
He began his career as a gladiators' doctor, but eventually became physician
to the Emperor Marcus Aurelius. His pathology was speculative and
based on the doctrine that health depended on the balance of the four
humours (black bile, yellow bile, blood and phlegm). His reliance on
philosophical premise and astrological prognostication has little
connection with modern scientific technique. Some of his anatomical
conclusions are based on inaccurate comparisons between animals, which
he dissected, and humans, whom he did not. But he made significant
contributions to diagnosis and prognosis.[1]

The female is less perfect than the male for one, principal reason –
because she is colder, for if among animals the warm one is the more
active, a colder animal would be less perfect than a warmer. A second
reason is one that appears in dissecting ...

All the parts, then, that men have, women have too, the difference
between them lying in only one thing, which must be kept in mind
throughout the discussion, namely, that in women the parts are within
[the body], whereas in men they are outside, in the region called the
perineum. Consider first whichever ones you please, turn outward the
woman's, turn inward, so to speak and fold double the man's, and you
will find them the same in both in every respect. Then think first, please,
of the man's turned in and extending inward between the rectum and
the bladder. If this should happen, the scrotum would necessarily take
the place of the uteri, with the testes lying outside, next to it on either
side; the penis of the male would become the neck of the cavity that had
been formed; and the skin at the end of the penis, now called the
prepuce, would become the female pudendum [the vagina] itself. Think
too, please of the converse, the uterus turned outward and projecting.
Would not the testes [the ovaries] then necessarily be inside it? Would it

not contain them like a scrotum? Would not the neck [the cervix], hitherto concealed inside the perineum but now pendent, be made into the male member? And would not the female pudendum, being a skin-like growth upon this neck, be changed into the part called the prepuce? It is also clear that in consequence the position of the arteries, veins, and spermatic vessels [the ductus deferentes and Fallopian tubes] would be changed too. In fact, you could not find a single male part left over that had not simply changed its position; for the parts that are inside in woman are outside in man. You can see something like this in the eyes of the mole, which have vitreous and crystalline humours and the tunics that surround these and grow out from the meninges, as I have said, and they have these just as much as animals do that make use of their eyes. The mole's eyes, however, do not open, nor do they project but are left there imperfect and remain like the eyes of other animals when these are still in the uterus ...

So too the woman is less perfect than the man in respect to the generative parts. For the parts were formed within her when she was still a foetus, but could not because of the defect in the heat emerge and project on the outside, and this, though making the animal itself that was being formed less perfect than one that is complete in all respects, provided no small advantage for the race; for there needs must be a female. Indeed, you ought not to think that our creator would purposely make half the whole race imperfect and, as it were, mutilated, unless there was to be some great advantage in such a mutilation.

Let me tell what this is. The foetus needs abundant material both when it is first constituted and for the entire period of growth that follows. Hence it is obliged to do one of two things; it must either snatch nutriment away from the mother herself or take nutriment that is left over. Snatching it away would be to injure the generant, and taking left over nutriment would be impossible if the female were perfectly warm; for if she were, she would easily disperse and evaporate it. Accordingly, it was better for the female to be made enough colder so that she cannot disperse all the nutriment which she concocts and elaborates ... This is the reason why the female was made cold, and the immediate consequence of this is the imperfection of the parts, which cannot emerge on the outside on account of the defect in the heat, another very great advantage for the continuance of the race. For, remaining within, that which would have become the scrotum if it had emerged on the outside was made into the substance of the uteri, an instrument fitted to receive and retain the semen and to nourish and perfect the foetus.

Forthwith, of course, the female must have smaller, less perfect testes, and the semen generated in them must be scantier, colder, and wetter (for these things too follow of necessity from the deficient heat). Certainly such semen would be incapable of generating an animal, and, since it too has not been made in vain, I shall explain in the course of my discussion what its use is: The testes of the male are as much larger as he is the warmer animal. The semen generated in them, having received the peak of concoction, becomes the efficient principle of the animal. Thus, from one principle devised by the creator in his wisdom, that principle in accordance with which the female has been made less perfect than the male, have stemmed all these things useful for the generation of the animal: that the parts of the female cannot escape to the outside; that she accumulates an excess of useful nutriment and has imperfect semen and a hollow instrument to receive the perfect semen; that since everything in the male is the opposite [of what it is in the female], the male member has been elongated to be most suitable for coitus and the excretion of semen; and that his semen itself has been made thick, abundant, and warm ...

It is clear that the left testis in the male and the left uterus in the female receive blood still uncleansed, full of residues, watery and serous, and so it happens that the temperaments of the instruments themselves that receive [the blood] become different. For just as pure blood is warmer than blood full of residues, so too the instruments on the right side, nourished with pure blood, become warmer than those on the left ... Moreover, if this has been demonstrated and it has been granted that the male is warmer than the female, it is no longer at all unreasonable to say that the parts on the right produce males and those on the left, females. In fact, that is what Hippocrates meant when he said, 'At puberty, whichever testis appears on the outside, the right, a male, the left, a female.'[2] That is to say, when the generative parts first swell out and the voice becomes rougher and deeper – for this is what puberty is – Hippocrates bids us observe which of the parts is the stronger; for of course, those that swell out first and have a greater growth are the stronger.

212. *Pregnancy. Rome, 1st cent. A.D. (Pliny the Elder, Natural History 7. 38-43, 48-51. Tr. H. Rackham (LCL))*

While pursuing the public career of a Roman knight, which culminated in command of the fleet at Misenum, Pliny wrote on many and varied subjects. His only surviving work, the *Natural History*, consists of thirty-six books on the arts and sciences. Pliny casts a wide net in gathering his scientific 'facts'.

All the other animals have a fixed season for copulation and for bearing offspring, but human reproduction takes place all the year round and the period of gestation varies – in one case it may exceed six months, in another seven, and it may even exceed ten; a child born before the seventh month is usually still born. Only those conceived the day before or the day after a full moon, or when there is no moon, are born in the seventh month. It is a common thing in Egypt for children to be born even in the eighth month; and indeed in Italy also for such cases to live, contrary to the belief of old times. These matters vary in more ways also. Vistilia the wife of Glitius and subsequently of Pomponius and of Orfitius, citizens of the highest distinction, bore these husbands four children, in each case after six months' pregnancy, but subsequently gave birth to Suillius Rufus after ten months and Corbulo after six – both of these became consuls – and subsequently bore Caesonia, the consort of the Emperor Gaius, after seven months. Infants born in this number of months are weakest in health during the first six weeks, the mothers in the fourth and eighth months of pregnancy; and abortions in these cases are fatal. Masurius states that Lucius Papirius as praetor in a suit for an estate brought by an heir presumptive gave judgment for the defendant; the plaintiff's case was that the heir apparent's mother said that he had been born after thirteen months' pregnancy, and the ground for the judgment was that there appeared to be no fixed period of pregnancy.

On the tenth day from conception pains in the head, giddiness and dim sight, distaste for food, and vomiting are symptoms of the formation of the embryo. If the child is a male, the mother has a better colour and an easier delivery; there is movement in the womb on the fortieth day. In a case of the other sex all the symptoms are the opposite: the burden is hard to carry, there is a slight swelling of the legs and groin, but the first movement is on the ninetieth day. But in the case of both sexes the greatest amount of faintness occurs when the embryo begins to grow hair; and also at the full moon, which period is also specially inimical to infants after birth. The gait in walking and every thing that can be mentioned are so important during pregnancy that mothers eating food that is too salt bear children lacking nails, and that not holding the breath makes the delivery more difficult; indeed to gape during delivery may cause death, just as a sneeze following copulation causes abortion.[3]

One feels pity and even shame in realizing how trivial is the origin of the proudest of the animals, when the smell of lamps being put out usually causes abortion! ...

Few animals except woman ever have sexual intercourse when pregnant – at all events superfetation only occurs with animals in very few cases. In the records of the medical profession and of writers who have been interested in collecting such occurrences, there is a case of miscarriage in which twelve infants were still-born at once. When, however, a moderate interval of time separates two conceptions, both may be successful, as was seen in the instance of Hercules and his brother Iphicles and in the case of the woman who bore twins of whom one resembled her husband the other an adulterer; and also in that of the maidservant of Marmara who, as a result of intercourse on the same day, bore one twin resembling her master and another resembling his steward, and that of another woman who bore one twin at the proper period and the other a five-months' child, and again of another who after bearing a seven months' child was delivered of twins three months later.

It is also well known that sound parents may have deformed children and deformed parents sound children or children with the same deformity, as the case may be; that some marks and moles and even scars reappear in the offspring, in some cases a birthmark on the arm reappearing in the fourth generation (we are told that in the Lepidus family three children were born, though not all in succession, with a membrane over the eyes); and indeed that other children have resembled their grandfather, and that also there has been a case of twins of which one resembled the father and the other the mother, and one of a child who resembled his brother like a twin although born a year later. Also that some women always bear children like themselves, some bear children like their husbands, some children with no family likeness, some a female child like its father and a male child like themselves.

213. *Menstruation, conception, contraception and abortion. Rome, 1st cent. A.D. (Soranus, Gynaecology 1. 24, 26, 34, 36, 39, 40, 60, 61, 64. Tr. O. Temkin)*

Soranus, a Greek from Ephesus in Asia Minor who practised in Rome, approaches his topic with more sympathy and common sense than his colleagues, and, unlike other practitioners, includes in his account of gynaecology all aspects of the female reproductive system, normal as well as abnormal.

Menstruation

24. One has to infer approaching menstruation from the fact that at the expected time of the period it becomes trying to move and there develops heaviness of the loins, sometimes pain as well, sluggishness, continual yawning, and tension of the limbs, sometimes also a flush of the cheeks which either remains or, having been dispersed, reappears after an interval; and in some cases approaching menstruation must be inferred from the fact that the stomach is prone to nausea and it lacks appetite. Menstruation which is about to occur for the first time must be inferred from the same signs but above all from the growth of the breasts which, broadly, takes place around the fourteenth year, and from the heaviness, irritation and pubescence in the region of the lower abdomen.

26. In women who have already menstruated often, each must be allowed to do according to her own custom. For some habitually take a rest, while others go on with moderate activities. But it is safer to rest and not to bathe especially on the first day. But in women who are about to menstruate no longer, their time for menstruation having passed, one must take care that the stoppage of the menses does not occur suddenly. For in regard to alteration, even if the body be changed for the better, all abruptness disturbs it through discomfort; for that which is unaccustomed is not tolerated, but is like some unfamiliar malaise. The methods we employ at the approach of the first menstruation must now be marshalled forth during the time when menstruation is about to cease; for that which is able to evoke the as yet absent excretion is even more able to preserve for some time menstruation which is still present. In addition, vaginal suppositories capable of softening and injections which have the [same] effect should be employed, together with all the remedies capable of rendering hardened bodies soft. But if the menstruation is too much for the strength of the patient, or again, if it is impeded by abnormal factors, then there is need for therapeutic measures which we shall elaborate in the section on 'things abnormal'.

Conception

34. One must judge the majority from the ages of fifteen to forty to be fit for conception, if they are not mannish, compact, and oversturdy, or too flabby and very moist. Since the uterus is similar to the whole [body], it will in these cases either be unable, on account of its pronounced hardness, easily to accept the attachment of the seed, or by reason of its extreme laxity and atony [let it fall again]. Furthermore they seem fit if their uteri are neither very moist or dry, nor too lax or constricted, and if they have their catharsis regularly, not through some moisture or ichors of various kinds, but through blood and of this neither too much nor, on the other hand, extremely little. Also those in whom the orifice of the uterus is comparatively far forward and lies in a straight line (for an orifice deviated even in its natural state and lying farther back in the vagina, is less suited for the attraction and acceptance of the seed).

36. The best time for fruitful intercourse is when menstruation is ending and abating, when urge and appetite for coitus are present, when the body is neither in want nor too congested and heavy from drunkenness and indigestion, and after the body has been rubbed down and a little food been eaten and when a pleasant state exists in every respect. (1) 'When menstruation is ending and abating,' for the time before menstruation is not suitable, the uterus already being overburdened and in an unresponsive state because of the ingress of

material and incapable of carrying on two motions contrary to each other, one for the excretion of material, the other for receiving.

39. (2) In order that the offspring may not be rendered misshapen, women must be sober during coitus because in drunkenness the soul becomes the victim of strange fantasies; this furthermore, because the offspring bears some resemblance to the mother as well not only in body but in soul ...

40. (3) Together with these points it has already been stated that the best time is after a rubdown has been given and a little food been eaten. The food will give the inner turbulence an impetus towards coitus, the urge for intercourse not being diverted by appetite for food; while the rubdown will make it possible to lay hold of the injected seed more readily. For just as the rubdown naturally aids the distribution of food, it helps also in the reception and retention of the seed, yesterday's superfluities, as one may say, being unloaded, and the body thoroughly cleansed and in a sound state for its natural processes. Consequently, as the farmer sows only after having first cleansed the soil and removed any foreign material, in the same manner we too advise that insemination for the production of man should follow after the body has first been given a rubdown.

Contraception

60. A contraceptive differs from an abortive, for the first does not let conception take place, while the latter destroys what has been conceived ... And an expulsive some people say is synonymous with an abortive; others, however, say that there is a difference because an expulsive does not mean drugs but shaking and leaping ... For this reason they say that Hippocrates, although prohibiting abortives, yet in his book 'On the Nature of the Child' employs leaping with the heels to the buttocks for the sake of expulsion.[4] But a controversy has arisen. For one party banishes abortives, citing the testimony of Hippocrates who says: 'I will give to no one an abortive'; moreover, because it is the specific task of medicine to guard and preserve what has been engendered by nature. The other party prescribes abortives, but with discrimination, that is, they do not prescribe them when a person wishes to destroy the embryo because of adultery or out of consideration for youthful beauty; but only to prevent subsequent danger in parturition if the uterus is small and not capable of accommodating the complete development, or if the uterus at its orifice has knobbly swelling and fissures, or if some similar difficulty is involved. And they say the same about contraceptives as well, and we too agree with them. And since it is safer to prevent conception from taking place than to destroy the foetus, we shall now first discourse upon such prevention.

61. For if it is much more advantageous not to conceive than to destroy the embryo, one must consequently beware of having sexual intercourse at those periods which we said were suitable for conception. And during the sexual act, at the critical moment of coitus when the man is about to discharge the seed, the woman must hold her breath and draw herself away a little, so that the seed may not be hurled too deep into the cavity of the uterus. And getting up immediately and squatting down, she should induce sneezing and carefully wipe the vagina all round; she might even drink something cold. It also aids in preventing conception to smear the orifice of the uterus all over before with old olive oil or honey or cedar resin or juice of the balsam tree, alone or together with white lead; or with a moist cerate containing myrtle oil and white lead; or before the act with moist alum, or with galbanum together with wine; or to put a lock of fine wool into the orifice of the uterus; or, before sexual relations to use vaginal suppositories which have the power to contract and to condense. For such of these things as are styptic, clogging and cooling cause the orifice of the uterus to shut before the time of coitus and do not let the seed pass into its fundus. [Such, however, as are hot] and irritating not only do not allow the seed of the man to remain in the cavity of the uterus, but draw forth as well another fluid from it.

62. And we shall make specific mention of some. Pine bark, tanning sumach, equal quantitites of each, rub with wine and apply in due measure before coitus after wool has been wrapped around; and after two or three hours she may remove it and have intercourse. Another: Of Cimolian earth, root of panax, equal quantities, rub with water separately and together, and when sticky apply in like manner. Or: Grind the inside of fresh pomegranate peel with water, and apply. Or: Grind two parts of pomegranate peel and one part of oak galls, form small suppositories and insert after the cessation of menstruation. Or: Moist alum, the inside of pomegranate rind, mix with water, and apply with wool. Or: Of unripe oak galls, of the inside of pomegranate peel, of ginger, of each 2 drachms, mould it with wine to the size of vetch peas and dry indoors and give before coitus, to be applied as a vaginal suppository. Or: Grind the flesh of dried figs and apply together with natron. Or: Apply pomegranate peel with an equal amount of gum and an equal amount of oil of roses. Then one should always follow with a drink of honey water. But one should beware of things which are very pungent, because of the ulcerations arising from them. And we use all these things after the end of menstruation ...

Abortion

64. In order that the embryo be separated, the woman should have [more violent exercise], walking about energetically and being shaken by

means of draught animals; she should also leap energetically and carry things which are heavy beyond her strength. She should use diuretic decoctions which also have the power to bring on menstruation, and empty and purge the abdomen with relatively pungent clysters; sometimes using warm and sweet olive oil as injections, sometimes anointing the whole body thoroughly therewith and rubbing it vigorously, especially around the pubes, the abdomen, and the loins, bathing daily in sweet water which is not too hot, lingering in the baths and drinking first a little wine and living on pungent food. If this is without effect, one must also treat locally by having her sit in a bath of a decoction of linseed, fenugreek, mallow, marsh mallow, and wormwood. She must also use poultices of the same substances and have injections of old oil, alone or together with rue juice or maybe with honey, or of iris oil, or of absinthium together with honey, or of panax balm or else of spelt together with rue and honey, or of Syrian unguent. And if the situation remains the same she must no longer apply the common poultices, but those made of meal of lupines together with ox bile and absinthium, [and she must use] plasters of a similar kind.

65. For a woman who intends to have an abortion, it is necessary for two or even three days beforehand to take protracted baths, little food and to use softening vaginal suppositories; also to abstain from wine; then to be bled and a relatively great quantity taken away. For the dictum of Hippocrates in the *Aphorisms*, even if not true in a case of constriction, is yet true of a healthy woman: 'A pregnant woman if bled, miscarries.' For just as sweat, urine or faeces are excreted if the parts containing these substances slacken very much, so the foetus falls out after the uterus dilates. Following the venesection one must shake her by means of draught animals (for now the shaking is more effective on the parts which previously have been relaxed) and one must use softening vaginal suppositories. But if a woman reacts unfavourably to venesection and is languid, one must first relax the parts by means of hip-baths, full baths, softening vaginal suppositories, by keeping her on water and limited food, and by means of aperients and the application of a softening clyster; afterwards one must apply an abortive vaginal suppository. Of the latter one should choose those which are not too pungent, that they may not cause too great a sympathetic reaction and heat. And of the more gentle ones there exist for instance: Of myrtle, wallflower seed, bitter lupines equal quantities, by means of water, mould troches the size of a bean. Or: Of rue leaves 3 drachms, of myrtle 2 drachms and the same of sweet bay, mix with wine in the same way, and give her a drink. Another vaginal suppository which produces abortion with relatively little danger: Of wallflower, cardamom, brimstone, absinthium, myrrh, equal quantities, mould with water. And she who intends to apply these things should be bathed beforehand or made to relax by hip-baths; and if after some time she brings forth

nothing, she should again be relaxed by hip-baths and for the second time a suppository should be applied. In addition, many different things have been mentioned by others; one must, however, beware of things that are too powerful and of separating the embryo by means of something sharp-edged, for danger arises that some of the adjacent parts be wounded. After the abortion one must treat as for inflammation.

214. *Childbirth: instructions for the midwife. Rome, 1st cent. A.D. (Soranus 1. 67-9 (excerpts). Tr. M.R.L.)*

For normal childbirth have the following ready: oil for injections and cleansing, hot water in order to wash the affected area, hot compresses to relieve the labour pains, sponges for sponging off, wool for covering the woman's body, and bandages to swaddle the baby in, a pillow so that the infant may be placed on it below the mother until the afterbirth has been taken away; scents, such as pennyroyal, sparganium, barley groats and quince, and if in season citron, or melon and anything similar to these, for the recovery of the mother's strength; a birthing stool so that the mother may be arranged on it ... a wide space in a crescent shape must be cut out in it [of a size appropriate] ... to prevent the woman from being pulled down beyond her thighs because the opening is too great, and on the contrary to prevent her from having her vagina pressured by its being too narrow (which is a greater problem); ... two couches, the one made up with soft coverings for rest after giving birth, the other hard for lying down on between labour pains ... When the mouth of the womb is open, and the midwife has washed her hands with hot oil, she should put in her forefinger (with the nail cut) of her left hand, and by gently drawing it arrange the opening so that the accessible part of the amniotic sac falls forward, and with her right hand she should apply oil to the area ... When the amniotic sac takes the size of an egg beneath the mouth of the womb, if the mother is weak and tense, one must deliver her while she is lying down there because this method is less disturbing and frightening ... Three women should stay ready who are able gently to calm the fears of the woman who is giving birth, even if they do not happen to have experience in childbirth. Two should stand on the sides, and one behind her so that the mother does not lean sideways because of the pain. If no birthing stool is available the same arrangement can be made if she sits on a woman's lap ... Finally the midwife, with her dress belted up high in an orderly way should sit down below beneath and opposite the mother ...

The midwife should then sit holding her thighs apart and with her left thigh leaning to support her left hand, in front of the mother as previously specified ... Then it is good for the midwife to be able to see the face of the mother, so she can calm her fears and assure her that there is nothing to worry about and that the childbirth is going well ... The midwife should guard against holding her face towards the mother's lap, lest she in modesty pull her body up; instead she should circle round the mouth of the womb with her finger ...[5] She should order the other woman who is holding her from behind to hold the mother's anus with a linen cloth, lest it be pushed out with her straining. If indeed the amniotic sac remains unbroken for a long time, she should break it with her fingernails and put her fingers in it and little by little open it wider. She should take care that the infant not fall out at once ... the helpers standing on the side, without shaking her and with open hands should bring the uterus downwards. When the infant tries to come out, the midwife should have a cloth in her hands to pick him up.

215. *The wandering womb. Cappadocia, 2nd cent. A.D. (Aretaeus, On the Causes and Symptoms of Acute Diseases 2 (excerpt). Tr. F. Adams)*

Aretaeus of Cappadocia, a contemporary of Galen, accepts the basic Hippocratic doctrines about hysteria but adds dramatic analogy to his account.

In the middle of the flanks of women lies the womb, a female viscus, closely resembling an animal; for it is moved of itself hither and thither in the flanks, also upwards in a direct line to below the cartilage of the thorax, and also obliquely to the right or to the left, either to the liver or spleen; and it likewise is subject to prolapsus downwards, and, in a word, it is altogether erratic. It delights, also, in fragrant smells, and advances towards them; and it has an aversion to fetid smells, and flees from them; and, on the whole, the womb is like an animal within an animal.

When, therefore, it is suddenly carried upwards, and remains above for a considerable time, and violently compresses the intestines, the woman experiences a choking, after the form of epilepsy, but without convulsions. For the liver, diaphragm, lungs and heart are quickly squeezed within a narrow space; and therefore loss of breathing and of speech seems to be present. And, moreover, the carotids are compressed from sympathy with the heart, and hence there is heaviness of head, loss of sensibility, and deep sleep.

And in women there also arises another affection resembling this form, with sense of choking and loss of speech, but not proceeding from the womb; for it also happens to men, in the manner of catalepsy. But those from the uterus are remedied by fetid smells, and the application of fragrant things to the female parts; but in the others these things do no good; and the limbs are moved about in the affection from the womb, but in the other affection not at all. Moreover, voluntary and involuntary tremblings ... but from the application of a pessary to induce abortion, powerful congelation of the womb, the stoppage of a copious haemorrhage, and such like.

If, therefore, upon the womb's being moved upwards, she begin to suffer: there is sluggishness in the performance of her offices, prostration of strength, atony, loss of the faculties of her knees, vertigo (and the limbs sink under her), headache, heaviness of the head, and the woman is pained in the veins on each side of the nose.

But if they fall down they have heartburn ... in the hypochondriac regions; flanks empty, where is the seat of the womb; pulse intermittent, irregular, and failing; strong sense of choking; loss of speech and of sensibility; respiration imperceptible and indistinct; a very sudden and incredible death, for they have nothing deadly in their appearance; in colour like that of life, and for a considerable time after death they are more ruddy than usual; eyes somewhat prominent, bright, not entirely fixed, but yet not very much turned aside.

But if the uterus be removed back to its seat before the affection come to a conclusion, they escape the suffocation. When the belly rumbles there is moisture about the female parts, respiration thicker and more distinct, a very speedy rousing up from the affection, in like manner as death is very sudden; for as it readily ascends to the higher regions, so it readily recedes. For the uterus is buoyant, but the membranes, its supporters, are humid, and the place is humid in which the uterus lies; and, moreover, it flees from fetid things, and seeks after sweet; wherefore it readily inclines to this side and to that, like a log of wood, and floats upwards and downwards. For this reason the affection occurs in young women, but not in old. For in those in whom the age, mode of life, and understanding is more mobile, the uterus also is of a wandering nature; but in those more advanced in life, the age, mode of living, understanding, and the uterus are of a steady character. Wherefore this suffocation from the womb accompanies females alone.

But the affections common to men happen also to the uterus, such as inflammation and haemorrhage, and they have the common symptoms, namely, fever, asphyxia, coldness, loss of speech. But in haemorrhage the death is even more sudden, being like that of a slaughtered animal.

216. *Inflammation of the womb. Cappadocia, 2nd cent. A.D. (Aretaeus, Therapeutics of Acute Diseases 2.11 (excerpt). Tr. F. Adams)*

The uterus in women has membranes extended on both sides at the flanks, and also is subject to the affections of an animal in smelling; for it follows after fragrant things as if for pleasure and flees from fetid and disagreeable things as if for dislike. If, therefore, anything annoy it from above, it protrudes even beyond the genital organs. But if any of these things be applied to the os, it retreats backwards and upwards. Sometimes it will go to this side or to that – to the spleen and liver, while the membranes yield to the distension and contraction like the sails of a ship.

It suffers in this way also from inflammation; and it protrudes more than usual in this affection and in the swelling of its neck; for inflammation of the fundus inclines upwards; but if downwards to the feet, it protrudes externally, a troublesome, painful and unseemly complaint, rendering it difficult to walk, to lie on the side or on the back, unless the woman suffer from inflammation of the feet. But if it mount upwards, it very speedily suffocates the woman, and stops the respiration as if with a cord, before she feels pain, or can scream aloud, or can call upon the spectators, for in many cases the respiration is first stopped, and in others the speech. It is proper, then, in these cases, to call the physician quickly before the patient die. Should you fortunately arrive in time and ascertain that it is inflammation, you must open a vein, especially the one at the ankle, and pursue the other means which prove remedial in suffocation without inflammation: ligatures of the hands and feet so tight as to induce torpor; smelling of fetid substances – liquid pitch, hairs and burnt wool, the extinguished flame of a lamp, and castor, since, in addition to its bad smell, it warms the congealed nerves. Old urine greatly rouses the sense of one in a death-like state, and drives the uterus downwards. Wherefore we must apply fragrant things on pessaries to the region of the uterus – any ointment of a mild nature, and not pungent to the touch, nard, or Egyptian bacchar, or the medicine from the leaves of the malabathrum, the Indian tree, or cinnamon pounded with any of the fragrant oils. These articles are to be rubbed into the female parts. And also an injection of these things is to be thrown into the uterus. The anus is to be rubbed with applications which dispel flatus; and injections of things not acrid, but softening, viscid, and lubricant, are to be given to the expulsion of the faeces solely, so that the region of the uterus may be emptied – with the juice of marsh mallow, or of fenugreek, but let melilot or marjoram be boiled along with the oil. But, if the uterus stands in need of support rather than evacuation, the abdomen is to be compressed by the hands of a strong woman, or of an expert man, binding it round also with a roller, when you have replaced the part, so that it may not ascend upwards again. Having produced sneezing, you must compress the nostrils; for by the sneezing and straining, in certain cases, the uterus has returned to its place. We are to blow into the nostrils also some of the root of soapwort, or of pepper, or of castor. We are also to apply the instrument for dry-cupping to the thighs, loins, the ischiatic regions, and groins, in order to attract the uterus. And, moreover, we are to apply it to the spine, and between the scapulae, in order to relieve the sense of suffocation. But if the feeling of suffocation be connected with inflammation, we may also scarify the vein leading along the pubes, and abstract plenty of blood ... Should the patient partially recover, she is to be seated in a decoction of aromatics, and fumigated from below with fragrant perfumes. Also before a meal, she is to drink of castor, and a little quantity of the hiera with the castor. And if relieved, she is to bathe, and at the proper season is to return to her accustomed habits; and we must look to the woman that her menstrual discharges flow freely.

217. *Treatment for hysterical suffocation. Cappadocia, 2nd cent. A.D. (Soranus, Gynaecology 3. 26, 28, 29. Tr. O. Temkin)*

Unlike some of his medical colleagues, Soranus did not believe in the theory of the wandering womb; he prescribes instead reassuring attention and physical therapy with soothing medicaments.

26. Hysterical suffocation has been named after both the affected organ and one symptom, viz. suffocation. But its connotation is: obstructed respiration together with aphonia and a seizure of the senses caused by some condition of the uterus. In most cases the disease is preceded by recurrent miscarriages, premature birth, long widowhood, retention of menses and the end of ordinary childbearing or inflation of the uterus. When an attack occurs, sufferers from the disease collapse, show aphonia, laboured breathing, a seizure of the senses, clenching of the teeth, stridor, convulsive contraction of the extremities (but sometimes only weakness), upper abdominal distention, retraction of the uterus, swelling of the thorax, bulging of the network of vessels of the face. The whole body is cool, covered with perspiration, the pulse stops or is very small. In the majority of cases they recover quickly from the collapse and usually recall what has happened; head and tendons ache and sometimes they are even deranged ...

28. [The disease] is of the constricted and violent class and exists both in an acute and chronic form; therefore the treatment must be suitable to these characteristics. During the initial stage one should lay the patient down in a room which is moderately warm and bright and, without hurting her, rouse her from the collapsed state by moving the jaw, placing warm compresses all over the middle of her body, gently straightening out all the cramped parts, restraining each extremity, and warming all the cool parts by the touch of [the] bare hands. Then one should wash the face with a sponge soaked in warm water, for sponging the face has a vitalising effect.

If, however, the state of aphonia persists, we also use dry cupping over the groin, pubes and the neighbouring regions; then we put on covers of soft clean wool. We also moisten these parts freely with sweet olive oil, keeping it up for some time, and swathe each extremity in wool (for this conducts the relaxation from the extremities toward the centre). Then we instill warm water into the opened jaws, and afterwards honey water too, and prescribe movement in a hammock. When the initial stage has ended we bleed, provided that weakness does not prevent it, or it is not long since food was given. Afterwards we give an injection of warm, sweet olive oil, moisten the parts, offer warm water as a mouthwash and drink, and make her abstain from food until the third day. On this day we first rub the patient down and afterwards we offer gruel-like food and give this from now on, every second day, until the dangerous condition regarding the uterus has safely subsided. [But every day] we use poultices like those prescribed for women who suffer from painful menstruation and apply hot sponge baths and relaxing hip-baths, the material for which we have mentioned above, and suppositories made of fat, marrow, fenugreek, mallow, and oil of lilies or henna oil, and injections by means of a clyster of olive oil or oil mixed with water, particularly if faeces are retained (for the excrement bruises the adjacent uterus). When the condition has abated we make use of wax salves and suppositories of a relatively high emollient power, then we give varied food, later on a bath, and finally wine.

29. But the majority of the ancients and almost all followers of the other sects have made use of ill-smelling odours (such as burnt hair, extinguished lamp wicks, charred deer's horn, burnt wool, burnt flock, skins and rags, castoreum with which they anoint the nose and ears, pitch, cedar resin, bitumen, squashed bedbugs, and all substances which are supposed to have an oppressive smell) in the opinion that the uterus flees from evil smells. Wherefore they have also fumigated with fragrant substances from below, and have approved of suppositories of spikenard and storax, so that the uterus fleeing the first-mentioned odours, but pursuing the last-mentioned, might move from the upper to the lower parts. Besides, Hippocrates[6] made some of his patients drink a decoction of cabbage, others asses' milk; and he, believing that the uterus is twisted like the intestines are in intestinal obstruction, inserted a small pipe and blew air into the vagina by means of a blacksmith's bellow, thus causing dilation. Diocles, however, in the third book *On Gynaecology*, pinches the nostrils, but opens the mouth and applies a sternutative; moreover, with the hand he pushes the uterus toward the lower parts by pressing upon the hypochondriac region; and applies warm fomentations to the legs. Mantias gives castoreum and bitumen in wine to drink, and if the arousal is imminent he orders playing on the flute and drumming. Xenophon proposes torchlight and prescribes the making of greater noise by whetting and beating metal plates. And

Asclepiades[7] applies a sternutative, constricts the hypochondriac region
with bandages and strings of gut, shouts loudly, blows vinegar into the
nose, allows sexual intercourse during remissions, drinking of water
[and pouring cold water over the head]. We, however, censure all these
men who start by hurting the inflamed parts and cause torpor by the
effluvia of ill-smelling substances. For the uterus does not issue forth like
a wild animal from the lair, delighted by fragrant odours and fleeing bad
odours; rather it is drawn together because of the stricture caused by the
inflammation. Also upsetting the stomach, which suffers from
sympathetic inflammation, with toxic and pungent potions makes
trouble. Forcing air by means of the smith's bellows into the vagina –
this inflation makes the uterus even more tense, which is already
rendered sufficiently tense by reason of the inflammation. Moreover, the
use of sternutatives, through their shaking effects and the pungency of
the drugs, produces a metasyncrisis in chronic conditions, thus
aggravating the condition of the patient who during the initial stage
needs not force but gentleness. Sounds and the noise of metal plates have
an overpowering effect and irritate those who are made sensitive by
inflammation. At any rate, even many healthy persons have been given
headaches by such sounds. Vinegar blown in is also harmful, for just
as external inflammations, so internal inflammations are increased by
every astringent. Furthermore, it is injurious to constrict externally with
strings or bandages the inflamed uterus which cannot even bear a
poultice without feeling it burdensome, because of the intensification
caused by the pressure. And drinking of water is not only not helpful but
sometimes even noxious, since the patient needs strengthening, not
metasyncrisis; moreover, metasyncrisis is produced again by switching
to diluted wine. Intercourse causes atony in everybody and is therefore
not appropriate; for without giving any advantage it affects the body
adversely by making it atonic. Pouring cold water over the head in order
to stop aphonia is obviously a technical mistake. For if the body is
rendered dense by the cold, the arousal necessarily becomes more
difficult to accomplish on account of the increased inflammation.

218. *Treatments for diseases of the womb. Rome, 1st cent. A.D. (Celsus, On
Medicine 6. 27; 5. 21; Tr. W.G. Spencer (LCL))*

Celsus, an encylopaedist, not a physician, wrote for other laymen.

From the womb of a woman, also, there arises a violent malady; and
next to the stomach this organ is affected the most by the body, and has
the most influence upon it. At times it makes the woman so insensible
that it prostrates her as if by epilepsy. The case, however, differs from

epilepsy, in that the eyes are not turned nor is there foaming at the mouth nor spasm of sinews; there is merely stupor. In some women this attack recurs at frequent intervals and lasts throughout life. When this happens, if there is sufficient strength, bloodletting is beneficial; if too little, wet cups should be applied to the groins. If she lies prostrate for a long while, or if she has done so at other times, hold to her nostrils an extinguished lamp wick, or some other of these materials which I have referred to as having a specially fetid odour to arouse the woman.[8] For the same end, affusion with cold water is also effectual. And there is benefit from rue pounded up in honey, or from a wax-salve made up with cyprus oil or from hot moist plasters of some sort applied to the external genitals as far as the pubes. At the same time also the hips and the backs of the knees should be rubbed. Then when she has come to herself, she should be cut off from wine for a whole year, even if a similar attack does not recur. Friction should be applied daily to the whole body, but particularly to the abdomen and behind the knees. Food of the middle class[9] should be given: every third or fourth day mustard is to be applied over the hypogastrium until the skin is reddened. If induration persists, a convenient emollient appears to be bitter-sweet steeped in milk, then pounded and mixed with white wax and deer marrow in iris oil, or suet of beef or goat mixed with rose oil. Also there should be given in draught either castory, or git,[10] or dill. If the womb is not healthy, it is cleaned with square rushes; but if it is actually ulcerated a wax-salve is made with rose oil, mixed with fresh lard and white of egg, and applied to it, or else white of egg mixed with rose oil, with pounded rose-leaves added to give it consistence. When painful the womb should be fumigated from below with sulphur. But if excessive menstruation is doing harm to the woman, the remedy is to scarify and cup the groins, or even to apply cups under the breasts. If the menstrual discharge is bad, the following medicaments are applied to evoke blood: costmary, pennyroyal, white violet, parsley, catmint and savory and hyssop. Let her include what is suitable in her diet: leeks, rue, cummin, onion, mustard, or any other acrid vegetable. If blood bursts out from the nose at a time when it should do so from the genitals, the groins are to be scarified and cupped, repeating this every thirtieth day for three or four months, then you may be sure that this affection has been cured. But if there is no show of blood, you may be sure that there are pains coming in the head. Then blood is to be let from the arms, and you have given relief at once ...

But there are other useful compositions, such as those which are introduced into women from below, the Greeks call them *pessoi*.[11] Their characteristic is that the component medicaments are taken up in soft wool, and this wool is inserted into the genitals.

A pessary for inducing menstruation contains 2/3 of a denarius[12] soda, added to two Caunean figs; or garlic seeds are pounded, a little myrrh added, and these are mixed with Susine lily ointment; or the pulp of a wild cucumber is diluted in woman's milk.

To mollify the womb a yolk of egg, fenugreek, rose-oil and saffron are mixed together. Or 1/6 denarius elaterium, the same quantity of salt, and 6 denarii of black bryony berries are taken up with honey.

The pessary invented by Boethus consists of saffron and turpentine resin, 4 denarii each, 1/3 denarius myrrh, 1 denarius rose-oil, 1 1/6 denarii calf's suet, 2 denarii wax, mixed together.

But against inflammations of the womb the composition of Numenius is the best; it consists of 1/4 denarius saffron, 1 denarius wax, 8 denarii butter, 12 denarii goose-fat, 2 yolks of egg boiled, and of rose-oil less than 1 cyathus.[13]

If the foetus is dead, to render its expulsion easier, pomegranate rind should be rubbed in water and so used.

If a woman is liable to fits owing to genital disease, snails are to be burnt with their shells and pounded up together; then honey added to them.

If a woman does not conceive, lion's fat is to be softened by rose-oil.

219. *Psychological origins of hysteria. Pergamum, 2nd cent. A.D. (Galen, On Prognosis 6. Tr. A.J. Brock)*

A rare case history of elegant deductive analysis; that the causes of hysteria are primarily psychological was not rediscovered until the twentieth century.[14]

I was called in to see a woman who was stated to be sleepless at night and to lie tossing about from one position to another. Finding she had no fever, I made a detailed inquiry into everything that had happened to her, especially considering such factors as we know to cause insomnia. But she either answered little or nothing at all, as if to show that it was useless to question her. Finally, she turned away, hiding herself completely by throwing the bedclothes over her whole body, and laying her head on another small pillow, as if desiring sleep.

After leaving I came to the conclusion that she was suffering from one of two things: either from a melancholy dependent on black bile, or else trouble about something she was unwilling to confess. I therefore deferred till the next day a closer investigation of this. Further, on first arriving, I was told by her attendant maid that she could not at present be seen; and on returning a second time, I was told the same again. So I went yet a third time, but the attendant asked me to go away, as she did not want her mistress disturbed. Having learned, however, that when I left she had washed and taken food in her customary manner, I came back the next day and in a private conversation with the maid on one subject and another I found out exactly what was worrying the patient. And this I discovered by chance.

After I had diagnosed that there was no bodily trouble, and that the woman was suffering from some mental uneasiness, it happened that, at the very time I was examining her, this was confirmed. Somebody came from the theatre and said he had seen Pylades dancing. Then both her expression and the colour of her face changed. Seeing this, I applied my hand to her wrist, and noticed that her pulse had suddenly become extremely irregular. This kind of pulse indicates that the mind is disturbed; thus it occurs also in people who are disputing over any subject. So on the next day I said to one of my followers that, when I paid my visit to the woman, he was to come a little later and announce to me, 'Morphus is dancing today.' When he said this, I found that the pulse was unaffected. Similarly also on the next day, when I had an announcement made about the third member of the troupe, the pulse remained unchanged as before. On the fourth evening I kept very careful watch when it was announced that Pylades was dancing, and I noticed that the pulse was very much disturbed. Thus I found out that the woman was in love with Pylades, and by very careful watch on the succeeding days my discovery was confirmed.

Similarly too I diagnosed the case of a slave who administered the household of another wealthy man, and who sickened in the same way. He was concerned about having to give an account of his expenses, in which he knew that there was a considerable sum wanting; the thought of this kept him awake, and he grew thin with anxiety. I first told his master that there was nothing phsyically wrong with the old man, and advised an investigation to be made as to whether he feared his master was about to ask an account of the sums he had entrusted to him and for this reason was worried, knowing that a considerable amount would be found wanting. The master told me I had made a good suggestion, so in order to make the diagnosis certain I advised him to do as follows: he was to tell the slave to give him back all the money he had in hand, lest, in the event of his sudden death, it should be lost, owing to the administration passing into the hands of some other servant whom he did not know: for there would be no use asking for an account from such a one. And when the master said this to him, he felt sure he would not be questioned. So he ceased to worry, and by the third day had regained his natural physical condition.

Now what was it that escaped the notice of previous physicians when examining the aforesaid woman and the aforesaid slave? For such discoveries are made by common inductions if one has even the smallest acquaintance with medical science. I suppose it is because they have no clear conception of how the body tends to be affected by mental conditions. Possibly also they do not know that the pulse is altered by quarrels and alarms which suddenly disturb the mind.

1. See below, p. 232, and J. Scarborough, *The Historian* 39 (1977) 213-27.

2. *On Common Diseases* 6. 6. 21.

3. Cf. Soranus's suggestion of sneezing as a contraceptive measure, p. 222.

4. See above, no. 88.

5. Since the Greek text is defective here, the description of bringing the baby out is taken from the 6th cent. Latin summary by Muscio, 1.66a.

6. Cf. p. 93.

7. 1st cent. B.C., a theoretical rather than experimental physician; virtually nothing is known about Mantias or about Xenophon of Cos.

8. The list of ingredients (in another context, 3. 20.1) consists of: burning pitch, unscoured wool, pepper, hellebore, castoreum, vinegar, garlic, onion.

9. Celsus (2. 18) defines foods of the middle class as nourishment for moderately strong people, relatively easy to digest, e.g., plant roots and bulbs, rabbit, birds (smaller than a flamingo), all unsalted fish, small whole salted fish, pork feet and brains, vinegar, and wine.

10. *Nigella sativa*, melanthium, melanospermum or black cumin. Its seeds were used both as a spice and as a medication for various ills.

11. Pessaries.

12. The denarius, or dram, was a measure of weight equal to one-seventh of an *uncia* (one-twelfth of a Roman pound). The pound equalled about 333 metric grams, the denarius about 4 grams. (Metric equivalents from *LCL*.)

13. The *cyathus* was a liquid measure equivalent to about 42cc.

14. On the history of this 'disease', see especially I. Veith, *Hysteria* (Chicago 1965).

XVII

Daily Life

220. *The need for educated parents. Rome, 1st cent. A.D. (Quintilian, Institutes of Oratory 1. 1.6. Tr. M.B.F.)*

As for parents, I should like them to be as well educated as possible, and I am not speaking just of fathers. We know that Cornelia, the mother of the Gracchi, contributed greatly to their eloquence, for the erudition of her speech has been handed down even to the present day in her letters. Laelia, too, daughter of Gaius [Laelius],[1] is said to have brought back the elegance of her father's speech in her own; and the oration which Hortensia, Quintus' daughter, made before the triumvirs is read not merely as an honour to her sex.[2]

221. *A good example. Hierapolis, 2nd cent. AD.? (Pseudo-Plutarch, Moralia 14b-c. Tr. M.R.L.)*

We ought therefore to try every appropriate means of disciplining our children, following the example of Eurydice. She was an Illyrian and a complete barbarian, but late in life she became involved in education because of her children's studies. The epigram she set up to the Muses provides adequate documentation of her love for her children: 'Eurydice of Hierapolis set up this tablet, when she had satisfied her desire to I become learned; for she worked hard to learn letters, the repository of speech, because she was a mother of growing sons.'

222. *An apprenticeship agreement. Oxyrhynchus, 2nd cent. A.D. (Oxyrhynchus papryus 1647. Tr. M.R.L.)*

An agreement between Platonis, also called Ophelia, daughter of Horion, of the city of Oxyrhynchus, with her full brother Plato as guardian, and Lucius son of Ision and Tisasis, of Aphrodisium in the Small Oasis: Platonis, also called Ophelia, has apprenticed to Lucius her slave Thermuthion, who is under age, to learn the weaver's trade, for four years starting at the beginning of the coming month Tubi of the present year, during which time she is to feed and clothe the girl and bring her to her instructor every day from sunrise to sunset so that the girl can perform all the duties assigned to her by him that are relevant to the aforesaid trade; her pay for the first year to be eight drachmas a month, for the second similarly twelve, for the third sixteen, for the fourth twenty. The girl is to have each year eighteen days off for festivals, but if she does no work or is sick for some days, she is to remain with her instructor for an equal number of days at the end of her time of service. The instructor is to pay for trade taxes and expenses.

223. *Management of an estate. Egypt, 2nd cent. A.D. (Hamburg papyrus 86. Tr. A.S. Hunt and C.C. Edgar (LCL))*

Ptolema to Antas her brother greeting. You write to Longinus [?] to look out for the prefect. Lo, the prefect has gone up. If you extricate yourself successfully, come here quickly before the prefect, in order that we may be able to have the youngster examined. All the fields are in good condition. The southern basin of the seventeen *arurae* has been sold for the use of the cattle. Your cattle have eaten one *arura* and gone off to Pansoue. All the land there has been given over to the cattle. The west of the vegetable plot has been given over for grass-cutting. We have sold the grass in the cleruchies, excepting the six eastern basins, for 112 drachmas. Grass is exceedingly [?] cheap. Three *arurae* were bought for you through Vetranius·for 130 drachmas for growing grass, and they have been sold through him again for the use of sheep for 68 drachmas. Longinus and Sarapion and all at home salute you. Vibius has gone off to Psenuris to sell the corn. Your people are well. Goodbye. Mecheir 30.

224. *Loss of a teacher. Oxyrhynchus, 2nd/3rd cent. A.D. (Oxyrhynchus papyrus 9.30. Tr. A.S. Hunt and C.C. Edgar (LCL))*

... do not hesitate to write to me about anything which you require from here. I was grieved to learn from the daughter of our teacher Diogenes that he had gone down the river; for my mind was easy with regard to him, as I knew that he intended to look after you to the best of his power. I took care to send and inquire about your health and to learn what you were reading. He said it was the sixth book, and he testified at large to the conduct of your attendant. So now, my child, you and your attendant must take care to have you placed under a suitable teacher. Many salutations from your sisters and the children of Theonis, whom the evil eye shall not harm, and from all our friends by name. Salute from me your esteemed attendant Eros ... (*Addressed*) ... to her son Ptolemaeus.

225. *Moving house. Egypt, 3rd cent. A.D. (PSI 1080. Tr. A.S. Hunt and C.C. Edgar (LCL))*

Diogenis to her brother Alexander greeting. In accordance with your instructions to Taamois about a house for us to move into, we found the one which we let go before moving over to Agathinus. The house is beside the Iseum, adjoining the house of Claudianus ... We move into it in Phamenoth. I wish you to know that I received from Bottus 120 drachmas. I have sent you ... of purple dye by Sarapiacus. The letter which you forwarded to me to deliver to Bolphius I have delivered. Many salutations to the little Theon. Eight toys have been brought for him by the lady to whom you told me to give your salutations, and these I have forwarded to you ... (*Addressed*) To Aurelius Alexander.

226. *Calpurnia and Pliny the Younger. Rome, A.D. 104-8 (Pliny the Younger, Letters 4. 19; 6. 4 and 7; 7. 5; 8. 10. Tr. B. Radice)*

Calpurnia, Pliny's third wife, was an orphan and several years his junior. She was a native of Pliny's home town, Comum in northern Italy. His letters to her (and about her) should be regarded not as private correspondence, but as representations of his beliefs and attitudes intended for publication.

To Calpurnia Hispulla, his wife's aunt and nearest living female relative

You are a model of family affection, and loved your excellent and devoted brother as dearly as he loved you; you love his daughter as if she were your own, and, by filling the place of the father she lost, you are more than an aunt to her. I know then how glad you will be to hear that she has proved herself worthy of her father, her grandfather and you. She is highly intelligent and a careful housewife, and her devotion to me is a sure indication of her virtue. In addition, this love has given her an interest in literature: she keeps copies of my works to read again and again and even learn by heart. She is so anxious when she knows that I am going to plead in court, and so happy when all is over! She arranges to be kept informed of the sort of reception and applause I receive, and what verdict I win in the case. If I am giving a reading she sits behind a curtain near by and greedily drinks in every word of appreciation. She has even set my verses to music and sings them, to the accompaniment of her lyre, with no musician to teach her but the best of masters, love.

All this gives me the highest reason to hope that our mutual happiness will last for ever and go on increasing day by day, for she does not love me for my present age nor my person, which will gradually grow old and decay, but for my aspirations to fame; nor would any other feelings be suitable for one brought up by your hands and trained in your precepts, who has seen only what was pure and moral in your company and learned to love me on your recommendation. For you respected my mother like a daughter, and have given me guidance and encouragement since my boyhood; you always foretold that I should become the man I am now in the eyes of my wife. Please accept our united thanks for having given her to me and me to her as if chosen for each other.

To his wife Calpurnia

Never have I complained so much about my public duties as I do now. They would not let me come with you to Campania in search of better health, and they still prevent me from following hard on your heels. This is a time when I particularly want to be with you, to see with my own eyes whether you are gaining in strength and weight, and if the pleasures of your holiday and the luxuries of the district are doing you no harm. Indeed, I should worry when you are away even if you were well, for there are always anxious moments without news of anyone one loves dearly, and, as things are, I have the thought of your health as well as your absence to alarm me with fluctuating doubts and fears. I am full of forebodings of every imaginable disaster, and like all nervous people dwell most on what I pray fervently will not happen. So do please think of my anxiety and write to me once or even twice a day – I shall worry less while I am reading your letters, but my fears will return as soon as I have finished them.

To Calpurnia

You say that you are feeling my absence very much, and your only comfort when I am not there is to hold my writings in your hand and often put them in my place by your side. I like to think that you miss me and find relief in this sort of consolation. I, too, am always reading your letters, and returning to them again and again as if they were new to me – but this only fans the fire of my longing for you. If your letters are so dear to me, you can imagine how I delight in your company; do write as often as you can, although you give me pleasure mingled with pain.

To Calpurnia

You cannot believe how much I miss you. I love you so much, and we are not used to separation.[3] So I stay awake most of the night thinking of you, and by day I find my feet carrying me (a true word, carrying) to your room at the times I usually visited you; then finding it empty I depart, as sick and sorrowful as a lover locked out. The only time I am free from this misery is when I am in court and wearing myself out with my friends' lawsuits. You can judge then what a life I am leading, when I find my rest in work and distraction in troubles and anxiety.

To Calpurnius Fabatus, his wife's grandfather

I know how anxious you are for us to give you a great-grandchild, so you will be all the more sorry to hear that your granddaughter has had a miscarriage. Being young and inexperienced she did not realise she was pregnant, failed to take proper precautions, and did several things which were better left undone. She has had a severe lesson, and paid for her mistake by seriously endangering her life; so that although you must inevitably feel it hard for your old age to be robbed of a descendant already on the way, you should thank the gods for sparing your granddaughter's life even though they denied you the child for the present. They will surely grant us children later on, and we may take hope from this evidence of her fertility though the proof has been unfortunate.

I am giving you the same advice and encouragement as I use on myself, for your desire for great-grandchildren cannot be keener than mine for children. Their descent from both of us should make their road to office easy; I can leave them a well-known name and an established ancestry, if only they may be born and turn our present grief to joy.[4]

227. *Advice on marriage. Boeotia, 2nd cent. A.D. (Plutarch, Moralia 138a-146a. (excerpts). Tr. R. Warner)*

Suggestions to a young friend and his wife; the husband is urged to be understanding and faithful, but it is expected that most adjustments will be made by the wife.

Now you two have been brought up together in philosophy, and so, by way of a wedding present for you both, I have made and am sending you a summary of what you have often heard. I have put things down briefly and side by side, to make them easier to remember. I pray that the Muses may stand by Aphrodite and help her! For they know that it is no more important for a lyre or a lute to be properly tuned than it is for the proper care of marriage and family life to be set to harmony by reason, mutual adjustment, and philosophy. Indeed, the ancients gave Hermes a place at the side of Aphrodite, indicating that in the pleasures of love reason is especially valuable; and they also gave a place to Persuasion and to the Graces, so that married people should have what they want from each other through persuasion and not by quarrelling and fighting with each other.

1. Solon advised the bride to eat a quince before getting into bed with her husband, and by this, I think, he meant that from the very beginning the pleasures coming from the lips and the voice should be harmonious and delightful.

2. In Boeotia after they have veiled the bride they put a garland of asparagus on her head, this being a plant with very rough spines and yet with an extremely pleasant taste. So the bride will make gentle and sweet her partnership with her husband if he does not shrink from her and get angry with her when in the early stages she is difficult and disagreeable. The people who cannot put up with girlish tantrums at the beginning are just like those who because unripe grapes are sour leave the bunches of ripe grapes for others to eat. Many newly married women, too, who get angry with their husbands in the first days find themselves in the position of people who put up with being stung by the bees, but never reach out for the honey comb.

9. When the moon is a long way from the sun, she looks large and bright to us; but when she comes near she fades away and hides. With a good wife it is just the opposite; she ought to be most conspicuous when she is with her husband, and to stay at home and hide herself when he is not there.

11. When music is played in two parts, it is the bass part which carries the melody. So in a good and wise household, while every activity is carried on by husband and wife in agreement with each other, it will still be evident that it is the husband who leads and makes the final choice.

18. A young Spartan girl was once asked whether she had yet started making advances to her husband. She replied: 'I don't to him; he does to me.' This, I think, is how a married woman ought to behave – not to shrink away or object when her husband starts to make love, but not herself to be the one to start either. In the one case she is being over-eager like a prostitute, in the other she is being cold and lacking in affection.

19. A wife ought not to make friends of her own, but to enjoy her husband's friends together with him. And the first and best friends are the gods in whom her husband believes and to shut her door to all magic ceremonies and foreign superstitions. For no god can be pleased by stealthy and surreptitious rites performed by a woman.

20. Man and woman are joined together physically so that the woman may take and blend together elements derived from each and so give· birth to a child which is common to them both, so that neither of the two can tell or distinguish what in particular is his or hers. It is very right too that married people should have the same kind of partnership in property. They should put everything they have into a common fund; neither of the two should think of one part as belonging to him and the other as not belonging; instead each should think of it all as his own, and none of it as not belonging to him.

27. The economical woman ought not to neglect cleanliness and the wife who is devoted to her husband should also show a cheerful disposition; for economy ceases to please when it is combined with dirt, as does the most proper behaviour in a wife when combined with an austere manner.

34. It should be the same with married people – a mutual blending of bodies, property, friends and relations. Indeed what the Roman law-giver had in mind, when he prohibited an exchange of presents between man and wife, was not to deprive them of anything, but to make them feel that everything belonged to both of them together.

35. In the African city of Leptis there is an old custom that on the day after her marriage the bride sends to her husband's mother and asks her for a pot. She does not give it and says that she hasn't got one, the idea being that the bride should recognise from the beginning a step-motherly attitude in her mother-in-law and, if something worse happens later on, should not be angry or resentful. A wife ought to realise what the position is and try to do her best about it. Her mother-in-law is jealous of her because her son loves her. And the only way of dealing with this is for her to win her husband's affection for herself and at the same time not to detract from or lessen his affection for his mother.

39. At all times and in all places wives and husbands should try to avoid quarrelling with each other, but they ought to be especially careful of this when they are together in bed. There was a woman in labour who, when the pains were on her, kept saying to those who were trying to get her to bed 'What's the good of going to bed? It was by going to bed that I got this.' But it is not easy to escape the disagreements, harsh words and anger that may arise in bed except just then and there.

48. But it is a finer thing still for a man to hear his wife say 'My dear husband, "but to me you are" guide, philosopher and teacher in all that is most beautiful and most divine.' In the first place these studies will take away a woman's appetite for stupid and irrational pursuits. A woman who is studying geometry will be ashamed to go dancing and one who is charmed by the words of Plato or Xenophon is not going to pay any attention to magic incantations. For if they do not receive the seed of a good education and do not develop this education in company with

their husbands they will, left to themselves, conceive a lot of ridiculous ideas and unworthy aims and emotions.

228. *The disadvantage of a rich wife. Rome, late 1st cent. A.D. (Martial, Epigram 8. 12. Tr. M.B.F.)*

A satirist looks at the husband-wife relationship.

Are you asking why I don't want to take a rich wife? I don't want a husband for a wife. Let the matron, Priscus, stay beneath the husband: otherwise woman and man can't be equals.

229. *Bereavement. Rome, late 1st cent. A.D. (Martial, Epigram 9.30. Tr. M.B.F.)*

Antistius Rusticus died on the savage shores of Cappadocia. O land guilty of a doleful crime! Nigrina brought back her husband's bones in her arms and complained that the journey was not long enough; and as she gave the sacred urn to the tomb, which she was jealous of, she saw herself twice bereft of her stolen spouse.

230. *Attempts to explain marriage customs. (Plutarch, Moralia 288-9; 276, 2nd cent. A.D. Tr. F.C. Babbitt (LCL))*

For what reason is it not the custom of maidens to marry on public holidays, but widows do marry at this time?

Is it, as Varro has remarked, that maidens are grieved over marrying, but older women are glad, and on a holiday one should do nothing in grief or by constraint?

Or is it rather because it is seemly that not a few should be present when maidens marry, but disgraceful that many should be present when widows marry? Now the first marriage is enviable; but the second is to be deprecated, for women are ashamed if they take a second husband while the first husband is till living, and they feel sad if they do so when he is dead. Wherefore they rejoice in a quiet wedding rather than in noise and processions. Holidays distract most people, so that they have no leisure for such matters.

Or, because they seized the maiden daughters of the Sabines at a holiday festival, and thereby became involved in war, did they come to regard it as ill-omened to marry maidens on holy days?

Why did the priest of Jupiter[5] resign his office if his wife died, as Ateius has recorded?

Is it because the man who has taken a wife and then lost her is more unfortunate than one who has never taken a wife? For the house of the married man is complete, but the house of him who has married and later lost his wife is not only incomplete, but also crippled.[6]

Or is it because the wife assists her husband in the rites, so that many of them cannot be performed without the wife's presence, and for a man who has lost his wife to marry again immediately is neither possible perhaps nor otherwise seemly? Wherefore it was formerly illegal for the flamen to divorce his wife; and it is still, as it seems, illegal, but in my days Domitian once permitted it on petition. The priests were present at that ceremony of divorce and performed many horrible, strange, and gloomy rites.

One might be less surprised at this resignation of the flamen if one should adduce also the fact that when one of the censors died, the other was obliged to resign his office; but when the censor Livius Drusus died, his colleague Aemilius Scaurus was unwilling to give up his office until certain tribunes ordered him to be led away to prison.

231. *A wedding invitation. Oxyrhynchus, 3rd cent. A.D. (Oxyrhynchus papyrus 111. Tr. M.R.L.)*

Herais requests your company at dinner in celebration of the marriage of her children at her house tomorrow, the fifth, at nine o'clock.

232. *An Italian benefactress. Tarracina, 2nd cent. A.D. (CIL X. 6328/ILS 6278. Tr. J.C. Fant)*

Caelia Macrina left money for the construction of the building to which this inscription was originally attached, and at the same time endowed an alimentary fund (i.e. to provide cash grants for food) for 200 children of her city. Alimentary grants could be either private or governmental, and were customarily larger for boys than for girls.[7] Caelia follows this pattern but is slightly more generous to girls than was usual. The shorter period allowed for girls to receive support reflects their younger age at marriage (often 13 or 14 years old).

Caelia Macrina, daughter of Gaius, by her will ordered 300,000 sesterces to be used [for the construction of this building]. She left ... sesterces for its decoration and maintenance. To the people of Tarracina, in memory of her son Macer, she left 1,000,000 sesterces, so that the income from the money might be given to 100 boys [and to 100 girls] under the title of 'alimenta': 5 denarii [= 20 sesterces] each month to each citizen boy up to the age of 16, and 4 denarii [= 16 sesterces] each month to each citizen girl up to the age of 14, so that 100 boys and 100 girls might always be receiving [the grant] in succession.

Women's organisations

233. *A women's club. Alexandria, 1st cent. A.D. (JEA 4 (1917) 253f. Tr. M.R.L.)*

The many analogous extant inscriptions are for men's clubs.

... for the women's [club] from the common treasury ... the president and Tetiris the ... have [dedicated a statue] of ... aris the high priestess.

Allusions in inscriptions to groups of women are a bit mysterious. In some cases they seem to indicate women's burial societies or perhaps a sort of unofficial ladies' auxiliary for the purpose of keeping feast days and honouring the dead. Not all the contexts, however, are funerary. At the least, the texts show that women organised outside the home for some social or religious purpose. If Elagabalus' *senaculum* did exist, it would have been at far too exalted a level to bear any resemblance to the organisations referred to in the inscriptions, with one perplexing exception, which in any case antedates his reign.

234. *The curia of women.*[8] *Lanuvium, 2nd cent. A.D. (CIL XIV. 2120/ILS 6199. Tr. M.B.F.)*

To Gaius Sulpicius Victor, father of Roman knights, a most blameless man, patron of the city, the senate and people of Lanuvium, on account of his incomparable service and immense generosity towards them, voted that an equestrian statue of him should be erected and dedicated it. On account of this dedication, he distributed to each man of the decurions, Augustales, and *curiae* twenty-four sesterces, and to the *curia* of women he gave a double banquet.

235. *The women's collegium. Rome, 1st/2nd cent. A.D. (CIL VI. 10423. Tr. M.B.F.)*

To well-deserving Ti ...[9] The women's *collegium* [put this up].

236. *A grant for funeral rites.*[10] *Feltria, 2nd cent. A.D. (CIL V. 2072. Tr. M.B.F.)*

To the gods of the dead. To Lucius Veturius Nepos, who, in order that they might carry out his funeral rites, gave the Ciarnenses 1600 sesterces, likewise the Herclanenses 400 sesterces, and the women 400 sesterces, so that the Ciarnenses might celebrate his birthday with incense, sausage, and wine, the Herclanenses the *parentalia,* and the women the roses.[11] He did this while he was still alive.

237. *The matrons. Trajan's Forum, Rome, 3rd cent. A.D. (CIL VI. 997/ILS 324. Tr. M.B.F.)*

Julia Augusta,[12] mother of emperors and camps, restored this for the matrons. Sabina Augusta[13] [put this up] for the matrons.

238. *Raising money. Rome, 3rd cent. B.C. (Livy, History of Rome 27. 37. 8-9. 1st cent. A.D. Tr. M.B.F.)*

In 206 B.C. the temple of Juno on the Aventine hill was struck by lightning.

When the soothsayers said that the omen had to do with the matrons and that the goddess must be appeased with a gift, those matrons who lived in the city or within the tenth milestone were called together on the Capitoline Hill by an edict of the curule aedile, and they elected from among themselves twenty-five to whom they would bring a sum of money from their dowries. From that the gift of a golden bowl was made and carried to the Aventine and was purely and chastely dedicated by the matrons.

239. *A meeting of married women. Rome, 1st cent. A.D. (Suetonius, Galba 5.1. Tr. M.B.F.)*

Although a formally constituted body of women cannot be inferred from the following, the *conventus* referred to *may* be more than a casual gathering in someone's drawing room.

[The Emperor Galba] did his duty by matrimony, but when he lost his wife Lepida and his two sons by her, he remained celibate and could no more be tempted by any prospect, not even Agrippina [the Younger], who, widowed by the death of Domitius, had gone after the still-married Galba with every means to such a degree that in a meeting of married women[14] Lepida's mother chastised her and even slapped her.

240. *A women's 'senate'. 3rd cent. A.D. (Hist. Aug. Elag. 4. 3-4. 4th cent. A.D. Tr. D. Magie (LCL))*

That the Emperor Elagabalus (A.D. 218-22) instituted a senate of women for the extremely frivolous purposes described below is unlikely. The text, from an often imaginative collection of imperial biographies, is worth noting, however, for its allusion to an earlier organisation.[15]

He established a *senaculum*, or women's senate, on the Quirinal Hill. Before his time, in fact, a congress of matrons[16] had met there, but only on certain festivals, or whenever a matron was presented with the insignia of a 'consular marriage' – bestowed by the early emperors on their kinswomen, particularly on those whose husbands were not nobles, in order that they might not lose their noble rank. But now under the influence of Symiamira[17] absurd decrees were enacted concerning rules to be applied to matrons, namely, what kind of clothing each might wear in public, who was to yield precedence and to whom, who was to advance to kiss another, who might ride in a chariot, on a horse, on a pack-animal, or on an ass, who might drive in a carriage drawn by mules or in a litter, and whether the litter might be made of leather, or of bone, or covered with ivory or with silver, and lastly, who might wear gold or silver on her shoes.

241. *A plan to restore the 'senate'. Rome, A.D. 270-5. (Hist. Aug. Aurel. 49. 6, 4th cent. A.D. Tr. D. Magie (LCL))*

The same source credits the Emperor Aurelian (A.D. 270-5) with remembering Elagabalus' brainchild (if it existed).

He had planned to restore to the matrons their senate, or rather *senaculum*, with the provision that those should rank first therein who had attained to priesthoods with the senate's approval.

---

1. Nicknamed *Sapiens*, the wise. Laelius was a hero of the Third Punic War and consul in 140 B.C. Cf. above, p. 206.

2. Cf. above, pp. 206-7.

3. One writer disposes of this sentiment thus: 'What he seems most to have loved in Calpurnia was her admiration for his writings, and we soon come to the conclusion that he was readily consoled for the absences he complains of by the pleasure of polishing the phrases in which he so gracefully deplores them.' J. Carcopino, *Daily Life in Ancient Rome* (New Haven and London 1940) 89, who adds the evidence from 9. 36: Pliny slept alone and first thing in the morning summoned his secretary, not his wife.

4. Pliny and Calpurnia never were able to have children.

5. *Flamen dialis*.

6. For the strange rituals and regulations attached to the priest and his wife, see Aulus Gellius 10. 15.

7. Cf. Fornara, No. 45: among Ionian women at Persepolis *c.* 500 B.C., mothers of boys received twice the allotment of women who had girls.

8. On this inscription and, briefly but with bibliography, the question of the women's *curia*, see Angela Donati, 'Sull' iscrizione lanuvina della curia mulierum', *Rivista storica dell' antichità* 1 (1971) 235-7.

9. Possibly Tigrides, as Mommsen suggests ad loc., and certainly a name of humble origin.

10. Three groups receive grants in this text, the Ciarnenses, the Herclanenses and 'the women'. The names of the men's groups may denote cult associations and the women's a burial society like the *collegium* in the document above. The Herclanenses were probably devoted to Hercules and the Ciarnenses (a name which occurs nowhere else) to a local deity. We are grateful to Professor S. Panciera for giving us the benefit of his singular expertise about this unique inscription.

11. Festivals of the dead. Other grants to women: *CIL* IX 4697, X. 5853, XIV. 2110.

12. Julia Domna. Cf. pp. 145-7.

13. The wife of Hadrian, who built in the first place whatever Julia restored.

14. *Conventu matronarum.*

15. No other evidence has been found for earlier rituals of this sort; but 'precedent' was often sought for new practices established in the late Empire. See Jean Gagé, 'Matronalia: essai sur les dévotions et les organisations culturelles des femmes dans l'ancienne Rome', *Collection Latomus* 60 (Brussels 1963), pp. 101f., note 1. See also J. Straub, 'Senaculum, id est mulierum senatus', in *Bonner Historia Augusta Colloquium 1964-65* (Bonn 1966) 221-40.

16. *Conventus matronalis.*

17. His mother, Julia Soaemias Bassiana, niece of Julia Domna.

XVIII

Religion

242. *Vestal virgins. Rome, 7th cent. B.C. (Plutarch, Life of Numa Pompilius 9-10, 2nd cent. A.D. Tr. J. Dryden)*

The goddess of the hearth, Vesta, was served by six virgins, whose duty it was to keep the sacred fire which took the place of a cult statue. Vesta's temple was a round building in the Roman Forum. Its institution was attributed to Numa Pompilius, the pious second king of Rome (715-673 B.C.), who succeeded the warlike Romulus.

The office of Pontifex Maximus, or chief priest, was to declare and interpret the divine law, or, rather, to preside over sacred rites; he not only prescribed rules for public ceremony, but regulated the sacrifices of private persons, not suffering them to vary from established custom, and giving information to every one of what was requisite for purposes of worship or supplication. He was also guardian of the vestal virgins, the institution of whom, and of their perpetual fire, was attributed to Numa, who, perhaps, fancied the charge of pure and uncorrupted flames would be fitly entrusted to chaste and unpolluted persons, or that fire, which consumes but produces nothing, bears an analogy to the virgin state. In Greece, wherever a perpetual holy fire is kept, as at Delphi and Athens, the charge of it is committed, not to virgins, but widows past the time of marriage.
... Some are of the opinion that these vestals had no other business than the preservation of this fire; but others conceive that they were keepers of other divine secrets concealed from all but themselves. Gegania and Verenia, it is recorded, were the names of the first two virgins consecrated and ordained by Numa; Canuleia and Tarpeia succeeded; Servius afterwards added two, and the number of four has continued to the present time.
The statutes prescribed by Numa for the vestals were these: that they should take a vow of virginity for the space of thirty years, the first ten of which they were to spend in learning their duties, the second ten in performing them, and the remaining ten in teaching and instructing others. Thus the whole term being completed, it was lawful for them to marry, and, leaving the sacred order, to choose any condition of life that

pleased them; but this permission few, as they say, made use of; and in cases where they did so, it was observed that their change was not a happy one but accompanied ever after with regret and melancholy; so that the greater number, from religious fears and scruples, forbore and continued to old age and death in the strict observance of a single life.

For this condition he compensated by great privileges and prerogatives; as that they had power to make a will in the lifetime of their father; that they had a free administration of their own affairs without guardian or tutor, which was the privilege of women who were the mothers of three children,[1] when they go abroad, they have the fasces carried before them; and if in their walks they chance to meet a criminal on his way to execution, it saves his life, upon oath made that the meeting was an accidental one and not concerted or of set purpose. Any one who presses upon the chair on which they are carried, is put to death. If these vestals commit any minor fault, they are punishable by the high priest only, who scourges the offender, sometimes with her clothes off, in a dark place, with a curtain drawn between; but she that has broken her vow is buried alive near the gate called Collina, where a little mound of earth stands inside the city, reaching some little distance, called in Latin *agger*; under it a narrow room is constructed, to which a descent is made by stairs; here they prepare a bed, light a lamp, and leave a small quantity of victuals, such as bread, water, a pail of milk; and some oil; so that body which had been consecrated and devoted to the most sacred service of religion might not be said to perish by such a death as famine. The culprit herself is put in a litter, which they cover over, and tie her down with cords on it, so that nothing she utters may be heard. They then take her to the Forum; all people silently go out of the way as she passes, and such as follow accompany the bier with solemn and speechless sorrow; and indeed, there is not any spectacle more appalling, nor any day observed by the city with greater appearance of gloom and sadness. When they come to the place of execution, the officers loose the cords, and then the high priest, lifting his hands to heaven, pronounces certain prayers to himself before the act; then he brings out the prisoner, being still covered, and placing her upon the steps that lead down to the cell, turns away his face with the rest of the priests; the stairs are drawn up after she has gone down, and a quantity of earth is heaped up over the entrance to the cell, so as to prevent it from being distinguished from the rest of the mound. This is the punishment of those who break their vow of virginity.

243. *Bacchic rites. Rome, 186 B.C. (CIL I² 581/ILS 18/ILLRP 511. Tr. ARS)*

The worship of the god Dionysus spread through Italy from the Greek cities of the south and was particularly popular among the lower classes and slaves.[2] While the exaggerated reports of orgiastic rites were shocking to conservative Romans, far more alarming was the organisational nature of this new religion. Secret societies of any sort, and especially of the lower classes, always held for the Romans the threat of sedition. The senate's decree which follows applied to all Italy and placed strict limitations on the worship of Bacchus, though it did not prohibit it entirely.

The consuls Quintus Marcius, son of Lucius, and Spurius Postumius, son of Lucius, consulted the Senate on October 7 in the Temple of Bellona, Marcus Claudius, son of Marcus, Lucius Valerius, son of Publius, and Quintus Minucius, son of Gaius, assisted in drafting the decree.

Regarding the Bacchanalia the senators proposed to issue a decree as follows to those who are allied with us: 'No one of them shall have a place devoted to the worship of Bacchus: and if there are any who say that they have a need for such a place, they shall appear in Rome before the urban praetor; and when the pleas of these men have been heard, our Senate shall make a decision regarding these matters, provided that not less than 100 senators are present when the matter is discussed. No Roman citizen or man of Latin rights or anyone of the allies shall associate with the Bacchae, unless they have appeared before the urban praetor and he has given permission, in accordance with the opinion of the Senate, delivered while not less than 100 senators were present when the matter was discussed.' The proposal passed.

'No man shall be priest of, nor shall any man or woman be master of, such an organisation; nor shall anyone of them have a common fund; nor shall anyone appoint any man or woman to be master of such an organisation or to act as master; nor hereafter shall anyone take common oath with them, shall make common vows, shall make stipulations with them; nor shall anyone give them surety or shall take surety from them. No one shall perform their rites in secret; nor shall anyone perform their rites in public, in private, or outside the city, unless he has appeared before the urban praetor and he has given permission, in accordance with the opinion of the Senate, delivered while not less than 100 senators were present when the matter was discussed.' The proposal passed.

'No one in a company of more than five persons altogether, men and women, shall perform such rites; nor in that company shall more than two men or three women be present, unless it is in accordance with the opinion of the urban praetor and the Senate, as has been written above.'

You shall publish these decrees in public assembly for not less than three market days, that you may know the opinion of the Senate. For the opinion of the senators is as follows: 'If there are any persons who act contrary to what has been written above, it is our opinion that a proceeding for a capital offence must be made against them'; and you shall inscribe this on a bronze tablet, for thus the Senate voted was proper; and you shall order it to be posted where it can be read most easily; and, as has been written above, you shall provide within ten days after these tablets have been delivered to you that those places devoted to the worship of Bacchus shall be dismantled, if there are any such, except in case something sacred is concerned in the matter.

244. *The festival of Agrionia. (Plutarch, Moralia 299e-300a, 2nd cent. A.D. Tr. F.C. Babbitt (LCL))*

As a historian, Plutarch had a keen interest in ancient practices of all kinds; but he reports this incident also as a pious believer in the traditional gods.[3]

The story is that the daughters of Minyas, Leucippe and Arsinoe and Alcathoe, went crazy.[4] They developed a craving for human meat and drew lots to choose among their children. Leucippe won and offered up her son Hippasos to be torn to pieces. Their husbands were called 'Psoloeis'[5] because in their pain and grief they were shabbily dressed. The daughters of Minyas were called Oleiae[6] because they were destructive.

Today the people of Orchomenus still call women in this family by that name. Every year at the festival of Agrionia the Oleiae flee and are pursued by the priest of Dionysus, sword in hand. If he captures one of the women he is permitted to kill her, and in my day the priest Zoilus did kill one. But the killing did the people of Orchomenus no good. Zoilus became sick as a result of a small wound he had, which became gangrenous, and eventually died. The people of Orchomenus were beset by suits for damages and adverse judgments. They took the priesthood away from Zoilus' family, and picked as new priest the best man in the city.

245. *Rules in the cult of Dionysus. Physcus, Locris, 2nd cent. A.D. (IG IX² 670/Sokolowski, LSCG 181.[7] Tr. A. Henrichs)*

With a Good Omen.

The Law of the thiasos of Amandus has been [ratified?] in two [meetings?].

The [...?] must pay to the association fourteen obols and no less.

The association has to provide three lamps.

A Maenad must not get excited over another Maenad nor rail at her. Likewise a Cowherd must not get excited or rail. If someone does, he or she shall give to the association a fine of four drachmas for each word.

For someone who does not attend the meetings although he is in town, the same. Someone who does not join the others on the mountain shall pay five drachmas to the association. [If] a Maenad does [not] bring fifteen [??] for the Holy Night, she shall pay five drachmas [to the association]. The same if (a Cowherd) does not bring ... (*The rest is lost.*)

For two years in a row, during the late Republic, a women's religious ritual is connected with political events.

246. *A divine portent. Rome, 63 B.C. (Plutarch, Life of Cicero 19.3, 20. 1-2, 2nd cent. A.D. Tr. J. Dryden)*

Plutarch records a story which demonstrates how Cicero had divine support in his prosecution of the Catilinarian conspirators.

It being evening and the common people in crowds expecting without, Cicero went forth to them, and told them what was done,[8] and then, attended by them, went to the house of a friend and near neighbour; for his own was taken up by the women, who were celebrating with secret rites the feast of the goddess whom the Romans call Bona Dea (Good Goddess), and the Greeks Gynaecea (Women's Goddess). For a sacrifice is annually performed to her in the consul's house, either by his wife or mother, in the presence of the vestal virgins. And having got into his friend's house privately, a few only being present, he began to deliberate how he should treat these men ...

Whilst Cicero was doubting what course to take, a portent happened to the women in their sacrificing. For on the altar where the fire seemed wholly extinguished, a great and bright flame issued forth from the ashes of the burnt wood; at which others were affrighted, but the holy virgins called to Terentia, Cicero's wife, and bade her haste to her husband, and command him to execute what he had resolved for the good of his country, for the goddess had sent a great light to the increase of his safety and glory. Terentia, therefore, as she was otherwise in her own nature neither tender-hearted nor timorous, but a woman eager for distinction (who, as Cicero himself says, would rather thrust herself into his public affairs, than communicate her domestic matters to him), told him these things, and excited him against the conspirators.

247. *Desecration of the Bona Dea. Rome, 62 B.C. (Plutarch, Life of Caesar 9-10,[9] 2nd cent. A.D. Tr. J. Dryden)*

But there was no disturbance during [Caesar's] praetorship, only what misfortune he met with in his own domestic affairs. Publius Clodius[10] was a patrician by descent, eminent both for his riches and eloquence, but in licentiousness of life and audacity exceeded the most noted profligates of the day. He was in love with Pompeia, Caesar's wife, and she had no aversion to him. But there was strict watch kept on her apartment, and Caesar's mother, Aurelia, who was a discreet woman, being continually about her, made any interview very dangerous and difficult. The Romans have a goddess whom they call Bona,[11] the same whom the Greeks call Gynaecea. The Phrygians, who claim a peculiar title to her, say she was mother to Midas. The Romans profess she was one of the Dryads, and married to Faunus. The Grecians affirm that she is that mother of Bacchus whose name is not to be uttered, and, for this reason, the women who celebrate her festival cover the tents with vine-branches, and, in accordance with the fable, a consecrated serpent is placed by the goddess. It is not lawful for a man to be by, nor so much as in the house, whilst the rites are celebrated, but the women by themselves perform the sacred offices, which are said to be much the same as those used in the solemnities of Orpheus. When the festival comes, the husband, who is either consul or praetor, and with him every male creature, quits the house. The wife then taking it under her care sets it in order, and the principal ceremonies are performed during the night, the women playing together amongst themselves as they keep watch, and music of various kinds going on.

As Pompeia was at that time celebrating this feast, Clodius, who as yet had no beard, and so thought to pass undiscovered, took upon him the dress and ornaments of a singing woman, and so came thither, having the air of a young girl. Finding the doors open, he was without any stop introduced by the maid, who was in the intrigue. She presently ran to tell Pompeia, but as she was away a long time, he grew uneasy in waiting for her, and left his post and traversed the house from one room to another, still taking care to avoid the lights, till at last Aurelia's woman met him and invited him to play with her, as the women did among themselves. He refused to comply, and she presently pulled him forward, and asked him who he was and whence he came. Clodius told her he was waiting for Pompeia's own maid, Abra, being in fact her own name also, and as he said so, betrayed himself by his voice. Upon which the woman shrieking, ran into the company where there were lights, and cried out she had discovered a man. The women were all in a fright. Aurelia covered up the sacred things and stopped the proceedings, and having ordered the doors to be shut, went about with lights to find Clodius, who was got into the maid's room that he had come in with, and was seized there. The women knew him and drove him out of doors, and at once, that same night went home and told their husbands the story. In the morning, it was all about the town, what an impious attempt Clodius had made, and how he ought to be punished as an offender, not only against those whom he had offended, but also against the public and the gods. Upon which, one of the tribunes impeached him for profaning the holy rites, and some of the principal senators combined together and gave evidence against him, that besides many other horrible crimes, he had been guilty of incest with his own sister, who was married to Lucullus. But the people set themselves against this combination of the nobility, and defended Clodius, which was of great service to him with the judges, who took alarm and were afraid to provoke the multitude. Caesar at once dismissed Pompeia, but being summoned as a witness against Clodius, said he had nothing to charge him with. This looking like a paradox, the accuser asked him why he parted with his wife. Caesar replied, 'I wished my wife to be not so much as suspected.' Some say that Caesar spoke this as his real thought, others, that he did it to gratify the people, who were very earnest to save Clodius. Clodius, at any rate, escaped; most of the judges giving their opinions so written as to be illegible that they might not be in danger from the people by condemning him, nor in disgrace with the nobility by acquitting him.

Witchcraft

Many papyri and tablets survive to testify to a pervasive faith, among all strata of society, in the efficacy of magic. Although both men and women were practitioners, sexual motives were considered particularly unnatural in females, who are portrayed in such works as Apuleius' *Golden Ass* as capable of murdering children and husband to attain their evil desires. Such things at least were believed to have happened in real life: cf. the epitaph for Iucundus (*CIL* VI 19747 / *ILS* 8522, Rome, *c.* A.D. 20): 'As I was approaching my fourth birthday I was seized and put in the ground, when I could have been sweet to my mother and father. A magic hand (*saga manus*) stole me away, everywhere cruel. While she is on earth she can also harm you and your children; guard them, parents, lest sorrow be driven into your hearts.' Horace composed a dramatic poem about a similar event: a young boy is killed to provide ingredients for a love charm to bring back Varus, the lover of the witch Canidia; the text follows.

248. *Ingredients for a love charm. Rome, 1st cent. B.C. (Horace, Epodes 5. Tr. M.R.L.)*

'Oh, by all the gods in the sky who rule earth and the human race, what does this noise mean, why are all of you looking at me savagely? I beg you, by your children, if you ever called on Lucina[12] and she came to bring you successful childbirth – by this purple band on my toga, insignia of innocent childhood; by Jupiter, who will not approve of this –

why are you looking at me like a stepmother, like a wild animal facing a spear?'

This is what the boy said in protest, with his lips trembling. He stood there (they had torn off his children's insignia), a young body, the sort that would soften the sacrilegious heart of a Thracian. Canidia, who had twined little snakes in her dishevelled hair, gave orders to burn in her witch's fire wild fig trees uprooted from tombs and funeral cypresses, eggs dipped in the blood of foul frogs, a night owl's feather, herbs from Iolchus[13] and Spain with its rich poisons, and bones torn from the mouth of a hungry bitch.

Now Sagana, with her skirts tied up, sprinkles water from Lake Avernus[14] through the whole house, with her rough hair standing on end, like a sea-urchin or some bristling wild boar. Vera, who lacks any conscience, had been digging up the ground with thick hoes, groaning with the effort, so the boy could be placed in the ditch and die from watching, throughout the long day, meals brought in two and three times – only his face would remain unburied, like a swimmer hanging in water by his chin. All this so his marrow could be cut out and his liver dried, to make a love charm, once his eyeballs had melted away from staring at the food.

Folia of Ariminum was there also, with her man's lust – so the resort town of Naples and all the neighbouring towns believed – she can bring down the stars and the moon from the sky with her Thessalian incantations. Then Canidia, gnawing her nails – what did she say (or not say?):

'Oh faithful witnesses to my deeds, Night and Diana, you who rule the silent time, when the secret rites are enacted, come to me now, and turn your divine anger on my enemy's house. While wild beasts lie hidden in the treacherous woods, relaxed in sweet slumber, that old man, whom everyone laughs at, my lover Varus – have Subura's[15] dogs bark at him – he has been rubbed with an ointment, the most perfect my hands have yet made. What has happened? Why does my cruel poison work less well than barbarian Medea's, the poisons she used when she went into exile, after taking revenge on her royal rival, high Creon's daughter, when the robe she prepared, a gift steeped in poison, carried off the new bride in fire? No herb, no root hidden in inaccessible places has escaped me. He is lying asleep on his couch, forgetting all of his lovers. But no! He's free to move around, thanks to an incantation by some more knowledgeable poisoner! No, Varus, I won't use ordinary potions. You'll regret what you've done; you'll come back to me, and your devotion to me will return with no help from Marsian spells.[16] I'll prepare a stronger potion, made stronger because you disdain me. You'll see heaven sinking beneath the sea, below the earth's surface, before you'll fail to burn with love for me, just like pitch in dark flames.'

After she said this the boy stopped trying (as he had earlier) to mollify the sacrilegious women with kind words and, uncertain how he should break the silence, he threw out Thyestean curses: 'Your magic poisons don't have the power to invert right and wrong, to stop a man's vengeance. I'll pursue you with curses; no sacrifice can atone for my angry curse. No, when I die the death you have determined, I'll come as a Fury by night,[17] as a shade I'll find your face with my hooked talons, the gods of the Dead[18] have this power, and I'll set on your restless hearts and drive your sleep off in terror. People will pursue you in turn and hit you with stones, you dirty old hags, and the wolves and the birds on the Esquiline hill[19] will scatter your unburied remains – a sight my parents (who alas will survive me)[20] will not fail to enjoy.'

249. *Epitaph with a curse. Rome, 1st cent. A.D. (CIL VI. 20905. Tr. R. Lattimore)*

An epitaph set up by a father to his daughter, with a curse added against the girl's mother, Acte, who had left him.

To the gods of the dead, the tomb of Junia Procula, daughter of Marcus. She lived eight years, eleven months, five days. She left in sorrow her unhappy father and mother. Marcus Junius Euphrosynus put up this altar for himself and_____e (*name erased*).

You, may your daughter's bones and your parents' rest together without you. Whatever you have done to us, may you get the same yourself. Believe me, you will be witness to your [fate]: here are inscribed the marks of eternal shame of Acte, a freedwoman, a treacherous, tricky, hard-hearted poisoner. [I leave her] a nail and a hempen rope to fasten about her neck, and burning pitch to sear her evil heart. Manumitted gratis, she went off with an adulterer, cheated her patron, and took away his servants, a maid and a boy, as he lay in bed, leaving him a lonely, despoiled man, broken-hearted. And the same curse [is laid upon] Hymnus and those who went away with Zosimus.

Defixiones ('bindings') usually give the names of the victim and the author of the curse (cf. no. 131, although the authors' names are omitted here) and list the parts of the body to be affected by the malediction. The reason for the curse is not always given.

250. *A comprehensive curse. Rome, late 2nd/3rd cent. A.D. (ILS 8751. Tr. M.R.L. and M.B.F.)*

This text, written on a thin sheet of lead, was discovered in a cinerary urn in a tomb north of Rome along with the cremated woman's remains.

Rufa Publica: her hands, her teeth, her eyes, her arms, her belly, her tits, her chest, her bones, her marrow, her belly, her legs, her mouth, her feet, her forehead, her nails, her fingers, her belly, her navel, her cunt, her womb, her groin; I curse Rufa Publica on these tablets.

251. *A curse against Aristo. Athens, Roman period. (IG III. iii. 97. 34-41. Tr. M.R.L.)*

I take Aristo and bind her hands and feet and soul; may she not utter an evil word about Philo, but may her tongue become lead and *you* [the *daimon*] bite her tongue!

252. *A curse against Aristocydes. Athens, 4th cent. A.D. (IG III. iii. 78. Tr. M.R.L.)*

Aristocydes and the women who accommodate him; may he never marry another woman; nor a boy either.

253. *A remedy for induration of the breasts. (P.Mag. VII, 208-9/Preisendanz-Henrichs² II, p. 9. Tr. J. Scarborough)*

[A remedy] against induration[21] of the breasts: take a fine linen rag and write on it in black ink: THERTTHARTHRL.[22]

254. *A remedy for ascent of the womb. (P.Mag. VII, 260-71/Preisendanz-Henrichs² II, p. 12. Tr. M.R.L.)*

[A remedy] against ascent of the uterus: 'I swear to you, Womb of the Origin of the World, by him who has been set over the underworld, before Heaven and Earth and Sea came into being, who created the angels, from whom first (*magic words: amichamchou kai chochao cheroei oueiacho odou proseionges*); by him who sits with the Cherubim and who bears his appointed throne; return again back to your seat, [and] do not bite into the heart like a dog, but stop and remain in your proper place; do not rage; as long as I swear to you by him who in the Beginning created the heaven and earth and all that is in them. Halleluia. Amen.' Write that on a plate [or strip] of tin and clothe it in seven colours.[23]

255. *Eumachia. Pompeii, 1st cent. A.D. (CIL X. 810/ILS 3785; 813/ILS 6368; A. Maiuri, Pompeii*[7] *(Rome 1965) 83. Tr. M.B.F.)*

Eumachia was priestess and prominent citizen of the city of Pompeii. She was patroness of the guild of fullers (cleaners, dyers, and clothing makers), one of the most influential trade-guilds of the city because of the importance of the wool industry in Pompeii's economy. Although her ancestry was humble, the fortune she inherited from her father, a brick manufacturer, enabled her to marry into one of Pompeii's older families. She provided the fullers with a large and beautiful building which was probably used as the guild's headquarters.

Over each of the two entrances to the Building of Eumachia in the Civil Forum (the dedication refers to the Emperor Tiberius and his mother, Livia, whose statue was found inside the building):

Eumachia, daughter of Lucius (Eumachius), public priestess, in her own name and that of her son, Marcus Numistrius Fronto, built with her own funds the porch, covered passage, and colonnade and dedicated them to Concordia Augusta and to Pietas.

On the base of a statue (now in the Museo Nazionale, Naples) of Eumachia, with her head veiled as a priestess:

To Eumachia, daughter of Lucius, public priestess, the fullers [dedicated this statue].

On her tomb in the cemetery outside the Porta Nuceria:

Eumachia, daughter of Lucius, [built this] for herself and for her household.

256. *Mamia. Pompeii, 1st cent. A.D. (CIL X. 816; 998/ILS 6369. Tr. M.B.F.)*

From a small temple on the side of the Portico of Concord:

Mamia, daughter of Publius, public priestess, [built this] to the genius of Augustus on her own land and with her own money.

From a monumental tomb on the Street of Tombs:

To Mamia, daughter of Publius, public priestess, the place of burial was given by decree of the decurions.[24]

257. *Cassia Victoria. Misenum, late 2nd cent. A.D. (Unpublished.*[25] *Tr. M.B.F.)*

An inscription from a shrine of the Augustales, a college of freedmen who
kept the emperor's cult.

Cassia Victoria, daughter of Gaius,[26] priestess of the Augustales,
dedicated in her own name and in that of her husband, Lucius
Laecanius Primitivus, a pronaos with columns and epistyle,[27] because of
[the Augustales'] extraordinary goodwill toward them. She gave a
banquet and to each man twelve sesterces.

Priestesses in the Greek East

258. *Flavia Ammon. Phocaea, 1st cent. A.D. (Pleket 11. Tr. M.R.L.)*

The tribe of the Tethades to Flavia Ammon, daughter of Moschus, who
is called Aristion, high priestess of the temple of Asia in Ephesus,
president, twice *stephanephorus*, priestess of Massilia, president of the
games, wife of Flavius Hermocrates, for her excellence and decorous life
and her holiness.

259. *Tata. Aphrodisias, 2nd cent. A.D. (Pleket 18. Tr. M.R.L.)*

The council and the people and the senate honour with first-rank honours
Tata, daughter of Diodorus son of Diodorus son of Leon, reverend
priestess of Hera for life, mother of the city, who became and remained
the wife of Attalus son of Pytheas the *stephanephorus*, herself a member of
an illustrious family of the first rank, who, as priestess of the imperial
cult a second time, twice supplied oil for athletes in hand-bottles, filled
most lavishly from basins for the better part of the night as well [as in the
day], who became a *stephanephorus*, offered sacrifices throughout the year
for the health of the imperial family, who held banquets for the people
many times with couches provided for the public, who herself, for dances
and plays, imported the foremost performers in Asia and displayed them
in her native city (and the neighbouring cities could also come to the
display of the performance), a woman who spared no expense, who loved
honour, glorious in virtue and chastity.

260. *Theano the arrhephoros. Athens, 2nd cent. A.D. (Kaibel 861/IG II²*
3634. Tr. B. Nagy)

Little girls, 'carriers of dew' (*arrhephoroi*), brought a robe and basket to
Athena in an ancient puberty rite. This little girl appears deliberately to
have been named for a Homeric priestess.[28]

My father Sarapion, my mother Chresime, and my five brothers and sisters, o mistress, have dedicated me, Theano the arrhephoros to you, goddess. Grant that my brothers and sisters may reach adulthood successfully and that my parents may grow old safely.

261. *Thesmophane. Athens, 2nd cent. A.D. IG II² 11674/Kaibel 153. Tr. M.R.L.)*

My dear father and mother as well²⁹ gave me the name Thesmophane before I met my sad death. For me the fates spun seven complete years with their threads and then cut them off. And indeed my renowned father lavished on me all the good things that belong to the noblest children. He did not omit libations or anything owed to the gods of the dead for my life. The priests of Eumolpus made a sacred branch for me and gave me great honour. The *thiasōtai* of Dionysus wove me a crown, and I was initiated into the mysteries of torch-bearing Demeter. I won a good honour, since the saying is true that children the gods love die.³⁰ Therefore, father, you were good to me; do not distress your dear heart longer in sorrow.

262. *A priestess of Demeter at Eleusis. Athens, 2nd cent. A.D. (Kaibel 863. Tr. M.R.L.)*

I am Marcianus' mother and Demetrius' daughter; my own name may not be spoken. I locked it away when the Athenians made me sacred priestess of Demeter, and myself hid it in the unconquerable depths. I did not initiate [into the Eleusinian mysteries] the children of Spartan Leda, nor Asclepius who discovered cures that healed diseases, nor Heracles who completed by his efforts all twelve labours for Eurystheus; [instead I initiated] the ruler of the wide earth and sea, the sovereign of innumerable mortals, Hadrian, who lavishes the cities with his boundless wealth, and above all these the famous land of Cecrops.³¹

263. *Berenice. Syros, 2nd/3rd cent. A.D. (Pleket 25. Tr. M.R.L.)*

The resolution of the prytaneis approved by the council and the people: Whereas Berenice, daughter of Nicomachus, wife of Aristocles son of Isidorus, has conducted herself well and appropriately on all occasions, and after she was made a magistrate, unsparingly celebrated rites at her own expense for gods and men on behalf of her native city, and after she was made priestess of the heavenly gods and the holy goddesses Demeter and Kore and celebrated their rites in a holy and worthy manner, has given up her life – meanwhile she had also raised her own children. Voted to commend the span of this woman's lifetime, to crown her with the gold wreath which in our fatherland is customarily used to crown good women. Let the man who proposed this resolution announce at her burial: 'The people of Syros crown Berenice daughter of Nicomachus with a gold crown in recognition of her virtue and her good will towards them.'

264. *Flavia Vibia Sabina. Thasos, late Empire (Pleket 29. Tr. M.R.L.)*

With good fortune. The senate honours Flavia Vibia Sabina, most noteworthy high priestess, and because of her ancestors uniquely mother of the council: she is the only woman, first in all time to have honours equal to those of the senators.

Christianity

Christianity was, for the Romans, another foreign religion (in this case an offshoot of Judaism) to be regarded with suspicion. Like the cult of Bacchus, the Christian religion brought members of the lower classes together in assemblies, which was particularly worrisome to the authorities. Christians were also victims of wildly exaggerated stories and false accusations based upon misinterpretation: incest and cannibalism, for example. Still, the Roman concern was for security of the state; the opposition to Christianity was not theological.

265. *Paul of Tarsus on women. 1st cent. A.D. (I Corinthians 7:1-16, 25-40, 11:2-16, 14:34-35; I Timothy 2:8-14. Tr. New English Bible)*

And now for the matters you wrote about.

It is a good thing for a man to have nothing to do with women; but because there is so much immorality, let each man have his own wife and each woman her own husband. The husband must give the wife what is due to her, and the wife equally must give the husband his due. The wife cannot claim her body as her own; it is her husband's. Equally, the husband cannot claim his body as his own; it is his wife's. Do not deny yourselves to one another, except when you agree upon a temporary abstinence in order to devote yourselves to prayer; afterwards you may come together again; otherwise, for lack of self-control, you may be tempted by Satan.

All this I say by way of concession, not command. I should like you all to be as I am myself; but everyone has the gift God has granted him, one this gift and another that.

To the unmarried and to widows I say this: it is a good thing if they stay as I am myself; but if they cannot control themselves, they should marry. Better be married than burn with vain desire.

To the married I give this ruling, which is not mine but the Lord's: a wife must not separate herself from her husband; if she does, she must either remain unmarried or be reconciled to her husband; and the husband must not divorce his wife.

To the rest I say this, as my own word, not as the Lord's: if a Christian has a heathen wife, and she is willing to live with him, he must not divorce her, and a woman who has a heathen husband willing to live with her must not divorce her husband. For the heathen husband now belongs to God through his Christian wife, and the heathen wife through her Christian husband. Otherwise your children would not belong to God, whereas in fact they do. If on the other hand the heathen partner wishes for a separation, let him have it. In such cases the Christian husband or wife is under no compulsion; but God's call is a call to live in peace. Think of it: as a wife you may be your husband's salvation; as a husband you may be your wife's salvation.

However that may be, each one must order his life according to the gift the Lord has granted him and his condition when God called him. That is what I teach in all our congregations. Was a man called with the marks of circumcision on him? Let him not remove them. Was he uncircumcised when he was called? Let him not be circumcised. Circumcision or uncircumcision is neither here nor there; what matters is to keep God's commands. Every man should remain in the condition in which he was called. Were you a slave when you were called? Do not let that trouble you; but if a chance of liberty should come, take it. For the man who as a slave received the call to be a Christian is the Lord's freedman, and, equally, the free man who received the call is a slave in the service of Christ. You were bought at a price; do not become slaves of men. Thus each one, my friends, is to remain before God in the condition in which he received his call.

On the question of celibacy, I have no instructions from the Lord, but I give my judgment as one who by God's mercy is fit to be trusted.

It is my opinion, then, that in a time of stress like the present this is the best way for a man to live – it is best for a man to be as he is. Are you bound in marriage? Do not seek a dissolution. Has your marriage been dissolved? Do not seek a wife. If, however, you do marry, there is nothing wrong in it; and if a virgin marries, she has done no wrong. But those who marry will have pain and grief in this bodily life, and my aim is to spare you.

What I mean, my friends, is this. The time we live in will not last long.

While it lasts, married men should be as if they had no wives; mourners should be as if they had nothing to grieve them, the joyful as if they did not rejoice; buyers must not count on keeping what they buy, nor those who use the world's wealth on using it to the full. For the whole frame of this world is passing away.

I want you to be free from anxious care. The unmarried man cares for the Lord's business; his aim is to please the Lord. But the married man cares for worldly things; his aim is to please his wife; and he has a divided mind. The unmarried or celibate woman cares for the Lord's business; her aim is to be dedicated to him in body as in spirit; but the married woman cares for worldly things; her aim is to please her husband.

In saying this I have no wish to keep you on a tight rein. I am thinking simply of your own good, of what is seemly, and of your freedom to wait upon the Lord without distraction.

But if a man has a partner in celibacy and feels that he is not behaving properly towards her, if, that is, his instincts are too strong for him; and something must be done, he may do as he pleases; there is nothing wrong in it; let them marry. But if a man is steadfast in his purpose, being under no compulsion, and has complete control of his own choice; and if he has decided in his own mind to preserve his partner in her virginity, he will do well. Thus, he who marries his partner does well, and he who does not will do better.

A wife is bound to her husband as long as he lives. But if the husband die, she is free to marry whom she will, provided the marriage is within the Lord's fellowship. But she is better off as she is; that is my opinion, and I believe that I too have the Spirit of God ...

I commend you for always keeping me in mind, and maintaining the tradition I handed on to you. But I wish you to understand that, while every man has Christ for his Head, woman's head is man, as Christ's Head is God. A man who keeps his head covered when he prays or prophesies brings shame on his head; a woman, on the contrary, brings shame on her head if she prays or prophesies bare-headed: it is as bad as if her head were shaved. If a woman is not to wear a veil she might as well have her hair cut off; but if it is a disgrace for her to be cropped and shaved, then she should wear a veil. A man has no need to cover his head, because man is the image of God, and the mirror of his glory, whereas woman reflects the glory of man. For man did not originally spring from woman, but woman was made out of man; and man was not created for woman's sake, but woman for the sake of man; and therefore it is woman's duty to have a sign of authority on her head, out of regard for the angels. And yet, in Christ's fellowship woman is as essential to man as man to woman. If woman was made out of man, it is through woman that man now comes to be; and God is the source of all.

Judge for yourselves: is it fitting for a woman to pray to God bareheaded? Does not Nature herself teach you that while flowing locks disgrace a man, they are a woman's glory? For her locks were given for covering.

However, if you insist on arguing, let me tell you, there is no such custom among us, or in any of the congregations of God's people ...

As in all congregations of God's people, women should not address the meeting. They have no licence to speak, but should keep their place as the law directs. If there is something they want to know, they can ask their own husbands at home. It is a shocking thing that a woman should address the congregation.

It is my desire, therefore, that everywhere prayers be said by the men of the congregation, who shall lift up their hands with a pure intention, excluding angry or quarrelsome thoughts. Women again must dress in becoming manner, modestly and soberly, not with elaborate hair-styles, not decked out with gold or pearls, or expensive clothes, but with good deeds. as befits women who claim to be religious. A woman must be a learner, listening quietly and with due submission. I do not permit a woman to be a teacher, nor must woman domineer over man; she should be quiet. For Adam was created first, and Eve afterwards; and it was not Adam who was deceived; it was the woman who, yielding to deception, fell into sin.

266. *St Perpetua (Acts of the Christian Martyrs 8.2-10. Tr. H. Musurillo)*

In 203 Septimius Severus banned conversion to either Judaism or Christianity, and as a result of this ban, St Perpetua was martyred in Carthage. Greek and Latin versions of her story were circulated; the account is atypical (and thus, perhaps authentic) because it contains a long narrative attributed to Perpetua herself.[32]

A number of young catechumens were arrested, Revocatus and his fellow slave Felicitas, Saturninus and Secundulus, and with them Vibia Perpetua, a newly married woman of good family and upbringing. Her mother and father were still alive and one of her two brothers was a catechumen like herself. She was about twenty-two years old and had an infant son at the breast. Now from this point on the entire account of her ordeal is her own, according to her own ideas and in the way that she herself wrote it down.

While we were still under arrest, she said, my father out of love for me was trying to persuade me and shake my resolution.

'Father,' said I, 'do you see this vase here, for example, or waterpot or whatever?'

'Yes, I do,' said he.

And I told him: 'Could it be called by any other name than what it is?' And he said: 'No.'

'Well, so too I cannot be called anything other than what I am, a Christian.'

At this my father was so angered by the word 'Christian' that he moved towards me as though he would pluck my eyes out. But he left it at that and departed, vanquished along with his diabolical arguments.

For a few days afterwards I gave thanks to the Lord that I was separated from my father, and I was comforted by his absence. During these few days I was baptized, and I was inspired by the Spirit not to ask for any other favour after the water but simply the perseverence of the flesh. A few days later we were lodged in the prison; and I was terrified, as I had never before been in such a dark hole. What a difficult time it was! With the crowd the heat was stifling; then there was the extortion of the soldiers; and to crown all, I was tortured with worry for my baby there.

Then Tertius and Pomponius, those blessed deacons who tried to take care of us, bribed the soldiers to allow us to go to a better part of the prison to refresh ourselves for a few hours. Everyone then left that dungeon and shifted for himself. I nursed my baby, who was faint from hunger. In my anxiety I spoke to my mother about the child, I tried to comfort my brother, and I gave the child in their charge. I was in pain because I saw them suffering out of pity for me. These were the trials I had to endure for many days. Then I got permission for my baby to stay with me in prison. At once I recovered my health, relieved as I was of my worry and anxiety over the child. My prison had suddenly become a palace, so that I wanted to be there rather than anywhere else.

Then my brother said to me: 'Dear sister, you are greatly privileged; surely you might ask for a vision to discover whether you are to be condemned or freed.'

Faithfully I promised that I would, for I knew that I could speak with the Lord, whose great blessings I had come to experience. And so I said: 'I shall tell you tomorrow.' Then I made my request and this was the vision I had.

I saw a ladder of tremendous height made of bronze, reaching all the way to the heavens, but it was so narrow that only one person could climb up at a time. To the sides of the ladder were attached all sorts of metal weapons: there were swords, spears, hooks, daggers, and spikes; so that if anyone tried to climb up carelessly or without paying attention, he would be mangled and his flesh would adhere to the weapons.

At the foot of the ladder lay a dragon of enormous size, and it would attack those who tried to climb up and try to terrify them from doing so. And Saturus was the first to go up, he who was later to give himself up of his own accord. He had been the builder of our strength, although he was not present when we were arrested. And he arrived at the top of the staircase and he looked back and said to me: 'Perpetua, I am waiting for you. But take care; do not let the dragon bite you.'

'He will not harm me,' I said, 'in the name of Christ Jesus.'

Slowly, as though he were afraid of me, the dragon stuck his head out from underneath the ladder. Then, using it as my first step, I trod on his head and went up.

Then I saw an immense garden, and in it a grey-haired man sat in shepherd's garb; tall he was, and milking sheep. And standing around him were many thousands of people clad in white garments. He raised his head, looked at me, and said: 'I am glad you have come, my child.'

He called me over to him and gave me, as it were, a mouthful of the milk he was drawing; and I took it into my cupped hands and consumed it. And all those who stood around said: 'Amen!' At the sound of this word I came to, with the taste of something sweet still in my mouth. I at once told this to my brother, and we realised that we would have to suffer, and that from now on we would no longer have any hope in this life.

A few days later there was a rumour that we were going to be given a hearing. My father also arrived from the city, worn with worry, and he came to see me with the idea of persuading me.

'Daughter,' he said, 'have pity on my grey head – have pity on me your father, if I deserve to be called your father, if I have favoured you above all your brothers, if I have raised you to reach this prime of your life. Do not abandon me to be the reproach of men. Think of your brothers, think of your mother and your aunt, think of your child, who will not be able to live once you are gone. Give up your pride! You will destroy all of us! None of us will ever be able to speak freely again if anything happens to you.'

This was the way my father spoke out of love for me, kissing my hands and throwing himself down before me. With tears in his eyes he no longer addressed me as his daughter but as a woman. I was sorry for my father's sake, because he alone of all my kin would be unhappy to see me suffer.

I tried to comfort him saying: 'It will all happen in the prisoner's dock as God wills; for you may be sure that we are not left to ourselves but are all in his power.'

And he left me in great sorrow.

One day while we were eating breakfast we were suddenly hurried off for a hearing. We arrived at the forum, and straight away the story went about the neighbourhood near the forum and a huge crowd gathered. We walked up to the prisoner's dock. All the others when questioned admitted their guilt. Then, when it came my turn, my father appeared

with my son, dragged me from the step, and said: 'Perform the sacrifice
– have pity on your baby!'

Hilarianus the governor, who had received his judicial powers as the
successor of the late proconsul Minucius Timinianus, said to me; 'Have
pity on your father's grey head; have pity on your infant son. Offer the
sacrifice for the welfare of the emperors.'

'I will not,' I retorted.

'Are you a Christian?' said Hilarianus.

And I said: 'Yes, I am.'

When my father persisted in trying to dissuade me, Hilarianus
ordered him to be thrown to the ground and beaten with a rod. I felt
sorry for father, just as if I myself had been beaten. I felt sorry for his
pathetic old age.

Then Hilarianus passed sentence on all of us: we were condemned to
the beasts, and we returned to prison in high spirits. But my baby had got
used to being nursed at the breast and to staying with me in prison. So I
sent the deacon Pomponius straight away to my father to ask for the baby.
But father refused to give him over. But as God willed, the baby had no
further desire for the breast, nor did I suffer any inflammation; and so I was relieved of any anxiety for my child and of any discomfort in
my breasts.

Some days later when we were all at prayer, suddenly while praying I
spoke out and uttered the name Dinocrates. I was surprised; for the
name had never entered my mind until that moment. And I was pained
when I recalled what had happened to him. At once I realised that I was
privileged to pray for him. I began to pray for him and to sigh deeply for
him before the Lord. That very night I had the following vision. I saw
Dinocrates coming out of a dark hole, where there were many others
with him, very hot and thirsty, pale and dirty. On his face was the
wound he had when he died.

Now Dinocrates had been my brother according to the flesh; but he
had died horribly of cancer of the face when he was seven years old, and
his death was a source of loathing to everyone. Thus it was for him that I
made my prayer. There was a great abyss between us: neither could
approach the other. Where Dinocrates stood there was a pool full of
water; and its rim was higher than the child's height, so that Dinocrates
had to stretch himself up to drink. I was sorry that, though the pool had
water in it, Dinocrates could not drink because of the height of the rim.
Then I woke up, realising that my brother was suffering. But I was
confident that I could help him in his trouble; and I prayed for him every
day until we were transferred to the military prison. For we were
supposed to fight with the beasts at the military games to be held on the
occasion of the Emperor Geta's birthday. And I prayed for my brother
day and night with tears and sighs that this favour might be granted me.

On the day we were kept in chains, I had this vision shown to me. I saw the same spot I had seen before, but there was Dinocrates all clean, well dressed, and refreshed. I saw a scar where the wound had been; and the pool that I had seen before now had its rim lowered to the level of the child's waist. And Dinocrates kept drinking water from it, and there above the rim was a golden bowl full of water. And Dinocrates drew close and began to drink from it, and yet the bowl remained full. And when he had drunk enough of the water, he began to play as children do. Then I awoke, and I realised that he had been delivered from his suffering.

Some days later, an adjutant named Pudens, who was in charge of the prison, began to show us great humour, realising that we possessed some great power within us. And he began to allow many visitors to see us for our mutual comfort.

Now the day of the contest was approaching, and my father came to see me overwhelmed with sorrow. He started tearing the hairs from his beard and threw them on the ground; he then threw himself on the ground and began to curse his old age and to say such words as would move all creation. I felt sorry for his unhappy old age.

The day before we were to fight with the beasts I saw the following vision. Pomponius the deacon came to the prison gates and began to knock violently. I went out and opened the gate for him. He was dressed in an unbelted white tunic, wearing elaborate sandals. And he said to me: 'Perpetua, come; we are waiting for you.'

Then he took my hand and we began to walk through rough and broken country. At last we came to the amphitheatre out of breath, and he led me into the centre of the arena.

Then he told me: 'Do not be afraid. I am here, struggling with you.' Then he left.

I looked at the enormous crowd who watched in astonishment. I was surprised that no beasts were let loose on me; for I knew that I was condemned to die by the beasts. Then out came an Egyptian against me, of vicious appearance, together with his seconds, to fight with me. There also came up to me some handsome young men to be my seconds and assistants.

My clothes were stripped off, and suddenly I was a man. My seconds began to rub me down with oil, as they are wont to do before a contest. Then I saw the Egyptian on the other side rolling in the dust. Next there came forth a man of marvellous stature, such that he rose above the top of the amphitheatre. He was clad in a beltless purple tunic with two stripes, one on either side, running down the middle of his chest. He wore sandals that were wondrously made of gold and silver, and he carried a wand like an athletic trainer and a green branch on which there were golden apples.

And he asked for silence and said: 'If this Egyptian defeats her he will slay her with the sword. But if she defeats him, she will receive this branch.' Then he withdrew.

We drew close to one another and began to let our fists fly. My opponent tried to get hold of my feet, but I kept striking him in the face with the heels of my feet. Then I was raised up into the air and I began to pummel him without as it were touching the ground. Then when I noticed there was a lull, I put my two hands together linking the fingers of one hand with those of the other and thus I got hold of his head. He fell flat on his face and I stepped on his head.

The crowd began to shout and my assistants started to sing psalms. Then I walked up to the trainer and took the branch. He kissed me and said to me: 'Peace be with you, my daughter!' I began to walk in triumph towards the Gate of Life.[33] Then I awoke. I realised that it was not with wild animals that I would fight but with the Devil, but I knew that I would win the victory. So much for what I did up until the eve of the contest. About what happened at the contest itself, let him write of it who will.

267. *Persecution under Diocletian. (Acts of the Christian Martyrs 22. Tr. H. Musurillo)*

When the Emperor Diocletian became ill in 303, a sacrifice for his health was required of all citizens, and those who did not cooperate were executed.

Since the advent and the presence on earth of our Lord and Saviour Jesus Christ, the greater the grace of the men of old, so much the greater was the victory of holy men. For instead of those visible enemies, we have now begun to crush enemies that cannot be seen with bodily eyes, and the invisible substance of the demons has been handed over to the flames by pure and holy women who were full of the Holy Spirit. Such were the three saintly women who came from the city of Thessalonica, the city that the inspired Paul celebrated when he praised its faith and love, saying, *Your faith in God has gone out to every place.*[34] And elsewhere he says, *Of charity for your brothers I have no need to write to you; for you yourselves have learned from God to love one another.*[35]

When the persecution was raging under the Emperor Maximian, these women, who had adorned themselves with virtue, following the precepts of the Gospel, abandoned their native city, their family, property, and possessions because of their love of God and their expectation of heavenly things, performing deeds worthy of their father Abraham. They fled the persecutors, according to the commandment, and took refuge on a high mountain. There they gave themselves to prayer: though their bodies resided on a mountain top, their souls lived in heaven.[36]

At any rate, they were here captured and brought to the official who was conducting the persecution, that, by thus fulfilling the rest of the divine commands and loving their Master even unto death, they might weave for themselves the chaplet of immortality. Of these girls one had preserved the shining purity of her baptism according to the holy prophet who said: *You will wash me and I shall be whiter than snow,*[37] and she was called Chione.[38] The second girl possessed the gift of our God and Saviour within herself and manifested it to everyone according to the word, *My peace I give you,*[39] and she was called Irene[40] by everyone. The third girl possessed the perfection of the Gospel, loving God with her whole heart and her neighbour as herself, in accord with the holy Apostle who says, *The aim of our charge is love,*[41] and she was appropriately named Agape.[42] When these three girls were brought before the magistrate and refused to sacrifice, he sentenced them to the fire, in order that thus by a short time in the fire they might overcome those that are devoted to fire, that is, the Devil and all his heavenly host of demons, and, attaining the incorruptible crown of glory, they might endlessly praise along with the angels the God who had showered this grace upon them. The record that was taken down in their case is the material of our account.

The prefect Dulcitius was sitting on the tribunal, and the court clerk Artemisius spoke: 'With your permission, I shall read the charge which was sent to your *genius* by the guard here present, in connection with the parties in court.'

'You may read it,' said the prefect Dulcitius. And the charge was duly read: 'To you, my lord, greetings from Cassander, staff-officer. This is to inform you, sir, that Agatho, Irene, Agape, Chione, Cassia, Philippa, and Eutychia refuse to eat sacrificial food, and so I have referred them to your genius.'

'What is this insanity,' said the prefect Dulcitius, 'that you refuse to obey the order of our most religious emperors and Caesars?' And turning to Agatho, he said: 'When you came to the sacrifices, why did you not perform the cult practices like other religious people?'

'Because I am a Christian,' said Agatho.

The prefect Dulcitius said: 'Do you still remain in the same mind today?'

'Yes,' said Agatho.

The prefect Dulcitius said: 'What do you say, Agape?'

'I believe in the living God,' replied Agape, 'and I refuse to destroy my conscience.'

'What do you say, Irene?' asked the prefect Dulcitius. 'Why did you disobey the command of our lords the emperors and Caesars?'

'Because of my fear of God,' said Irene.

'What do you say, Chione?' asked the prefect.

'I believe in the living God,' replied Chione, 'and I refuse to do this.'

The prefect said: 'And how about you, Cassia?'

'I wish to save my soul,' said Cassia.

The prefect said: 'Are you willing to partake of the sacrificial meat?'

'I am not,' said Cassia.

The prefect said: 'And what say you, Philippa?'

'I say the same,' said Philippa.

'What do you mean, the same?' said the prefect.

Said Philippa: 'I mean, I would rather die than partake.'

'Eutychia,' said the prefect, 'what do you say?'

'I say the same,' said Eutychia; 'I would rather die.'

The prefect said: 'Do you have a husband?'

'He is dead,' said Eutychia.

'When did he die?' asked the prefect.

'About seven months ago,' said Eutychia.

The prefect said, 'How is it then that you are pregnant?'

Eutychia said: 'By the man whom God gave me.'

The prefect said: 'But how can you be pregnant when you say your husband is dead?'

Eutychia said: 'No one can know the will of almighty God. So God willed it.'

The prefect said: 'I urge Eutychia to cease this madness and to return to sound reason. What do you say? Will you obey the imperial command?'

'No, I will not,' said Eutychia. 'I am a Christian, a servant of almighty God.'

The prefect said: 'Since Eutychia is pregnant, she shall be kept meanwhile in jail.' Then he added: 'What say you, Agape? Will you perform all the actions which religious persons perform in honour of our lords the emperors and Caesars?'

Agape replied: 'It is not at all in Satan's power. He cannot move my reason; it is invincible.'

The prefect said: 'What say you, Chione?'

Chione said: 'No one can change my mind.'

The prefect said: 'Do you have in your possession any writings, parchments, or books of the impious Christians?'

Chione said: 'We do not, sir. Our present emperors have taken these from us.'

'Who was it who gave you this idea?' asked the prefect.

'God almighty,' said Chione.

The prefect said: 'Who was it who counselled you to commit such folly?'

'It was almighty God,' answered Chione, 'and his only begotten Son, our Lord Jesus Christ.'

The prefect Dulcitius said: 'It is clear to all that you are all liable to the crime of treason against our lords the emperors and Caesars. But seeing that you have persisted in this folly for such a long time, in spite of strong warnings and so many decrees, sanctioned by stern threats, and have despised the command of our lords the emperors and Caesars, remaining in this impious name of Christian, and seeing that even today when you were ordered by the soldiers and officials to deny your belief and signify this in writing, you refused – therefore you shall receive the punishment appropriate for you.'

Then he read the sentence written on a sheet: 'Whereas Agape and Chione have with malicious intent acted against the divine decree of our lords the Augusti and Caesars, and whereas they adhere to the worthless and obsolete worship of the Christians which is hateful to all religious men, I sentence them to be burned.' Then he added: 'Agatho, Irene, Cassia, Philippa, and Eutychia, because of their youth are to be put in prison in the meanwhile.'

After the most holy women were consumed in the flames, the saintly girl Irene was once again brought before the court on the following day. Dulcitius said to her: 'It is clear from what we have seen that you are determined in your folly, for you have deliberately kept even till now so many tablets, books, parchments, codices, and pages of the writings of the former Christians of unholy name; even now, though you denied each time that you possessed such writings, you did show a sign of recognition when they were mentioned. You are not satisfied with the punishment of your sisters, nor do you keep before your eyes the terror of death. Therefore you must be punished.

'It would not, however, seem out of place to show you some measure of mercy: if even now you would be willing to recognise the gods you will be released from all danger and punishment. Now what do you say? Will you do the bidding of our emperors and Caesars? And are you prepared to eat the sacrificial meats and to sacrifice to the gods?'

'No,' said Irene, 'I am not prepared, for the sake of the God almighty who *has created heaven and earth and the seas and all that is in them.*[43] For those who transgress the word of God there awaits the great judgment of eternal punishment.'

The prefect Dulcitius said: 'Who was it that advised you to retain those parchments and writings up to the present time?'

'It was almighty God,' said Irene, 'who bade us to love him unto death. For this reason we did not dare to be traitors, but we chose to be burned alive or suffer anything else that might happen to us rather than betray the writings.'

The prefect said: 'Was anyone else aware that the documents were in the house where you lived?'

'No one else,' said Irene, 'saw them, save almighty God who knows all things. But no stranger. As for our own relatives, we considered them worse than our enemies, in fear that they would denounce us. Hence we told no one.'

'Last year,' said the prefect, 'when this edict of our lords the emperors and Caesars was first promulgated, where did you hide?'

'Wherever God willed,' said Irene. 'We lived on the mountains, in the open air, as God is my witness.'

'Whom were you living with?' asked the prefect.

Irene answered. 'We lived out of doors in different places among the mountains.'

The prefect said: 'Who supplied you with bread?'

Irene answered: 'God, who supplies all men.'

'Was your father aware of this?' asked the prefect.

Irene answered: 'I swear by almighty God, he was not aware; he knew nothing at all about it.'

'Were any of your neighbours aware of this?' asked the prefect.

Irene answered: 'Go and question our neighbours, and inquire about the area to see whether anyone knew where we were.'

The prefect said: 'Now after you returned from the mountain where you had been, as you say, were any persons present at the reading of these books?'

Irene answered: 'They were in our house and we did not dare to bring them out. In fact, it caused us much distress that we could not devote ourselves to them night and day as we had done from the beginning until that day last year when we hid them.'

Dulcitius the prefect said: 'Your sisters, in accordance with my commands in their regard, have received their sentence. Now you were guilty even before you ran away and before you concealed these writings and parchments, and hence I do not wish you to die immediately in the same way. Instead I sentence you to be placed naked in the brothel with the help of the public notaries of this city and of Zosimus with the executioner; and you will receive merely one loaf of bread from our residence, and the notaries will not allow you to leave.'

And so, after the notaries and the slave Zosimus, the executioner, were brought in, the prefect said: 'Be it known to you that if ever I find out from the troops that this girl was removed from the spot where I have ordered her to be even for a single instant, you will immediately be punished with the most extreme penalties. The writings we have referred to, in the cabinets and chests belonging to Irene, are to be publicly burned.'

After those who were put in charge had taken the girl off to the public brothel in accordance with the prefect's order, by the grace of the Holy Spirit which preserved and guarded her pure and inviolate for the God who is the lord of all things, no man dared to approach her or so much as tried to insult her in speech. Hence the prefect Dulcitius called back this most saintly girl, had her stand before the tribunal, and said to her: 'Do you still persist in the same folly?'

But Irene said to him: 'It is not folly, but piety.'

'It was abundantly clear from your earlier testimony,' said the prefect Dulcitius, 'that you did not wish to submit religiously to the bidding of the emperors; and now I perceive that you are persisting in the same foolishness. Therefore you shall pay the appropriate penalty.'

He then asked for a sheet of papyrus and wrote the sentence against her as follows: 'Whereas Irene has refused to obey the command of the emperors and to offer sacrifice, and still adheres to a sect called the Christians, I therefore sentence her to be burned alive, as I did her two sisters before her.'

After this sentence had been pronounced by the prefect, the soldiers took the girl and brought her to a high place, where her sisters had been martyred before her. They ignited a huge pyre and ordered her to climb up on it. And the holy woman Irene, singing and praising God, threw herself upon it and so died. It was in the ninth consulship of Diocletian Augustus, in the eighth of Maximian Augustus, on the first day of April, in the kingship of our Lord Jesus Christ, who reigns for ever, with whom there is glory to the Father with the Holy Spirit for ever. Amen.

268. *Gnostic ritual. Lugdunum, 2nd cent. A.D. (Irenaeus, Against Heresies 1. 13. 1-4. (excerpts). Tr. M.R.L.)*

Irenaeus, a second-century bishop of Lugdunum (Lyons), in describing the initiation of a woman into a Gnostic sect, emphasises as the most dangerous aspects of this heretical cult its appeal to women and the priest Marcus' use of magic tricks. The important role played by a female essence (grace) in the ritual, a characteristic of Gnostic Christian belief, is significantly absent from the conversion literature of the 'right-thinking' or orthodox church in this period.[44]

There is another one of those Gnostics who prides himself on having improved on his teacher. His name is Marcus. He is skilled in the art of false magic, and has used it to deceive many men and not a few women and to convert them to his cult, on the grounds that he is the most knowledgeable and has the greatest access to hidden and indescribable places. One could call him the One before the Antichrist (if such a person existed).[45] ... He pretends to say grace over a cup with wine in it; while he strings out his prayer at great length, he makes the wine turn red and purple, so that they will believe that the true Grace of the Company of the Most High is letting her blood drop into his cup during his prayer, and that those present should strongly desire to taste of that cup so that into them too Grace would drop, because she is summoned by that magician.[46] Again, he gives women cups full of wine and orders them to say grace in his presence. When this is done he offers another cup much larger than the one over which the deceived woman has said grace; he then pours from the smaller cup (over which the woman said grace) into the much larger one which he has brought forward; at the same time he says as follows: 'May grace who is before all things, who cannot be known or imagined, fill your inner person and multiply in you her understanding, sowing her mustard seed in good soil.'[47] By saying this sort of thing he makes the poor woman insane, while he appears to be working wonders, since the bigger cup is filled up by the smaller cup, so that it spills over. By performing other tricks like that he has destroyed many people, and steals them for his cult ...

He spends his time mainly with women, and particularly with those who come from good families and who have fine clothes and are very rich. He frequently deceives them with flattery, and seduces them by saying: 'I want you to share in my grace, since the Father of All always sees your angel before his face.[48] The place of your greatness is in *us*; it is right that we come together into one being. Take grace first from me and through me. Prepare yourself as a bride to receive your bridegroom so that you may be what I am, and I be what you are. Set in your bridal chamber the seed of light. Receive from me your bridegroom, take him, and be taken in him. Behold grace descends on you. Open your mouth and prophesy.' But when the woman answers 'I have never prophesied and I have nothing to prophesy,' he offers new prayers, to the bewilderment of the woman who is being deluded: 'Open your mouth and speak whatever comes to you, and you will prophesy.' And she in her delusion, excited by what has already been said, her courage stimulated by the notion that she can prophesy, with her heart pounding harder than it should, takes the chance, and speaks in her delirium, and all sorts of things come out, foolishly and brazenly ... From that time on she thinks she is a Prophetess and gives thanks to Marcus because he shared his grace with her. She offers to pay him, not only by giving him her possessions (by which means he has amassed a huge amount of wealth) but also by intercourse with her body, and in addition she seeks to be united with him in everything so that she may enter with him into the One ... This same Marcus uses love potions and aphrodisiacs so that he can inflict violence on the bodies of some women – not of all. Those who return to the Church of God very often confess that not only have their bodies been corrupted by him but that they were passionately in love with him ...

269. *Celibacy. Palestine, 4th cent. A.D. (St Jerome, Against Jovinianus 47. Tr. W.H. Fremantle)*

In the process of marshalling evidence against marriage (and women) the priest Jerome, who often appears to be more concerned with making an effective case than with historical accuracy, cites an otherwise unknown treatise on marriage by Aristotle's successor Theophrastus (fourth century B.C.). Such treatises had been in circulation since the late fifth century B.C., and it is interesting that even in the context of Christian theology Greek and Roman misogyny did not lose its currency.

A book *On Marriage*, worth its weight in gold, passes under the name of Theophrastus.[49] In it the author asks whether a wise man marries. And after laying down the conditions – that the wife must be fair, of good character, and honest parentage, the husband in good health and of ample means, and after saying that under these circumstances a wise man sometimes enters the state of matrimony, he immediately proceeds thus: 'But all these conditions are seldom satisfied in marriage. A wise man therefore must not take a wife. For in the first place his study of philosophy will be hindered, and it is impossible for anyone to attend to his books and his wife. Matrons want many things, costly dresses, gold, jewels, great outlay, maid-servants, all kinds of furniture, litters and gilded coaches. Then come lectures the livelong night: she complains that one lady goes out better dressed than she: that another is looked up to by all: "I am a poor despised nobody at the ladies' assemblies." "Why did you ogle that creature next door?" "Why were you talking to the maid?" "What did you bring from the market?" "I am not allowed to have a single friend, or companion." She suspects that her husband's love goes the same way as her hate. There may be in some neighbouring city the wisest of teachers; but if we have a wife we can neither leave her behind, nor take the burden with us. To support a poor wife, is hard: to put up with a rich one, is torture.

'Notice, too, that in the case of a wife you cannot pick and choose: you must take her as you find her. If she has a bad temper, or is a fool, if she has a blemish, or is proud, or has bad breath, whatever her fault may be – all this we learn after marriage. Horses, asses, cattle, even slaves of the smallest worth, clothes, kettles, wooden seats, cups, and earthenware pitchers, are first tried and then bought: a wife is the only thing that is not shown before she is married, for fear she may not give satisfaction. Our gaze must always be directed to her face, and we must always praise her beauty: if you look at another woman, she thinks that she is out of favour. She must be called my lady, her birthday must be kept, we must swear by her health and wish that she may survive us, respect must be paid to the nurse, to the nursemaid, to the father's slave, to the foster-child, to the handsome hanger-on, to the curled darling who manages her affairs, and to the eunuch who ministers to the safe indulgence of her lust: names which are only a cloak for adultery.

'Upon whomsoever she sets her heart, they must have her love though they want her not. If you give her the management of the whole house, you must yourself be her slave. If you reserve something for yourself, she will not think you are loyal to her; but she will turn to strife and hatred, and unless you quickly take care, she will have the poison ready. If you introduce old women, and soothsayers, and prophets, and vendors of jewels and silken clothing, you imperil her chastity; if you shut the door upon them, she is injured and fancies you suspect her. But what is the good of even a careful guardian, when an unchaste wife cannot be watched, and a chaste one ought not to be? For necessity is but a faithless keeper of chastity, and she alone really deserves to be called pure, who is free to sin if she chooses. If a woman be fair, she soon finds lovers; if she be ugly, it is easy to be wanton. It is difficult to guard what many long for. It is annoying to have what no one thinks worth possessing. But the misery of having an ugly wife is less than that of watching a comely one. Nothing is safe, for which a whole people sighs and longs. One man entices with his figure, another with his brains, another with his wit, another with his open hand. Somehow, or sometime, the fortress is captured which is attacked on all sides.

'Men marry, indeed, so as to get a manager for the house, to solace weariness, to banish solitude; but a faithful slave is a far better manager, more submissive to the master, more observant of his ways, than a wife who thinks she proves herself mistress if she acts in opposition to her husband, that is, if she does what pleases her not what she is commanded. But friends, and servants who are under the obligation of benefits received, are better able to wait upon us in sickness than a wife who makes us responsible for her tears (she will sell you enough to make a deluge for the hope of a legacy); who boasts of her anxiety, yet drives her sick husband to the distraction of despair. But if she herself feels ill, we must fall sick with her and never leave her bedside. Or if she be a good and agreeable wife (how rare a bird she is!), we have to share her groans in childbirth, and suffer torture when she is in danger.'[50]

A wise man can never be alone. He has with him the good men of all time, and turns his mind freely wherever he chooses. What is inaccessible to him in person he can embrace in thought. And, if men are scarce, he converses with God. He is never less alone than when alone.

264a. *Paulina, priestess of several mystery cults. Rome, A.D. 384 (ILS 1259-61. Tr. M.R.L.)*

Wife of Vettius Agorius Praetextatus, an important imperial official and leader of the pagans in the Senate, a devout adherent of traditional religion.[51] Cf. nos 258-64.

To the gods of the dead. Vettius Agorius Praetextatus, augur, priest of Vesta, priest of the Sun, quindecemvir,[52] curialis of Hercules, initiate of Liber and the Eleusinian [mysteries], hierophant, neocorus, tauroboliatus, father of fathers.[53] In public office imperial quaestor, praetor of Rome, governor of Tuscia and Umbria, governor of Lusitania, proconsul of Achaia, praefect of Rome, senatorial legate on seven missions, prefect of the praetorian guard twice in Italy and Illyrica, consul ordinarius elect,[54] and Aconia Fabia Paulina,[55] initiate of Ceres and the Eleusinian [mysteries], initiate of Hecate at Aegina, tauroboliata, hierophant. They lived together for forty years.

(*On the right side of the tomb*). Vettius Agorius Praetextatus to his wife Paulina. (*In verse*) Paulina, conscious of truth and chastity, devoted to the temples and friend of the divinities, who put her husband before herself, and Rome before her husband, proper, faithful, pure in mind and body, kindly to all, helpful to her family gods ... (*On the left side*) Vettius Agorius Praetextatus to his wife Paulina. (*In verse*) Paulina, the partnership of our heart is the origin of your propriety; it is the bond of chastity and pure love and fidelity born in heaven. To this partnership I entrusted the hidden secrets of my mind; it was a gift of the gods, who bind our marriage couch with loving and chaste bonds. With a mother's devotion, with a wife's charm, with a sister's bond, with a daughter's modesty; with the great trust by which we are united with our friends, from the experience of our life together, by the alliance of our marriage, in pure, faithful, simple concord; you helped your husband, loved him, honoured him, cared for him.

(*On the back of the monument. Paulina is speaking, in verse*) My parents' distinction did nothing greater for me than that I even then seemed worthy of my husband. But all glory and honour is my husband's name, Agorius. You, descended from noble seed, have at the same time glorified your country, senate, and wife with your mind's judgment, your character and your industry, with which you have reached the highest pinnacle of excellence. For whatever has been produced in either language by the skill of the sages to whom the gate of heaven is open, whether songs that poets composed or writings in prose, these you make better than when you took them up to read.[56] But these are small matters; you as pious initiate conceal in the secrecy of your mind what was revealed in the sacred mysteries, and you with knowledge worship the manifold divinity of the gods;[57] you kindly include as colleague in the rites your wife, who is respectful of men and gods and is faithful to you. Why should I speak of your honours and powers and the joys sought in men's prayers? These you always judge transitory and insignificant, since your title to eminence depends on the insignia of your priesthood. My husband, by the gift of your learning you keep me pure and chaste from the fate of death; you take me into the temples and devote me as the servant of the gods. With you as my witness I am introduced to all the mysteries; you, my pious consort, honour me as priestess of Dindymene and Attis with sacrificial rites of the taurobolium; [58] you instruct me as minister of Hecate in the triple secret and you make me worthy of the rites of Greek Ceres. On account of you everyone praises me as pious and blessed, because you yourself have proclaimed me as good through the whole world; though unknown I am known to all.[59] For with you as husband how could I not be pleasing? Roman mothers seek an example from me, and think their offspring handsome if they are like yours.[60] Now men, now women want and approve the insignia that you as teacher have given me. Now that all these have been taken away I your wife waste away in sorrow; I would have been happy, if the gods had given me a husband who had survived me, but still I am happy because I am yours and have been yours and will now be yours after my death.

(*Another inscription*) To Fabia Aconia Paulina, daughter of Aco Catullinus formerly prefect and consul, wife of Vettius Praetextatus prefect and consul elect, initiate at Eleusis to the god Iacchus, Ceres and Cora, initiate at Lerna to the god Liber and Ceres and Cora,[61] initiate at Aegina' to the two goddesses, tauroboliata, priestess of Isis, hierophant of the goddess Hecate, and initiate in the rites of the Greek Ceres.[62]

(*Inscription on a statue base*) In honour of Coelia Concordia, chief vestal virgin, Fabia Paulina arranged that a statue be made and set up first on account of her distinguished chastity and celebrated holiness concerning the divine cult, and chiefly because [Coelia Concordia] first had set up a statue to [Paulina's] husband Vettius Agorius Praetextatus, who was a man in all ways exceptional and deserving of honour even by virgins and by priestesses of this [high] rank.[63]

---

1. The *ius trium liberorum* or 'right of three children' was part of the Augustan marriage legislation (cf. above, p. 181. A mother of three children (four if a freedwoman) was released from *tutela*, or guardianship.

2. See also Livy. 39. 8-18.

3. Cf. D.A. Russell, *Plutarch* (London 1973) 83.

4. Cf. the description of the women worshippers of Dionysus in Euripides' *Bacchae* (especially 134-66), rushing through the mountains, freed from the constraints of home and domestic life.

5. 'Sooty'.

6. 'Destroyers'.

7. Cf. Dionysiac rituals, above, p.113.

8. I.e. that the Catilinarian conspiracy had been discovered and the conspirators arrested.

9. Plutarch tells the same story in shorter form in his *Life of Cicero*, 28.

10. P. Clodius Pulcher, whose sister Clodia is condemned by Cicero in the *Pro Caelio* (above, p. 147).

11. 'Good'; see no. 246.

12. An epithet of Juno as goddess of childbirth.

13. A town in Thessaly, known for witchcraft. Cf. *Odes* 1.27.21.

14. A volcanic lake in Campania, thought to be the entrance to the underworld.

15. The Subura was a crowded, dirty section of Rome between the Viminal and Esquiline Hills. Though it was notorious for containing many brothels, it also contained respectable merchants and residents.

16. The Marsi inhabited the mountains east of Rome. They practised magic, but it was, apparently, not strong enough for Canidia.

17. That is, an avenger.

18. The Manes (above, p. 211), who are invoked on many tombstones.

19. The land outside the Esquiline Gate (on the east side of the city) was used as a cemetery for paupers. Unlike other Roman corpses of this period, those placed here were not cremated, hence the reference to limbs. It is interesting to note that Maecenas, Horace's patron, built his villa in this area: cf. Horace, *Satires* 1.8.

20. The conventional conclusion to a dying victim's curse (e.g. Dido's, *Aeneid* 4.620). Throughout antiquity critical significance was attached to burial procedures and places by pagan and Christian, rich and poor.

21. Hardening.

22. A series of magic letters.

23. The tin strip or plate would be worn on the arm like an amulet.

24. The local senate.

25. For the archaeological context of the inscription, see A. de Franciscis in *Atti del decimo convegno di studi sulla Magna Grecia* (Taranto 1970), pp. 447-9. We are indebted to Professor J.H. D'Arms for bringing the inscription to our attention.

26. This indicates free birth. Her husband, however, was a freedman.

27. On which this inscription is carved.

28. See W. Burkert, *Hermes* 94 (1966) 1-25. She bears the name of the famous priestess in Homer's *Iliad*; see B. Nagy, *CJ* 74 (1979) 261.

29. Usually the father named the child. As in the case of Theano (p. 260), her name indicates her parents may have wanted her to become a priestess, in this case of Demeter, for whom the festival of Thesmophoria was celebrated.

30. Menander's line 'Those whom the gods love die young' (Fr. 111 Koerte) had by the 2nd cent. B.C. become proverbial.

31. Attica.

32. See esp. E.R. Dodds, *Pagan and Christian in an Age of Anxiety* (Cambridge 1965) 47-53.

33. Arenas had two gates, the .Porta Sanavivaria (Gate of Life) for gladiators who survived, and the Porta Libitina (Gate of Death). On the political significance of her death, see M.R. Lefkowitz, *Journ. Amer. Acad. of Religion* 44 (1976) 417-21 and G.E.M. de Ste. Croix, *Past and Present* 26 (1963) 6-37.

34. I Thessalonians 1:8.

35. I Thessalonians 4:9.

36. Cf. Matthew 10:23. In Euripides' *Bacchae* the women's being 'on the mountain' is also construed as a serious social threat (e.g. 217-20).

37. Psalm 51:7.

38. 'Snow'.

39. John 14/27.

40. 'Peace'.

41. I Timothy 1:5.

42. 'Love'.

43. Acts 4:24.

44. On the role of women in Gnostic cults, see E.H. Pagels, *The Gnostic Gospels* (New York 1979) 48-69; on women in orthodox practice, A. Cameron, *Greece and Rome* 27 (1980) 60-8.

45. As if he were John the Anti-Baptist.

46. Cf. the conversion language used by Jesus in the Gnostic *Gospel of Thomas*: 'He who will drink from my mouth will become as I am' (50.28).

47. Cf. Mark 4: 31.

48. Matthew 18:10.

49. The fragment of 'Theophrastus' has also been attributed to Seneca (Fr. 13, 47ff.) The anthologist Stobaeus preserves some theoretical abstracts from ethical treatises for and against marriage by Antiphon the Sophist (5th cent. B.C., 87 B 49 Diels-Kranz). and the Hellenistic Neopythagoreans (collected in Thesleff), and the Stoics Antipater (1st cent. B.C.) and Hierocles (1st cent. A.D.).

50. Cf. Antiphon (see note 49): 'Is it not clear that a wife, if she is to his mind, gives her husband no less cause for love and pain than he does to himself, for the health of two bodies, the acquisition of two livelihoods, and for respectability and honour? Suppose children are born: then all is full of anxiety, and the youthful spring goes out of the mind, and the countenance is no longer the same' (tr. K. Freeman, *Ancilla to the Pre-Socratic Philosophers* (Cambridge, Mass. 1957) 149-50).

51. See esp. H. Bloch, 'The last pagan revival in the West,' *Harvard Theol. Review* 38 (1945) 199-244.

52. These last three titles signify that Praetextatus was a member of three out of the four ancient priestly colleges; priest of the Sun could refer to the cult either of Mithras (cf. *ILS* 4152) or Sol Invictus; for Praetextatus (as for the Emperor Julian) the Sun represented the Twelve Gods (Macrobius, *Sat.* 1. xvii, 1-xxiv.1).

53. These titles refer respectively to the cult of the oriental gods Serapis, Magna Mater and Mithras. In the ritual of the taurobolium a bull (*tauros*) was slaughtered over the head of the initiate while he/she stood below in a pit. Through the shower of blood the initiate was reborn for eternity (e.g. *ILS* 4152); cf. the metaphorical rebirth of Christians through drinking the wine that represents the blood of the Saviour.

54. Praetextatus was proconsul of Achaea in 362 under the philhellenic pagan Emperor Julian the 'Apostate', a particular honour. He was prefect of Rome in 367 under the Emperor Valentinian, when Christian factions were disputing the papacy. During this period he restored the Portico of the Twelve Gods with its statues in the Roman Forum. He was prefect of the Praetorian guard when he died in 384, and consul elect for 385, the year of his wife's death.

55. She has the honorary title of 'woman of distinction'.

56. Praetextatus translated Themistius' paraphrases of Aristotle's *Prior and Posterior Analytics*, but Paulina's words suggest that he also had better editions prepared of works of Latin literature.

57. See n.52 above on the Twelve Gods.

58. Dindymene, i.e. the Magna Mater. Praetextatus showed an unusual concern for the religious education of his wife; see P. Brown, *Religion and Society in the Age of Augustine* (London 1972) 172. Cf. *ILS* 4154, an inscription on an altar set up in 340 by Caecina Lolliana and her son Ceionius Rufus Volusianus; his sister Sabina was an initiate of some of the same mystery cults as Paulina.

59. The reverse of Clodia's situation; see no. 155, p. 147.

60. A variation on the usual praise of close resemblance of father and son; see pp. 104, 162.

61. As governor of Achaea Praetextatus had protected these cults against the Christian government.

62. I.e. the Magna Mater; with Isis, this represents her participation in Oriental cult, cf. n. 53.

63. This action had been opposed by the prefect of Rome of 385, the prominent pagan Symmachus, on the grounds that it was untraditional to bestow such honours on men (Symm., *Ep.* 2. 36). In general see esp. H. Bloch, 'The pagan revival in the West at the end of the fourth century,' in A. Momigliano, ed., *The Conflict between Paganism and Christianity in the Fourth Century* (Oxford 1963) 193-218.

ABBREVIATIONS

AP	*Greek Anthology,* ed W.R. Paton, LCL (Cambridge, Mass. 1916)
ARS	A.C. Johnson, P.R. Coleman-Norton, F.C. Bourne, *Ancient Roman Statutes* (Austin, Texas, 1961)
BGU	*Ägyptische Urkunden aus den Museen zu Berlin: Griechische Urkunden*
CIL	*Corpus Inscriptionum Latinarum* (Berlin 1863-)
FGH	F. Jacoby, *Die Fragmente der griechischen Historiker* (Berlin 1923-50)
FH	P. Friedländer, with H.B. Hoffleit, *Epigrammata: Greek Inscriptions in Verse* (Berkeley, Calif. 1948)
FHG	C. Muller, *Fragmenta Historicorum Graecorum,* 5 vols (Paris, 1848-70)
Finley	M.I. Finley, *Studies in Land and Credit in Ancient Athens, 500-200 B.C.* (New Brunswick, N.J. 1951)
FIRA	S. Riccobono et al., *Fontes Iuris Romani Antejustiniani,* 2nd ed., 3 vols (Florence 1940-43)
GHI	R. Meiggs and D. Lewis, *A Selection of Greek Historical Inscriptions* (Oxford 1969)
GLP	*Select Papyri* III, ed. D.L. Page, LCL (Cambridge, Mass. 1941)
IG	*Inscriptiones Graecae* (Berlin 1873-)
ILLRP	A. Degrassi, *Inscriptiones Latinae Liberae Rei Publicae,* I² (Florence 1965), II (Florence 1963)
ILS	H. Dessau, *Inscriptiones Latinae Selectae,* 3 vols (Berlin 1892-1916)
I. Magn.	O. Kern, *Die Inschriften von Magnesia am Maeander* (Berlin 1900)
JEA	*Journal of Egyptian Archaeology*
JÖAI	*Jahreshefte des Österreichischen Archäologischen Instituts*
Kaibel	G. Kaibel, *Epigrammata Graeca ex lapidibus conlecta* (Berlin 1878)
P. Cattaoui	B.P. Grenfell and A.S. Hunt, 'Papyrus Cattaoui,' *Archiv für Papyrusforschung* 3 (1903-6) 55ff.
P. Eleph.	O. Rubensohn, *Elephantine-Papyri* (*BGU*, Sonderheft)
Peek	W. Peek, *Griechische Vers-Inschriften,* I, *Grab-epigramme* (Berlin 1955)
P. Fam. Tebt.	B.A. van Gronigen, *Papyrologica Lugduno-Batava* (Leiden 1950)
P. Hibeh	B.P. Grenfell and A.S. Hunt, *The Hibeh Papyri*
Pleket	H.W. Pleket, *Epigraphica II: Texts on the Social History of the Greek World* (Leiden 1969)
P. Mag.	K. Preisendanz, *Papyri Graecae Magicae* (Leipzig 1928)
P. Mich.	J.G. Winter, *Papyri in the University of Michigan Collection* (Ann Arbor 1936)
P. Oxy.	B.P. Grenfell and A.S. Hunt, *The Oxyrhynchus Papyri,* 17 vols (1896-1927)
PSI	G. Vitelli et al., *Papiri della Società Italiana,* 10 vols (1912-32)
P. Tebt.	B.P. Grenfell, A.S. Hunt et al., *The Tebtunis Papyri*
SB	F. Preisigke et al., *Sammelbuch griechischer Urkunden aus Ägypten* (Strassburg et al., 1915-)
SEG	*Supplementum Epigraphicum Graecum* (Leiden 1923-)
Sokolowski, *LSAM*	F. Sokolowski, *Lois sacrées de l'Asie Mineure* (Paris 1955)
Sokolowski, *LSCG*	F. Sokolowski, *Lois sacrées des cités grecques* (Paris 1969)
Sokolowski, *LSCG*, Supp.	F. Sokolowski, *Lois sacrées des cités grecques,* Supplément (Paris 1962).
Syll.	W. Dittenberger, *Sylloge Inscriptionum Graecarum,* 3rd ed., 4 vols (Leipzig 1915-24)
Thesleff	H. Thesleff, ed., *The Pythagorean Texts of the Hellenistic Period* (Abo 1965)
UPZ	U. Wilcken, *Urkunden der Ptolemäerzeit (Ältere Funde)* (Berlin-Leipzig 1927-)

Concordance of Sources

References in bold type are to the numbers allocated to translations in this book unless otherwise indicated.

ANCIENT AUTHORS

Acts of the Christian Martyrs 8.2-10, **266**; 22, **267**
Aeschylus, *Eumenides* 658-61, **p. 98 n. 2**
Alcman, fr. 1.5-101, **122**
Alexis, fr. 18 Pickard-Cambridge, **53**; fr. 146 Kock, **35**
Antipater of Thessalonica, *AP* VII. 413, **p. 25 n. 7**
Antiphon, *Against a Stepmother on a Charge of Poisoning* (exc.), **76**
Anyte, *AP* VII. 486, **14**; 490, **12**; 492, **11**; 649, **13**
AP XIII. 16, **44**
Apollodorus, *Against Neaera* (excs), **77**
Apollonius of Rhodes, *Argonautica* 3.838-67, **129**
Appian, *Civil War* 4.32-4, **206**; 4.39-40, **208**
Archilochus, *P. Colon.* 7511, **104**
Aretaeus: *On the Causes and Symptoms of Acute Diseases* 2 (exc.), **215**; *On the Therapeutics of Acute Diseases*, **216**
Aristotle: *On Dreams* 459b-460a, **95**; *On the Generation of Animals* 716a5-23, 727a2-30, 727b31-33, 728b18-31, 765b8-20, 766a17-30, 783b26-784a12, **92**; *Politics* 1254b3-1277b25 (excs), 1313b33-39, 1335a8-17, **86**
Aulus Gellius, *Attic Nights* 10.23, **189**

Callimachus, *Hymns* 6.119-33, **118**
Celsus, *On Medicine* 5.21, 6.27, **218**
Cicero: *Pro Caelio* 13-16 (exc.), **155**; *Brutus* 58.211, **204**
Corinna, 654P, **7**; 664P, **8**

Demosthenes 23.53, **p. 76 n. 19**; *Against Macartatus* (43).51, 54, **68**; 45.28, **66**
Dio Cassius, *History of Rome* 54.16.1-2, **192**; 78.2, 78.18 (excs), 79.23 (excs), **154**
Diogenes Laertius 5.11-16, **67**; 6.96-8, **43**

Erinna, *GP* 3.120, **9**; *AP* VII.710, 712, **10**
Eubulus, fr. 116, 117 Kock, **34**
Euripides, *Cretans, GLP* 11, **33**

FGH 257a, fr. 6, **45**
FHG III. 520ff., **166**
FIRA p. 3 (excs), **187**; p. 23 (excs), **188**

GLP 11, **33**; 185-7, **38**; 3.120, **9**
Gaius, *Institutes* 1.97-117, 136-7a, **194**
Galen: *On Prognosis* 6, **219**; *On the Usefulness of the Parts of the Body* 14.6-7 (excs), **211**

Herodas, *Mimes* 1, **108**; 6, **109**
Herodotus, *Histories* 8.87-8, **40**
Hesiod, *Works and Days* 42-105, **28**; 695-705, **29**
Hippocrates: *Diseases of Women* 1.1, 2, 6, 7, 21, 25, 33, 62, **96**; 2.123, 126, **97**; *Epidemics* 5.12, 25, **101**; *Nature of Women* 2, **99**; 3, 8, **98**; 98, **94**; *On the Generating Seed and the Nature of the Child* 407, 13, 30, **93**; *On Virgins*, **100**
Hipponax, fr. 68 West, **31**
Historia Augusta: Aurelian 49.6, **241**; Elagabalus, 4.3-4, **240**
Homeric Hymn to Demeter 370-495, **117**
Horace, *Epodes* 5, **248**

Irenaeus, *Against Heresies* 1.13.1-4 (excs), **268**
Isaeus 3.39, **71**; 3.64, **69**; 6.18-24, **74**; 8.18-20, **73**; 10.10, **70**

St. Jerome, *Against Jovinianus* 47, **269**
Justinian
  Codex 9.1, 8, 11, 17, 18, 20, 22-5, 27, 29, **193(ii)**; 9.10.1, **195(i)**; 9.12.1, **196(ii)**; 11.11.pr., **197(ii)**
  Digest 5.3.27.pr.-1, **197(ii)**; 12.4.9.pr., **196(ii)**; 23.2.13, **197(ii)**; 23.2.34.1, 3, **196(ii)**; 23.2.36, **195**; 23.2.41.pr.-1, **193(iii)**; 23.2.42.pr.-1, **196(ii)**; 23.2.43.pr.-6; 23.2.44.pr.-1, 6-8; 23.2.45.pr., **193(iii)**; 23.2.70; 24.1.31.pr.-1; 24.2.1, 3, **196(ii)**; 26.7.1.pr.-1, 4; 26.7.2.pr.; 48.2.2; 48.2.8; 48.5.1.pr.; 48.5.2.2; 48.5.2.8; 48.5.7.pr.; 48.5.8.pr.; 48.5.10.pr.-2; 48.5.11.8-9; 48.5.11.12-13; 48.5.13.pr.; 48.5.13.3; 48.5.13.8; 48.5.19.3; 48.5.20; 48.5.21; 48.5.22.pr.-2, 4; 48.5.23-25 pr; 48.5.26.pr.-1, **193(iii)**
  Institutes 1.9, **195(i)**; 1.10.pr. (exc.), **196(ii)**; 1.11.pr.,10, **195(i)**
Juvenal, *Satires* 6 (excs), **157**

Livy 21.27.8-9, **238**; 34.1-8 (abridged), **191**
Lysias, *On the murder of Eratosthenes* 9-33,
37-50, **73**

Martial, *Epigrams* 1.13, **p. 155 n. 9**; 8.12,
228; 9.30, **229**
Menander, fr. 15, **36**; fr. 333 Koerte, **37**;
Anon. apud M., Sandbach p. 328, **38**

Nossis, *AP* VI.265, **15**; 273, **17**; 275, **16**;
332, **18**; IX. 604, **19**; 605, **20**

Paul of Tarsus: I Corinthians 7:1-16, 25-40;
11:2-16; 14:34-5; I Timothy 2:8-14, **265**
Paulus, *Opinions* 2.1-9, 2.20.1, **196(i)**;
2.21.1-4, 2.21.9-13, 2.21.16, **197(i)**; 2.22.1,
196(i); 2.24.1-9, **197(i)**; 2.26.1-17, **193(i)**;
3.10.1-2, **196(i)**
Plato: *Laws* 6.780e-781d, 7.804c-806c,
8.838a-839b, **88**; *Republic* 5.451c-452c,
455c-456b, 457a, 457c, 458c-d, 459d-461e,
87; *Timaeus* 91 (excs), **91**
Pliny the Elder, *Natural History* 7.38-43,
48-51, **212**; 35.40, **181**
Pliny the Younger, *Letters* 3.16, **150**; 4.19,
226; 4.21, **151**; 5.16, **152**; 6.4, 6.7, 7.5,
226; 7.19, **209**; 8.10, **226**
Plutarch: *Lives*: Mark Antony 25-9, **156**;
Caesar 9-10, **247**; Cicero 19.3, 20.1-2,
246; Gaius Gracchus 19, **147**; Tiberius
Gracchus 1.2-2, **146**; Lycurgus 14-16
(excs), **89**; Numa Pompilius 9-10, **242**;
Moralia, 14b-c (Pseudo-Plutarch), **221**;
138a-146a (excs), **227**; 240c-242d (excs),

90; 245c-f, **39**; 249d, **103**; 276, **230**;
288-9, **230**; 299e-300a, **244**

Quintilian, *Institutes of Oratory* 1.1.6, **220**

Sallust, *Conspiracy of Catiline* 24-5, **203**
Sappho, fr. 1, **1**; 16, **3**; 31, **2**; 44, **6**; 94, **4**;
96, **5**
Semonides of Amorgos, *On Women*, **30**
Seneca, *To Helvia on Consolation* 16, **148**
Sophocles, *Tereus* (fr. 583 Radt), **32**
Soranus, *Gynaecology* 1.19-20, **178**; 1.24, 26,
34, 36, 39, 40, 60-2, 64-5, **213**; 1. 67-9,
214; 3.26, 28-9, **239**
Suetonius, *Galba* 5.1, **239**
Sulpicia (apud Tibullum) 3.13, 15-18, **133**;
3.14, **132**

Tacitus: *Annals* 4.53, **167**; *Dialogue* 28 (exc.),
149
Theocritus, *Idylls* 2 (exc.), **130**; 15 (exc.),
110
Thesleff 123-4, **111**; 151-4, **107**
Thucydides 6.59, **22**

Ulpian, *Rules* 5.8-10, 5.11.1̄, **195(ii)**; 6.1, 2,
4, 6, 7, 9, 10, 12, 7.2, **196(iii)**

Valerius Maximus, *Memorable Deeds and
Sayings*, 4.4.pr., **145**; 6.3.9-12, **190**;
6.7.1-3, **153**; 8.3, **205**

Xenophon: *Memoirs of Socrates* 2.7, **105**;
Oeconomicus 7-10 (excs), **106**

PAPYRI

P. Antinoop., **36**
BGU 1104, **83**; 1107, **179**; 1210 (excs), **198**
P. Cattaoui 3, 4, **201**
P. Colon. 7511, **104**
P. Eleph. 3, **84**
P. Fam. Tebt. 21, **199**
P. Hamb. 86, **223**
P. Hibeh 54, **116**
P. Mag. 7. 208-9, **253**; 260-71, **254**

P. Mich. 6551, **200**
P. Oxy. 91, **180**; 111, **231**; 744, **112**; 930,
224; 1647, **222**; 2082, **45**
Preisendanz-Henrichs² *II* p. 9, **253**; p. 12, **254**
PSI 1080, **225**
P. Tebt. 104, **82**; 776, **85**
SB X.10756 (excs), **202**
UPZ 19, **128**

GREEK INSCRIPTIONS

Agora XVII.913, **61**
Finley 8, **80**; 9, **78**; 130, **81**; 155, **79**
FH 132, **p.20 n. 3**; 138, **22**; 139, **23**; 152,
42; 177m, **41**
GHI 44, **120**
HSCP 82(1978)148, **114**
Hesperia 28(1959) 208-38: (A) 221, 255, 259,

328, 468, 472, 493, 497, 505, 518; (B) 91,
112, 114f., 212, 214, **58(i)**
Hesperia 37(1968) 368-80: 49.4-5, 50.34,
58(ii)
Inscr. Creticae IV.72, cls II. 45-9, V. 9-28,
VII.15-29, VIII.42-3, 12-20, **64**
IG I² 24, **120**; 473, **50**; 756, **119**

LATIN INSCRIPTIONS

Indexes

References are to page numbers in both indexes.

WOMEN AND GODDESSES

GENERAL INDEX

Index

Index   291

Bacchic rites, 250-3; *see also* Dionysus
Baiae, 149, 156n. 26
bareheadedness, 176, 264-5
battles, involving women, 21, 22
bedmaking, 103
bee, woman compared to, 15-16, 102
benefactresses, private, 135, 209; public,
    157-9, 243-4, 259, 260
bigamy, 183
birth defects, 219
birthing stool, 244
bleeding (therapeutic), 223, 228, 231
bondsman, female, 41
bread-making, 103
breasts, 99, 153; cancer of, 147; induration
    of, 258; *see also* wet-nurses
brides, rituals of, 120; *see also* marriage,
    weddings
brothels, 51, 188; *see also* prostitution
buildings, built by women, 243-4, 259, 260
burial societies, 244-5

carding contest, 22
Catiline, conspiracy of, 205, 253
Cato, M. Porcius, 175, 176-8
celibacy, 263-4, 277-8; *see also* chastity
chastity, 104-5, 134, 154-5, 260, 279-80; *see also*
    vestal virgins
childbirth, age for, 70; clinical instructions
    for, 224-5; pains of, 155; pollution of, 121;
    see also labour pains, miscarriage
childlessness, 25, 180
choking (hysterical), 95; *see also* suffocation
Christianity, 262-78
Cicero, 253
citizenship, laws concerning, 199, 200-1
Clodius Pulcher, P., 254-5
clothing, 9, 105, 110, 265; immodest, 140; of
    Roman matron, 135, 177; of Roman
    prostitute, 132
clubs, women's, 244
coemptio, 190-1, 199
cognates, 173; *see also* guardianship
coitus interruptus, 99
coldness, characteristic of females, 215-17; *see*
    also heat
collegium, of women, 244
Colline Gate (Rome), 154, 250
conception, 82-5, 86; best conditions for,
    220-1; remedy for difficulty in, 232
concubines, 45, 48, 174, 188; adultery of,
    185; different from wives, 193; Lacaina,
    171; prohibited, 59; rights of children of,
    37, 40-1; transfer of, 60-1; *see also*
    prostitution
confarreatio, 190-1; *see also* marriage
confinement indoors, 176; *see also* seclusion
contraception, 88, 99, 173, 221-2; different
    from abortion, 221

contracts, forbidden to women, 38; *see also*
    marriage, property
conventus matronalis, 245
cooking, 67
cosmetics, 43, 102-3, 105, 140
courage, of women, 21, 22, 210, 211-12; in
    illness, 144; in proscriptions, 145; in
    Second Punic War, 154
courtesans, 25n. 4, 51-7, 125; *see also*
    prostitution
curia of women, 244, 247n. 8
curses, 29, 126, 171, 257-8

dancing, 76, 205, 241
daughter: father's love for, 133, 265-8;
    mother's, 134
death: in childbirth, 143; before marriage, 8,
    9, 11, 133, 136, 144
death penalty, 173, 175, 197, 250
defixiones, see curses
depilation, 137
deviousness, of women 12-14, 15, 22, 72, 152
devotion, in marriage, 138-9, 142-3, 145,
    208-19, 237-9
Diocletian, persecution under, 270-5
dildoes, 107-9
Diocles, *On Gynaecology*, 229
Dionysus, 113-14, 261; *see also* Bacchic rites
dissection, 215
divorce, 59-60, 173, 209, 210; of *flamen dialis*,
    243; forbidden to Christians, 263; and
    property, 33; as punishment, 176; by
    repudiation, 174, 189; by wife, 175, 191
doctors, *see* physicians
douche (vaginal injection), 95, 222, 227, 229
dowries, 38, 55, 57-8, 65, 194-5, 199-200;
    contributions from, 245; in marriage
    contract, 59; provided by female relative,
    209; repayment of, 60, 61; of widow, 36
dressmakers, 170
drinking, 51, 105, 107, 154, 184, 221;
    abstinence after uterine disease, 231;
    before abortion, 223; death for, 173, 176;
    forbidden to women, 175; during
    intercourse, 221; not advised for
    wet-nurses, 165
dropsy, 95
drugs, 155, 173; *see also* love potions, magic,
    witchcraft
dysmenorrhea, 89, 229

ecstatic rites, 116, 250-2, 275-6
education, 4, 66-8, 72-4, 101, 133, 205, 235,
    241-2; in Sparta, 76; of wife by husband,
    100-4; mother's role in children's, 141-2,
    206, 235
Egnatius Metellus, 176
Elagabalus, 244, 246